R. Gupta's

POPULAR
Dictionary of
LEGAL TERMS

by
RPH Editorial Board

Ramesh Publishing House, New Delhi

Published by
O.P. Gupta *for* Ramesh Publishing House

Admin. Office
12-H, New Daryaganj Road, Opp. Officer's Mess,
New Delhi-110002 ☏ 23261567, 23275224, 23275124

E-mail: info@rameshpublishinghouse.com
Website: www.rameshpublishinghouse.com

Showroom
● Balaji Market, Nai Sarak, Delhi-6 ☏ 23253720, 23282525
● 4457, Nai Sarak, Delhi-6, ☏ 23918938

© *Reserved with the Publisher*

No Part of this book may be reproduced or transmitted in any form or by any means, electronic or mechanical including photocopying, recording or by any transformation storage and retrieval system without written permission from the Publisher.

Indemnification Clause: *This book is being sold/distributed subject to the exclusive condition that neither the author nor the publishers, individually or collectively, shall be responsible to indemnify the buyer/user/possessor of this book beyond the selling price of this book for any reason under any circumstances. If you do not agree to it, please do not buy/accept/use/possess this book.*

Book Code: R-287
10th Edition: 1807
ISBN: 978-93-5012-879-4
HSN Code: 49019100

Dictionary of
LEGAL TERMS

Q. Who is an abandonee?

A. abandonee means not "one who is abandoned"—as the suffix-**EE** might suggest—but "one to whom property rights [in a thing] are relinquished." Leff writes that "there are numerous circumstances in which, abandonment of something by one person would have the practical or even legal effect of vesting that thing in a particular other person, who thus may usefully be called an *abandonee."* Leff, *The Leff Dictionary of Law,* 94 Yale L.J. 1855, 1856 (1985).

Q. What is meant by Abandonment?

A. abandonment = Relinquishment of an interest, claim of right voluntarily.

Q. What is meant by abate?

A. abate is a Formal Word, common in legal contexts, meaning either: (1) "to nullify; quash; demolish" (to abate a legal action); or (2) "to diminish" (to abate a debt). The *OED* records a technical legal sense that is rarely used today, "to intrude or thrust oneself forcibly or tortiously into a tenement between the death of the owner and the accession of the legal heir (abatement of free hold)." Today, *abate* is used primarily in the sense explained in (1), e.g., "In suits for abatement of a nuisance, courts have directed an officer of the court to engage a contractor specifically to *abate* the nuisance."

The adjective is *abatable,* as in, "Appellants further contend that where a nuisance is *abatable,* the damages assessed must be limited to the rental value of the property."

Q. In what reference, the terms aberration and aberrance are used?

A. aberration, aberrance (-cy), aberrant, n. *Aberrant,* almost always used with reference to persons, means "a deviant; one deviating from an established norm." *Aberration* is not limited to persons, and means: (1) "a deviation or departure from what is normal or correct," or (2) "a mental derangement." *Aberrance* and -cy are Needless Variants of *aberration.*

aberrational, aberrant, adj., **aberrative.** *Aberrational* = of or pertaining to an aberration, e.g., "It is our duty to allow a decision to be made by the Attorney General's delegate, as long as it is not so *aberrational* that it is arbitrary rather than the result of any perceptible rational approach." *Aberrant* = deviating from behavioural or social norms. *Aberrative* = tending to be aberrational.

Q. What is meant by Abet?
A. abet means, to aid in the commission of an offence.

Q. What do you mean by Abettor?
A. abettor is, one who encourages or aid the commission of an offence.

Q. What is meant by the word abdicate?
A. abdicate may mean: (1) "to disown"; (2) "to discard"; or (3) "to renounce." In legal writing, it usually takes on the third meaning listed. e.g., "How can so massive a negation of democracy, so total an *abdication* of law-making power to judges, be permitted to continue in a nation supposedly still devoted to the principles of self-government?" "Until these devices begin to work, I do not believe that the criminal law can *abdicate* its responsibility simply because the problem is massive and complex."

abduce, abduct. These words overlap in meaning but are not interchangeable. Both may mean "to draw away (a limb etc.) from its natural position" *(OED)*. Yet, the more common meaning of *abduct* is "to lead/..................... away by force."

Q. What is called abduction?
A. abduction; kidnap(p)ing; child-stealing. *Abduction* = the act of leading (someone) away by force. It constitutes a statutory offense in many states. e.g., *abduct* is statutorily defined in one state as "to restrain a person with an intent to prevent his liberation by: (a) secreting or holding him in a place where he is not likely to be found; or (b) using or threatening to use deadly force."

In G.B., *abduction* is generally given a narrower sense, "the offence of taking an unmarried girl under the age of 16 from the possession of her parents or guardians against her will" *(CDL)*. The *OCL* additionally defines *abduction* in English law as taking "a girl under 18 or a defective woman of any age from the possession of her parent or guardian for the purpose of unlawful sexual intercourse or a girl under 21 with property or expectations of property from such a possession to marry or have unlawful sexual intercourse or ..... taking away and detaining any woman with the intention that she shall marry or have unlawful sexual intercourse with a person, by force or for the sake of her property or expectations of property." Whereas in the U.S., *abduction* has virtually no connotations relating to the sex of the victim, in G.B. the victim is almost invariably a woman. *Abduction of voters* is also a criminal offense in G.B.

Kidnapping = the act or an instance of stealing, abducting or carrying away a person by force or fraud, often with a demand for ransom *(W3)*. *Kidnapping* (the *-pp-* spelling is preferred) is not restricted in application to children as victims, though the etymology suggests it. *Child-stealing* is the technical statutory term for the abduction of children.

Q. What is meant by the word abide?

A. abide. A. General Sense. *Abide* = (1) to stay (the right of entering and abiding in any state of the Union): (2) to tolerate, withstand; (3) to obey; (4) to await; or (5) to perform or execute (in reference to orders or judgements).

Abide also commonly takes on the sense "to await," as in the following legal construction, "The judgement should be reversed and a new trial granted, with costs to *abide* the event."

Abide by is a Phrasal Verb, meaning "to acquiesce in or conform to.", e.g., "Jurors must *abide by* the oath with respect to both sentencing and determining guilt or innocence."

Abiding = lasting, enduring, e.g., "The two gifts are both of a kind that indicates and *abiding* and unconditioned intent—one to a church, the other one to a person whom she called her adopted son."

B. Past tense and Past-Participal Forms. With the meanings most probably to be found in legal texts ('await' and 'execute'), *abided* is the preferred past tense and past participle. In the archaic sense "to stay, dwell," *abode* is the preferred in the past tense and either *abode* or *abided* in the past participle tense. For most ordinary purposes, *abided* serves well without seeming to be stilted.

Q. What do you understand by ab initio?

A. ab initio, in initio. The former means "from the beginning" (an act beyond one's legal competence is void *ab initio*) while the latter means, as its prefix suggests, "in the beginning." Neither Latinism seems to be quite justified in ordinary contexts, though *ab initio,* which—in legal writing—is used commonly in the phrase *void ab initio,* is common enough not to be particularly objectionable.

Q. What is abjudge?

A. abjudge, adjudge. These words are anti-thetical in one sense. *Abjudge* is a rare term (not in most abridged dictionaries), meaning "to take away by judicial decision"

adjudicate is synonymous with *abjudge,* q.v.

Q. Who is an abjure?

A. abjure, adjure. The former may mean either: (1) "to renounce"; or (2) "to avoid." The latter means: (1) "to charge or entreat solemnly, as if under oath or under the penalty of a curse". The nominal forms are *abjuration* (or *abjurement*—now defunct) and *adjuration.* The adjectival forms end in *-tory.*

abjurer, -or. The *-er* spelling is preferred.

Q. What is meant by abeyance?

A. abeyance has a general sense ("a state of suspension, temporary nonexistence, or inactivity" *[OED])* and a technical legal sense ("expectation or contemplation of law; the position of waiting for or being without a claimant or owner" *[OED]).* Even in legal contexts, however, the general lay sense is commonly used, as in, "Texas would not consider his claim if this action were held in *abeyance."*

Q. What is meant by the term abhorrent?

A. abhorrent, meaning literally "shrinking from in abhorrence" or "strongly opposed to," is frequently used for things in legal context to mean "so far removed from as to be repugnant or inconsistent" *(OED).*

-ABLE. A. Choice of *-able* or *-ible.* Many adjectives have competing forms ending in *-able* and *-ible.*

It should be noted that *-able* (in contrast with *-ible*) is a living suffix, which may be added to virtually any verb without an established suffix in either *-able* or *-ible.* These are some of the adjectives preferably spelled *-able: actionable, addable, advisable, affectable, allegeable, analyzable, annexable, arrestable, assessable, averageable, bailable, blamable, changeable, chargeable, circumscribable, commensurable, committable, condensable, conductable, connectable, contestable, contractable, conversable, convictable, correctable, definable, demurrable, detectable, diagnosable, diffusable, endorsable, enforceable, excisable, excludable, expandable, extendable, garnishable, ignitable, immovable, improvable, includable, inferable, movable, noticeable, patentable, perfectable, persuadable, ratable, redressable, retractable, salable, suspendable, tractable, transferable, willable.*

The following words, limited in number because *-ible* is not now a living combining form in English, are spelled with the *-i* as follows: *accessible, adducible, admissible, audible, avertible, collapsible, collectible, combustible, commiscible, compactible, compatible, comprehensible, compressible, concussible, contemptible, controvertible, convertible, corrodible, corruptible, credible, deducible, deductible, defeasible, defensible, descendible, destructible, digestible, discernible, divisible, edible, educible, eligible, erodible, exhaustible, expressible, fallible, feasible, flexible, forcible, fusible, horrible, impressible, incorrigible, indelible, intelligible, inventible, invincible, irascible, irresistible,* *legible, negligible, omissible, ostensible, perceptible, permissible, plausible, possible, producible, protectible, reducible, reprehensible, repressible, responsible, reversible, revertible, risible, seducible, sensible, submersible* (or *submergible*), *suggestible, suppressible, susceptible, terrible, transfusible, vendible, visible.*

Some adjectives with the variant suffixes have different meanings. Thus *impassable* means "closed, incapable of being traversed"; its twin, *impassible*, means "unable to feel pain," or, less distinctively, "impassive, emotionless," *Passable* and *passible* have correspondingly positive meanings. (These pairs are formed from different Latin roots (L. *passus* "having suffered" and L. *passare* "to step"). Similarly, *impartible* means "not subject to partition" and *impartable* "capable of being imparted." *Conservable* means "oral," whereas *conversible* is a Needless Variant of *convertible. Forcible* means either "effected by means of force" (forcible entry) or "characterised by force"; *forceable,* much less frequently encountered, would be the better term to describe a door that is "capable of being forced open."

Q. Who is an able bodied seaman?

A. able-bodied seaman; able seaman. The former, though of far more recent vintage, seems to be the usual term in admiralty law, meaning "a merchant seaman certified for all seaman's duties".

Q. What is abolishment?

A. abolishment, admonishment. These nouns are inferior to the organically derived *abolition* and *admonition;* is there no longer any difference in meaning between the *-ment* and the *-tion* forms. The *-ment* forms persist in much legal writing, e.g., "The Securities Industry Association issued a 'legal alert' that refers to the NYSE memo and its strongly worded *admonishment* [read *admonition*] to have securities loan arrangements covered by written agreement." "The Legislature must be given a fair opportunity to take whatever action it should deem advisable before the *abolishment* [read *abolition*] of the long-accepted immunity."

Q. What is aborticide?

A. aborticide = the act of destroying a live fetus. One might think that this is a Needless Variant *of abortion.* But that term, technically, refers to something rather different, "the expulsion of a nonviable fetus" *(W3). Aborticide* is, however, an ill-formed equivalent of *feticide.* If, as the dictionaries suggest, it is formed upon the verb *abort,* then ironically, it is what Fowler called an abortion but here, it is termed as a **Morphological Deformity**. If it were formed on the noun *abortus* (= an aborted fetus), then it would be illogical, for one does not "kill" *(-cide)* a fetus that has already been aborted. *Aborticide* is to be avoided in favour of the superior alternative, *feticide* (BrE *foeticide*).

Q. What is abortive?

A. abortive, aborted. *Abortive* may mean (1) "unsuccessful," or (2) "inchoate." With the first meaning listed, it takes on the figurative sense of *aborted* (= cut short), as *an abortive trial, i.e.,* one cut short before the verdict by, e.g., settlement of the dispute. (Note that *-ive,* an active suffix here, has a passive sense.) e.g., "A jury convicted appellants of various offenses arising out of an *abortive* scheme to import a large quantity of Marijuana into the United States from Mexico." In the following sentence, *abortive* has the sense 'unsuccessful' without the connotations of "cut short." "More cross-examinations with well-chosen objectives are rendered *abortive* by the pursuit of "will o' the wisp" decoys than by any other single factor."

Abortive is archaic in reference to abortions of foetuses, except in the sense "causing an abortion"; and in that sense, it is a Needless Variant of *abortifacient.*

Q. Explain about.

A. about; approximately. *Approximately* is a Formal Word *about* is the ordinary, perfectly good equivalent, *About* should not be used, as it often is, with other terms of approximation such as *estimate* or *guess,* because it means "roughly" or "approximately." Hence, "roughly about $10,000" is redundant.

Q. What is meant by above?

A. above. A. *Above* meaning "more than" or "longer than." This usage is to be restricted to informal contexts. *"Above [read more than]* six-hundred lawsuits have been filed since the tragedy." "Should the piano remain, by mutual consent, *above [read longer than]* the term of four months, it is understood that the company is to pay Stieff interest at the rate of six percent per annum."

B. *Above* is an acceptable ellipsis for *above mentioned* if clear in context, e.g., "The *above* arguments apply only to judicial disqualification under section 455(a)." After all, one rarely sees *below-mentioned* or *undermentioned;* some phrase such as *discussed below* is far more natural.

Q. What is above-made?

A. above-made. Above-made is an unnecessary word and an ugly one, e.g., "The following decisions of this court fully sustain the *above-made* statements [read *these statements* or *the above statements].*"

Q. What is above quoted?

A. above-quoted, above-styled, above-mentioned, above-captioned and other such compounds must be hyphenated; one sees the tendency nowadays to spell *above-quoted* and *above-mentioned* as single words. Actually, it is best to avoid these compounds altogether, when possible, by using more specific terms of reference; *i.e.,* instead of writing *the above-mentioned court,* one should name the court (or, if it has just been named, write the *court that court* or some similar identifying phrase).

Q. What is abridge?

A. abridge, violate. Constitutional and other rights are often said to be *abridged* or *violated.* A connotative distinction is possible, however. *Violate* is the stronger word; when rights are *abridged,* they are the merely diminished; when rights are *violated,* they are flouted outright.

Q. What is meant by abrogate?

A. abrogate, obrogate, arrogate. *Abrogate,* far more common than *obrogate,* means "to abolish (a law or established usage) by authoritative or formal action; annul; repeal." *Abrogate* is occasionally confused with *arrogate* (= to usurp).

Obrogate is a civil-law term meaning "to repeal (a law) by passing a new one" *(OED).*

Arrogate (= to usurp) is properly used in the following sentence. "Courts may *arrogate* the authority of deciding what the individual may say and may not say and there may be readily brought about the very condition against which, the constitutional guarantee was intended as a permanent protection."

Q. What is abscond?

A. abscond is both transitive ("to hide away, conceal (anything)" *[OED])* and intransitive ("to depart secretly or suddenly; to hide oneself").

abscondence, abscondment, absconsion.

The second and third are Needless Variants, rarely found; *abscondence* is the preferred nominal form corresponding to the verb *abscond* q.v.

Q. Explain the term absent.

A. absent (= in the absence of; without) is commonly used as a preposition in legal writing. It can be effective if sparingly used, e.g., "The statute, in permitting a verdict of guilty *absent* a finding of a design to effect death, allows the imputation of intent from one defendant to another." "In the absence of a clear manifestation of a contrary intent, it is presumed that the settlor intended the trustee to take a fee simply because in selling he could pass title as owner rather than as donee of a power."

Q. Who is an absentee?

A. absentee, used as an adverb, is a new and useful linguistic development, e.g., "Our inquiry as to [read *into*] why the defendants took Alaniz and her son and daughter to vote *absentee* has to begin with whether or not the request came from Alaniz herself." It would be cumbersome in that context to have to write, "to vote as absentees." *W3* records *absentee* as a noun only but the adverbial usage is increasingly widespread. The word may function also as an adjective, as in *absentee landlord.*

Q. What are absolute constructions?

A. Absolute Constructions. Nominative absolutes, increasingly rare in modern prose, allow the writer to vary his syntax while concisely subordinating incidental matter. Such phrases do not bear an ordinary grammatical relationship to the rest of the sentence, inasmuch as the noun or noun phrase does not perform any one of the function (subject, object, apposition etc.) that ordinarily attach nouns grammatically to other words in the sentence. Yet, the whole absolute phrase acts as an adverbial modifier of some verb; e.g., *the court adjourning, we left the court room* = when the court adjourned, we left the courtroom.

Q. How to absolve one from financial liability?

A. absolve, depending upon the context, takes either *of* or *from*. One is absolved *of* financial liability and absolved *from* wrongdoing—assuming that the courts treat the accused kindly. In the following sentence, *from* appears wrongly in place of *of*: "If the mother contributed nothing to his support because she was absolved *therefrom* [read, if we must, *thereof*] under the act, no expectation of pecuniary advantage exists."

Here, the opposite error appears: "Cnudde considered that Hardgrave's letter completely *absolved* her *of* [read *from*] any charges of improper behaviour in her teaching methods or in the context of her course."

Q. Explain abstract.

A. abstract, v.t.; **abstractify.** *Abstract* is the Chameleon-hued verb meaning (1) "to separate," (2) "to summarise" (to abstract a judgement), (3) "to divert," (4) "to steal" or (5) "to take (something concrete) abstract." In sense (4), *abstract,* more particularly, means "to withdraw, deduct, remove, or take away (something)" *(OED)*. The *OED* labels this word a Euphemism in the sense "to take away secretly, slyly or dishonestly; to purloin." In this sense, *abstract* is a Formal Word that really beclouds the act it describes: "Universal's funds were surreptitiously *abstracted* and deposited in Richfied's account." A more common word, such as *remove* or *withdraw,* would be preferable.

Abstractify is not listed in the dictionaries, though it has appeared in legal texts. It serves as a pejorative alternative for sense (5) of *abstract.* Perhaps, it is a useful invention, for there is no reason for *abstract* to undergo any further degeneration of meaning.

Q. What is abutment?

A. abutment, abuttals. An *abutment* is the place at which, two or more things abut. *Abuttals*—a term used only in the plural—means "land boundaries." *Abuttals* is usually used of abstract boundaries and *abutments* are usually of physical structures (e.g., the walls of bridges adjoining land). *Abbuttals* is a variant spelling to be avoided.

Q. What is abysmal?

A. abysm(al), abyss(al). The nouns are synonymous in signifying "a bottomless gulf." *Abyss* is the more current form, and is, therefore, to be preferred. Though *abysm* is obsolescent, *abysmal* thrives (indeed, has become trite) as a figurative term for 'deep' or "immeasurably great" *(W3)* (abysmal benightedness). *Abyssal* is a technical oceanographic term.

Q. What is meant by accede?

A. accede, exceed. *Accede* = (1) "to agree or consent"; (2) "to come into office or a position of stature;" or (3) "to enter a treaty or an accord." It is an intransitive verb that takes the preposition *To Exceed,* a transitive verb, means (1) "to surpass" or (2) "to go beyond the proper limits." The first syllable of *accede* should be pronounced with a short -*a*- so as to differentiate its sound from *exceed.*

Q. What is an accent?

A. accent, v.t.; **accentuate.** These synonyms have a latent distinction that might be observed usefully. Fowler notes that *accent* is more common in literal and *accentuate* in figurative senses. Hence, one properly *accents* the third syllable of *appellee* and *accentuates* the weakness in an opponent's legal arguments, e.g., "These elements, though *accentuating* the wrong, are not the essence of the same."

Q. Explain acceptance in legal terms.

A. acceptance, -cy, acceptation. The first one is used to express the active sense of the verb (to accept), and the second one, the passive sense (to be accepted). *Acceptance* = the act of accepting; *acceptation* = the state of being accepted (widespread acceptation of the doctrine of strict liability in tort was long in coming). *Acceptancy* is a Needless Variant of *acceptance,* just as *acception* is for *acceptation.*

Acceptance is a common word. Following are examples of acceptation used correctly: "In actions of slander, words are to be taken in their common *acceptation.*" "That there is no right of property in a dead body in the ordinary *acceptation* of that term [which term: *property* or *dead body*?] is undoubtedly true when limited to a property right in the commercial sense."

acceptance for honour; acceptance supra protest. Both terms mean "a form of acceptance of a bill of exchange to save the good name of the drawer or an endorser" *(CDL).* Both are Terms of Art, *acceptance for honour* perhaps being the more generally comprehensible of the two. *Acceptance supra protest* ought to be avoided.

Q. Who is an acceptor in your view?

A. accepter, -or. "The first form is now generally used for one who accepts. The second (earlier) form is the legal term, one who accepts or undertakes the payment of, a bill of exchange." M. Nicholson, *A Dictionary of American-English Usage* 6 (1957).

Q. What is an accessory?

A. accessory, n.; **accessary,** n. *Accessory* now predominates in AmE and BrE in meaning both 'abettor' and "a thing of lesser importance."

These words should be pronounced with the first -*c*- as a hard -*k*- sound; a common mispronunciation is /ă-ses-ă-ree/. The same is true of *accession,* which should have a hard -*c*- followed by a soft one.

Q. Explain an accident.

A. accident; incident. "Available statistics establish that flight engineers have rarely been a contributing cause or factor in commercial aircraft *accidents* or *incidents.*" Here *incident* apparently means "near-accident" and for the purposes of nonce-differentiation, it may be justified. *Incident* should be avoided, however, as a Euphemism for *accident.*

Q. What is accidentally?

A. accidentally. So spelled; *accidently* is a solecism. The confusion may arise from the form of *evidently* and patently. Cf. **incidentally.**

Q. Who is an accomplice?

A. accomplice, accessory. *Accomplice* is the broader term, meaning "one who is a party to a crime, either as a perpetrator or as an accessory" *(CDL).* Thus *accessory* is a subclass of *accomplice,* meaning "one who is a party to a crime that is actually committed by someone else (the perpetrator)" *(CDL).*

Q. What is an accord?

A. accord, accordance. To be *in accord* is to be in agreement, e.g., "This holding was in *accord* with the overwhelming weight of authority in the state courts as reflected in Wigmore's classic treatise on the law of evidence."

This phrase should not be used in place of a more direct statement, e.g., "The adoption of this method was based on the premise that the order in point of time of deposits and withdrawals was essential to proof and that the burden was upon claimant; we are *not in accord with* [read *we reject* (or *disagree with*)] that view."

To be *in accordance* is to be in conformity or compliance. *In accordance* is sometimes cumbersome but often useful, e.g., "The search was conducted *in accordance* with FCI regulations and without excessive use of force." *Out of accordance with* = not in conformity with.

Accord is wrongly used for *accordance* in the following sentences: "The agency disbursed funds in *accord* [read *accordance*] with the plan." "In *accord* [read *accordance*] with the approach taken by this court in these decisions, we hold that the presentation of an administrative claim in excess of $1,00,000 is a sum certain under 28 C.F.R. § 14.2."

Q. What is an accord?

A. accord, v.t.; **afford,** v.t. These are **Chameleon Hued** words that share the meaning "to furnish or grant," as commonly used in legal texts (accorded or afforded) all the rights due to him under due process). Yet some differentiation is possible: *Accord* has the nuance of granting something because it is suitable or proper (accord litigants a stay of costs pending appeal), e.g., "Where the challenged law operates to the peculiar disadvantage of a suspect class, the court *accords* the distinction no presumption of constitutionality." "The children were not *accorded* procedural due process before school officials reached the conclusion that they could not continue to attend school."

Accord in this sense should usually, take a personal object, not an inanimate one; this error occurs when *accord* is used as a high-sounding substitute for *give:* "I cannot subscribe to the court's sweeping refusal to *accord* [read *give*] the equal protection clause any role in this entire area of the law." "Courts generally *accord* [read *give*] statutory language its commonsense meaning." The origin of the correct usage of *accord* lies in the historical (and still current) sense "to grant (a thing asked) *to* (a person), to give with full consent, to award" *(OED).*

Afford, in contrast, is the more general term, meaning "to furnish (something) as an essential concomitant" (*afford to* the indigent defendant legal representation), e.g., "The Sixth Amendment guarantees that a person brought to trial in any federal court must be *afforded* the right to assistance of counsel before he can be validly convicted." "If we *afford* relief *to* this town, will we have to do likewise as each unincorporated village decides to incorporate?"

Intransitively, *accord* takes the prepositions *in, to* or *with,* depending upon the context (we *accord in* our opinions but we *accord to* plaintiff his due and this *accords with* the prevailing view).

Q. Who is an accused?

A. a person becomes an accused immediately after he has been arrested by the police for an offence which forms the subject matter of investigation by them.

Q. Distinguish between accord as well as between satisfaction and compromise and settlement.

A. accord and satisfaction, compromise and settlement. The former appears usually in contractual contexts. Though the two phrases may overlap to some extent, *compromise and settlement* is used in the context of a dispute, more probably, giving rise to litigation. It applies to all disputes, not just to those arising from contracts. The two substantive words in *compromise and settlement* are broader than those in *accord and satisfaction* but *compromise* is roughly analogous to *accord* and *settlement* is analogous to *satisfaction.*

An *accord* is an agreement to substitute for an existing debt or obligation some alternative form of discharging that debt; a *satisfaction* is the actual discharge of the debt by the substituted means. Stated otherwise, an *accord* is the agreement to perform (in an alternative way) and the *satisfaction* is the actual performance. Any claim (whether disputed, unliquidated or undisputed and liquidated) may be discharged by an *accord and satisfaction.*

But only a disputed or uniliquidated claim may be the basis for a *compromise and settlement.* Though the two words in this phrase have been used with a variety of meanings and even synonymously, at base *compromise* means "an agreement between two or more persons to settle matters in dispute between ally, however, one should use the term adverbially without the preposition and spell it as one word (he rested awhile).

Q. What is meant by acquittal?
A. Acquittal = The order of discharge of courts. If a court satisfied with the evidence that the accused is not guilty, he shall record an order of acquittal (Cr.P.C. 1973, Secs. 248 and 255).

Q. What is an act of God?
A. act of God means an accident, which occurs due to the operation of natural forces, which no human foresight could provide against.

Q. What is an act of state?
A. act of state means, act done by Government in the exercise of its sovereign powers.

Q. What is meant by Actionable wrong?
A. actionable wrong = A wrongful act which an action lies in a court of law.

Q. What is meant by Actus Reus?
A. actus reus = wrongful act.

Q. What is meant by adjourn ?
A. adjourn = To defer the hearing of a case to another date in the court.

Q. What is adjudication?
A. adjudication = Decision of the court, e.g., the order of a court which declares a debtor to be a bankrupt.

Q. What do you mean by Ad Idem?
A. ad idem = with a common understanding.

Q. What do you mean by Ad valorem?
A. ad valorem= According to the valuation.

Q. What is meant by Administrative law?
A. administrative law = The branch of public law which deals with the various organs of the sovereign power and rules made by him.

Q. What is Adultery?

A. adultery is voluntary sexual intercourse between a married man and some other than his wife or between a married woman and some other than her husband.

Q. What do you mean by Adverse claim?

A. a claim put forward against the interest of another person.

Q. What is an affidavit?

A. affidavit = A written statement under an oath, which is sworn to by person making it, as true.

Q. What is meant by affray?

A. affray = unlawful fighting or use of force to intimidate others.

Q. What do you understand by the age of capacity?

A. age of capacity = The age at which a person becomes legally capable of entering into a contract, executing a will, maintaining a law suit etc.

Q. What do you understand by the age of majority?

A. age of majority = the age at which a person attains full legal rights e.g., 18 years in India.

Q. What is meant by agnates ?

A. agnates = Relatives whose relationship can be traced exclusively through males.

Q. What is alibi?

A. alibi = (Elsewhere) A defence, where an accused alleges that at the time when the offence with which he is charged was committed, he was elsewhere.

Q. Who is Alien enemy?

A. alien enemy = A person owing allegiance to an adverse belligerent state.

Q. What is alimony?

A. alimony = the maintenance given by husband to his divorced wife.

Q. What is meant by assault?

A. assault = sudden violent attack to hurt another person by striking at him with or without weapon.

Q. Who is an amicus curiae?
A. amicus curiae = the friend of the court is the name is given to the lawyer appointed by a court to represent a poor litigant.

Q. What is meant by Amnesty?
A. amnesty = A general pardon given by government.

Q. What is annuity?
A. annuity = an amount that is payable yearly after a certain period.

Q. What do you understand by an appeal?
A. appeal = application to a higher court to examine against a case decided by a lower court and possibly given a different decision.

Q. What is meant by arbitration?
A. arbitration = settling disputes by referring them to independent third parties.

Q. What is meant by arrest?
A. arrest = the lawful restraining of the liberty of a person in order to compail obedience to the order of a court or to prevent the commission of a crime.

Q. What is arson?
A. arson = crime of unlawfully damaging or destroying by fire.

Q. What is meant by assay?
A. assay usually used to denote examination of weight and measures by officials.

Q. What do you mean by attach?
A. attach = to take, seize or apprehend property by order of court.

Q. What is meant by autrefois?
A. autrefois = a person cannot be tried for the same offence twice.

Q. What is an axiom?
A. axiom = an established principle that is universally accepted within a given framework of reasoning or thinking. The term should not be used of propositions argued for by advocates; if the issue is the subject of controversy, it is not an *axiom,* unless the question is the applicability of an axiom to a given situation.

Q. Explain the term *backberend*.

A. backberend, backberand, backbearing. This Anglo-Saxon term (meaning "having in one's possession" and used of a person carrying off stolen property [lit., "bearing it on his back"]) is now preferably spelled as *backberend*. The other spellings are **Needless Variants**.

Q. What is *back of* in legal terms?

A. back of, in back of. These colloquial phrases are inferior to *behind* in literal and figurative usage, e.g., "Before negligence can be predicated on a given act, *back of* [read *behind*] the act must be sought and found a duty to the individual complaining, the observer of which, would have averted or avoided the injury."

Q. What are different meanings of the word *bail*?

A. bail is a Chameleon-hued legal term, As a noun, it means (1) "the person who acts as a surety for a debt;" (2) "the security or guaranty agreed upon;" or (3) "release on bail of a person in custody." As a verb, *bail* means (1) "to set free for security on one's own recognizance for appearance on another day;" (2) "to become a surety for;" or (3) "to guarantee."

Modern idiom requires *release on bail*, though formerly *in bail* was not uncommon: "Mr. Bartletta was then, taken before the recorder and released in bail to await the act of the grand jury."

Q. What is meant by *bailable*?

A. bailable = admitting of or entitled to bail. Thus it may refer to persons or to offenses, e.g., "Furthermore, the record shows that Dovalina's attempted murder charge was not *bailable*." (One might as naturally have written that Dovalina himself was not *bailable* because he had been charged with attempted murder.) "Even if Congress is free to define *nonbailable* offenses, certainly the allowable justifications are limited and cannot include punishing a defendant before the final determination of his guilt."

Q. Who is a *bailee*?

A. bailee, bailie. *Bailee* = one to whom property is bailed or delivered in trust, e.g., "*Bailees* alone could sue for a conversion and were answerable over for the chattel to their bailor" (Holmes, J.). *Bailie* is a term for a Scottish magistrate; it is also a dialectal variant of *bailiff,* q.v.

Dictionary of Legal Terms

Q. Explain bailiery?

A. bailiery, bailiary. The former is the preferred form of this word, meaning "the jurisdiction of a bailie."

Q. What is a bailiff?

A. bailiff has come, perhaps only in law school mock trials and moot court, to be used as a verb meaning "to act as a bailiff." If that is so, it would, perforce, soon infiltrate the speech of the profession. It is an acceptable colloquialism but should not appear in serious print.

bailiwick, sheriffwick. *Bailiwick* = the office, jurisdiction, or district of a bailiff. Figuratively, it has become synonymous with *domain*. *Sheriffwick* = the office, jurisdiction or district of a sheriff.

Because in one sense, *bailiff* and *sheriff* are synonymous, the derivatives in *-wick* have become synonyms. *Bailiwick* is the more common of the two: "At common law, a sheriff has no jurisdiction beyond the borders of his country, the rule being that the acts of an officer outside his country or *bailiwick* are un-official and necessarily void unless expressly or impliedly authorised by statute." *Bailiffry* is a Needless Variant and *bailivia* is an obsolete variant of *bailiwick*. *Sheriffdom* is a variant form of *sheriffwick*.

Q. What is bailment?

A. bailment = when goods are left by one person with another to hold accordance with instructions.

Q. Who is a bailor?

A. bailor, -er, bailee. *Bailor* and *-er* are not at all clearly distinguished in actual legal usage, though they might easily and usefully be given clear differentiation. *Bailor* and *bailee* (*i.e.*, the persons on the giving and receiving ends of a bailment) are correlative personal nouns, e.g., "No *bailee* is permitted to deny that the *bailor* by whom, any goods were entrusted to him, was entitled to those goods at the time when they were so entrusted." (Eng.)

Bailer (*or bail bondsman*) should be reserved for the sense "one who attaches bail (the surety in criminal law)." Nevertheless, the spelling *bailor* is often used in that sense and *bailer* appears occasionally in civil contexts. With the certain advent of objections to *bail bondsman* on grounds of Sexism, we ought to encourage wider usage of *bailer* in this sense.

Q. Explain the term banish.

A. banish, v.t., generally takes the preposition *from* (he was banished from the country). Krapp cites the usage "The king *banishes* you his presence," with two objects but this usage is archaic.

Q. Who is bankrupt?

A. bankrupt, bankrout. The latter is an obsolete form of the word. During the English Renaissance, scholars re-spelled French borrowings such as *bankrout* on the Latin model, hence *bankrupt*. Many of these respellings did not survive (e.g., accompt for account); *bankrupt* is one of the few that did.

Q. Who is a bankruptee?

A. bankruptee, n., is an unnecessary Neologism equivalent to the well-established *bankrupt*, n., = one that has declared bankruptcy, e.g., "For legal purposes, the family homestead can include up to 200 acres (100 for a single adult) of real property that aren't located within city, town or village limits, and/or one acre of land, plus any temporary residence if the *bankruptee* [read *bankrupt*] has not acquired another home." shorpshire, *The Nouveau Broke,* D Magazine, Nov. 1986, at 89 (inset).

Q. Explain a bar in various terms.

A. bar. In the U.S., all lawyers are members of a bar, whether they are litigators or office practitioners. In G.B., only barristers, as opposed to solicitors, make up the *Bar* (the word is customarily capitalised in G.B.)

bar, debar, disbar. The first two have closely related meanings. *Bar* means "to prevent (often by legal obstacle)" e.g., "The English Statute of Westminster II *barred* dower of a wife who deserted her husband and committed adultery; and some states have statutes *barring* an elective share on a similar principle." "The court concluded that these warranty disclaimers did not necessarily *bar* a breach of contract claim." "Legislative immunity does not, of course, *bar* all judicial reviews of legislative acts." *Bar* also serves as a noun (a bar to all claims).

Debar, a somewhat archaic Formal Word, means "to preclude from having or doing" e.g., "It would required very persuasive circumstances enveloping congressional silence to *debar* this court from re-examining its own doctrines." "There is no reason why the plaintiff should be confined to his action on the special agreement and be *debarred* his remedy on the assumpsit implied by law." (Eng.) *Disbar* means "to expel from the legal profession." The corresponding nouns are *debarment* and *disbarment.*

bargained-for exchange. This phrase is sometimes erroneously termed as *bargain for exchange*. Here, its variations are correctly used: "The doing of the act constitutes acceptance, the *bargained-for* consideration and the offeree's performance." "If the termination of obligations were an immediate *bargained-for* right of consequence, he would presumably have taken advantage of his freedom from testamentary obligation to make a new will."

The origin of the phrase *bargained-for exchange* may be seen from this sentence: "Consideration is something bargained for and given in exchange."

bargainee (= the purchaser in a bargained-for exchange) is more obscure than *purchaser* but the word is perhaps a necessary correlative of *bargainor*.

Q. Who is a bargainer?

A. bargainer, -or. The two forms are not synonymous, as one might suspect. *Bargainer* means "one who bargains." *Bargainor* has a more specific legal, meaning: "the seller in a bargained-for exchange."

Q. Who is a bargee?

A. bargee is illogically formed with the *-ee* suffix but it is established. *Bargee* (17th c.) is a variant of *bargeman* (14th c.), without the inefilicity of Sexism, e.g., "The story of the Elmhurst's *bargee* was that off Bedloe's Island a third tug of the railroad ..... came alongside, struck the barge a heavy blow on her port quarter, nearly capsizing her, driving her forward against the barge ahead and breaking some planks forward." *Sinram v. Pennsylvania R.R.*, 61 F.2d 767, 768 (2d Cir. 1932) (per L. Hand, J.)

Q. What is meant by barter?

A. barter = to exchange one commodity for another.

Q. Explain the term basis.

A. basis is sometimes wrongly used for *reason*, e.g., "The court, after a full review of the authorities, concluded that there was now no sound *basis* [read *reason*] why the value of life insurance coverage, as well as the cash surender value, might not be considered in a property division between parties to a divorce action."

This word may also be mischief in adverbial constructions (on a ..... basis), where a simple adverb would serve better. "The commission was set up *on a provisional basis* [read *provisionally*]." "Those issues must be *determined on a case-by-case basis* [read *determined case by case*]." "The attorney represented his clients *on a contingent-fee basis* [read *for a contingent fee*]."

The plural of *basis*, as well as *base*, is *bases;* the pronounciations differ, however: for *basis,* the plural is pronounced ***bay**-seez*, for base ***bays**-ez*.

Q. Who is a bastard?

A. bastard, a term of abuse generally, is still used with technical neutrality in the law, e.g., "Although a *bastard* cannot inherit from his parents or other ancestors at common law, statutes or judicial decisions permit a *bastard* to inherit from his mother and the mother to inherit from her *bastard.*" This technical neutrality is not, however, today without comic overtones.

Q. Who is bastardy?

A. bastardy = (1) the condition of a bastard; illegitimate birth; or (2) the begetting of bastards; fornication *(OED).* Today in sense (1), *illegitimacy* is the more usual term and the preferable one for avoiding unduly derogatory connotations. Sense (2) is not common.

Q. What is meant by bathos?

A. bathos; pathos. Thse two words frequently cause confusion. *Bathos* means "a sudden descent from the exalted to the trite or from the sublime to the ridiculous." *Pathos* means "sympathetic pity" and is useful, e.g., in reference to juries.

battery connotes to the layman physical violence. The legal meaning, however, is "the intentional or negligent application of physical force to or the offensive contact with someone without his consent" e.g., "[T] he *battery* here was a technical one and was accompanied by neither physical injury nor violence. It was a mere touching of the person of the plaintiff, a mere incident of the restraint, the false imprisonment." *Fisher v. Rumler,* 239 Mich. 224, 214 N.W. 310, 311 (1927).

beak is a BrE slang term for a magistrate or justice of the peace.

because causes problems when used as a conjunction after *reason.* Here, the construction is inverted: *"Because* [read *That*] the lessor accepted the first payment is no reason to conclude that the corporation existed by estoppel."

before for *by.* Cases come *before* courts, which then *review* those cases (i.e., *review* is *by* those courts). "We note that such a determination is a matter placed within the sound discretion of the district judge and review *before* [read *by* us] is very limited."

beg is occasionally used in dissenting opinions in the phrases *beg to differ* and *beg to advise.* These are **Archaisms** to be eschewed.

Q. What is beget?

A. beget is today used only figuratively, e.g., "The services and gifts must have been rendered with a frequency that *begets* an anticipation of their continuance." In its literal sense, *beget* is an **Archaism**, e.g., "When proof has been given of the non-access of the husband at any time when his wife's child could have been *begotten,* the wife may give an, evidence as to the person by whom it was *begotten.* " (Eng.) The more usual term today, is *to conceive or to father.*

Q. What is begging the question?

A. begging the question does not mean "evading the issue" or "inviting the obvious questions," as some mistakenly believe. The proper meaning of *begging the question* is "basing a conclusion on an assumption that is as much in need of proof or demonstration as the conclusion itself." The formal name for this logical fallacy is *petitio principii*. In the following sentence, the writer mangled this Set Phrase and misapprehended its meaning: "This explanation begs the issue."

As for an example of *begging the question,* here is a classic one: "Reasonable men are those who think and reason intelligently." *Patterson v. Nutter,* 78 Me. 509, 7 A. 273, 275 (1886). This statement begs the question, "What does it mean to think and reason intelligently?"

Q. What is meant by begin?

A. begin. A. *To begin.* As an introductory phrase used to enumerate reasons, the idiomatic phrase is *to begin with,* not *to begin.* In the following sentence, the lack of the preposition *with* makes *to begin* sound narrowly chronological, as if *A* actually began something and then, at some indeterminate point, stopped: "To begin, A played a substantial role in negotiating both agreements." [Read *To begin with, A played a substantial role in negotiating both agreements.*] "*To begin* [add *with*], it was clear that Dixon suffered a permanent injury and that he died of an unrelated disease."

B. *Commence and start. Begin* is the usual word, to be preferred to nine times out of ten *Commence* is a Formal Word; ceremonies and exercises are likely to *commence,* as are legal proceedings. *Start* is usually used of physical movement (to start running).

Q. What is meant by behalf?

A. behalf. A distinction exists between *in behalf of* and *on behalf of.* The former means "in the interest or in defense of" (he fought in behalf of a just man's reputation); the latter, *on behalf of,* means "as the agent of, as representative of" (on behalf of the corporation, I would like to thank .....) (he appeared on behalf of his client).

Upon behalf of is now considered much inferior to *on behalf of.* "We conclude that the public interest involved in this dispute compels us to look beyond the immediate interests of the named litigants and to consider the situation of the natural gas consumers *upon* [read *on*] whose behalf, the Mississippi Power Service Commission has intervened."

behaviour(al)ism. The correct name for the doctrine that human behavior provides the only significant psychological data is *behaviourism.*

Q. What is behest?

A. behest is a stronger word than **request**; it means (1) "a command" or (2) "a strong urging." *Bequest,* q.v., is sometimes misused for *behest.* An example follows: "It is enough that a writing, defamatory in content, has been read and understood at the *bequest* [read *behest*] of the defamer." "At his *bequest* [read *behest*], I undertook this onerous task but have been thankful to him for so urging me." This is a **Malapropism**.

Q. What is behoof?

A. behoof is the noun, *behoove* (AmE) or *behove* (BrE) the verb. Both noun and verb have an archaic flavour. Historically, the verb in BrE was pronounced, as it now is in AmE, to rhyme with *move* and *prove*. In BrE today, "it is generally made to rime with *rove* or *grove,* by those who know it only in books" *(OED)*.

Q. What is called belated?

A. belated has made its way into legal language as a synonym of *untimely,* e.g., "We must decline to entertain appellant's *belated* cross-points." Its use in this context is perfectly acceptable.

Q. What is to belie?

A. belie = (1) to disguise, give a false idea of; (2) to leave unfulfilled; or (3) to contradict or prove the falsity of. Sense (3) is by far the commonest in legal contexts, e.g., "The Court suggests that the search for valuables in the closed glove compartment might be justified as a measure to protect the police against lost property claims; again, this suggestion is *belied* [i.e., *contradicted*] by the record." "Appellant contends that his lawyer's failure to put on evidence at the penalty stage prejudiced his ability to avoid the death sentence; but the nature of the evidence appellant asserts his attorney should have presented *belies* [*i.e., proves the falsity of*] the argument."

Q. What do appellate courts mean by courts below?

A. below. It is often used by appellate courts to mean "at the trial-court stage" e.g., "As the district court noted *below,* this litigation involves only that portion of the contract relating to the actual construction of the platform."

Q. What is below-mentioend?

A. below-mentioned, under-mentioned. The former is AmE or BrE while the latter is BrE only. *Below,* like *above,* q.v., is frequently used as an ellipsis for *below-mentioned.*

Q. What is meant by bemuse?

A. bemuse; amuse. The former is frequently taken to be a fancy variant of the latter; the meanings differ significantly, however. *Bemuse* = (1) to plunge into thought, preoccupy; or (2) to muddle (one's mind); bewilder. Here, sense (2) of *bemuse* applies: "It is easy to see why an equity court, *bemused* by the expression "Equity, acts in personam and not in rem," would be tempted to say that an equity court has no 'power' to affect directly land titles in another state." *Amuse* needs no definition here.

Q. What is a bench?

A. bench, like *court,* q.v., has come to stand through metonymy, for judges collectively, as in the phrase *bench and bar.*

Q. Who is a bencher?

A. bencher, in England, means "one who sits on a bench" *(OED)* and usually refers to a member of the governing body of one of the Inns of Court, e.g., "I happen to be a *Bencher* of the Inner Temple and whilst the former glories of the Inns of Court have in a large measure departed, some things abide throughout the centuries." (Lord Justice Birkett) "There was thus little occasion for controversies as to discipline to be brought before the judges, unless the *benchers* failed in the performance of their duties." *People v. Culkin,* 162 N.E. 487, 490 (n.Y. App. 1928) (per Cardozo, C.J.). *Benchers* are also known as *Masters of the Bench.* Archaically, the term was used more generally in reference to magistrates, judges, assessors and senators.

Q. What is a bench trial?

A. bench trial has become a common equivalent of *trial to the bench* (= a nonjury trial).

Q. What is beneficient?

A. beneficent, beneficial, benevolent. The etymological difference between *beneficent* and *benevolent* is that between deeds and sentiments. *Beneficent* = doing good, charitable (benefic now being merely a Needless Variant). *Benevolent* = well-wishing, supportive, (emotionally) charitable. The differentiation should be cultivated; we should reserve *beneficent* for "doing good" and *benevolent* for "inclined or disposed to do good."

Beneficial has the general meaning "favourable, producing benefits" and the specialised legal meaning "consisting in a right that derives from something (as a contract or an expectancy) other than legal title" (beneficial interest), a sense that derives from the older legal meaning "of or pertaining to usufruct" *(OED),* e.g., "An alien may generally become trustee of property that he can own *beneficially."* "The supervised administration embraces a determination of the persons *beneficially* entitled to the estate after debts, expenses and taxes are paid."

Q. What is a benefit and who are the benefittees?

A. benefit. Invariably, the passive form of this verb can be advantageously made into an active construction: "Defendant has an adverse interest because he would *have been benefited by* [read *have benefited from*] a ruling in favour of the insurance company."

benefit(t)ed, benefit(t)ing. These words should be spelled with one -t-, not two.

benefittees has not yet made its way into the dictionaries, though it has appeared in American legal prose, e.g., "The final House version of the bill included no mention of existing seniority systems and the *benefittees* thereunder." The double -tt- is incorrect (cf. *benefited*) because the accent does not fall on the penultimate syllable. The better spelling of the word, if we are to have it at all, is *benefitee.*

Q. What is benign?

A. benign, benignant. The latter is a Needless Variant. The antonym of *benign,* however, is *malignant.*

Q. To bequeath means to give personal property by will, explain.

A. bequeath, devise, devolve. *Bequeath* = to give personal property by will. Laymen and lawyers alike use this term metaphorically: "While its origins are somewhat obscure, we know that the marital privilege is *bequeathed* to us by the long evolution of the common law, not by constitutional adjudication."

Devise = to give real property by will. As a noun, *devise* refers to the realty so given—the analogue for personal property is *bequest.* The Uniform Probate code uses only the term *devise* to describe giving property by will whether the property is real personal; it would be bootless to call this well-ensconced terminological shift incorrect.

Devolve = to pass on (an estate, right, liability or office) from one person to another. In the context of estates, *devolve* usually takes the preposition *upon* and sometimes *to.*

Q. What is a bequest in your view?

A. bequest, bequeathal, bequeathment. *Bequest* = (1) the act of bequeathing; or (2) personal property (usually other than money) disposed of in a will. *Bequeathal* and *bequeathment* are Needless Variants of sense (1) of *bequest.*

Bequest should not be used as a verb, as I once used it in this sentence: "And by so felicitiously using the words newly *bequested* [read *bequeathed*] to English, [Shakespeare], more than any other writer of the English Renaissance, validated the efforts of earlier and contemporary neologists." B. Garner, *Shakespeare's Latinate Neologisms,* 15 Shakespeare Stud. 149, 151 (1982).

Bequest is sometimes confused with *behest,* q.v.

Q. Define bereave.

A. bereave, v.t., yields past-tense forms *bereft* or *bereaved* and the same forms as past participles. *Bereaved* is used in reference to loss of relatives by death. *Bereft* is used in reference to loss of immaterial possessions or qualities.

As Bryson has observed, to be *bereft of* something is not merely to lack it but to have been dispossessed of it. *Dictionary of Troublesome Words* 26 (1984). Hence this use is incorrect: "The Mann Act was not designed to cover voluntary actions *bereft of* [read *lacking*] sexual commercialism."

Q. What is bestiality?

A. bestiality = act of having intercouse with an animal. It is prohibited and punishable.

Q. What is a bestowal?

A. bestowal; bestowment. The latter is a Needless Variant, e.g., "We held that a change in judicial interpretation or view of applicable law after final judgement has been entered does not furnish a basis for a bill of review and the *bestowal* of equitable relief." "The term 'endowment' has been defined as the *bestowment* [read *bestowal*] of money as a permanent fund, the income of which, is to be used in the administration of a proposed work."

Q. Who is a bettor?

A. bettor is the standard spelling for "one who bets or wagers." *Better* has also been used in this sense but is liable to confusion with the comparative form of *good.* Cf. **abettor.**

Q. Explain the meaning of between.

A. between. A. *Between and among. Between* is commonly said to be better with two and *among* with more than two things. Fowler calls this a "superstition" and quotes the OED: "In all senses *between* has been, from its earliest appearance, extended to more than two ..... It is still the only word available to express the relation of a thing to many surrounding and individually; *among* expresses a relation to them collectively and vaguely; we should not say *the space lying* *among the three points or a treaty among three Powers."* The rule, as generally enunciated, is merely simplistic. Although it is an accurate guide for the verb *divide* (*between* with two objects, *among* with more than two), the only iron-clad distinction is the one stated by the *OED*. *Between* expresses one-to-one relations of many things and *among* expresses collective and undefined relationships.

In the same case, in which, Justice Marshall writes, "*among* the defendant, the forum and the litigation," Justice Brennan, in his concurring and dissenting opinion, writes: "*between* the controversy, the parties and the forum state." Refer *Shaffer v. Heitner.* 433 U.S. 186 (1977). The latter phrase might be said to express a more specific individual relationship between each one of the named things, the former phrase (perhaps consciously) expressing a vaguer relation.

B. *Between* and Numbers. This may cause problems, if the numbers at either end of the spectrum are intended to be included, e.g., "If three petitioners and one respondent advance to Round Three from a bracket, then those four teams' names will be placed in a hat, and *between one and three* [read *from one to three*] teams will be chosen to switch sides." Two is the only whole number between one and three.

C. *Between you and I.* A commentator has pointedly termed this locution "a grammatical error of unsurpassable grossness." One can add little to that judgement.

D. *Between; as between.* Sometimes *as between* (= comparing; in comparison of) is misused for the straightforward preposition, e.g., "The contractual *provisions as between* [read *provisions between*] the parties are as follows." Cf. **as against.**

E. Fewer Than Two Objects. This construction is a peculiar brand of **Illogic**, as in *between each house* or *between each speech* (instead of properly, *between every two houses* and *between speeches*). Another manifestation of this error is *between ..... or,* with two prepositional objects, rather than *between ..... and;* the misuse results from confusion between *either ..... or* and *between ..... and.*

Q. Define be-verbs.

A. Be-Verbs. A. Wrongly Omitted in Non-Finite Uses. *Be*-verbs, usually in the infinitive or participal form, are often omitted from sentences in which, they would add clarity. One explanation is that they are intended to be 'understood.' But this explanation does not excuse the ambiguities and awkwardnesses often caused by such omissions. The bracketed verbs in the following sentences were originally omitted: "These devices can be used to intercept a wire or oral communication; specifically designated as not */being/* such devices are telephone or telegraph equipment furnished to a user and used in the ordinary course of business, and hearing aids." "The annotation necessarily starts with the assumption that the process or information involved was regarded as [*being*] of a secret or confidential nature." "If the western film offer were found [*to be*] difference [*from*] or inferior to the musical film offer, it makes no difference whether Parker reasonably or unreasonably refused the second offer." "Because this instruction was substantially similar to the willful instruction at the end of the trial, which we have previously held *[to be]* proper, the instruction was not erroneous." "If I thought those two cases *[to be]* in point, I should have to consider them very carefully but I do not." (Eng.)

B. Circumlocutory Uses. Verb phrases containing *be*-verbs are often merely circumlocutory ways of saying something better said with a simple verb. Thus *be determinative of* for *determine* is verbose. But *be determinative* is all right where there is no object, as in Judge Learned Hand's statement: "All such attempts are illusory and if serviceable at all, are so only to center attention upon which, one of the factors may *be determinative* in a given situation."

The following circumlocutory uses of *be*-verbs are common in legal writing; the simple verb is ordinarily to be preferred: *be abusive of (abuse), be amenda-tory of (amend), be benefited by (benefit from), be conducive to (conduce to), be decisive of (decide), be derived from (derive from), be desirous of (desire or want), be determinative of (determine), be dispositive of (dispose of), be in agreement (agree), be in attendance (attend), be indicative of (indicate), be in dispute (dispute* or *disagree). be in error (err), be in exercise of due care (exercise due care), be in existence (exist), be influential on (influence), be in receipt of (have received), be operative (operate), be persuasive of (persuade), be possessed of (possess), be productive of (produce), be probative of (prove), be promotive of (promote), be violative of (violate).*

Many such wordy constructions are more naturally phrased in the present tense singular: *is able to (can), is authorised to (may), is binding upon (binds), is empowered to (may), is unable to (cannot).*

C. Unidiomatically Used in Place of Action Verbs. One should always use the specific verb that conveys the idea of the action described, rather than an unspecific *be*-verb: "Some agencies adopt procedures that permit some public participation; understandable pressures from interested outsiders *are* [read demand] that more should or in some cases, must do so."

Q. What is the difference between bi and semi.

A. bi-; semi-. One can remember the proper prefix in a given context by noting that *bi-* means 'two,' and *semi-* 'half.' Hence *bi-monthly* = every two months (not "twice a month") and *semimonthly* = every half month or twice a month. *Biweekly* and *semi-weekly* work similarly. Still. *bi-* has been used to mean "occurring twice in a (specified span of time)" so often (and so legitimately, e.g., in *biennial*) that, for the sake of clarity, it may be better to avoid the prefix altogether when possible. See the next entry.

Q. Differentiate between biannual, biennial and semiannual.
A. biannual; biennial; semiannual. *Biannual* and *semiannual* both mean "occurring twice a year." *Biennial* means "occurring once every two years." The distinction between these words becomes important, for example, when employment contracts provide for *"biannual* meetings of the committee to dispose of accident and bonus questions, and any other agreements." It is imprudent, however, to rely upon a word like *biannual* for such a contractual provision.

Q. What is a bid?
A. bid (= to offer a bid) forms *bid* in the past tense. In the sense of *bid farewell,* the past tense is *bade,* rhyming with *glad* and the past particple is *hidden.* "She did as she was *bid* [read *bidden*]."

bid, n.; **tender,** n. In AmE, both terms are used, whereas in BrE only the latter would appear, in the sense "a submitted price at which one will perform work or supply goods."

Q. What is biennial?
A. biennial = every two years. If we scale the numerical summit, we have *triennial* (3), *quadriennial* (4), *quinquennial* (5), *sexennial* (6), *septennial* (7), *octennial* (8), *novennial* (9), *deceddial* (10), *vicennial* (20), *centennial* (100), *millennial* (1000).

Q. Explain bigamy.
A. bigamy, polygamy, digamy, deuterogamy. *Bigamy* = going through a marriage ceremony with someone when one is already lawfully married to someone else *(CDL).* It may be committed knowingly or unknowingly; if knowing, *bigamy* is a criminal offense.

Digamy and *deuterogamy* both mean "a legal second marriage occurring after divorce from or death of the first spouse." *Deuterogamy* is the more common term (to the extent that either might be called common!) and is not, like *digamy,* liable to confusion with *bigamy.* Hence, *digamy* should be considered a Needless Variant.

Polygamy is the generic term for "multiple marriages" and encompasses *bigamy;* it is much used by anthropologists, describing both *polygyny* (the practice of having several wives) and *polyandry* (the practice of having several husbands).

Q. What is a bilateral promise?

A. bilateral, unilateral. A *unilateral* contract is one in which, a promise is given by one party in exchange for the actual performance by the other party. A *bilateral* contract is one in which, each party promises a performance so that each party is an obligator on his own promise and an obligee on the other's promise.

Q. How much is a billion?

A. billion. In the U.S. and France, *billion* means "one thousand millions" (= 1,000,000,000); but in G.B., Canada, and Germany, it means "one million millions" (= 1,000,000,000,000). An American *trillion,* q.v., equals the British *billion.* In BrE, however, the AmE meaning is gaining ground, esp, in journalism and technical writing.

Q. What is a birth in legal terms?

A. birth, v.i., was used with some frequency in the Middle Ages as a verb. It fell into disuse, however and only recently it has been revived in AmE. Some dictionaries label it as dialectal. Given its usefulness and its long standing in the language, there can be substantial objections to it.

Q. Explain Blackacre.

A. blackacre is the proverbial example of real estate in hypothetical property problems. Abutting tracts are usually called *Whiteacre, Browancre* or some other colorined denomination. These terms have long been a part of the common-law tradition: "Where as devise is of *blackacre* to A, and of *whiteacre* to B, in tail, and, if they both die without issue, then to C, in fee, here A and B have cross remainders by implication." (Blackstone)

Q. Explain the term blame.

A. blame, v.t., should take a person as the direct object, as in, "I *blame him* for the fires," rather than "I *blame the fires* on him." In the best usage, one *blames* a person; one does not, properly, *blame* a thing *on* a person.

Q. Who is blameworthy?

A. blameworthy. A. And *culpable.* Though the two words are etymologically equivalent, in twentieth-century usage the Anglo-Saxon *blameworthy* has tended to be used in noncriminal, the Latinate *culpable* in criminal contexts. Hence, *blameworthy* in civil contexts, can be used as follows: "The indemnitee's conduct is sufficiently *blameworthy* to preclude indemnity." "Plaintiff is not *blameworthy* in failing to bring suit earlier; thus laches does not apply," "We also consider whether there was trickery or *blameworthy* action by the police."

And *culpable* in criminal contexts: "The court's focus must be on the defendant's *culpability,* not on those who committed the robbery and shot the victims." "The defense of mistake of fact was not available as a defense to negate the *culpable* mental state of criminal negligence." "It is reasonable to presume that the sentencing judge, who revokes probation, takes a fresh look at the defendant's *culpability* and circumstances and considers at that point the amount of time the defendant should be required to serve."

Occasionally, however, *culpability* creeps into civil contexts, as here in the context of punitive damages, a hybrid remedy: "Exemplary damages are awarded only in cases of extreme *culpability* and are limited to the plaintiff's demonstrable litigation expenses." Nevertheless, the writer of that sentence was describing egergious conduct and *blameworthiness* today, hardly seems appropriate for flagrant conduct.

B. And *blameful; blamable. Blameworthy* and *blamable* both mean "deserving to be blamed." The latter is a Needless Variant. *Blameful* (= imputing blame; blaming) has been mistakenly used for *blameworthy.* We need not use up more words for the meaning replicated by *blameworthy* and *blamable.*

Q. What is blandish?

A. blandish, brandish. The former means "to cajole; to persuade by flattery or coaxing." The latter means "to wave or shake in a menacing or threatening way."

Q. What is blasphemy?

A. blasphemy = the public or criminal libel of speaking matter relating to God Jesus christ, the Bible or the book of common prayer, intending to wound the feelings of manking or to excite contempt and hatred against the church.

Q. What is blatant?

A. blatant, flagrant. There is a well-defined distinction but each word is frequently misused in place of the other. What is *blatant* stands out glaringly or repugnantly; what is *flagrant* is deplorable and shocking; the latter term connotes outrage. A perjurer might tell *blatant* lies to the grand jury to cover up for his *flagrant* breach of trust. Egregious criminal acts are *flagrant* (flagrant arson), not *blatant,* e.g., "For any *flagrant* dereliction or disregard of professional duty on the part of the attorney, the license, by which, he was admitted to practice, may be revoked." "The court could have properly determined, as it did, that Batson's conduct was so *flagrant* as to justify severe sanctions."

Blatant is correctly used in this sentence: "The question concerning the blinding of the Libyan in the Colorado shooting was *blatantly* improper." Here, *flagrant* is misused for *blatant:* "The constitutional violation is *flagrantly* [read *blatantly*] apparent in a case involving the imposition of a maximum sentence after reconviction." "No matter how infrequently the special counsel has brought Hatch Act charges in the past, federal employees can hardly be faulted for concluding that registering voters in *flagrant* [read *blatant*] disregard of the special counsel's advice is not worth the grave risk to their livelihoods."

Black defines *flagrant necessity* as "a case of urgency rendering lawful an otherwise illegal act" and *flagrantly against the evidence* as "so much against the weight of the evidence as to shock the conscience and clearly indicate passion and prejudice of the jury." *Flagrant* is the wrong choice of word in the first phrase, though arguably correct in the second one because of the element of shock. *Blatant necessity* would be the better wording for the first Less Variant. When writing or speaking for laymen, however, *case* is the term that would not confuse.

Black notes that **Differentiation** is possible between these terms, though if it does exist at all it is little heeded: "*case* not infrequently has a more limited signification, importing a collection of facts, with the conclusion of law thereon" whereas "*cause* imports a judicial proceeding entire and is nearly synonymous with *lis* in Latin or *suit* in English."

B. And *action.* Although *cause* and *action* are nearly synonymous, yet the legal idioms in which, the phrases are used differ. Thus an *action* or *suit* is said to be commenced' but a *cause* is not. Similarly, a *cause* but not an *action* is said to be 'tried.' Any substantive distinction between the words is subtle: broadly, *action* connotes legal procedure and *cause* denotes the merits of the dispute.

C. Disposition by Courts, *Causes* (or *cases*) are *on dockets;* they may be *remanded* (by an appellate court) or *disposed of* (by any court). But they may not be *reversed* or *affirmed,* e.g., "This is the keystone of the opinion below: If it is in error, the *cause must be reversed* [read *judgement must be reversed*]."

Q. What is meant by Body corporate?
A. body corporate = An association or collection of person having rights and duties distinct from those of the individual persons who form it from time to time.

Q. What is meant by Bonafide?
A. bona fide = In good faith.

Q. What is a Bond?
A. bond means a legal instrument by which a person undertakes to do or not to do something.

Q. What do you understand by a borstal?
A. borstal = A reformatory, where youth offenders are kept.

Q. What is meant by breach?
A. breach means the infringing or violation of right, duty or law, agreement etc.

Q. What do you understand by breach of contract?
A. breach of contract is failure to perform the obligation under the contract.

Q. What is meant by brief in legal terminology?
A. brief = An abbreviated statement of acts and points of law drawn up for counsel in charge of a case.

Q. What is breach of trust?
A. Breach of trust means a breach of any duty imposed on a trusted. As such, by any law for the time being in force (Indian Trust Act 1882 Sec. 3)

Q. What is buggery?
A. buggery = sodomy, the offence committed by a person consisting of anal penetration punishable by the sexual offences Act 1956. It is prohibited by law as an unnatural offence.

Q. What do you understand by burden of proof?
A. burden of proof = the duty of a party to prove a disputed assertion or charge.

Q. What is meant, by stander?
A. By stander = one who is present at the place of occurrence but does not participate in it.

Q. What do you understand by law?
A. by law = Regulations made by the local authority or corporation or company for its members for their day to day work.

Q. What is a case?

A. case = A legal action or trial, argument put in legal proceedings.

Q. What is cause of action?

A. cause of action; right of action. These terms should be distinguished. *Cause of action* has been interpreted by the courts in two distinct ways: to refer to *the facts* and to refer to *the rights*. Generally, it refers to facts, "the grounds that entitle a person to sue" *(CDL)*. Sometimes, *the cause of action* is misused for *prima facie case* q.v., as here: "Plaintiff failed to make out his *cause of action* [read *prima facie case*] and therefore, his claim must fall."

Right of action has two senses: (1) "the right to take a particular case to court" *(CDL)*; and (2) "a chose in action." Here, sense (1) obtains: "The foundation of the *right of action* was a family relationship with the deceased."

Q. What is a cautionary note?

A. cautionary; cautious. *Cautionary* = encouraging or advising caution, e.g., 'This time we do not award damages but sound a *cautionary* note to those who would persistently raise arguments against the income tax that have been put to rest for years." *Cautious* = exercising caution.

Q. What is caveat?

A. caveat = A warning

Q. What do you understand by Caveat Emptor?

A. caveat emptor is a legal maxim. It means let the purchaser beware.

Q. How will you distinguish cede from concede?

A. cede; concede. The distinctions are as follows. *Cede* = to give up, grant, admit or surrender: "By the Treaty of October 4, 1864, the Klamath Indian Tribe *ceded* approximately twenty million acres of aboriginal land to the government of the United States." *Secede* = to withdraw formally from membership or participation in. *Concede* = (I) to admit to be true; (2) to grant (as a right or a privilege); or (3) to admit defeat in (as an election).

Q. What is a ceiling in your view?

A. ceiling, used in the sense of 'maximum,' is in itself unobjectionable but can sometimes lead to unfortunate mixed metaphors, e.g., "The task force recommended a general *increase* in the *ceilings*." One *raises* a ceiling rather than *increases* it. An English writer on usage quotes a preposterous example about "a ceiling price on carpets." In using words figuratively, one must keep in mind their literal meanings. Cf. **Catapult.**

Q. What is censor?

A. censor, v.t.; **censure,** v.t., To *censor* is to oversee and revise, to selectively suppress or edit, e.g., "The right of the superintendent in the exercise of a reasonable discretion to *censor* the ordinary mail written by a patient, who has been adjudged insane, is not challenged."

To *censure* is to criticise severely, to castigate, e.g., "In 1978, the Alabama Court of the Judiciary *censured* a judge for merely associating with a former convict." "The SEC may remove from officer or *censure* any officer or director of a self-regulatory organisation if it finds that he has willfully violated the rules or abused his position."

Q. Define centennial.

A. Centennial, centenary. In all the anniversary designations (*bi-, sesqui-* etc.), whether as an adjective or as a noun, the *-ial* forms are preferred in AmE, the *-ary* forms in BrE.

Q. What is certain?

A. certain can cloy as readily as almost any other word; *said,* q.v., surpasses it, but not by much: "[The plaintiff] was lawfully possessed of a *certain* donkey, which said donkey of the plaintiff was then lawfully in a *certain* highway and the defendant was then, possessed of a *certain* wagon and of *certain* horses drawing the same." *Davies v. Mann,* 152 Eng. Rep. 588 (Ex Ch. 1842). The *OED* labels this usage of *certain,* as well as the phrase *certain of* (certain of his possessions) "somewhat archaic." The latter phrase has been used here: "She brought suit under section 1983 in the United States District Court against Rotramel and the city, alleging that their actions had deprived Tuttle of *certain of* his constitutional rights."

Q. What is certitude?

A. certainty; certitude. *Certainty* = (1) an undoubted fact; or (2) absolute conviction. Sense (2) is very close to that reserved for *certitude,* which means "the quality of feeling certain or convinced" e.g., "The only thing that gives us slight pause is the question how much *certitude* the agents must have that the premises they are entering, though not listed on the dealer's license as his place of business, really are such." Holmes states, rather memorably, "*Certitude* is not the test of *certainty*. We have been cock-sure of many things that were not so." O.W. Holmes, *Natural Law,* in *Collected Legal Papers* 311 (1920).

Q. What is certiorari?

A. a writ from superior court which quashes the decision of a lower court because it is based on irregular procedure.

Q. What is cesser in legal terms?

A. cesser is a **Legalism** meaning "the premature termination of some right or interest" *(CDL).* It usually appears in the phrase *cesser clause* or *cesser provision,* e.g., "The oldest method of protecting the beneficiary from his own indiscretions is the *cesser* provision or forfeiture clause, which provides that the interest of the beneficiary ceases if he assigns or his creditors attempt to reach his interest by legal process."

Q. What is cession?

A. cession, session. *Cession* = a giving up, granting; the act of ceding, e.g., Powell, *Professional Divestiture: The Cession of Responsibility for Lawyer Discipline,* 1986 Am. B. Found. Res. J. 31. It is used often for nations or people who *cede* land. *Session* = a meeting or gathering and is used for deliberative bodies (court is in session).

Q. Explain the term cestui.

A. cestui |*sed-ee*| (= beneficiary) commonly appears as an elliptical form of *cestui que trust,* q.v. For example, "The only person who can object to the disposition of the trust property is the one having some definite interest in the property; he must be a trustee, a *cestui* or have some reversionary interest in the trust property." "If the *cestui* has the transaction with the trustee set aside, of course he must return any consideration paid by the trustee to him." As with the full phrase, *beneficiary* is a preferable term.

Q. What is the meaning of cestui que use?

A. cestui que use (originally, in Law French, *cestui a que use,* lit., "that person for whose use") refers to the beneficiary of a use, q.v. Today, the term appears primarily in historical contexts, inasmuch as uses have been abolished in England. For example, "The *cestui que use* of a freehold estate had no action at common law to enforce his claim against the foeffee." "The person, who enjoyed a use, was known as the *cestui que use;* the feoffor to use and the *cestui que use* might be the same person or different persons." Some American jurisdictions retain the term, however; as with *cestui que trust, beneficiary* is a preferable term in modern contexts.

Q. What is ceteris paribus?

A. ceteris paribus (= other things being equal or the same) is an unnecessary Latinism, since we have the common English phrase. Cf. **mutatis mutandis.**

Q. What is a chamber?

A. chambers. This word refers to the private office of a judge or magistrate. In G.B., it additionally has the sense "the offices occupied by a barrister or group of barristers" *(CDL).* The word is always plural in form, regardless of the number of rooms denoted. Laymen sometimes wrongly make the word singular, as in *judge's chamber.* See, e.g., M. Nicholson, *A Dictionary of American-English Usage* (1957), under camera.

The one use in which, the singular *chamber* is correct, is as an adjective: "During this period, however, other events not formally reflected in the record took place; these include *chambers conferences* [read *chamber conferences* or *conferences in chambers*], which were, of course, known to the district court."

Q. What is champerty?

A. champerty, maintenance. "It would seem that in England, contingent fees are held to be within the inhibition of the statutes of *champerty* and *maintenance.*" These words denote related but distinct offenses. *Champerty* is "the illegal proceeding, whereby a party [often a lawyer] not naturally concerned in a suit engages to help the plaintiff or defendant to prosecute it, on condition that, if it be brought to a successful issue, he is to receive a share of the property in dispute" *(OED). Maintenance* is "the action of wrongfully aiding and abetting litigation; sustentation of a suit or suitor at law by a party who has no interest in the proceedings or who acts from any improper motive." *(OED).*

The element of pecuniary return is absent from the notion of *maintenance.* Pollock noted at the turn of this century that "actions for maintenance are in modern times rare, though possible." Pollock, *The Law of Torts* 321 (1887) (quoted in *OED).* The same might now be said of *champerty,* although *contingent fees,* q.v., which might be said to fit within the traditional definiton of *champerty,* are common in the U.S.; they have been excepted from the prohibition of *champerty* and in most of the cases, are proper under the canons of ethics.

The adjectival form of *champerty* is *champertous and the agent noun is champertor* (labeled obsolete by the *OED* but with no such notation in *W3*). Following is an example of the adjective: "For an agreement to be *champertous,* the financier must have no interest in the litigation to be financed." *United States v. Algernon Blair, Inc.* 795 F. 2d 404, 409 (5th Cir. 1986).

Q. Explain the term character.

A. character, reputation. These words are frequently used in the law of defamation and of evidence. Very simply, the semantic distinction is that *character* is what one is whereas *reputation* is what one is thought by others to be.

Q. What is a charge?

A. charge, n. & v.t. **A.** In the sense "accusation." To write that someone has been *accused* of a *charge* is a **Redundancy**. For example, "In announcing Mr. X's suspension, the [newspaper] management pointed out that Mr. X *had neither been accused nor convicted of any charge* (read *had neither been charged nor convicted).*" (Follett, *Modern American Usage* 47 (1966).

B. Active & Passive Use. *In charge of,* Nicholson writes, may be used both actively and passively, e.g., "The livestock were left *in charge of* the foreman; the foreman was left *in charge of* the livestock." The usual way of wording the passive construction is *in the charge of,* which prevents any possible ambiguities, e.g., "The truck was *in charge of* [read *in the charge of*] Mack Free, who was instructed not to permit any person to ride upon or drive it." To one not accustomed to *in charge of* in the passive construction, subject and object appear to have been confused, *i.e.,* the sentence seems to say that the truck had control of or authority over Mack Free. One more example: "It had been the practice in Texas to assign a Pullman conductor to trains with two or more sleeping cars while in trains with only one sleeping car that car was *in charge of* [read *in the charge of*] a porter."

C. *That-*phrase Objects. It is permissible to write, "He charged that the prosecutorial misconduct was of constitutional dimensions," although in G.B. *charge* generally takes a direct object, either a person or a thing, e.g., "Count one *charged* the defendant that on or about October 27, 1969, being an undischarged bankrupt, he had obtained credit to the extent of £451 13s. 9d. from Lloyds Bank Ltd without informing the said bank that he was then, an undischarged bankrupt." *Regina v. Hartley,* [1972] 2 Q.B. 1.

Both direct objects and *that*-phrase objects are common in the U.S. Here is another example of the latter type: "The complainant further *charged* that the above-mentioned book was printed by defendant."

D. *Charge the jury.* When the trial judge *charges* the jury or gives the jury its *charge,* he instructs the jurors on the standards to be applied in their decision. "The trial judge, in *charging the jury,* required no less than this." The nominal phrase is *jury charge* (= the judge's instructions).

Q. What do you understand by a charge sheet?
A. It is the process in which the officer in charge of a police station or lockup enters the accusation or charges against person brought there in custody whether arrested with or without warrant.

Q. What is meant by chattel?
A. chattel = Movable property.

Q. What is circumstantial evidence?
A. circumstantial evidence = A series of circumstances from which an inference of suit can be drawn.

Q. What is class action?
A. A law suit brought by a representative member of a group of person on behalf of all others.

Q. What is meant by cognate.
A. cognate = Blood relation other than an agnate and includes a female relation only.

Q. What is cognizable offence?
A. An offence in which arrest can be made without a warrant.

Q. What is meant by cognizance?
A. cognizance means the acceptance of a cause for hearing and decision to take notice of a dispute or controversy, taking judicial notice by court.

Q. What is meant by cohabitation?
A. cohabitation = Living together as husband and wife even if not married.

Q. What is commutation?
A. commutation = the change of a penaltyor punishment from a greater to a less punishment.

Q. What is confession?

A. confession is a written acknowledgement of guilt by a party, accused of an offence.

Q. What is meant by condonation?

A. condonation = the pardoning of an offence.

Q. What is conjugal right?

A. conjugal right = Rights of husband/wife to the consortium of the other.

Q. What is consanguinity?

A. cansanguinity = Relationship by blood.

Q. What is consideration?

A. consideration means the price for the promise to do or not to do something. Every contract requires consideration to be legally enforceable.

Q. What is consummation?

A. consummation = voluntarily sexual intercourse to make marriage complete.

Q. What do you understand by the contempt of court?

A. contempt of court = willful disregard, disobedience or disrespect to a court of law.

Q. What is meant by contraband Goods?

A. contraband goods = Goods prohibited by law.

Q. What is a contract?

A. contract = A legally binding agreement between two or more parties.

Q. What is conversion?

A. conversion = The action of wrongfully converting something to one's own use.

Q. What is convenant?

A. convenant = An agreement in writing between two persons, whereby one is enjoying to do or not to do something.

Q. What is conveyance?

A. conveyance = A written document transferring ownership of land from one person to another.

Q. What do you understand by conviction?

A. conviction = An act of a court awarding a person guilty of a criminal offence and awarding a punishment.

Q. What is meant by coparcener?

A. coparcener = one who shares (equally) with other inheritance in the state of a common ancestor.

Q. What is copyright?

A. The exclusive right of printing or otherwise multiplying copies of published literary work; that is the right of preventing all others from doing so the infringement of this right is called piracy. Copy right is extends to original, artistic, dramatic and musical works and to recordings films and broadcast etc.

Q. Who is a coroner?

A. coroner = An officer who inquires into any violent of unnatural death.

Q. What is corpus?

A. corpus = A body, human body.

Q. Define countenance.

A. countenance, give ..... to is usually an unnecessary Peripheasis for *countenance,* v.t., e.g., "Courts have indeed used language that *seems to give countenance to* [read *seems to countenance*] the notion that, if a plot is worked out, it cannot be copyrighted."

Q. What is countersignature?

A. countersignature = a second signature on an instrument attesting to its authenticity. The verb is *to countersign.*

Q. Explain the term countervail.

A. countervail = to counterbalance; to compensate for, e.g., "The interests of nonminorities in not taking another test do not sufficiently *countervail* these needs."

The word, most often, appears as a participal adjective, e.g., "Vidrine filed no *countervailing* affidavits." "Nevertheless, *countervailing* policy considerations have been evident ever since the Statutes of Mortmain, restricting the amounts of wealth that may be transferred out of the normal channels of social organisation." There is nothing inherently wrong with the words but *countervailing considerations* is on the verge of becoming a legal **Cliche**.

Q. What is countless in legal terms?

A. countless applies only to **Count Nouns**, e.g., "Porters recently have been carrying *countless* baggage to and from passengers' cars." One may have *countless bags* but not *countless baggage*.

Q. What is a court of appeal?

A. court of appeal(s). Both forms appear but *appeals* is more common in the U.S., whereas *appeal* is more common in G.B. The correct form is the statutorily prescribed or the customary form of a given jurisdiction. Following is an example of the less usual American form: "In 93 Cal. App. 2d 43, the Court of *Appeal* affirmed the judgement."

Q. What is meant by court fee?

A. court fee = the fee payable on filling of a suit, application, appeal etc. in the court of law.

Q. Define court of first instance.

A. court of first instance = (1) a court, in which, any proceedings are initiated or (2) the trial court as opposed to an appellate court. The *CDL* marks sense (2) as a loose usage.

Q. What is a court of law?

A. court of law is a formal phrase for *court*, which suffices in ordinary legal contexts, e.g., "The word 'say' is important in this context: because when a document is under scrutiny in a *court of law*, attention will be paid only to what, as a piece of natural language, it appears actually to declare." (Eng.) Today, *court of law* often merely emphasises the dignity of the judicial institution referred to; but in a few jurisdictions and certainly in historical contexts, it may usefully distinguish a law-court from a court of equity or from some other type of court.

Q. What is Court Martial?

A. court martial = A tribunal for the administration of military law.

Q. What is cousinhood?

A. cousinhood; cousinage. *Cousinage* has the disadvantage of possible confusion with *cozenage* (= fraud); thus *cousinhood* might be considered as a preferable word.

Q. Define couth?

A. couth, a Back-Formation from *uncouth,* has never been accepted by authorities as a proper word.

Q. What is a real covenant?

A. covenant v.i. & v.t. To *convenant* is to enter into a covenant or formal agreement, to agree or subscribe to by covenant, e.g., "A father *covenants* to transfer an estate to his daughter and her husband-to-be."/ "Other claims made by the appellant in respect of dispositions made by himself were allowed but the claim to deduct Mrs. Reynolds's *covenanted* payments was disallowed." (Eng.) Nonlawyers are unaccustomed to the verbal uses of the word.

Q. What are coverages?

A. coverages. "Mr. P. is being paid a salary of approximately $61,000 per year including certain insurance *coverages*." This plural of what has traditionally been a mass noun is now common.

Q. What is covert?

A. covert, overt. *Covert* is best pronounced like *covered,* except with a -*t*- at the end *kuv-ert.* Still, *koh-vert/,* nearly rhyming with *overt* (but for the accent), is the more common pronunciation in AmE nowadays.

Q. Define coverture.

A. coverture = the condition or position of a woman during her married life when she is, by law, under the authority and protection of her husband *(OED).* The word reeks of **Sexism**, though it is unobjectionable in historical contexts. Traditionally used only in reference to wives, this word has recently been applied to husbands as well: "In community-property jurisdictions, with some exceptions, the spouse has an interest during *coverture* in the community fund." "At common law, dower attached only to an estate of inheritance of which, the husband was seised at some time during *coverture*."

Usually, in contemporary contexts, some phrase such as *during marriage* would suffice in place of the legalistic *during coverture,* e.g., "Community property is a system of regulating rights and obligations of husband and wife *during coverture* [read *during marriage*]."

Dictionary of Legal Terms 47

Q. What is Cozen?

A. cozen is a literary and archaic word meaning "to cheat." The word has never been used as a specific legal term, and is generally to be avoided in legal writing.

Q. Who is a creator?

A. creator is a somewhat exalted name for one who establishes a trust, e.g., "The second type of statute provides that where the *creator* of such trust reserves to himself for his own benefit a power of revocation, a court, at the suit of any creditor of the *creator,* may compel the exercise of such power of revocation so reserved, to the same extent and under the same conditions that such *creator* could have exercised them."

Q. What is a creature?

A. creature. Legal idiom has developed a peculiar kind of taxonomy in which, legal doctrines or principles are described as *creatures,* e.g., "Adoption, in this country, is entirely a *creature of statute* and is unknown at common law." "The cause of action is wholly a *creature of equity."* The *OED* quotes the following English example from 1855: "The railway and the rights of the railway are the *creatures* of the Act of Parliament." A useful phrase, *creature of* etc., should not be so overworked as to become another tiresome legal Cliche.

Q. Who is credible?

A. credible, credulous, creditable. *Credible* = believable; *credulous* = gullible, tending to believe and *creditable* = worthy of credit, laudable.

Q. What is credit?

A. credit (= to give credence to) for *believe* is now almost peculiar to legal writing but is an acceptable legal idiom: "Black and Danley contradicted each other in their testimony and the court *credited* Danley." "It may be that the court below did not consider such evidence substantial or did not *credit* its validity but we are unable to determine from a silent record the thought processes of the court below." "The trial judge was entitled to *credit* her testimony."

Q. Who is a crier?

A. crier (= a court officer who calls the court to order) has the variant spelling *cryer,* which is to be eschewed. Today, the bailiff usually acts as crier; hence, *bailiff* has almost supplanted the term *crier.*

Q. What is criminality?

A. criminality = the quality or fact of being criminal. "Underlying this specific issue are more fundamental principles regarding the creation of criminal liability and the extent to which, a defendant's belief in the *criminality* of his acts affects such liability." This term has the variants *criminalness* and *criminalty,* neither of which, should appear in modern legal writing.

Q. What exactly is a criterion?

A. criterion, -ria. *Criteria* is the plural, *criterion* the (originally Greek) singular. A Ph.D. in linguistics once defended *criteria* as a singular because "not everyone knows that the singular is *criterium*"! (Infrequently one even sees, though not infrequently enough, *criterias.*) The plural *criterions* was tried for a time but failed to become a standard. Here, the correct forms are used: "The test is whether a handicapped individual who meets all employment *criteria,* except for the challenged discriminatory *criterion,* can perform the essential functions of the position in question without endangering the health and safety of others."

The following are the examples of *criteria* wrongly made singular: "The determining *criteria* [read *criterion*] is the function of the attorneys' fees in the litigation process." "Appellant contends that the trial court used an improper *criteria* [read *criterion*] and denied appellant due process by basing its decision on its prior belief."

It has even happened that *criterion* has been mistaken as a plural, perhaps because *criteria* is so frequently misused as a singular: "In *Johnson,* a panel of this court noted that it was appropriate to carefully review the basis upon which the district court made its award, upon finding that improper *criterion* [read *criteria*] were utilised."

Q. What is meant by Culpable?

A. culpable = criminal, blame worthy.

Q. What is meant by Custody?

A. custody = confinement or imprisonment, e.g., Remand (of accused person) in custody control and possession of something or person, e.g., to surrender ourself into the custody of the court.

Q. Explain the Custom.

A. custom = An unwritten law dating back to civilization. This is a conduct which is observed uniformly and voluntarily by the people.

———◇◇◇———

Q. What is meant by damages?
A. damages = A sum of money paid to the plaintiff as compensation for breach of contract or tort.

Q. What is meant by De Facto?
A. de facto = In fact, actually

Q. What is meant by De Jure?
A. de Jure = According to the law.

Q. What is declaratory decree?
A. declaratory decree = A decree which simply declares the rights of the parties to express the opinion of the court on any question without ordering to be done.

Q. What is a decree?
A. decree = A judgement delivered by a court.

Q. What is a deed?
A. deed = A written statement which is signed, sealed and delivered.

Q. What do you understand by defamation?
A. defamation = Publication of a false or derogatory statement regarding a person, which lowers his reputation in the eyes of members of the society.

Q. Who is a defendant?
A. defendant = A person sued in a court of law.

Q. Explain the delegated legislation.
A. This consists of orders, rules regulations, bylaws etc. Which is made by a person or body other than the legislative authority by virtue of powers conferred by the statute. It is also called subordinate legislation or administrative legislation.

Q. What is demise?
A. demise = The grant of lease.

Q. What is deposition?
A. **deposition** = The giving of testimony upon oath in court of law.

Q. Who is a deponent?
A. **deponent** = a person who makes an affidavit or deposition.

Q. What is meant by desertion?
A. **desertion** = Abandonment by one spouse or the other.

Q. What is meant by devise?
A. **devise** = A gift of land in a will.

Q. What is diction?
A. **diction** = (1) enunciation, distinctness of pronunciation or (2) word-choice. Often sense (2) is overlooked. This book addresses, in a large measure, the problems of legal diction.

Q. What is a dictum?
A. **dictum. A.** Full Phrase. *Dictum* is a shortened form of *obiter dictum* (= a nonbinding, incidental opinion on a point of law given by a judge in the course of a written opinion delivered in support of a judgement). The full phrase still occasionally appears: "The principle of stare decisis impliedly imposes upon the writer of the opinion the obligation to refrain from *obiter dicta* and to confine himself to the precise questions involved." Judge Posner has aptly defined *dictum* as "as statement in a judicial opinion that could have been deleted without seriously impairing the analytical foundations of the holding that, being peripheral, may not have received the full and careful consideration of the court that uttered it." *Sarnoff v. American Home Products Corp.,* 798 F. 2d 1075. 1084 (7th Cir. 1986).

Q. Define the word differ.
A. **differ (from, (with).** To *differ from* is to be unlike whereas to *differ with* is to express a divergent opinion, e.g., "With respect to legacies out of the personal estate, the civil law, which in this respect has been adopted by courts of equity, *differs* in some respects *from* the common law in its treatment of conditions precedent."

Q. What is different from and what is different than?
A. **different (from, than).** *Different than* is often considered to be inferior to *different from.* The problem is that *than* should follow a coparative adjective

(e.g., *larger than, sooner than,* etc.) and *different* is not comparative—though, to be sure, it is a word of contrast. Writers should generally prefer *different from. Than* implies a comparison, *i.e.,* a matter of degree; but *differences* are ordinarily qualitative not quantitative, and the adj. *different* is not strictly comparative, e.g., "Minors are treated differently *than* [read from] adults in the criminal justice system."

Still, it is indisputable that *different than* is sometimes idiomatic and even useful insofar as *different from* frequently is not interchangeable with it, as here: "Corporate residency is *different* for venue *than* for diversity purposes." Also, *different than* may properly begin clauses where attempting to use *different from* would be so awkward as to require another construction: "The record establishes that Wakefield is a *different* person mentally and emotionally *than* he was before his loss of hearing."

Where, however, *from* nicely fills the slot of *than,* it is to be preferred: "The fact that the injury occurred in a *different* manner *than* [read *from*] that which might have been expected, does not prevent the chauffeur's negligence from being in law the cause of the injury." (Andrews, J., in *Palsgraf.*)/ "If the testator makes a gift of property that is of a different nature *than* [read *from*] that of the property bequeathed, an application of the doctrine of ejusdem generis gives rise to a presumption that he did not intend to adeem." The *Oxford Guide* (p. 102) notes that when the adverb *differently* is used, *than* is "especially common ..... and has been employed by good writers since the seventeenth century" e.g., "A civil-rights suit is to be treated no differently *than* any other civil action."

Different to is a common British construction, unobjectionable when used by British writers: "He may say that the other has wholly failed in performance and given him a thing *different* in kind *to* that which was bargained for or of no substantial value." (Eng.)

Frequently, writers will use *different* superflously with *other than:* "The right of the district court to require the commissioners' court, by mandamus, to place a *different* [delete] valuation on the property of the railway company *other than* the value therefore placed on said property by the commissioners' court is discussed in the case of *Dillon v. Bave.*"

Q. What is differentia?

A. differentia (= distinguishing mark or characteristic) is a technical biological term that was long ago appropriated by legal writers, though often, it is used merely to mean "a distinction." The term is more common in G.B. than in the U.S., e.g., "The only *differentia* that can exist must arise, if at all, out of the fact that the acts done are the joint acts of several capitalists and not of one capitalist only." (Eng.) "The question in every case is whether the tribunal in question has similar attributes to a court of justice or acts in a manner similar to that in which, such courts act. This is of necessity a *differentia* that is not capable of precise limitation." (Eng.) The plural is *differentiae*.

Q. What is a differential?

A. differential. A. For *difference.* The *OED* records the noun *differential* only in specialised mathematical and biological senses. As a popularised technicality, it was extended to mean "a difference in a wage or salary" e.g., "Payment [may be] made pursuant to ..... a *differential* based on any other factor other [sic] than sex." Equal Pay Act, 29 U.S.C. § 206 (d) (1) (1982) (emphasis added).

The intrusion of this word into the domain of *difference* should stop there, however. The following usage of *differential* was ill advised: "Most of the foreign news reaches this country at the City of New York and because of this and of time *differentials* [read *differences*] due to the earth's rotation, the distribution of news matter throughout the country is principally from East to West."

B. And *different. Differential,* adj = (1) of, exhibiting, depending upon, a difference or (2) constituting a specific difference. The adjective is not nearly as often misused as the noun see (A) above: "*Differential* treatment of parties, who are similarly situated, raises questions about whether the agency is administering its program in a fair, impartial and competent manner." "I am unhappily aware that this ruling will create anomalies through *differential* recognition of the acts of judges appointed respectively before and after U.D.I." (Eng.) "This tactic enables the court to characterise state goals that have been legitimated by Congress itself as improper solely because it disagrees with the concededly rational means of *differential* taxation selected by the legislature."

C. And *deferential.* These near-homophones sometimes trip up semiconscious writers and speakers. *Deferntial* = showing deference; respectful.

Q. What is difficult of?

A. difficult of, an archaic construction, is common still in legal prose, e.g., "The complications that can arise when divorces are invalid are *difficult* of solution." Formerly this phrase was seen in literary as well as in legal writing.

Q. What is digital?

A. digital is commonly used as the adjective corresponding to *finger* to contexts such as the following: The issue of *digital* rape was raised at trial." *State v. Roden,* 380 N.W. 2d 669, 670 (S.D. 1986)./ "He argues that officials subjected him to a *digital* rectal search that violated his fourth, fifth and eighth amendment rights."

Dictionary of Legal Terms 53

Q. What is dignitas?

A. dignitas is a preposterous **Latinism** in place of the ordinary word *dignity*, e.g., "I accept the fact, therefore, that the applicant has suffered an injury to his *dignitas* [read *dignity*] by the respondent's actions." (Rhod.)

Q. Does dignity exist in law?

A. dignity exists in law in a sense obsolete in nonlegal contexts. It is used to mean "rank; magnitude," esp. in the phrase *of constitutional dignity*, e.g., "A statute and a constitution, although of unequal *dignity*, are both laws and rest on the will of the people." "The constitutional requirement of substantial equality and fair process can be attained only where counsel acts in the role of an active advocate in behalf of his client, as opposed to that of amicus curiae; the no-merit letter and the procedure it triggers do not reach that *dignity*." "The duty that Botkin owed defendant, in making those payments, was of a *dignity* with, if not superior to, any which he owed to plaintiff."

Q. What is the meaning of the word to dilate?

A. dilat(at)ion. The better nominal form of the verb *to dilate*, from an etymological point of view, is *dilatation*. But *dilation* is common in AmE medical contexts. In other senses, *dilatation* (= [1] speaking or writing at length or [2] expansion) should be used.

Q. What is dilatory?

A. dilatory = tending to cause delay (dilatory pleas or exceptions). This word is little known to laymen.

Q. What exactly is a dilemma?

A. dilemma = a choice between two unpleasant or difficult alternatives. This word should not be used by **Slipshod Extension** for *plight or predicament*. The adjective is *dilemmatic*.

Q. Who is a dilutee?

A. dilutee = an unskilled worker added to a staff of skilled workers.

Q. Define diminution.

A. diminution, diminishment. The latter is a **Needless Variant**: "But there are procedural safeguards against *diminishment* [read *diminution*] of the infant's award." *Diminution dim-i-**nyoo-**shon* or ***noo**-shon* is often mispronounced /*dim-yoo-**nish**-on*/, by metathesis and sometimes is erroneously spelled as *dimunition*.

Q. What is meant by diminutive?

A. diminutive, meaning "small" is not pronounced /di-***min***-û-tiv/ but rather di-***min***-yû tiv, with a liquid -*u*-.

Q. What is diplomatic privilege?

A. diplomatic privilege = Legal immunity accorded to ambassadors and representatives of foreign governments.

Q. What is direct in legal terms?

A. direct is often used as an ellipsis for *direct examination*. e.g., "His testimony on *direct* did not relate to any inculpatory or exculpatory comments by Mr. P."

Q. What is a directory?

A. directory, imperative. These words have been used distinctively for purposes of statutory interpretation. "Mandatory provisions [in a statute] have ..... frequently been classified as either *imperative* (when failure to comply renders all subsequent proceedings void) or *directory* (when the subsequent proceedings are valid, though the persons failing to carry out the action enjoined [i.e., mandated] by Parliament may sometimes be punishable)." *F.v.F.,* [1971] P. 1, 11 (Prob. Div. & Adm. Div.), e.g., "It has been held that a violation is a substantial and not a mere technical error, since such a statute is *imperative* and not *directory.*"

In the U.S., frequently, the distinction is rather different; *directory* is opposed to *mandatory* and is only a little stronger than *precatory*, q.v.: "Statutes that regulate and prescribe the time in which, public officers shall perform specified duties, are generally regarded as *directory* only."

In the following sentence, *directional* (= of or relating to, or indicating, spatial direction) is wrongly used for *directory:* "The sentence is a *directional* [read *directory*] provision indicating when and how she is to receive the payments." *Coker v. Coker,* 650 S.W.2d 391, 395 (Tex. 1985) (Spears, J., dissenting).

Q. Define legal disability.

A. disability. A. And *liability; inability.* These words, which overlap only slightly but are infrequently confounded, are best keenly distinguished. *Disability* = (1) the lack of ability to perform some function or (2) in capacity in the eyes of the law. *Liability* = (1) probability (2) a pecuniary obligation or (3) a drawback. *Inability* = the lack of power or means.

B. And *disablement. Disablement* = (1) the action of disabling or (2) the imposition of a legal disability. Here, sense (1) applies: "Under a credit insurance policy the beneficiary is the creditor and upon the death or

Dictionary of Legal Terms 55

disablement of the insured, the benefits or proceeds of the policy automatically accrue to the creditor for the purpose of discharging the debtor's financial obligations." See (A) for the senses of *disability*.

Q. What is a directed verdict?

A. directed verdict; instructed verdict. The phrases are synonymous. The (U.S.) Federal Rules of Civil Procedure use *directed verdict*. Both phrases exemplify Hypallage, in as much as the jury—and not the verdict—is what is directed or instructed.

Q. Define direct-evidence.

A. direct evidence, original evidence. Both of these phrases are used as antonyms of *hear-say evidence* and *circumstantial evidence* (or *indirect evidence*). *Direct evidence* is more common. As an opposite of *hearsay,* it means "a statement in reference to another's previous words, made by a witness in court to prove the truth of the matter asserted." As an antonym of *circumstantial evidence, direct evidence* = a statement of a witness that he perceived a fact in issue with one of his five senses or that he was in a particular physical or mental state *(CDL)*.

It would be helpful by way of differentiation to use *original evidence* as an antonym of *hearsay evidence* and *direct evidence* as an antonym of *circumstantial evidence*.

Q. What is direct examination?

A. direct examination examination-in-chief. The latter is a chiefly British variant of the former.

Q. What are directional words?

A. directional words. A. In *-ward(s)*. BrE has an affinity for *-wards* words. "There was a taxicab proceeding *Westwards* whose driver was called as a witness." (Eng.) In AmE *-ward* is the preferred form across the broad. Hence, *toward* is preferred in the U.S., *towards* in G.B.

B. Verbose Constructions. Use of such words as *easterly* and *northerly* in phrases like *in an Easterly direction* is prolix. In fact, the simple word for the direction *(East)* usually suffices in place of the words ending in either *-erly* or *-wardly*. "The appellee was riding his bicycle *Northwardly* [read *North*] on 29th Street just before the accident; appellant was driving his car *in a southerly direction* [read *south*] on Jackson Street." The one useful distinctive sense that *Southwardly* and *Southerly* convey is "in a direction more or less south."

Q. What is disadvantage in law?

A. disadvantage, v.t., appears regularly in legal writing but generally, only in the past participle form *disadvantaged* appears in lay writing. Usually functioning as an adjective (disadvantaged student). Following are the examples of typical legal usage: "The statute *disadvantages* those who would benefit from laws barring racial, religious or ancestral discrimination." "The state may no more *disadvantage* any particular group by making it more difficult to enact legislation in its behalf than it may dilute a person's vote." "The district court judge held that the EEOC could not show sex discrimination violating section 703(d) (1) of Title VII because females had not been *disadvantaged* with respect to males."

Q. What is disaffirmation?

A. disaffirmation, disaffirmance. For the word meaning 'repudiation' the distinction drawn at *affirmance,* q.v., would recommend the form *disaffirmation.* The *COD* recommends *-tion,* but *W9* records only *-ance,* a common form in AmE. Try as we might for consistency, we are unlikely to achieve it here. *Disaffirmation* is better but *disaffirmance* cannot be strongly criticized, e.g., "The common-law method for reaching this remedial goal is through an out-of-court *disaffirmance* of the contract followed by a legal restitutionary action." "The tentative trust becomes absolute and irrevocable on the death of the depositor before the beneficiary without revocation or some decisive act or declaration of *disaffirmance,* entitling the beneficiary to the balance remaining at the time of the depositor's death but not to anything more than such balance."

Q. Define the term disappoint.

A. disappoint (of (in). *Disappoint* is used in legal contexts is a sense rare in lay contexts, namely, "to deprive; to frustrate in one's expectations" e.g., "A court of equity will then, sequester the benefits intended for the electing beneficiary, to secure compensation to those persons whom his election *disappoints."* "The courts will not *disappoint* the interest of those for whose benefit, the party is called upon to exercise the power."

Usually, the term *disappointed* refers to heirs who take neither an intestate share of an estate nor a share by will, e.g., "Under such circumstances, the gift to the class is implied and the testator could not have intended the objects of the power to be *disappointed* of his bounty by the failure of the donee to exercise such power in their favour." To be *disappointed* in a thing, as opposed to of it, is to have received or attained it but to consider it as not measuring up to one's expectations.

Often *disappointed* is used as a past participial adjective: "He is known in the law as a *disappointed* legatee and the doctrine of acceleration of remainders should be adopted at the expense of *disappointed* legatees."

Q. What is disapprobation?

A. disapprobation is an especially Formal Word meaning "disapproval." It is perhaps allowable in weighty contexts: "On the opening of the cause, Lord Kenyon expressed his *disapprobation* of the action; but his lordship permitted the cause to proceed." (Eng.) But in ordinary prose it leads to topheaviness: "Employees may feel the need to sign the petition in order to curry favor with or avoid *disapprobation* [read *disapproval*] by company officials."

Q. What is meant by the term to disapprove.

A. disapprove, like *approve,* q.v., may be transitive as well as intransitive. "We *disapprove* the dicta in that case." This usage of the word is far more common in legal than in non-legal writing.

Q. Define disassociate.

A. disassociate, dissociate. Though common, *disassociate* is inferior to *dissociate,* q.v., of which, it is a **Needless Variant**.

Q. What is disasterous?

A. disasterous is a fairly common misspelling of *disastrous.* Refer Leff, *The Leff Dictionary of Law,* 94 Yale L.J. 1855, 2038 (1985), s.v. *aphrodisiac.*

Q. What is disbarment and what is disbarring?

A. disbarment, disbarring. Both mean "the action of expelling a lawyer from the bar." *Disbarment* is the more common noun in the U.S.A., e.g., "A threat of personal chastisement made by an attorney to a judge out of court for his conduct or rulings during the trial of a cause pending is strictly unprofessional and furnishes grounds for *disbarment.*" "The effect of a *disbarment* is the utter extinction of professional character."

In G.B., the gerund in *-ing* is common: "*Disbarring* may be imposed by the benchers as the ultimate punishment on a barrister guilty of conduct unbecoming the profession." (Eng.)

Q. What is disbelief?

A. disbelief, unbelief, nonbelief, misbelief. *Disbelief* is the mental rejection of something after considering its plausibility; it results from active, conscious decision. *Unbelief* denotes the state of doubt but of not having made up one's mind. *Nonbelief* is a Needless Variant of *unbelief.* "*Nonbelief* [read *Unbelief*] of the prosecutor in the guilt of the person charged with crime is evidence of want of probable cause for the prosecution." A *misbelief* is an erroneous or false belief.

Q. Explain the term to disburse.

A. disburse, disperse. *Disburse* is used only in reference to distribution of money (the directors disbursed dividends to the stockholders). *Disperse* is used in reference to distribution of all other things, such as crowds or diseases.

Q. What is the meaning of the term to discharge?

A. discharge was formerly common as a variant of *dismiss* in mandates, e.g., "Case *discharged.*"

Q. What do you understand by disclaimer?

A. disclaimer is an express denial or complete renouncing one's legal right or claim.

Q. What is distress?

A. distress = The seizure chattal to satisfy out of the proceeds of its sale, some debt or claim.

Q. What is disciplinary?

A. disciplinary, disciplinatory. The latter is a Needless Variant. *Disciplinary* = (1) related to discipline or (2) carrying out punishment. Here, sense (2) applies: "The special master considered the company's disparate enforcement of its no-solicitation policy to be mitigated by the legality of the warning, apology, mistake, or failure to result in *disciplinary* action."

Q. What is the meaning of the term to disclose?

A. disclose, expose. There are important differences. *Disclose* = to reveal any factual matter. *Expose* = (1) to lay bare or unmask something bad or (2) to place in a perilous condition.

Q. What is discomfiture?

A. discomfit(ure). *Discomfit* (= to frustrate, disconcert) is best used only as a verb. The preferred noun is *discomfiture*. Ill-trained writers use phrases such as *much to his discomfit* in which, either *discomfort* or *discomfiture* is intended.

Q. Is discommend the opposite of recommend?

A. discommend is the opposite of *recommend*, not of *commend*.

Q. Discover is to uncover, reveal, explain.

discover is, except in legal **Argot**, obsolete in the sense "to uncover, reveal". The verb now generally means "to find, detect."

Q. What is discoverable?

A. discoverable, in American law, means "subject to pretrial discovery" (discoverable documents of the corporation). This sense goes beyond the general meaning of "ascertainable."

Q. Explain discovert.

A. discovert is not an opposite of *covert* as ordinarily used—*overt* is. *Discovert* means "unmarried, whether widowed, divorced or never having married," or, more technically, "not subject to the disabilities of coverture" e.g., "She united with her husband in making a sale to her brother of the land put into their possession by her father's executor and she subsequently acknowledged it when *discovert*."

Q. What is discrete?

A. discrete, discreet. The former means "separate, distinct" whereas the latter means "cautious, judicious," *Discreet* is most commonly used of speaking or writing. The usual error is to misuse *discreet*, the more common term in non-legal language for *discrete*. Here, in this quotation from a casebook, the opposite blunder is committed: "Consider again Pound, ante, p. 64, Hierarchy of Sources and Forms in Law. *Compare* Keeton's discussion of overruling precedents—rules vis-a-vis principles—ante, pp. 839-40, *with* Pound. Is the average opinion writer this *discrete* [read *discreet*]?"

Q. What is meant by divorce?

A. divorce = Dissolution of marriage.

Q. What do you understand by donicile?

A. domicile = The place where one has his permanent residence to which if absents, he has the intention of returning.

Q. Who is a donee?

A. donee = To whom gift is made.

Q. Who is a donor?

A. donor = one, who makes a gift.

Q. Who is drawee?

A. drawee = payor (drawee bank). Inasmuch as lawyers understand *drawee* and *payor* to be synonymous, *drawee/payor* makes little sense. "A payee or other true owner of an instrument that is cashed under a forged endorsement may sue directly *the drawee/payer* [read either *the drawee* or *the payor*] bank."

Q. What is drought?

A. drouth, drought. The former is archaic in BrE but still frequently appears in AmE texts. Nevertheless, *drought* is the preferred form in both linguistic communities.

Q. What is a drug?

A. drug for *dragged* is a nonstandard dialectal form common in the South (U.S.): "He then *drug* [read *dragged*] the body into the house."

Q. Who is drunk?

A. drunk, drunken. In older and literary usage, the *Oxford Guide* notes, *drunk* and *drunken* were "the predicative and attributive forms respecitvely; now usually allocated to distinct senses, namely 'intoxicated' and "given to drink."

We do, however, have the fixed idiom *drunken driving,* defined by the *CDL* as "driving while affected by alcohol." *Drunken* here means "exhibiting or evidencing intoxication" e.g., "This was the year the courts joined the legislatures in earnest in the five-year-old crackdown on *drunken* driving." "Smith, a *drunken* driver, travelling at eighty miles an hour or faster, weaving from side to side of the road, tried to pass the plaintiff's automobile."

Q. What is dubitante?

A. dubitante = doubting. The term is used in law reports of a judge who is doubtful about a legal proposition but is loath to declare it wrong, e.g., "Mr. Justice Retledge acquiesces in the Court's opinion and judgement *dubitante* on the question of equal protection of the laws."

Some judges use this term after their names in separate opinions, as if it were analogous to *concurring* or *dissenting*. Apparently the purpose of doing so is to signal that the judge has grave doubts about the soundness of the majority opinion but not so grave as to cause him to dissent.

Q. What is due process of law?

A. due process of law. When applied to judicial proceedings, this phrase traditionally "mean[s] a course of legal proceedings according to those rules and principles, which have been established in our system of juris-prudence for the protection and enforcement of private rights." *Pennoyer v. Neff,* 95 U.S. 714, 733 (1877).

Q. Where do we use due to?

A. due to should be used to mean "attributable to" and often follows the verb *to be* (sometimes understood in context). The phrase is commonly misused as a conjunctive adverb for *because of, owing to, caused by* and *on grounds of,* e.g., "The trial was lost *due to* [read *because of*] his damaging admissions." "*Due to* [read *Because of*] the close interrelation between these two rights, we believe that Wiggins's petition fairly raised the issue of his right to counsel." "Because the state court did not specify whether it denied habeas relief on the merits or *due to* [read *on grounds of*] procedural default, we must interpret the state court's silence." "*Due in part to* [read *In part because of*] the widespread enactment of pretermitted heir statutes, the majority of the courts have been unwilling to hold that birth of issue alone revokes a will."

Here, the phrase is correctly used: "We conclude that since the defendant knew of his right to a speedy trial, the failure of the government *due to* clerical error or oversight to request the Indiana prison authorities to advise the defendant of his right does not violate the statute." "A distinction must be drawn between cases in which the difficulties are *due to* uncertainty as to the causation of the damage, in which questions of remoteness arise and those which are *due to* the fact that the assessment of damages cannot be made with any mathematical accuracy." (Eng.)

Due followed by an infinitive is not a form of the phrase *due to*, though it looks deceptively similar, e.g., "Because "security center" is a generic term, not entitled to service mark protection, the district court decision is *due to be* reversed."

Q. Define duplicitous.

A. duplicitous, duplicative, -ory. *Duplicitous* (= marked by duplicity) is a twentieth-century coinage generally understood to mean "deceitful." The American courts have latched onto the word in the sense of doubleness, from the old legal meaning of *duplicity* (= double pleading). Hence, "A *duplicitous* indictment is one charging two separate crimes in the same count." *United States v. Ellis,* 595 F. 2d 154, 163 (3d Cir. 1979). The following are other typical examples: "The grounds of the motion insisted on here are that the indictment is *duplicitous* and that the weapon is not so described." *Davis v. State,* 46 Fla. 137, 35 So. 76, 76 (1903). "The allegation in a single count of a conspiracy to commit several crimes is not *duplicitous.*" *Braverman v. United States,* 317 U.S. 49, 54 (1942). "Acosta argues further that the indictment was *duplicitous* because it joined separate conspiracies into one count." *United States v. Acosta,* 763 F. 2d 671, 696 (5th Cir. 1985). "An indictment charging rape in one count in having intercourse with a female under the statutory age of consent and in another count, in having intercourse with a female whose mind was so weak as to render her incapable of consenting, both referring to the same transaction, is not *duplicitous.*" A literate layman would be utterly confused by this use of the word.

Duplicitous should not be extended beyond its sense of doubleness in pleading, indictments etc., as it is here: "There is a suggestion that some of the work performed by counsel for Baxter was *duplicitous* [read *duplicative*] because of a change in counsel during the preparation stages of the litigation." *Baxter v. Savannah Sugar Refinning Corp.,* 495 F. 2d 437, 447 (5th Cir. 1974).

Duplicative, which one might have preferred in the sense to *duplicitous,* has been adopted for other uses in the law. "As between federal district courts ..... the general principle is to avoid *duplicative* litigation." *Colorado River Water Conservation Dist. v. United States.* 424 U.S. 800, 817 m(1976)./ "Recent Supreme Court decisions have emphasised the risk of *duplicative* recoveries and other factors without mentioning antitrust standing as a distinct inquiry." "The policy of minimization of *duplicative* enforcement might well prevail over concerns of centralisation." "We realised at the time of the decision that unifying school systems often would cause elimination of *duplicative* jobs." *Duplicatory* is a Needless Variant.

Q. What is duplicity in law?

A. duplicity is frequently used in law for *duplication,* e.g., "The defendant suggested that the 340 billable hours resulted from a *duplicity* of time spent by the plaintiff's attorney and his five associates." "The country prosecutor was even heard boasting to a member of the press that he had a *'duplicity'* of evidence!" These uses of the word are poor; they derive from the true legal meaning "the pleading of two (or more) matters in one plea; double pleading" *(OED.)* The word should not, by Slipshod Extension, be used of other types of doubleness.

The non-legal sense of *duplicity* (= deceitfulness, double-dealing) is also quite common in legal contexts: "When a lawyer's falsehood and *duplicity* is established he becomes a professional outcast." "The trial judge stated that he doubted the plaintiff's veracity; but the right of a party to have his own statement is not diminished when the district court suspects *duplicity.*"

Q. What is duress?

A. duress, durance. *Duress* = (1) the infliction of hardship; (2) forcible restraint; or (3) compulsion illegally exercised to force a person to perform some act. *Durance* is an archaic Legalism sharing sense (2) of *duress*. Neither word is needed in that sense, however.

Q. Who is dutiable?

A. dutiable = subject to the levy of a duty, e.g.: "The dual purpose of the search is to ascertain whether an illegal alien is seeking to cross the border and whether contraband or *dutiable* property is being smuggled."

Q. Who is dutiful?

A. dutiful; duteous. The usual term is *dutiful*. Although formerly in good use, yet *duteous* is an archaic Needless Variant.

Q. Who is duty bound?

A. duty(-) bound. This term of American legal Argot, an adjectival rendering of the phrase *bounden duty,* should be hyphenated, e.g.: "Seamen, of course, are wards of admiralty whose rights federal courts are *duty-bound* to be jealously protect." "As long as the Supreme Court of the United States adheres to its long-standing construction of the Second Amendment, this court and all other Texas courts are *dutybound* [read *duty-bound*] to follow and apply that construction." "The appellant advances a rule to the effect that because of the engagement of the parties a confidential relationship resulted whereby decedent was *duty bound* [read *duty-bound*] to make a full disclosure to appellant of the exient, nature and value of his property." Usually a simple *bound* suffices.

Q. Who is dynamic?

A. dynamic, n., is a Vogue Word generally best avoided, e.g., "In the first case, a negotiation is stipulated. In the second, the *dynamic* leads almost inevitably in that direction." [Read *In the second, a negotiation is almost inevitable.*]

Q. What do you mean by dysfunctional?

A. dysfunctional (= functioning abnormally) is so spelled; *disfunctional* is a not uncommon misspelling.

Q. Explain *each.*

A. each. A. Number. *Each* takes a singular verb and pronouns having *each* as an antecedent must be in the singular, e.g., "*Each is* entitled to benefits under this program." "A high-water mark was reached in *Morris Trusts v. Commissioner,* in which *each* of ten trusts *were* [read *was*] held to create two separate trusts." "Persuasive arguments exist that *each* of the first two criteria *is* satisfied."

Sometimes, *each* is mistaken as the subject in a sentence in which, it acts in apposition, as in "A and B each *withdraw* [not *withdraws*]." Here, the mistake is made: "Smith and Jones *each has his reason* [read *each have their reasons*] for not complying with the request for production."

B. Delimiting the Application of *each.* Especially, in contexts in which, *all* appears before *each,* it may be important to use defining words after *each.* Thus "suppose a statute required *all directors* to take an oath of secrecy and imposed a penalty on *each director* in the event of a violation. If half the directors took the oath and half failed, could they all be prosecuted or only those who failed?" E.A. Dreidger, *The Composition of Legislation* 78 (1957). The remedy lies, of course, in writing that the penalty is imposed on *each director who fails to take the oath,* assuming that is the intended meaning.

Q. Who are *each and every?*

A. each and every. This trite phrase should generally be eschewed but especially, it should not be plugged in where only one of the adjectives properly modifies what follows, e.g., "Plaintiff has performed *each and every* of his obligations under the contract." *Each* works fine here, but not *every,* for one cannot say, "He has performed *every* of his obligations." One who insists on being bromidic should write: "Plaintiff has performed *each and every one* of his obligations under the contract." Cf. and/or & If, as, and when.

Q. Define *each other* and *one another.*

A. each other, one another. The former phrase is used of two persons or entities; the latter is best confined to contexts involving more than two, e.g., "One of us would turn to the foregoing comment and find that the two terms cancel *one another* [read *each other*]."

While using these phrases, it is important to know precisely what is being compared. In the following sentence, *elements constituting the basis of damages* are being compared, though the writer mistook *causes of action* as the units of comparison: "Having examined the jury instructions and the special verdict in this case, we find that the elements constituting the basis of damages of *each* of the two causes of action were not sufficiently distinguished *from one another* [read *from those of the other*] to ensure that there was no double compensation." The use of *each* before *one another* is what caused the problem; the writer was guilty of Swapping Horses from *each other* to *one another*.

Q. What is early on?

A. early on is not the odious locution that some people think. Slightly informal, it is perfectly idiomatic in both AmE and BrE.

Q. What is easement?

A. easement, right of way. The former term is now obsolete in all but the legal sense, whereas the latter is common among laymen. An *easement* is either a legal or an equitable right enjoyed by a landowner to benefit from nearby land. Often, *easements* take the form of *rights of way* (= rights to pass over another person's land). But a *right of way* may be granted by license (to the person) as well as by easement (inuring to the land).

Q. What is ecclesiastical law?

A. ecclesiastical law, canon law. Although these generic terms overlap a great deal, *ecclesiastical law* broadly covers all laws relating to a church, whether from state law, divine law, natural law or societal rules; *canon law* is more restricted, referring only to the body of law constituted by ecclesiastical authority for the organisation and governance of a Christian Church.

Q. What is meant by the term economic?

A. economic, economical. *Economical means "thrifty"* or, in the current jargon, "cost-effective." *Economic* should be used for every other meaning possible for the words, almost always in reference to the study of economics. Hence, we have *economic studies* and *economic interest* but not *economical shopping.*

Q. What are edly words?

A. -EDLY. Words ending in this way are more pervasive in law than elsewhere. Often, the classic adverbial formula *in a ..... manner* does not work with these words; thus *allegedly* does not mean "in an alleged manner," *purportedly* does not mean "in a purported manner" and *admittedly* does not mean "in an admitted manner." Rather, the unorthodox formula for these words is *it is ..... -ed that,* i.e. *allegedly* (= it is alleged that) and so on. Instead of bewailing the unorthodoxy of these words in *-edly*, we should be thankful for their promotion of conciseness and continue to use them (if only sparingly). We have many of them, such as *supposedly, allegedly, assertedly, reportedly, admittedly, confessedly* and *concededly*.

Nonetheless, forms in *-edly* ought to be avoided if a ready substitute exists: "[A] bank may indeed be *liable for unauthorizedly revealing* [read *liable for revealing without authorisation*] the state of a depositor's accounts to his creditors." *Schuster v. Banco de Iberoamerica*, 476 So. 2d 253, 255 (Fla. App. 1985) (Schwartz, J., dissenting).

Q. What is educative?

A. educational, educative, -tory, educable. *Educational* = (1) having to do with education (educational issues) (2) serving to further education (educational films). *Educative* = tending to educate instructive (educative lectures). *Educatory* is a **Needless Variant** of *educative*. *Educable* = capable of being educated (educable pupils).

Q. Define educe.

A. educe, v., (= to elicit; evoke) should be distinguished from *adduce* (= to bring forward for analysis) and from *educt*, n. (= something educed), e.g., "In the present case, the factual showing thus *educed* [*i.e., developed, brought out*] does not so unequivocally point to a borrowed employee relationship as to permit a summary judgement." Here, the sense is correct but the word is matched with the wrong subject: "We need not reach this issue, because *no factual showing was educed* [read either *no showing was made* or *no facts were educed*] by the defendant to negate the allegations of her complaint that the failure to re-employ her resulted from gender-based discrimination."

Q. Who is educible?

A. educible, educable. The former means "capable of being educed or drawn out." The latter means "capable of being educated."

-EE. A. General Principles. This suffix (fr. French past participle *-é*) originally denoted "one who is acted upon" and the sense is inherently passive. Thus we have : *acquittee* (= one who is acquitted); *arrestee* (= one who is arrested); *conscriptee* (= one who is conscripted); *detainee* (= one who is detained); *educatee* (= one who is educated [by an *educator*]): *expellee* (= one who is expelled); *inauguree* (= one who is inaugurated); *indictee* (= one who is indicted); invitee (= one who is invited); *liberee* (= one who is liberated); *permittee* (= one who is permitted); *returnee* (= one who is returned); *selectee* (= one who is selected); *separatee* (= one who is separated); *shelteree* (= one who is sheltered); *smugglee* (= one who is smuggled); *telephonee* (= one who is telephoned).

The suffix has also a dative sense, in which, it acts as the agent noun for the indirect object; this is the sense in which, the suffix is most commonly used in law: *abandonee* (= one to whom property rights are relinquished); *advancee* (= one to whom something is allocated); and *allottee* (= one to whom something is allotted).

Q. What is meant by embezzlement?
A. embezzelment = Dishonest misappropriation of property by a person, who comes in possession thereof lawfully.

Q. What is eminent domain?
A. eminent domain = Power of the state to acquire private property for public use.

Q. What is enactment?
A. enactment = Act of Parliament.

Q. What is meant by encroachment?
A. encroachment = Unlawfully entering upon mother's rights or possessions.

Q. What is meant by equity?
A. equity = Fair and right, the recourse to general principles of justice to correct and supplement the ordinary law.

Q. What is meant by escheat?
A. escheat = The lapsing of property of the sovereign or state on the death of the owner intestate and without heir.

Q. What is estate?
A. estate = An interest in land.

Q. What do you understand by estoppels?
A. estoppels = A rule of evidence preventing a person from denying truth of statement which he has made previously by which he has led another to believe and act upon.

Q. What is eviction?
A. eviction = Dispossession, recovery of land by the application law.

Q. What is evidence?

A. evidence = The legal means exclusive of more argument, which tend to prove or disprove any matter of fact, the truth of which is submitted to judicial investigation.

Q. What is meant by execution?

A. execution = Enforcing a court's judgement with the force of law.

Q. Who is an executor?

A. executor, -er. The *-er* spelling is obsolete. An *executor* is either (1) "One who does or performs some act"; or (2) "one who, appointed in a testator's will, administers the estate." In sense (2), the accent falls (familiarly) on the second syllable |*ig-zek-yu-tor*|; in sense (1), the accent is on the first syllable |***ek***-*se-kyoot-er*|.

Q. What is executory?

A. executory, -torial. *Executory* = designed to take or capable of taking full effect only at a future time *(OED)* (an executory judgement) (executory contract). *Executorial* = of or pertaining to an executor.

Q. Define executrix.

A. executrix, -tress. The former is the usual feminine form of *executor,* which may itself serve as a neuter form covering both sexes. Legal writers usually distinguish between the sexes with this term, however.

Q. What is exegesis?

A. exegesis; epexegesis; eisegesis. Knowledge of these terms is useful to anyone having to interpret writings. *Exegesis* = explanation or exposition (as of a word or sentence), e.g., "In interpretation of federal statutes and congressional intent ..... semantic *exegesis* is not conclusive." *International Union v. Marshall,* 584 F.2d 390, 397 (D.C. Cir. 1978). *Epexegesis* = the addition of a word or words to convey more clearly the meaning implied or the specific sense intended, in a preceding word or sentence *(OED). Eisegesis* = the interpretation of a word or passage by reading into it one's own ideas *(OED Supp.).*

Q. What is exemplary?

A. exemplary has almost contradictory connotations: *exemplary damages* make an example out of a wrongdoer, whereas *exemplary behaviour* is model behaviour. *Exemplary* is sometimes misunderstood as meaning 'severe' in phrases such as *exemplary punishment.*

Q. Define exempt.

A. exempt appears not uncommonly in the U.S. as an ellipsis for *tax-exempt.* Usually, this usage occurs only in contexts in which, the reader has already learned that the subject at hand is tax exemptions and not other types of exemptions. Following is a typical specimen: "An *exempt* organisation has the privilege of preferred second-class or third-class mailing rates." Weinlein, *Federal Taxation of Not-for-Profit Arts Organizations,* 12 J. Arts, Mgmt., & Law 33 (Summer 1982).

Q. What is exercise for existence?

A. exercise for *existence* is a puzzling error, e.g., "A presumption of undue influence arises from proof of the *exercise* [read *existence*?] of a confindential relation between the testator and such a beneficiary, coupled with activity on the part of the latter in the preparation of the will." (A *confidential relation* is not *exercised.*)

Q. Who is exertive?

A. exertive, -tional. *Exertive* = tending to exert or rouse to action (*OED*) (resolve is an exertive emotion). *Exertional,* though recorded in none of the Oxford or Merriam-Webster dictionaries, has appeared (usually, in the negative form) in American law cases in the field of social security disabilities. *Exertional* = of or pertaining to exertion, e.g., "[H]e is unable to return to his past relevant work and suffers from a *non-exertional* impairment." *Warmoth v. Bowen,* 798 F.2d 1109, 1110 (7th Cir. 1986)./ "[W]henever a *nonexertional* impairment is presented the Secretary must introduce a vocational expert to testify that jobs in the workplace exist for a person with that particular disability." *Bapp v. Bowen,* 802 F.2d. 601, 604 (2d Cir. 1986).

Q. What is ex facie?

A. ex facie (= in view of what is apparent, lit., "from the face") is not justified as a legal **Latinism**, inasmuch as so many ordinary English words, such as *evidently, apparently* or *on its face,* suffice in its stead: "*Ex facie* [read *patently*] those transfers would be the same in form and in effect precisely as the instrument of transfer now before us." (Eng.) Here the phrase is wrongly made adjectival: "The Companies Act of 1948 brought into being that which was *ex facie* [read *evident*] in all its essential characteristics." (Eng.)

Q. What is meant by ex officio?

A. ex officio = By virtue of office.

Q. What is ex gratia?

A. ex gratia, a gratia. *Ex gratia* means "as a favour, not by legal necessity" (ex gratia payment). *A gratia* is a **Needless Variant**.

Q. What is existing?

A. existing. Legal drafters should beware of the **Ambiguity** of this word. It may mean "existing at the time of the writing" or "existing at some time after the writing," if not specifically put within a time frame.

Q. What is an exit?

A. exit has been an acceptable verb since the early seventeenth century. Those who object to it on grounds that one does not 'entrance' a building have a misplaced prejudice.

Q. What is exlex in legal terms?

A. exlex, ex lege. Good legal writers have little or no usage for these terms; nevertheless, it is well to known their meanings. *Exlex* is an adjective meaning "outside the law; without legal authority" (an exlex government), whereas *ex lege* is an adverb meaning "as a matter of law" (property forfeited ex lege).

Q. What is ex maleficio?

A. ex maleficio = (adv.) by malfeasance; (adj.) tortious, e.g., "We do not find these allegations sufficient, either on authority or on principle, to establish a constructive trust *ex maleficio* [read *resulting from malfeasance*]." "In the character of a trustee *exmaleficio* [read *by virtue of malfeasance*], he shall be held to make good the things to the person who would have the property."

Q. Define exnecessitate.

A. ex necessitate (= of necessity) is a Latinistic pollutant, e.g., "They argue that adoption of the doctrine would be a nullification of the rule that executory limitations are void unless they take effect *ex necessitate* [read *of necessity*] and in all possible contingencies within the prescribed period."

Q. What is an exodus?

A. exodus, a much abused word, refers to the simultaneous departure of many people. It is not the term to describe one lawyer's leaving a firm: "Likewise, negotiations failed on whether Poindexter's ex-firm was entitled to reimbursement of several thousand dollars in costs expended on the Nicol case upon Poin-dexter's *exodus* [read *exit*] or upon the conclusion of the case."

Dictionary of Legal Terms 71

Occasionally *exodus* is mistakenly thought to be the equivalent of *influx,* which is actually an antonym.

Exodus should be avoided as a verb: "Poor people have no ability to *exodus from* [read *leave en masse*] an improverished state for richer ones."

Q. In what sense, the word exonerate is used?

A. exonerate, in the sense "to free from responsibility," should be used only in reference to people. Hence, the following use is erroneous: "Held, affirmed for DuPont since there was no evidence that the booster [a component in an explosive device] was responsible for the explosion and the evidence offered by plaintiff tended to *exonerate* [read *rule out*] the booster." Cf. **exculpate.**

In the sense "to free from encumberances," of course, *exonerate* is used of liens, e.g., "We find that the decedent did not expressly signify any intention not to *exonerate* the property here from the mortgage lien." Whereas *acquit* takes *of exonerate* takes the preposition *from:* "We affirm the lower court's holding that it was the intention of the testator that this legacy be *exonerated from* all liens."

Q. What is called exorbitant?

A. exorbitant (lit., "having departed or deviated from one's track [*orbita*] or rut") is sometimes mistakenly spelled *exhorbitant,* perhaps out of confusion with *exhort.* E.g., "Daon's own appraiser agreed that this price was *exhorbitant* [read *exorbitant*]." *Foster v. Doan Corp.,* 713 F.2d 148, 149 (5th Cir. 1983).

Q. What is exparte order?

A. ex parte order = An order granted after hearing one party only.

Q. What is meant by expert witness?

A. expert witness = one who gives an opinion on a particular subject due to his special knowledge.

Q. What is extradition?

A. extradition = A process by which an offender is transferred from one country to another for a trial.

Q. What is meant by the term face, on its.

A. face, on its. In the expression *face* refers to the inscribed side of a document. It means "in the words of, in the plain sense of" (the document on its face indicates testamentary intent). The phrase is sometimes used figuratively of things other than documents, e.g., "A libel is harmful *on its face.*"

One must be careful of context with this shopworn phrase. When the subject is plural and the phrase becomes *on their face,* there is a technical failure of concord that can sometimes be risible: "Most laws, however, discriminate or mete out different treatment *on their face.*" (No one wants to see treatment meted out on anyone's face; though the sentence refers *to the face of* the statute, nonetheless the imagery suggests something different.)/ "*On their face,* the municipal historic preservation ordinances satisfy requisite due process criteria."/ "Some of these statutes were held to be unconstitutional *on their face* or as applied." (Note that in these last two sentences the plural form *on their faces* would be even worse.)

The *face* idiom is an old one in the law. "In our opinion the writ ought not to be allowed by the court if it appears for the *face* of the record that the decision of the federal question which is complained of was so plainly right as not to require argument." *The Anarchists' Case,* 123 U.S. 131, 164 (1887).

Q. What is facial?

A. facial = complete; on its face; as a whole, e.g., "The cases before us are governed by the normal rule that partial, rather than *facial,* invalidation is the required course for such statutes." The adverbial usage is almost as common as the adjectival use; *facially* does not mean "in a facial manner." but "on its face". An example follows: "The court of appeals erred by *facially invalidating the statute in its entirely* [*i.e., invalidating the statute on its face*]." "We hold that the plaintiff has standing to challenge the constitutionality of the ordinance and that the section in its present form is *facially overbroad and unconstitutional* [*i.e., overbroad and unconstitutional on its face*]."

Q. Define the term facilitate?

A. facilitate (= to aid, help) is a Formal Word to be used sparingly, for it often is jargonistic, as is the agent noun *facilitator* (= helper). "The commission's improved decision undoubtedly *facilitates* this court's review by clarifying the issues involved." As Fowler and others have noted, it is better to write that an *action* (e.g., the *court's review*, in the sentence just quoted) is facilitated rather than that the *actor* (e.g., *the court*) is facilitated.

Q. What is fact in law?

A. fact, adj., **factual.** In phrases such as *fact(ual) question*, the longer form is preferable. Notwithstanding that *fact question* is jaring, it is potentially misleading to the reader. In the following sentence, for instance, the usage of *factual* would have circumvented the reader's thinking that *existence of fact* is an unhyphenated phrasal adjective: "If the proceedings are characterised as a trial on a stipulated record, the existence of *fact questions* [read *factual questions*] will not undermine the result." The sentences that follow, illustrate the better usage: "We are directed by statute and Supreme Court precedent to accord a presumption of correctness to such state court *factual findings.*" "Petitioners contend that the ICC impermissibly substituted its judgement for the *factual findings* of the state commission."

Notably, *factual* has two meanings: (1) "of or involving facts" (factual issue); and (2) 'true' (a factual depiction). Here, sense (2) is illustrated in a sentence in which, *fact* would be not just inferior but wrong: "If this were a *factual* account of what happened, the plaintiff would not have a cause of action."

Sense (1) of *factual,* the more usual meaning, appears in the following sentences: "The ICC's section 1150(c) jurisdiction is not of a limited nature but, in a proper case, is plenary, and may allow the ICC to delve into the *factual* record before the state agency." "The rule contemplates that only *factual* questions will be submitted to the jury to which the judge will apply the law, supplementing, if necessary, any *factual* determinations not submitted to the jury."

Q. What is factum?

A. fact, n., **factum.** *Fact* (lit., "a thing done") means "an action performed, an event, an occurrence or a circumstance." In legal writing, *fact* has the additional particularized sense "an evil deed, a crime." Thus we have the expressions *before the fact, after the fact* and *confess the fact.*

Factum, the Latinate form of the word, has several meanings: (1) [regarding change in domicile] "a person's physical presence in a new domicile"; (2)"due execution of a will"; (3) "a fact or statement of facts; and (4) "an act or deed." In senses (3) and (4), the only ones contained in the *OED,* the word has no merit in modern contexts (except in the phrase *fraud in the factum* [senses 2 and 4]; few lawyers would understand *factum* when so used. In sense (1), *factum* is perhaps a Term of Art; nevertheless, the term calls for elucidation.

Sense (2) occurs frequently in the context of wills where it is generally, no more useful or specific than *execution:* "It might be argued that logically, the only question upon the probate was the *factum* [read *execution*] of the instrument." In the Set Phrase *fraud* or *mistake in the factum,* however, the use of *factum* is well ensconced: "There is a close analogy, however, to the situation in which, a provision in a will, by mistake, in the *factum* is denied effect." "When there has been a fraudulent representation concerning the nature of the instrument or its contents, usually described as a fraud in the *factum,* it is well settled that the will or a fraudulently induced part of a will should be denied probate."

Q. What is a fact finder?
A. fact(-) finder should be hyphenated, not spelled as two words. Likewise, *fact-finding* is best hyphenated rather than spelled out in two words. The trend is to make both terms solid but the trend is, at best, incipient.

Q. What do you understand by false imprisonment?
A. false imprisonment = The confinement of a person without just cause or excuse. There must be a total restraint of the person and the onus of proving reasonable cause is on the defendant.

Q. What is fact finding?
A. fact-finding = the finding of facts; *factual finding* = a finding of fact, e.g., "The agency's decision that an impact statement was not required pretermitted the *fact-finding* process designed by Congress." "The court's *factual finding* on that issue precluded recovery by the plaintiff."

Fact-finding is often mistakenly used not in reference to the process but to mean "a finding of fact" e.g., "The earlier ruling was a fact-finding [read *factual finding*]." "On the basis of the above *fact-findings* [read *factual findings*], plaintiff has failed to make out a prima facie case." "The magistrate declined to enter any meaningful [q.v.] *factfindings* [read *factual findings*] on the incidents surrounding the workover crew's hotel room arrangement, which appellant contended had precipitated the discharge."

Q. Differentiate between factional factious and fractious.
A. factional, factious, fractious. These words are confusingly similar. *Factional* = of or relating to a faction. *Factious* = given to faction; acting for partisan purposes. *Fractious* = refractory, unruly, fretful, peevish.

Q. What is factitious?
A. factitious, fictitious. Both have the basic sense "artificial." *Factitious* = (1) man-made and not natural; and (2) sham produced by contrivance. *Fictitious* = imaginary, not real. The latter term is often used of testimony, accounts of facts or stories.

Dictionary of Legal Terms

Q. What is called the fact of the matter?

A. fact of the matter, the. This phrase is trite **Fustian** that may serve as a filler in speech but that generally has no justification in writing. Infrequently, it gives the needed rhythm.

Q. What is a factor?

A. factor properly means "an agent or cause that contributes to particular result." It should not be used, by Slipshod Extension, in the sense "a thing to be considered; event; occurrence." In law *factor* is used also in the sense "consignee" or "commission agent."

Q. What is factotum?

A. factotum = a general servant with myriad duties. The preferred plural is *-tums* rather than *-ta.* "The agents suspected that the appellees were driving stolen vehicles, not that they served as *factota* - [read *factotums*] of illegal aliens." *United States v. Miranda-Perez,* 764 F. 2d 285, 289 (5th Cir. 1985).

Q. What are facts?

A. facts cannot literally be false; if something is a fact, then it is, by its very nature, true. Yet, in law, one often reads and hears of the "truth" or "flasity" of certain facts. E.g., "Presumably, there were good reasons in the interest of justice nearly 100 years ago, which impelled the court to fetter its own power to get at the *true facts.*" (Eng.) "No order shall recite *untrue facts.*" This is an acceptable practice, as *facts* in such a context is really an elliptical form of *alleged facts.* Hence: "Subject to later case development, the Texas measure of probative value, "tending to establish the presence or absence, *truth or falsity of a fact,"* does not seem functionally distinct from the federal definition, to make the existence of the *fact* more probable or less probable."

Q. What is a fact situation?

A. fact situation, factual situation. What is implied by these terms is that a *fact situation* = a situation with a given set of facts (hypothetical or actual) and that *factual situation* = a situation that exists or existed in fact. When coupled with the noun *situation, factual* tends to take on sense (1) listed in the entry under *fact,* adj. Cf. *fact(ual) determinations* in which, *factual* assumes sense (1).

Q. What are facts under the?

A. facts, under the is an acceptable legal idiom, e.g., "*Under the facts* of the case at bar, we cannot say that the district court erred in allowing the inclusion of this testimony." Cf. **circumstances, under the.**

Q. What is fact that?

A. fact that, the. It is imprudent to say, as some have, that this phrase ought never to be used. At times, it cannot reasonably be avoided. One writer has suggested that *because* will usually suffice for *the fact that.* See Vigilans, *Chamber of Horrors* 63 (1952). Yet rarely, if ever, is *because* a good substitute.

Where *the fact that* can be easily avoided, however, it should be. E.g.: "*The fact that* [read *That*] the right to protection was founded upon the doctrine of secondary meaning rather than, for example, upon common-law technical trademark law or statutory trademark law, generally has not been regarded as controlling a determination of the proper geographic scope of protection."

The pluralised form, as in "*The facts that* ..... " is usually unnecessary and awkward for the singular where the discrete facts discussed are easily considered part of an overall structure or pattern. "*The facts that* [read *The fact that or that*] the records in this case were made by the proprietor and were in his possession *were* [read *was*] irrelevant to the determination whether their creation was compelled, the majority said."

Q. What is fair use?

A. fair use, fair dealing. The defence of *fair use,* in actions for copyright infringement, is known also as *fair dealing* in G.B. The term *fair use* (not *fair usage*) is the one applied in 17 U.S.C § 107 to describe the kinds of limitations that the law places on the exclusive rights of copyright.

Q. What do you mean by the term fall due?

A. fall due is the idiomatic legal phrase, meaning "to become due" and is used in the context of negotiable instruments, e.g., "He paid the notes as they *fell due.*"

Q. What makes a false plea?

A. false plea, sham plea. Both term mean "an obviously frivolous or absurd pleading that is made only for purposes of vexation or delay." *Sham plea* (or *pleading*) has been the more common of the two in the U.S.; the *CDL* (British) contains the main entry under *false plea.*

Q. What is far-reaching?

A. far-reaching is one of our most overburdened adjectival phrases. This metaphor should be used cautiously; the phrase should always be hyphenated, e.g., "This argument, which is of *far-reaching* significance, was designed to show that the union was not in breach of the court's orders." (Eng.) "They had no notification that any complaint was being made under section 6(k), which is a different and, in this case, more *far-reaching* matter." (Eng.)

Q. Define farther and further.

A. farther, further. Both are comparative degrees of *far* but they have undergone Differentiation. In the best usage, the former refers to physical distances, the latter to figurative distances. "The Supreme Court looks no *farther* [read *further*] than whether the distinctions have some 'rational basis." "But the immunity goes *farther* [read *further*]." In BrE, *further* is used both physically and figuratively whereas *farther* is physical only.

The superlatives are *farthest* and *furthest. Furthermost* is rare for *farthest* (not *furthest*).

Q. What is fastly?

A. fastly is an obsolete form that now exists only as a barbarism, in the same manner in which, *fast* is used as an adverb and as an adjective.

Q. What is fatal in legal parlance?

A. fatal. In legal Argot, this word means "providing grounds for legal invalidity." This sense is common: "The court pointed out that uncertainty as to the fact of damage is *fatal.*" "While the parties have extensively argued and briefed a number of questions, one basic proposition is dispositive of—and *fatal* to—the position taken by the plaintiffs."

Q. What is Felony?

A. felony = Crime of any kind, legally graver than misdemeanors.

Q. What is meant by feme sole?

A. feme sole = unmarried woman.

Q. What is fiat?

A. fiat = A command, a decree, a short order or warrant of a judge or public officer that contains steps should be taken.

Q. What is fiduciary?

A. fiduciary = A relationship based on trust or good faith.

Q. What is meant by F.I.R.?

A. F.I.R. = First information report of grievance which is given to police.

Q. What is force majeure?

A. Force-Majeure = irresistible

Q. What is fore closure?

A. fore closure = A decree determines the equitable right of a mortgagor to redeem after the mortgagee's estate has become absolute at law.

Q. What is meant by forfeiture?

A. forfeiture = A punishment whereby the offender lost all his interests in his property.

Q. What do you understand by forma pauperis?

A. A suit may be instituted by a pauper who is a person not possessed to sufficient means to enable him to pay the fee prescribed by law for the plaint in such suit.

Q. What is franchise?

A. frenchise = The right of voting.

Q. What is meant by freehold?

A. freehold = the absolute ownership of land.

Q. What is frustration of the contract?

A. frustration of the contract = The cancellation of a contract due to impossibility of performance.

Q. What do you understand by full blood?

A. Two persons are said to be related to each other by full blood when they are descended from a common ancestor by the same wife.

Q. What is functus officio?

A. functus officio = An authority who has performed the act authorized so that the authority is exhausted.

Q. Define the term *gauntlet*?

A. gantlet, gauntlet. Although the latter is more common in most of the senses, yet the former is still preferred in one of them. One runs the *gantlet* (= a kind of ordeal or punishment) but throws down the *gauntlet* (= a glove). The trend is to use *gauntlet* for *gantlet*; like many trends, it is worth resisting. *Gauntlet* is correctly used here: "Jurists are free to state their personal views in a variety of forums but the opinions of this court are not proper occasions to throw down *gauntlets* to the Supreme Court."

Q. What is a *gaol*?

A. gaol, gaoler. These are variant BrE spellings of *jail* and *jailer*. The terms are pronounced the same regardless of their spellings.

Q. What is *garden-variety*?

A. garden-variety, adj., = of the ordinary or familiar kind. This phrase is becoming a garden-variety Cliche in legal prose, e.g., "Because *Eichelberger* was nothing more, nor less, than a *garden-variety* divorce case, one would normally have thought that the litigation had ended when the court of civil appeals overruled Mr. Eichelberger's motion for re-hearing."

Q. Define the term *garnish*.

A. garnish, garnishee, v.t. In American legal writing, the usual verb form is *garnish* (= to take property, usually, a portion of someone's salary, by legal authority). *Garnishee* is usually reserved for the nominal sense ("a person or institution such as a bank that is indebted for or is a bailee for another whose property has been subjected to garnishment". The noun corresponding to *garnish* is *garnishment*.

In G.B., however and in a few American jurisdictions, *garnishee* as well as *garnish* is used as a verb: "As it was composed entirely of money that did not belong to Smith, it could not be *garnisheed* by his creditor and this was sufficient to dispose of the case." (Eng.). The *OED* gives passing notice to *garnishee* as a verb and its corresponding noun *garnisheement;* the main entries are under *garnish* and *garnishment*.

Q. Who is a *garnisher*?

A. garnisher, -or. *Garnisher* is preferred; it is the only spelling listed in *W*3 and the prevalent spelling in legal texts.

Q. What are gases?

A. gases, not *gasses,* is the plural form of the noun *gas;* nevertheless, for the verb *to gas, gassed* is the accepted past tense and *gasses* is the third-person singular form. C.f. **bus.**

Q. What is the relationships of gender to sex?

A. gender has long been used as a grammatical distinction of a word according to the sex referred to. It has newly been established in the language of the law in phrases such as *gender-based discrimination*, a usage disapproved as jargonistic by some authorities.

Here, the better usage has been illustrated: "In the court's view, the ordinance creates a conflict between first amendment free speech guaranties and the fourteenth amendment right to be free from *sex-based* discrimination."

Q. What is generalised?

A. generalised (= made general) for *general*. "Some courts, refusing to find in the rather *generalised* [read *general*] language of the usual statute a legislative intent to abolish the concept of marital unity, have sought to adapt the incidents of ownership by the entirety to the principle that neither spouse has rights or powers superior to those of the other." The sentence does not intend to convey that the language was *made general* (by the legislature, presumably) but that it *is general*. Cf, **particularised.**

Q. What is the basic meaning of generally?

A. generally has three basic meanings: (1) "disregarding insignificant exceptions" (the level of advocacy in this court is generally very high); (2) "in many ways" (he was the most generally qualified applicant); (3) 'usually' (he generally left the office at five o'clock). Sense (3) is least good in formal writing, though at times it merges with sense (1).

A note must be made of generally accepted accounting principles, generally accepted accountancy principles. The former is the usual phrase in the U.S., the latter in G.B. *Accountancy* is, however, used in the U.S. in other phrases and contexts. The phrases are often abbreviated as *GAAP*.

Q. What is generative?

A. generative, generational. The distinction is clear; *generative* = procreative; *generational* = pertaining to generations. "The degree of kinship between a decedent and a claimant was reckoned by taking the number of *generative* [read *generational*] steps between them or by adding the numbers of such steps between both of them and their nearest common ancestor."

Q. Define genericalness.

A. generic(al)ness, genericism. *Genericness,* though odd-looking, is now the most widely used noun corresponding to *generic,* adj. It has been recorded from 1939 in the *OED Supp.* and appears most commonly in reference to trademarks, e.g., "Rovira's affirmative defense of *genericness* was not barred by the federal rules." *Keebler Co. v. Rovira Biscuit Corp.,* 624 F.2d 366, 374 n. 7 (Ist Cir. 1980). "Foreign words are translated into English and then, tested for descriptiveness or *genericness* by seeing whether that foreign word would be descriptive of the product to that segment of the purchasing public, which is familiar with that language." Despite its specialised currency, *genericness* retains a non-English appearance.

Genericalness is listed in the *OED* and *W2*; it does not, like *genericness,* flout principles of English word formation and might be preferred on that ground. It has been omitted from *W3*, which labels the adj. *generical* as archaic.

Genericism has also appeared, e.g., "There remain two defenses that licensees might make-descriptiveness and *genericism.*" Treece, *Licensee Estoppel in Trademark Cases,* 58 Trademark Rep. 728, 738 (1968). Labeled rare in the *OED, genericism* is perhaps the most realistic alternative to oust *genericness.*

Q. Who is a genius?

A. genius (= the prevailing character or spirit; characteristic method or procedure) is often used in reference to law, e.g., "A federal cause of action brought at any distance of time would be utterly repugnant to the *genius* of our laws." *Webb v. Board of Education,* 471 U.S. 234 (1985) (quoting *Adams v. Woods,* 2 Cranch 336, 341 (1805)). The pl. *geniuses* is preferred over *genii.*

Q. What is genocide?

A. genocide = Mass killing of a group of.

Q. Who is a gentleman?

A. gentleman should not be used indiscriminately as a genteelism for *man,* the generic term. *Gentleman* should be reversed for reference to a cultured and refined man.

Q. Where do you use a gerund?

A. Gerunds. The legal writer's prejudice against nouns in *-ing* is unfounded. When it comes to Cutting Out the Chaff, one effective method of reducing prolixity is to use gerunds directly. Thus *adjudicating that case was difficult* rather than *the adjudication of that case was difficult; presenting the arguments* rather than *the presentation of the arguments* etc.

Q. Explain to get.

A. get > got > gotten. In formal writing, *got* is the better past participle; *gotten* is by far, the more frequent from the AmE, however.

Q. Define gift in legal parlance.

A. gift, it may be surprising to learn, has acted as a verb since the sixteenth century, e.g., "All the property was *gifted* property [i.e., it took the form of gifts]." Though this usage is old, it is not a standard now. English has the uncanny ability, however, to transform nouns into verbs, and to revive moribund usages. Twenty years ago, *contact* was objected to as a verb, though it had been used that way since the early nineteenth century; few writers now feel uncomfortable using the word as a verb.

Gift may soon be in the same class but still, cautious writers may prefer to use it only as a noun if the verb causes discomfort, as it well may: "The stock may not be *gifted,* pledged or hypothecated without the board's approval." One is accustomed to thinking of *gifted children* but not of *gifted stock.*

Q. What is the legal meaning of gist?

A. gist began as a legal term meaning "the real ground or point (of an action, indictment etc.)" *(OED)* and has since passed into non-legal parlance. Yet, it is still (perhaps unwittingly) used in the legal sense: "The *gist* of the libel is that certain articles called lubricators are not good articles." Cf. **gravamen.**

Q. What is meant by giving evidence?

A. give evidence = to testify. "The defendant *gave evidence* that he was elsewhere at the time of the alleged sale and did not make it." *Dunn v. United States,* 284 U.S. 390, 392 (1931) (per Holmes, J.).

Q. What is meant by Good will?

A. good will = The benefit which arises from the establishment of particular business or occupations. Intrinsic value of the good repute and customs of an established trade or business.

Q. What is meant by gratuitous?

A. gratuitous = Without valuable or legal consideration.

Q. What is Gratuity?

A. gratuity = A lump sum paid by an employer to retiring employee.

Q. What is ground rent?
A. ground rent = The rent paid by the holder of a lease to do the freeholder.

Q. What do you understand by group litigation?
A. group litigation = A low suit, instituted on behalf of or against a group of persons recognised as one litigating entity.

Q. Who is guardian?
A. a person having right and duty to protect the property or right of a minor person.

Q. What do you understand by Habeas corpus?
A. It means have the body to present. A writ issued to bring person before a court to ensure that his imprisonment is not illegal.

Q. What is meant by half blood?
A. half blood = The children of the same mother, but have different fathers.

Q. What do you understand by hearsay?
A. It is not admissible as an evidence under evidence Act because witness makes statements of another, who was a direct witness to the event in question.

Q. What is hereto?
A. hereto (= to this) is sometimes misused for *heretofore* (= up to this time), e.g., "hedonic damages have not *hereto* [read *heretofore*] been recoverable in this state."

Q. What is heritable?
A. heritable, inheritable, hereditary. As between the first two, the second is the more common; it means "capable of being inherited": "The issue presented by this case is whether a husband's community interest in his surviving wife's civil service retirement benefits is *inheritable* upon his death by adult children of his former wife." "The grantee even in a deed deposited in escrow has an *inheritable* right." *Heritable* is infrequent enough today to be classed a Needless Variant for most purposes, though it persists in Scotland and in civil-law jurisdictions.

The negative form of the adjective has been rendered both *uninheritable (OED)* and *nonheritable (W3)*. The latter is more common in the U.S., e.g., "[I]t would create an estate in fee simple which ..... would be *nonheritable*." Frather, *Bequests of Orts,* 48 Mo. L.Rev. 476, 478 (1983).

Hereditary has a more restricted sense: "Descending by inheritance from generation to generation" *(OED):* "In the American states it is a fundamental principle that no man can be a magistrate, a legislator or a judge by *hereditary* right." (Eng.)

hesitancy -ce; hesitation. *Hesitancy* is a quality (the state of being hesitant; reluctance) whereas *hesitation* is an act (the act of hesitating). So: "The courts had no *hesitancy* in holding the defamatory matter libelous." "We have no *hesitation* [read *hesitancy,* i.e., reluctance] in declaring that public policy requires that the interest of the beneficiary of a trust should be subject to the claims for support of his children." *Hesitance* is a Needless Variant.

Q. Explain hew.

A. hew = (1) to chop, cut; or (2) to adhere or conform (to). Sense (1) is illustrated in this sentence: "The appellants contend that the wife took title to the estate of her husband in fee simple absolute, which is not *hewed* down to a lesser estate by words of weaker import."

Sense (2), which is more common in modern legal prose, occurs in the following sentence: "In any event, we *hew* to the Supreme Court's broad language; if that is to be trimmed, it is for the court to do, not for us."

The preferred past participle is *hewn* in BrE and *hewed* in AmE, e.g., "The substantive distinction between admonitions and instructions is not always clear or closely *hewn to* [read, in AmE, *hewed to*]."

Q. What is hiba?

A. hiba. perfect gift, one accompanied by delivery and acceptance (under Mohammadan law).

Q. What is a Higher Court?

A. higher court, upper court. Both phrases are used to denote an appellate court that reviews the judgement of a *lower court,* q.v. Following is a specimen of the less common form: "The *upper court,* on appeal, held that it was not error to admit parol evidence of extraneous facts."

Q. Explain the term hijack.

A. hijack. Vehicles and planes are *hijacked,* not people, e.g., "Lipsig spent two years trying to get political asylum for Tshombe who was mysteriously *hijacked* [read *abducted*?] to Algiers in the mid-sixties and detained in prison."

Dictionary of Legal Terms 85

Q. What is historical?

A. historical, historic. The former, meaning "of or relating to or occurring in history," is called upon for a more frequent usage. The latter means "historically significant" (the Alamo is a historic building). An event that makes history is *historic;* an event of no great importance that occurred in history is *historical.* Momentous happenings or developments are *historic;* merely documented happenings or developments are *historical.* Here, *historic* has been is correctly used: "Chief Justice Cardozo's *historic* and oft-quoted dissent in *Graf v. Hope Bldg. Corp.* has become equity's modern fount in cases in which, the tyrant demands his dollars and cents on legal time whatever the impact of sickening hardship his victim suffers on account thereof." "In *Brown II* the Court referred to its *historic* opinion in *Brown I* as declaring the fundamental principle that racial discrimination in public education is unconstitutional."

Q. Explain hitherto.

A. hitherto; thitherto. *Hitherto* = heretofore; *thitherto* = theretofore. Obviously, these Archaisms are not worth using if we define terms—*heretofore* and *theretofore*—that are less archaic and perfectly equivalent, e.g., here, a legal writer mistook the import of *hitherto,* which does not properly appear with the pluperfect tense: "The Superior Court, conceding that it *hitherto* [read *thitherto,* or, better, *theretofore*] had refused to enjoin such conduct, recognised the growing tendency in courts to grant equitable relief under such circumstances."

Q. Who are hoi polloi?

A. hoi polloi (= the common people, the masses). Inasmuch as *hoi* in Greek means "the," *the hoi polloi* is a technical Redundancy. Nevertheless, *the hoi polloi* predominates.

Q. When do we hold?

A. hold, v.t. When used property in the legal sense, this verb describes *what* judges do and is thus transitive. It should not be used intransitively to describe *how* judges do. In the following two sentences, the intransitive usage is wrong. "Without the scracity rationale, it seems unlikely that the *Red Lion* Court would have held *as it did,* even more unlikely that the present Court would do so." "This court's task, then, is to decide *how* [read *what*] the Oregon courts would hold when faced with the issue." (Courts hold *something,* they do not hold *in a certain manner.* Thus, in the second example, the noun *what,* not the adverb *how,* is the proper word). In general English usage, of course, the intransitive usage of *hold* is quite acceptable in such clauses as *the argument does not hold.*

Hold need not be followed by *to be* or *as*, though *to be* may sometimes add clarity, e.g., "We *hold permissible* [better: *hold to be permissible*] an award of extraordinary damages for frivolous appeal." In *Bryan v. Bigelow*, the unincorporated letter was *held testamentary* [better: *held to be testamentary*] and not admissible in evidence to rebut a resulting trust in favour of the residuary estate." But here the shorter form works better. "The defendant was *held to be liable* [read *held liable*] for breach of contract and conversion." *Held as* (the award was held as permissible) is idiomatically inferior.

As a noun, *holding* involves a determination of a matter of law that is pivotal to a judicial decision. Here, it is loosely used in a lay sense: "Justice Jacobs quoted an 1859 New Jersey *holding*, "Few statutes would stand if tried by standards of logic, grammar or rhetoric." The opinion may have made this *statement*; but, inasmuch as it is not a statement of law, it cannot be a *holding*.

Q. To hold means to defend. Explain.

A. hold a brief for (= to defend or support) is a lawyers' idiom that has passed into general usage.

Q. What is holden?

A. holden is an archaic past participate of *hold*, used as recently as 1850 in *Brown v. Kendall*, 60 Mass. (6 Cush.) 292 (1850): "There certainly are cases in the books where the injury being direct and immediate, trespass has been *holden* to lie, though the jury was not intentional." This Archaism has even found its way into the twentieth-century texts: "Perjury committed in a state court *holden* by prermission of state law and of federal officials in a federal building, is not outside the jurisdiction of the state to punish."

Q. What is holding over?

A. holding over is a legal Argot denoting "the action of a tenant continuing in occupation of premises after his lease has expired" *(CDL)*, e.g., "The tenant, *holding over* despite efforts to evict him, planted a crop that eventually, the landlord harvested."

Q. What is a holocaust?

A. holocaust (lit., "burnt hole." fr. Gk.) is one of our most hyperbolical words, beloved of jargonmongers and second-rate journalists. The historical sense from World War II, of course, is beyond question. Figurative applications of term, however, are often questionable. Here, it is used to no avail in reference to a scandal: "C.R. would soon be engulfed in a *holocaust of controversy and pain* [read *painful controversy*] that would maim several lives, including his own, wound hundreds of other people and jostle the foundations of the world's most glamorous industry." Inherent in the sense of the word, whether literal or figurative, is burning; it may be used appropriately of fires so, but not, for example, of floods.

Q. What is a holograph?

A. holograph. In the law of wills, a *holograph* is a will that is entirely written, dated and signed in the hand of the testator, e.g., "Unfortunately, much litigation is stimulated by other requirements for the execution of *holographs* and the difficulty in integrating *holographs* at probate is particularly acute."

This word is not to be confused with *hologram* (= a three-dimensional picture).

Q. Explain homage.

A. homage is best pronounced as ***hom**-ij*. It is a pretension to omit the *-h-* sound.

Q. What is a homestead?

A. homestead, v.t. The past tense of this verb is *homesteaded,* e.g., "The Chancellor adjudged the subject property *to be homestead* [read *to be homesteaded* or *to be a homestead*] under article X of the Florida Constitution." One who homesteads is *homesteader.* Congress enacted the Homestead Act in 1862.

Q. What is is homocide?

A. homocide = Killing of a human being, by another human being.

Q. What are the signs of a homogeneous thing?

A. homogen(e)ous. *Homogeneous* (five syllables) is the usual and the etymologically preferable form. *Homogeneal, homogenetic* and *homogenetical* are rare forms to be avoided; they have failed to become standard and should be laid tor rest.

Q. Is honourable a title of respect to judges? Explain.

A. Honourable is a title of respect given to juges, members of the U.S. Congress, ambassadors and the like. It should be used not with surnames only but with complete names (e.g., *The Honorable Antonin Scalia*) or with a little of courtesy (e.g., *The Honorable Mr. Scalia*). The abbreviation *Hon.* should be used only in mailing addresses.

Q. Which is a honorable court?

A. honorable court, this, is a phrase commonly sprinkled throughout briefs. It should be sparingly used, for it tends to nauseate even those judges most susceptible to flattery, e.g., "Review by *this Honorable Court* of the granting by the district court of the motion for preliminary injunction is a routine matter in which, *this Honorable Court* need determine only whether the district court abused its broad discretion in granting the preliminary injunction." The references should be to *the Court or this Court,* apart from the first reference in, e.g., the commencement of a pleading. (The capitalisation of *court* is a compliment enough.)

Q. What is hopefully?

A. hopefully. So much has been written of this word that little could be added here, except to advise the reader to strike this word from his vocabulary. Briefly, the objections are that: (1) *hopefully* properly means "in a hopeful manner" and should not be used merely to mean *I hope* or *it is to be hoped;* (2) in constructions such as, "Hopefully, it will rain today," The writer illogically attributes an emotion (*hopefulness*) to an inanimate object (*it*).

In 1932, the sense "it is to be hoped" would have been inconceivable; here, in an example from that year, the word is used in the sense "in a hopeful manner": "[D]efendant would be placed in a state of servitude, for which, she might *hopefully* expect as ignorance of the law is no excuse (rendered in Latin *ignorantia juris neminem excusat* [lit., "ignorance of law excuses no one"]), e.g., "The effect of this provision is to continue the *ignorantia legis* principle as part of the Model Code culpability structure." The full maxim itself, however, is best rendered in English.

Q. What do you understand by hostile witness?

A. hostile witness = The witness, who makes statement adverse to the party calling and examining him.

Q. What is hypothecation?

A. Hypothecation = A right of a creditor in which the pleader retains possession of the thing pledges.

Q. What is meant by Ibid?

A. Ibid = At the same place or from the same sources, in the same book or passage.

Q. What is ilk?

A. ilk correctly means "the same"; hence *of that ilk* means "of that same kind." Yet the word is commonly misapprrehended as relating to race or family; it is not that specefic.

Q. What is ill?

A. ill. The comparative form of this adjective is *worse,* the superlative *worst.* The adverb is *ill, illy* being an illiterate form. Yet illiteracies have been known to creep into legal writing and even into judicial opinions:

illation (= the act of inferring or something inferred) is a learned term little used today, though a few modern judges are quite fond of it. *Inference* serves just as well, and more understandably.

Q. What is illegal;

A. illegal, illicit, unlawful. These three terms are fundamentally synonymous, although *illicit* (illicit love affairs) carries moral overtones in addition to the basic sense "not in accordance with or sanctioned by law."

Q. What is illegible hand writing?

A. illegible, unreadable. *Illegible* = not plain or clear enough to be read (used of handwriting of defaced printing). *Unreadable* = too dull or obfuscatory to be read (used of bad writing).

Q. Explain the term illicit.

A. illicit for *elicit.* One might have thought this mistake impossible but it does occur. *Illicit* = illegal; *elicit* = to bring out, to call forth, e.g., "No testimony was *ilicited* [read *elicited*] that justified this breach."

Q. Who is an illiterate man?

A. illiterate = (1) unable to read or write; or (2) unlettered. Justice Holmes was wont to use this word in sense (2), the heightened sense of the word: "In the case at bar, we have an *illiterate* woman writing her own will. Obviously, the first sentence, 'I am going on a journey and may not ever return,' expresses the fact that was on her mind as the occasion and inducement for writing it." *Eaton v. Brown,* 193 U.S. 411, 414 (1904) (per Holmes,J.).

Q. What is illogic?

A. illogic is really a catchall category for writing that suffers from some sort of error in thinking or some logical fallacy. Often, it results from failing to be mindful of what the subject of the verb is and to make certain that the sentence properly expresses what it is that acts upon something else or who kicked whom.

A. Illogical Comparison. This lapse occurs commonly in locutions like *as large if not larger than,* which, when telescoped, becomes *as large than.* One should write *as large as if not larger than.* Similar problems occur with classes: when members of a class are being compared, a word such as *other* must be used to restrict the class, e.g., "Our system of justice is better than any [*other*] in the world."

Still another problem of comparison occurs when the writer forgets exactly what he is comparing, e.g., "The case involved facts virtually identical with *Ragan* [read *those in Ragan*].

Here is an example of inappropriate comparison of the subject with another noun: "May a defendant, who has settled with the plaintiff, recover contribution from other potential defendants?" The phrase *other potential defendants* is wrong because anyone, who has settled, is no longer a *potential* defendant.

B. Illogical Subject of a Participle. "Any definition is likely to distinguish between religion and mere conscientious belief, *construing* the first amendment to govern the former but not the latter."

C. Mistaken Subject of a Prepositional Phrase. "*Wallin was the school bus driver in which* [read *Wallin was driving the bus in which*] Hillman and Ellington and Kleven were passengers."

D. Insensitivity to Metaphor. "In my opinion that foundation is not weakened by the fact that *it is buttressed by other provisions that are also* [read *other provisions are also*] designed to avoid the insidious evils of government propaganda favouring particular points of view." (Buttresses can serve only to strengthen, not to weaken.) "The *erie* doctrine was bastardised by its progeny." (This makes no sense, because parents, not children, create bastards.) "The nineteenth century has provided new impetus to literary studies, putting them on untraveled roads." (Travel creates roads: they do not exist in vacuum.)

E. Poor Usage of Temporal Sequence. "Indeed, the condition of the plane after the crash *was such as to eliminate an air collision* [read *was such as to* *eliminate further speculation about an air collision*]." "The obligation of the deceased to transfer certain property, as a minimum, during his life, does not negate a desire to leave other property after death and more than the minimum, at least in the absence of new responsibilities." (A deceased person cannot have obligations to transfer property during his life.)

F. Vexatious Little Words with Plain Literal Meanings. "Acceptances must be communicated to offeror *after* [read *in*] a reasonable amount of time." (If *after* a reasonable amount of time, then the period has become *unreasonable!*) "Appellee argues forcefully *as did the district court below* [read *and the district court below held*] that because IBM and the third-party firms provide identical services, the third-party firms do not constitute a separate market." (The appellee may *argue* this on appeal; but the district court *held* in its opinion. Courts do not *argue*).

G. Complete Obliviousness in the Task of Writing. "The courts are more reluctant in considering extrinsic evidence to construe a will than to construe an *inter vivos* transfer." [Read *Courts are more reluctant to consider extrinsic evidence in construing a will than in construing an inter vivos transfer.*] (The original sentence suggests that courts have a choice of what to construe, as if a judge might say: "Well, here I am considering some extrinsic evidence. Why, I think I'll construe an *inter vivos* transfer that would be more fun than a will")

Q. What is an illusion?

A. illusion, delusion. These words are used differently despite their similar meanings. An *illusion* exists in one's fancy or imagination. A *delusion* is an idea or a thing that deceives or misleads a person.

Q. What is illusory?

A. illusory, -sive. The former is preferred, e.g., "Some courts, following the read of New York, invoked a test whether the arrangement was *illusory,* measured in terms of the substance of the arrangement."

Q. What is meant by illustrate in modern usage?

A. illustrate, in modern usage, means "to provide a good example of (something); to exemplify." In the following sentence, it has been used ambiguously: "Hohfeld's analysis *illustrates* the fallacy of accepting too literally the artificial entity theory." The writer is not claiming—as his sentences seem to do—that Hohfeld's analysis is itself a good example of "the fallacy of accepting too literally the artificial entity theory." Rather, he is pointing to Hohfeld's analysis as one that elucidates well the nature of this fallacy.

illustrate is usually accented on the first syllable. /**il**-u-strayt/.

Q. Where do we use illy?

A. illy is not an acceptable adverb in formal writing, perhaps not even in nondialectal informal writing. *Ill* itself acts as an adverb, e.g., "It is freely conceded that there are many decisions contrary to this view; but, when carried to the extent contended for by the appellant, we think they are unsafe, unsound, and *illy* [read *ill*] adapted to modern conditions."

Q. Who is an imbecile?

A. imbecile, adj.; **imbecilic.** The preferred adjectival form of *imbecile,* n., is *imbecile,* adj. The form in *-ic* should be avoided.

Q. What is meant by Imbezzle?

A. Imbezzle = To steal, where a person entrusted with goods, wastes and diminishes them.

Q. What is meant by the term to imbibe?

A. imbibe is a Formal Word meaning "to drink." It occurs more frequently in legal than in non-legal contexts, e.g., "In *Kelly v. Gwinnell,* the New Jersey Supreme Court took a major step in holding social hosts liable for the torts of their guests whom they have allowed to over*imbibe.*"

Q. What is immaterial in legal matters?

A. immaterial, nonmaterial. The former term is called for in most legal contexts. "Should even a *nonmaterial* [read *immaterial*] error, if made with the intent to deceive the magistrate, invalidate a warrant?" "A testator is not induced by the misrepresentation if he knows the facts or if the facts misrepresented are *immaterial.*" Although both may mean "not consisting of a material substance," yet *immaterial* tends to mean "of no substantial importance; inconsequential"; *nonmaterial,* in contrast, generally means ownership of property by two or more persons who have identical interests in the whole of the property, with a right of survivorship. *Tenancy in common* = equitable ownership of property by two or more persons in equal or unequal undivided shares, with no right of survivorship. The property for each of these tenancies may be either real (land) or personal (e.g., a bank account), although the *CDL,* which reflects British legal practices, confines its definitions to real property.

Q. What is immovable property?

A. immovable property = Property attached or embedded to the land.

Dictionary of Legal Terms 93

Q. What do you understand by immunity?
A. immunity = The condition of being exempt from some liability to which other are subject. For ex:—The immunity of a judge in respect of things done or said when exercising his judicial function.

Q. What is meant by Impeach?
A. impeach = Bring a charge against a person.

Q. What is meant by in camera?
A. in camera = Not in open court, in private.

Q. What is meant by in cest?
A. in cest = Sexual intercousse between persons related with blood. For ex. brother and sister etc.

Q. What is meant by in Limnie?
A. in limnie = At the outset, preliminary.

Q. What is meant by In Pari Delicto?
A. in pari delicto = In equal fault, cupable or criminal.

Q. What is meant by In Re?
A. in re = In the matter of.

Q. What is Indictment?
A. indictment = A written accusation, read out in court at the begining of a criminal trial.

Q. What is indemnity?
A. Formal leagal acceptance of responsibility against damage or loss.

Q. What is injunction?
A. injuction = An order or judgement by which a party to an action is required to do or refrain from doing a particular thing.

Q. What is meant by innuendo?
A. innuendo = Defamatory hint or remark.

Q. What is meant by insolvent?

A. insolvent = A person whose assets are in sufficient to pay his debt.

Q. What is meant by interalia?

A. inter alia = Among other things.

Q. What is meant by inter vivos?

A. inter vivos = Between living persons.

Q. What is inter locutory order?

A. inter locutory order= order which is made pending the cause and before a final hearing on the merit.

Q. What do you understand by international law?

A. international law = The body of rules regulating the relations among the nations, resolving the conflict between laws of diffirent nations.

Q. What is meant by interrogatories?

A. interrogatories = In the course of civil suit, these are particular permission in writing demanded of witnesses or parties brought in to be examined in a case.

Q. What is meant by intestate?

A. intestate = A person who dies without making a will.

Q. What is meant by Intra Virus?

A. intra virus = within the powers.

Q. What is meant by ipsofacto?

A. ipso facto = by the fact itself.

Q. When do we use the term *join together?*
A. A join together is a Redundancy that should be allowed to survive only in the marriage service and there only because it is a bonafide remnant of Elizabethan English.

Q. What is *joint tenancy?*
A. Where property is ancestral is owned by two or more persons under one instrument or act of the parties.

Q. In what conditions the terms, *jointly and severally* are used?
A. When persons jointly as well individually liable for their actions.

Q. What is a *journal* in the legal context?
A. journal, v.t.; **journalise.** Both terms are used in the sense "to record in a journal." *Journalise* is more usual in legal contexts, e.g.: "He filed an appeal after the district judge officially *journalised* the judgement." The verb *to journal* has additional, non-legal senses.

Q. Distinguish between *judex* and *Judge.*
A. judex, except in historical contexts (e.g., "English Chancery Courts, heavy borrowers from the civil law, may have derived the system of special masters from the civilian *judex* of the Roman Republic and Early Empire."), it is an unnecessary equivalent of *judge.*

Q. Who is a *judge?*
A. judge, justice. Judges often took unkindly on mistakes in their titles: "By two identical motions filed on January 3, 1985 in these related actions, defendant moves for an order disqualifying the Honorable Mr. Justice [*sic*] Charles L. Brieant from hearing this matter on the ground that said "Honorable Charles L. Brieant was the presiding justice [*sic*] in the trial of *Lany Optic Industries, Inc. v. Passport International Ltd."* *Tenzer v. Lewitinn.* 599 F. Supp. 973, 974 (S.D.N.Y. 1985) (per Brieant, J.). As a general rule, judges sitting on the highest appellate level of a jurisdiction are known as *justices.* Trial judges and appellate judges on intermediate levels are generally called *judges,* not *justices.* (New York and Texas depart from these rules of thumb; in New York. *Justices* sit on the trial court [the Supreme Court, oddly] and in Texas, *Justices* sit on the courts of appeals [between the trial court and the Supreme Court the latter being the highest court of appeal which is also composed of *justices*].)

Horwill wrote that "*Judge* carries with it-in America-by no means such dignified associations as it possesses in England. It may mean [in the U.S.] no more than a *magistrate* of a police court." Horwill, *Modern American Usage* 180 (1935). Justice may also denote in the U.S. a low-ranking judge, as in the phrases *justice of the peace and police justice.*

Q. What is judge-made law?

A. judge-made, adj., is used generally as an antonym of *statutory,* e.g., "Some time should also be devoted to discussion of legislative as opposed to *judge-made* tort law." "With limited exceptions, these sections of the restatement reflect no statutes or statutory developments; they purport to be precise statements of the prevailing or better *judge-made* law and the Reporter suggests that they may be implemented by judicial action or by statute."

Q. What is a judgement.

A. judgement = A decision of a court with legal reasoning in a legal proceeding.

Q. Define judgemental.

A. judgemental, judgmatic. *Judgemental* = (1) of or relating to judgement or (2) judging when uncalled for. Sense (2) is now more common (a judgemental critic), but sense (1) still appears. E.g., "The qualification is generally undertaken only in an effort to make meaningful [q.v.] a whole host of *judgemental* factors applicable at a particular time." *Judgematic,* called by Fowler a "facetious formation" because of its irregular formation on the analogy of *dogmatic,* is a **Needless Variant** of *judicious.*

Q. What is a judgement-book?

A. judgement-book, judgement-roll. A *judgement-book* is kept by the clerk of court for the entry or record of judgements. A *judgement-roll* is virtually the same in American practice, though some jurisdictions such as New York call for *entry* of judgements in the *judgement-roll* and mere record of judgements in the *judgement-book.* The usual term in G.B. is *judgement-roll.*

Q. What is meant by judgement debtor?

A. judgement debtor = A person against whom a decree has been passed.

Q. Define the term judgement non obstante veredicto?

A. *judgement non obstante veredicto,* **judgement notwithstanding the verdict, j.n.o.v.; judgement n.o.v.** Of these forms, perhaps, the best unabbreviated one is *judgement notwithstanding the verdict.* Its Latin equivalent is as often as not in

Dictionary of Legal Terms 97

the U.S. erroneously rendered *verdicto* rather than *veredicto*. We must not forget the Latin phrase, however, lest young lawyers come not to understand the import of *j.n.o.v.,* q.v.

Q. What are judgements in an appellate-court?

A. judgements, Appellate-court. By *judgement* in this article is meant the final decree of an appellate court that acts upon a lower-court judgement, whether affirming, reversing, vacating or whatever. The British ordinarily use *judgement* synonymously with *opinion,* whereas in the U.S. we distinguish between the *opinion* (which sets out the reasons for the disposition) and the judgement (the pronouncement of the disposition itself). This article, then, primarily reflects the American practices.

A cardinal principle of judgement-drafting is that appellate opinions should make explicit how the court is disposing of the judgement or order below. Appellate courts have sometimes, left the parties and the trial court uncertain about the status of a case by using vargue terms such as *so ordered* and *ordered accordingly,* without a clear statement of the disposition preceding these phrases. This practice is now obsolete.

A second important point is that judges should almost make a fetish of the following distinctions: an appeals court affirms, reverses or modifies *judgements* or *orders;* it agrees with, approves or disapproves *opinions* or *decisions;* and it remands *cases* (or causes) and *actions.* When the court lacks jurisdiction to hear the appeal, the proper disposition is usually *appeal dismissed.* Although an appellate court, in its opinions, may approve or disapprove the trial court's statement or use of legal propositions, the judgement proper operates only on the judgement or order appealed from-that is, appellate courts do not affirm or reverse opinions, only orders or judgements. (The appellate court may, for example, affirm the judgement below but substitute a rationale leading to that judgement.)

The terms *vacate* and *reverse* can be problematic. Practices vary; some courts *reverse* the judgement below when the trial court should have disposed of the case differently and *vacate* when the trial court may not have been incorrect but needs to be unconstrained by its former judgement as it carries out the further directions of the appellate court, e.g., "We *vacate the judgement of the district court and remand* the case for proceedings consistent with this opinion." Still other courts *vacate* only injunctions or administrative orders, *reversing* all other erroneous dispositions below. Courts ought to encourage consistency among their particular judges in these matters of usage.

With these guidelines in mind, it may be useful to consider a number of appellate court judgements as well as statements about judgements, that are illustrative of the pitfalls awaiting the unwary.

Some examples, related to the aforementioned discussion, follow.

Q. What is judgement in rem?

A. A Judgement in rem binds not only the parties of the action but all other persons.

Q. Explain mistaking the Lower court for its judgement.

A. 1. Mistaking the Lower Court for its Judgement. "We deny the petitions and *affirm* [read *affirm the order of*] the Interstate Commerce Commission." "In an opinion by Justice Brennan, the Supreme Court *affirmed* [read *affirmed the judgement of*] the fourth Circuit." "For these reasons, I am of the opinion that the evidence was sufficient to warrant revocation in this case and would *affirm* [read *affirm the judgement of*] the lower court." (The tribunal appealed from is not before the higher court for approval or disapproval affirmance or reversal; rather, its *judgement* or *order* is).

2. Mistaking the Case for the Judgement Below. "*The case* (or *cause*) [read *The judgement*] is affirmed." (The case or cause remains the same; an appellate-court judgement acts directly upon a previous judgement in the case, but not upon the case itself).

3. Mistaking the Lower Court's Opinion for Its Judgement. "The *opinion* [read *judgement*] of the trial court is affirmed." "The *decision* [read *judgement*] of the district court is reversed." "For reasons stated below, we affirm the *decision* [read *judgement*] of the trial court." (The appellate court may agree or disagree with the trial court's opinion or decision; again, however, it affirms or reverses the *judgement*).

4. Mistaking the Appellate Court's Judgement for the Trial Court's. "The judgement of the trial court is reversed and rendered." (Appellate courts ordinarily have no power or jurisdiction to render a trial court's judgement; yet, appellate courts are often authorised to render judgements that should have been rendered by the trial court. Read *The judgement of the trial court is reversed; on appeal, we render judgement for .....*)

5. Mistaking the Judgement for the Case. "The judgement of the trial court is reversed *and remanded* [read *and the case is remanded*]." (The judgement of the trial court may be reversed but only the *case* may be remanded.) "We vacate and remand the case for consideration of whether these errors were harmless." (Understood, perhaps, are the words *the judgement of the trial court* after the word *vacate;* it is generally best not to rely upon Understood Words in drafting judgements, however; yet see (10) below and the following discussion.) "The trial court's judgement is *affirmed in part and reversed and remanded in part* [read *affirmed in part, reversed in part and the case is remanded*]." (A case may not be remanded in part. If the judgement is not stated in sentence form, it is quite proper to write *affirmed in part, reversed in part and remanded.*)

6. Superfluously Granting Judgement After Reversal of a Plaintiff's Judgement. "The judgement for the plaintiff is reversed *and the judgement is here rendered for the defendant* [omit the italicised words]." (If no counterclaim has been interposed by the defendant, the judgement should end after the word *reversed;* the judgement is favourable to the defendant merely in denying the plaintiff recovery of the plaintiff.)

7. Wrongly Omitting a Remand. "The judgement that the plaintiff take nothing is reversed and is here rendered for the plaintiff." (This judgement is incomplete, unless there is only one possible form and measure of relief; if the plaintiff sought damages, the case would have to be remanded to the trial court for a determination of the measure of damages.)

8. Mistaking the Judgement for the Court Below or its Judgement. "The district court's *judgement held* [read *opinion held,* or, better, *The district court held*] that the oral contract was dissolved by virtue of appellee's breach for failure to provide or secure the promised financing."

Finally, it is worth noting that the terms *affirm, reverse, remand* etc. may have "understood" objects, as here: "We affirm on all issues with regard to Jack Ballard but *reverse* insofar as the court held Mary Ballard liable for the 1969 and 1970 deficiencies." "We hold that Ohio's law of trade secrets is not preempted by the patent laws of the United States and accordingly, we *reverse.*" "We *reverse* and *remand.*" These elliptical phrases are unexceptionable; when, however, one of these verbs of disposition is given an object, then all such verbs in the immediate context should have explicit objects (refer item 5 above).

Q. Explain judicative, judicatory and juditorial.
A. judicative, -tory, -torial. *Judicative* is a Needless Variant of *adjudicative,* q.v. *judicatorial* is a **Needless Variant** of *judicial,* q.v. *judicatory,* adj., = (1) of or relating to judgement; (2) by which a judgement may be made giving a decisive indication critical. For the nominal senses of *judicatory,*

Q. What is a court of judicature?
A. judicature, judicatory. *Judicature* = (1) a judge's term of office; or (2) a body a judges. It is sometimes used in G.B. where *judiciary,* q.v., usually appears in

the U.S.; hence, the U.S. statute is the Judiciary Act of 1789 whereas Britain has the Judicature Acts of 1873-75 and the Supreme Court of Judicature (Consolidation) Act of 1925. *Judicature* is used in the U.S. in names such as the American Judicature Society, which publishes the journal, *judicature,* by its own terms "a forum for fact and opinion relating to all aspects of the administration of justice and its improvement."

On the whole, however, *judicature* is far more common in G.B. than in the U.S., e.g., "The chancery division placed stress upon certain provisions of the *Judicature* Act." (Eng.) "This paragraph applies to all courts of *judicature,* criminal of civil and to all persons having by law or by consent of parties, authority to hear, receive and examine evidence." (Eng.) "It is a basic rule of English *judicature* that our courts do justice in public." (Eng.)

Judicatory = judiciary; judicature. Except in specialised senses in Scotland and in the Presbyterian Church, this term should be avoided as a Needless Variant. For its adjectival sense,

Q. What is judicial?

A. judicial, judicious. *Judicial* = (1) of, relating to or by the court (judicial officers); (2) in court (judicial admissions); (3) legal; (4) of or relating to a judgement. Here, sense (1) has been illustrated: "The requirements of this section had been *judicially* interpreted [*i.e.,* interpreted by the court] well before defendants' actions." "Far more imposing is the edifice of private remedies *judicially* extracted from the Securities and Exchange Act of 1934."

Following are the examples of sense (2) of *judicial:* "The record further revealed that the trial court erroneously apprised the defendant of the effect of his plea (i.e., by failing to inform him that his plea (i.e., by failing to inform him that his *judicial* stipulation had foreclosed a merit consideration of his appeal from the adverse ruling on the motion to supress)." "Appellant then took the witness stand and *judicially* confessed that she had committed the offense allegedly against her in the indictment."

And here, sense (3): "It is now well established by *judicial* precedent that where an atorney has taken a retainer to defend a prisoner, he is not at liberty to withdraw during the trial because he discovers that his client is guilty."

Sense (4), not recorded in unabridged or legal dictionaries, is not uncommon in legal contexts, especially in the U.S.

Todd's liability for Auto's attorneys' fees, therefore, is fundamentally different from, the example, liability for interest on a judgement, which we held, was not covered by the red-letter clause in *Alcoa Steamship Co. v. Charles Ferran & Co.,* relied on by the district court. Whereas an award of *judicial* interest is collateral to and independent of the action itself, attorneys' fees awarded as a result of breach of an implied warranty of workman like performance are an integral part of the merits of the case and the scope of relief. *Todd Shipyards Corp. v. Auto Transportation. S.A.,* 763 F. 2d 745, 756 (5th Cir. 1985)."

Though hardly unusual, this usage of the word is certainly suspect.

Judicious has a quite different meaning: "well considered, discreet, wisely circumspect" e.g., "The court *judiciously* exercised its inherent equitable power to fashion a remedy appropriate to the wrongs committed." "By *judicious* application of Rule 403, a trial judge can afford the defendant in an obscenity case a fair opportunity to prove that the community displays a reasonable degree of acceptance of comparable material." "My theory was expressed too widely in certain parts and not widely enough in others; and Mr. Whitworth's pamphlet appeared to me to have corrected and completed it in a *judicious* manner." (Eng.) *Judgematic* is a Needless Variant of *judicious*.

Q. How do courts judicialise?

A. judicialise = to treat judicially, arrive at a judgement or decision upon (*OED*). More recently it has evolved to mean "to take into the province of the courts" e.g., "Rule making proceedings have become more *judicialized*."

Q. What is Judicial Cognizance?

A. judicial notice, judicial cognizance. The former phrase (referring to the means by which, a court may take as proved certain facts without hearing evidence) is now the more common of the two in both the U.S. and G.B.

The verb phrase is *to notice judicially:* "While there are few absolutes in this area, we can *notice judicially*-if we need-that contemporary wills more often than not use the residuary clause to carry out the most important provision."

Q. What do you understand by judicial review?

A. judicial review = The power of the courts to review the legislative and executive section and determine their validity.

Q. Is judiciary a noun, explain?

A. judiciary, adj. Ordinarily, a noun, *judiciary* is used in *W*3 adjectivally in the phrase *with full judiciary authority* (in definition of *enbanc*). *W3* records *judiciary* as an adjective equivalent to *judicial.* It is rarely so used in legal contexts and should be avoided in that sense as a Needless Variant.

But in the sense "of or relating to the judiciary," which means something different from *judicial* (= of or realting to the court), q.v., the adjective *judiciary* is quite useful, e.g., "If the history of the interpretation of *judiciary* legislation teaches anything, it teaches the duty to reject treating such statutes as a wooden set of self-sufficient words." *Romero v. International Terminal Operating Co.,* 358 U.S. 354, 379 (1959).

Q. Judiciary is a judicial branch of government. Comment.

A. judiciary, n., (= the judicial branch of government) is used in G.B. as well as in the U.S., e.g., "Appellant has questioned the validity of the sections of the act relating to the last-mentioned objective upon the theory that they are unconstitutional enroachments by the legislative branch of the government upon the powers of the *judiciary.*" "In *Crouch v. Crouch,* we gave reasons for the federal *judiciary's* traditional refusal to exercise diversity jurisdiction in domestic relations cases."

Q. What is a jump bail?

A. jump bail = failure of the accused person, to appear before court at the time after getting a bail.

Q. What is the meaning of the phrase juncture?

A. juncture. The phrase *at this juncture* should be used in reference to a crisis or a critically important time; it is not equivalent merely to "at this time" or 'now.' When used with these latter meanings, it is a pomposity. Here, it is appropriate: "There can be no question the respondent was "in custody" at least as on the moment he was placed under arrest; because he was not informed of his constitutional rights at this *juncture,* respondent's subsequent admissions should not have been used against him." And here, it is inappropriate: "The controversy *at this juncture merely points up* [read *at this point merely illustrates*] the indefiniteness and uncertainty of the controversial portion of the decree." "Texas argues that delay of review is not all that it seeks to avoid by petitioning *at this juncture* [read *at this point* or *now*]."

Q. Explain jural.

A. jural, juridic, -idical, juratory, -atorial. *Jural* = (1) of or relating to law or its administration, legal, juristic; or (2) of or pertaining to rights and obligations. Today, *jural* is more common in sense (2): "The categories were cast in terms of *jural* relations, with a particular suit falling into one group or another depending on the character of the right sought to be enforced." "The same points and the same examples seem valid in relation to all possible kinds of *jural* interests, legal as well as equitable."

Sense (1), in which, *jural* is really only a Needless Variant of simpler terms, still sometimes appears: "Witnesses are often required to describe in meticulous detail a happening that occurred months and years before the *jural* finding of facts." "One legacy of the Enlightment is the belief that law is something separate from the state, a set of longstanding *jural* rules or immutable principles resting on God or 'nature' that the state supposedly enforces."

Q. What are judicial proceedings?

A. juridial = relating to judicial proceedings or to the law; the form in *-idical* is standard, e.g., "The line of departure will be set by that unifinished classic of *juridical* righteousness, the statement that for every wrong, there is a remedy." "The intent that must be manifested by the settlor is an intent to create the *juridical* relationship known to the law as a trust." "I cannot believe that the court ever meant, in listing the criteria that usually attend the creation of a remainder, to express an inflexible rule or an inexorable *juridical* formula by the use of which we would be able to derive an automatic answer in all cases." *Juridical* is sometimes, mispronounced as if it were spelled *jurjdical,* with a soft *-c-*.

Juratory, a rare term today, means "of or pertaining to an oath or oaths; expressed or contained in an oath" (*OED*). *Juratorial,* also rare, means "of or belonging to a jury" (*OED*).

Q. What is a jurat?

A. jurat, jurant. Both mean "one who has takes an oath"; except in Scottish history, *jurant* is a Needless Variant that is used rarely. *Jurat* usually refers to a public official, though historically, it could refer to a juror: "On his left, was a group of twelve sworn *jurats,* selected not for their ignorance of or impartiality for the matters at hand but precisely because they were more likely to know the truth in advance." (Eng.)

Jurat has an additional and perhaps, more common, sense: "a clause placed at the end of an affidavit stating the time, place and officer before whom, the affidavit was made" e.g., "It further appears that the *jurat* to the loyalty affidavit has been properly executed."

Q. Define jurisdiction.

A. jurisdiction = the *power* of a court to decide a case or enter a decree, e.g., "There is no *jurisdiction* to insert words in order to correct a mistake even though it is proved that the testator did not know and approve of the sense carried by deficient words actually appearing in the instrument." (Eng.) By transference of sense, *jurisdiction* has come to mean additionally "the territory within which, an authority may exercise its power" (the accused then fled the jurisdiction).

A. And *venue*. *Venue* refers to the possible or proper *places* for the trial of a lawsuit, as distinguished from the proper forums in which, *jurisdiction* (the *power* to hear the case) might be established.

B. Prepositions with. *Jurisdiction* takes of or *over*. "This court does not have *jurisdiction over* the appeal." "How such a magistrate can be said to have had no *jurisdiction over* the charge at all, it is hard to see." (Eng.) "This court has *jurisdiction of* the subject matter of the claims asserted in plaintiff's first amended complaint."

Q. Give the meaning of jurisdictional.

A. jurisdictional, -dictive. The latter means "having jurisdiction" (the court that is jurisdictive of this suit), the former "of or relating to jurisdiction" e.g., "The time limit fixed by Rule 59(e) is *jurisdictional:* it may not be extended by waiver of the parties or by rule of the district court." This Differentiation has emerged only recently, jurisdictive being, in its other senses, a Needless Variant of **jurisdictional**. Jurisdictive is rare in American legal prose.

Q. Who is a jurisprude?

A. jurisprude, recorded in neither the OED nor the *OED Supp.,* has been listed in *W3* as a Back-Formation from *jurisprudence* with the meaning "a person who makes ostentatious show of learning in jurisprudence and the philosophy of law or who regards legal doctrine with undue solemnity or veneration." The word deserves wider currency but not without recognition of its pejorative connotations. (For the neutral personal noun corresponding to *jurisprudence.* In the following sentence, *jurisprude* is wrongly used as if it were a neutral noun: "Yet all these scientific theories of law still leave contemporary *jurisprudes* [read *jurisprudents*] unsatisfied and for good reason." Forte, *Natural Law and Natural Laws,* 26 Univ. Bookman 75, 75-76 (1986).

Q. Explain the meaning of jurisprudence in detail.

A. jurisprudence. A. Practical or Theoretical Sense. This uncertain term has evolved curiously. The *OED* assigns three senses to it : (1) knowledge of or skill in law; (2) the science that treats of human laws (written or unwritten) in general; and (3) a system or body of law. The original sense (1) of practical skill in the law shifted to create the meanings (2 and 3) that emphasise the body of knowledge with which, skilled practitioners work.

Though derivatives of *jurisprudence* exist in a number of Western languages, this shift in meaning from the practical to the theoretical has apparently occurred only in English. Although both senses remain alive, the theoretical one, equivalent now roughly to "philosophy of the law," dominates at present. The result, one writer has argued, is that "a word of distinguished pedigree and a well-established English meaning not essentially different from that which it bears in other languages has been made to colour like a chameleon and finally, emerge as a self-contradictory chimera." Note, *A Note on the Word Jurisprudence*, 231 Law Q. Rev. 334, 339 (1942).

B. For *case law*. In AmE, *jurisprudence* has been extended even further from "body of law" to mean "court decisions or caselaw" e.g., "The seaman's cause of action against a shipowner for unseaworthiness of the vessel is largely a child of twentieth-century *jurisprudence*." Note, *The Doctrine of Unseaworthiness in the Lower Federal Courts,* 76 Harv. L. Rev. 819, 819 (1963). "This holding recognised and applied, as a part of the general maritime law, a principle previously applied by either statute or *jurisprudence* in other contexts." The French use their term *la jurisprudence* in precisely this sense. *Case law* and *decisional law* are less grandiose terms in English.

C. As a Count Noun. *Jurisprudence* is a proper count noun, e.g., "The courts, for many years, refused to acknowledge the existence of "administrative law" as *a jurisprudence* [read *a branch of jurisprudence*]."

Q. Who is jurisprudent?

A. jurisprudent, jurisprudential. *Jurisprudent,* though appearing to be an adjective, is a noun meaning "a jurist, or learned lawyer." (Cf. **jurisprude.**) *Jurisprudential* = of or relating to jurisprudence, e.g., "In a real and practical sense, when such an opportunity arises, the remedial considerations (not theoretical or *jurisprudential* concepts) totally dictate the course of action the plaintiff should pursue."

Q. Who is a Jurist?

A. jurist. In England, this word is reserved for those having made outstanding contributions to legal thought and legal literature. In the U.S., it is rather loosely applied to every judge of whatever level and sometimes, even to non-scholarly practitioners who are well respected.

Here, the term has been used correctly: "These topics would lead us into a very large inquiry, incompatible with the object of this summary sketch; but they deserve the attention of all students of the law of prize and it is to be hoped that some eminent *jurist* will, hereafter, examine them." Appendix on Prize Causes,

4 U.S. (2 Wheat.) 293 (1817)./ "For *jurist,* law teacher and judge, comparative law is becoming more than a part of his general culture." (R. Pound) "The apportionment picture in Pennsylvania has, indeed, degenerated into a sorry state, in spite of the lofty ideals of the many sincere and scholarly *jurists* who contributed to its development over the years."

The most common error in the U.S. is to suppose that *jurist* is merely an equivalent of *judge:* "We find no constitutional question concerning the validity of Charles Milton's conviction and sentence of death about which, reasonable *jurists* [read *judges*] could differ."

Q. What is juristic?

A. juristic, -istical. The form in *-istical* is a Needless Variant, e.g., "We can all profit by the advice this legal disciplinarian gave his students on effective *juristic* style.

Q. What do you understand by juristic person?

A. juristic person = A legal entity other than a natural person such as corporations, association, idols etc.

Q. Define jurocracy.

A. jurocracy = government by the courts. Refer D.L. Horowitz, *The Jurocracy: Government Lawyers, Agnecy Programs, and Judicial Decisions* (1977). The term is recorded in none of the major dictionaries, though certainly, it is a useful addition to the language.

Q. Who is a juror?

A. juror, juryman, -woman, jurator. *Juror* is the word to be used in all modern contexts. *Juryman* and *jurywoman* should be avoided on grounds of SEXISM, though occasionally, they appear, e.g., "A petty juror may not—and it is doubtful whether a grand juror may—give evidence as to what passed between the *jurymen* [read *jurors*] in the discharge of their duties." (Eng.) *Jurator* is an obsolete equivalent.

Q. Define a jury.

A. jury is a Collective Noun in the U.S.; hence it is governed, in most contexts, by a singular verb. To emphasise the individual members of the jury, we have the word *jurors. The jury was* is generally preferable in AmE to *The jury were,* e.g., "The jury *are* [read *is*] to decide according to the preponderance of the evidence." "Judges do not decide questions of fact; the jury *do* [read *does*] not decide questions of law." "The jury *have* [read *has*] little use for a smart-aleck cross-examiner." "The jury *are* [read *is*] instructed that the words contained in the publication sued on by the plaintiff imply that the crime of murder had been committed by the plaintiff and are actionable per se." "The jury *are* [read *is*] bound by the instructions of the court."

In G.B., however, where using plural verbs with collective nouns is common, *jury* usually takes a plural verb.

Q. Is jury adjective or a noun?

A. jury is both adjective and noun. Here it acts as an adjective: "*Dunn* still has a sound rationale, Justice Rehnquist declares: the possibility that the inconsistency was a product of *jury* lenity." The legal writer should be aware that, as a general English adjective, *jury* has, in addition to the ordinary legal meaning "of or relating to a jury," the meaning "make-shift" (a jury rig).

jury room is a beginning to be written as one word; the *OED* lists it in hyphenated form, and *W3* lists it as two words.

Q. Is Jus a legal right?

A. jus (= a legal right, rule, or principle of law) forms the plural *jura,* e.g., "Such a lien secures the creditor neither *jus in rem* nor *jus ad rem.*"/ "Rights to things, *jura in rem,* have for their subject some material thing, as land or goods, which the owner may use or dispose of in any manner he pleases within the limits prescribed by the terms of his right." The term is spelled also *ius.*

Q. Explain jus disponendi.

A. jus disponendi (= the right to dispose of property) is an unnecessary Latinism that masks as a Term of Art, e.g., "He has the entire *jus disponendi* [read *right to dispose of the property*], which implies that he may give it absolutely or may impose any restriction or fetters not repugnant to the nature of the estate that he gives." "Here, undoubtedly, the devisee is given an estate in fee simple by clear, unambiguous and explicit words; this carries the *jus disponendi* [read *right to dispose of the property*]."

jus in re(m), jus ad rem. The distinction is a simple one, though of decreasing importance: "A *jus in re* is a right, or property in a thing, valid as against all mankind. A *jus ad rem* is a valid claim on one or more persons to do something, by force of which, a *jus in re* will be acquired." *The Young Mechanic,* 30 F. Cas. 873, 876 (C.C.D. Me. 1855) No. 18, 180). The usual phrase is *jus in rem,* not *jus in re.*

Q. What is *jus sanguinis?*

A. jus sanguinis = a legal rule whereby, a child's citizenship is that of his parents. We have no other name for it.

Q. Define *just deserts?*

A. just deserts is occasionally misrendered *just desserts,* as here: "Nor can Horizon avoid its just *desserts* [read *deserts*] by its pleonastic harping on the fact that its conduct ..... has been impeccable since at least mid-June of 1983." *N.L.R.B. v. Horizon Air Services, Inc.,* 761 F.2d 22, 32 (Ist Cir. 1985).

Q. What is *jus tertii?*

A. jus tertii (= the right of a third party) generally is not a useful enough latinism to justify its presence in legal prose, e.g., "Recovery in trover by a mere possessor against the defense to title in a third party (*ius tertii*) [omit parenthetical phrase] is apparently allowed in most states in which, the question has been raised." "Respondents may be correct that petitioner does not possess standing *jus tertii* [read *as a third party*] but that is not the issue."

Q. Justiciable means liable to the determined in a court of justice. Explain.

A. justiciable, judiciable. The former is preferred in the sense "liable to be determined in a court of justice; subject to jurisdiction" (justiciable cases and controversies). Here, however, it is used non-sensically; the U.S. Supreme Court, in quoting this sentence, appropriately *sic*'d it: "There has not been enough time in which, *justiciably* [*sic*] to decide the case." *Judicable* is a Needless Variant.

Q. Who is *justiciar?*

A. justiciar, n., **justiciary.** These terms are obsolete in all but historical sense relating to medieval England.

Q. What is *justificatory?*

A. justificatory, justificative. The latter is a Needless Variant of the former: "The plaintiff should have *marshaled justificatory reasons for* [better: *justified*] allowance of the amount sought."

Q. Explain *justify.*

A. justify, like *warrant* q.v., generally takes as its object an action or belief, not a person, e.g., "The instant cases furnish sufficient additional indications of the settlor's intent to *justify* our giving effect to the language of the instrument limiting an estate to the grantor's heirs."

In legal prose, however, this verb frequently takes personal objects, e.g., "M. told the officer nothing that would *justify the officer in concluding* that T. was about to escape."

Q. What are juvenile courts?

A. juvenile courts = Magistrates exercising jurisdiction over offences committed by and other matters related to children and young persons.

Q. What is juvenile delinquency?

A. juvenile delinquency = An offence committed by a person who is under 16 years of age.

Q. What is meant by kidnapping?

A. kidnapping = An act of taking away or abducting a person out of another's custody or from lawful guardianship for unlawful purpose.

Q. What is meant by kin?

A. kin = Blood relatives.

Q. What is meant by laches?

A. laches = Neglect of a person to promptitude in pursuing a legal remedy.

Q. What is meant by laissez faire?

A. laissez faire = Government non-interference of the economic matters.

Q. When do we lament?

A. lament, v.t., should not be made intransitive by the addition of a preposition, e.g., "In this space we have often *lamented over* [omit *over*] the recent rise of ultraconservatism."

Q. What is lamentable?

A. lamentable is preferably accented on the first, not the second, syllable *lam-in-ta-bel*.

Q. Is landlocked (shut in by land). Explain.

A. landlocked (= shut in or enclosed by land; almost entirely surrounded by land) is usually used in literal senses in the law. But it has its figurative uses as well: "The Chancellor is no longer fixed to the woolsack: he may stride the quarter-deck of maritime jurisprudence and, in the role of admiralty judge, dispense as would his *landlocked* brother, that which equity and good conscience impel."

Q. What is the landmark of the law?

A. landmark of the law is, as the following quotation suggests, a **Cliche** to be sparingly bestowed on cases, e.g., "The critical decision is that of Lord Mansfield in *Moses v. MacFerlan* that truly merits the cliche, a *landmark of the law*"

Q. Define language.

A. language in the sense "wording (of a document)" is peculiar to the law, e.g., "Defendant points out that both sections 2223 and 2224 employ the *language* "one who gains a thin 8," and argues that the sense of the word 'gain' as thus used is to acquire a tangible benefit or an unconscionable thing.

Q. What is a lapse statute?

A. lapse statute; antilapse statute; nonlapse statute. All three phrases denote (in the U.S.) the same type of statute, the meaning of which, has been illuminated in the quotations: "Nearly all states have enacted *lapse statutes* designed to provide a substitute beneficiary for the deceased legatee in certain situations." "A majority of the states have held that a *nonlapse statute* does not apply to a member of a class who was dead at the time of the execution of the will." "If an *antilapse statute* applies to save gifts of persons living when the will is executed but not the gifts of persons who die before the will is executed, republication of the will by codicil after the death of a lagatee should not prevent an application of the statute to save the gift."

Today *lapse statute* is the most common phrase, even though it is the least logical (inasmuch as the effect of the statute is to *prevent* the lapse of testamentary gift(s). The best phrase, in tems of lucidity, *is antilapse statute.* There are judicial opinions in which, both *nonlapse* and *antilapse* appear in reference to the selfsame statute; yet the terms should not be varied in a single writing.

Q. Define lapsus calami.

A. lapsus calami = a slip of the pen. A very good example, though it may merely be a misprint, occurs in a judicial opinion that looks as if it represents a backslide in first amendment rights. A judge writes: "The First Amendment is not a fetish. *Reversed* it must be but this *reverence* must be tempered with a realistic approach to such problems as that now at bar." Without *reverence* to prompt the reader to understand that the judge means *Revered* and not *Reversed,* we might be quite confused about his purpose.

Q. Who is a larcenist?

A. larcenist; larcener. *Larcenist* (= one who commits larceny) is the ordinary term; *larcener* is a primarily BrE variant.

Q. What is larceny?

A. larceny = The taking and carrying away of mere personal goods of another with intent to steal the goods.

Q. What is largesse?

A. largess(e). The English spelling *larges* is preferred, but the French pronunciation *lahr-zhes* is a standard.

Q. Define last will and testament.

A. last will and testament. Much ink has been spilled by at least one well-known writer in opposition to this phrase. See D. Mellinkoff, *The Language of the Law* 77-79, 331-33 (1963). The argument against it is that coupling *testament* with *will* is redundant and that *last* is usually inaccurate. "When a testator has been made will-conscious and likes the habit, *last will* adds spice to a will contest. For example, here is an actual case: will No. 1 revoked by will No. 2; a later 'codicil to my last will held to refer to No. 1, reviving it and revoking No. 2. The testator was talking about his first—not his second—when he said his *last will (id.* 333).

A curious case, to be sure and one that might lead some to conclude that *last will and testament* "is redundant, confusing, and usually inaccurate" *(id).* Yet, laymen know the phrase well and understand it as a ceremonious equivalent of *will.* The doublet *will and testament* is no more disturbing than many others that exist undisturbed in our language and that even enrich it.

The only recommendation to be made here is that the phrase be confined to usage as a title to the document it refers to and that general references to the document be couched in the single word *will.* If our goal is to clean up legal writing, there are worthier objects of our reforms than *last will and testament.*

Q. What is later is legal parlance?

A. later. A. Without temporal context. *later* should not be used unless a proper temporal context has first been established, e.g., "As Charles Evans Hughes, *later a chief justice of the Supreme Court,* [read *who was to become a chief justice,*] stated in 1907, ..." Cf. **then-.**

B. *Later on.* This collocation is venially verbose for *later,* e.g., "That deed and the description therein contained will be considered more particularly *later on* [read *later*] in this opinion."

Q. What are Latinisms?

A. latinisms. "I think the cases are comparatively few in which much light is obtained by the liberal use of Latin phrases ..... Nobody can derive any assistance from the phrase *novus actus interveniens* until it is translated into English." *Ingram v. United Automobile Services, Ltd.,* [1943] 2 All E.R. 71 (per du Parcq, L.J.) (quoted in 59 Law Q. Rev. 293 (1943)). In legal writing, we must distinguish between Terms of Art for which, there are no ordinary English equivalents and those terms that are merely vestigial Latinisms with simple English substitutes. The former category comprises useful Latinisms such as *prima facie, ex parte, de minimis, habeas corpus, alibi* and *quorum.* Some words that do have ordinary English equivalents have nevertheless, become such standard terms that they are unobjectionable, e.g., *bonafide* (= good faith), *amicus curiae* (= friend of the court) and *versus* (= against). These words have become a part of the English language or at least necessary parts of the language of the law.

The rightful objects of our condemnation are the bombastic and vestigial Latinisms that serve no purpose but to give the writer a false sense of erudition. These terms convey no special legal meanings or no delicate nuances apprehended only by lawyers. So, the lawyer, who writes *sub suo periculo* instead of *at his own risk,* strikes his reader as a laughable, figure.

Q. Where do we use the word launch in legal proceedings?

A. launch has become trite as used in these sentences: "Most of the miscellaneous matters relating to the *launching* [read *beginning*] of a new corporation are accomplished at a meeting of the initial directors." "Those injured in their rights of property are not required to suffer successive inflictions of pecuniary injury until a criminal prosecution is *launched* [read *begun*]."

Q. What is a laundry list?

A. laundry list is the slang phrase American lawyers commonly use to denote any sort of statutory roster of covered items.

Q. Define Law.

A. law, the law. A distinction can be drawn between *a law* and its plural *laws,* on the one hand, words that point to one or more particular and concrete instances of legal precepts and, on the other hand, *the law,* a phrase that signifies something more general and abstract. Thus particular precepts such as those of the Sherman Antitrust Act (U.S.), the Theft Act (G.B.) and the like can each be called *a law. The law,* by contrast, is used for something much wider and more general, sometimes in conjunction with words descriptive of a recognised branch of legal science, e.g., the law of torts or with words descriptive of a particular system of law, e.g., the law of England. Sometimes *the law* means or includes the institutions and persons who represent and administer the law, the complex of courts and prisons, judges, lawyers, clerks and police (*OCL* 717).

In other words law, is a body of rules which regulates human conduct governs the relationship between two or more persons.

Q. Define law as an adjective?

A. law, adj. *Law* acts in conjunction with *legal* as the adjective for *law,* n. No strict Differentiation is possible, as we have *law studies* beside *legal studies, lawbooks* beside *legal books.* But *legal firm* is not good English if it is used in place of law *firm,* just as *law doctrine* is not used for *legal doctrine.* The *OED* and *OED Supp.* contain hundreds of examples of the attributive adjective *law.*

Q. Where do we use the word latterly?

A. latterly is an Archaism for *later* or *lately,* e.g., "But there is a notion that *latterly* [read *lately*] has been insisted on a good deal that a combination of persons to do what any one of them might lawfully do by himself will make the otherwise lawful conduct unlawful."

Q. Define laudatory.

A. laudatory, -tive; laudable. The synonymous adjectives *laudatory* and *laudative* mean "expressing praise." The latter is a Needless Variant of the former. *Laudable,* in contrast, means "deserving praise." The distinction is the same as that between *praiseworthy* (= *laudable*) and the active *praiseful* (= *laudatory*).

The misuse of *laudatory* for *laudable* is all too common: "That the decision may achieve a *laudatory* [read *laudable*] result is not a valid consideration."

Two specimens of the phrase follow, both of them from late in the nineteenth century: "If advice given *mala fide,* and loss sustained, entitle me to damages, why, though the advice be given honestly [*i.e., bonafide*], but under wrong information, with a loss sustained, am I not entitled to them [i.e., damages]?"/ "Therefore, we are all of opinion that the defendant ought in justice to refund this money thus *mala fide* recovered."

Q. What is lease?
A. lease = The contract between owner of property and a tenant who agrees to pay money for the use and possession of the property for a fixed period of time.

Q. What is legacy?
A. legacy = A gift of property by will.

Q. What is libel?
A. libel = A defamatory statement especially in writing but it includes also pictrures, signs or electronic broadcast.

Q. What is lien?
A. A right by which a person in possession of the property holds and retains it against the other is satisfied of a demand due to the party retraining it.

Q. What is meant by liquidated?
A. liquidated = Fixed or certained.

Q. What is a litigation?
A. litigation = The taking of legal action by a party who is known as a litigant.

Q. What do you understand by a lunatic?
A. lunatic = An idiot or person of unsound mind or insane.

———✧✧✧———

Q. What are Malapropisms?

A. malapropisms are words used incorrectly that produce a humorous effect. The term derives from the character Mrs. Malaprop in Sheridan's play *The Rivals;* Mrs. Malaprop loves big words but uses them ignorantly to create hilarious solecisms and occasionally embarrassing double entendres. One of Mrs. Malaprop's famous similes is *as headstrong as an allegory on the banks of the Nile.*

The following are the examples of legal malapropisms. One lawyer apparently mistook *meretricious* (= marked by falsity; superficially attractive but fake nevertheless) for *meritorious* with embarrassing consequences: a plaintiff's lawyer, he asked a judge to rule favourably on his client's "meretricious claim." Other illustrations are *nefarious* (= evil) for *multifarious* ("Ties, shirts, shoes, belts, socks and all the other *nefarious* parts of one's wardrobe") and *voracity* (= greediness with food) for *veracity* ("There would have been nothing to be gained by trying to impeach the truthfulness or *voracity* of those witnesses.")

Q. What is malefactor?

A. malefactor = criminal, felon. Although the term is now primarily literary, the *OED* contains the following quotation of Herbert Spencer from 1862: "By a *malefactor,* we now understand a convicted criminal, which is far from being the acceptation of evil-doer."

Q. What is malevolent and what is maleficent?

A. malevolent; maleficent. Whereas the former means "desirous of evil to others," the latter means positively "hurtful or criminal to previous standards." "A subsequently adopted program, no matter how *laudatory* [read *laudable*], is wholly irrelevant to the issue of racial discrimination at an earlier date."

Law shares with *legal* the sense "pertaining to the law as a body of rules or as a field of study." e.g., "The principal *law* question on the cross-appeals is whether the Supreme Court committed reversible error in awarding exemplary damages as incidental to injunctive relief." *Legal* has the additional sense others." Hence, *malevolent* has to do with malicious desires and *maleficent* with malicious actions.

Q. Define malefeasance.

A. malfeasance, -zance, malefeasance; misfeasance, malefactin. Usage of the words *malfeasance* and *misfeasance* is imprecise in AmE. Perhaps, it is best to begin this entry with the clear-cut BrE distinctions. In BrE, the distinction between *malfeasance* and *misfeasance* is sharper than in the U.S. and is somewhat different. *Malfeasance* = an unlawful act; *misfeasance* = the negligent or otherwise improper performance of a lawful act (*CDL*). *Misfeasance* also has the more specialised legal sense that is common in G.B.: "a legal act done in an improper or illegal way." *Malefeasance* and *malfeazance* are obsolete spellings of *malfeasance*.

In AmE, *malfeasance* is often confined to the sense "misprision; misconduct or wrongdoing by a public official." *Misfeasance* is a more general word meaning "transgression, trespass."

In the U.S., the notion in the word *malfeasance* of public office is sometimes important; but the word is often used for corporate as well as of public officials and sometimes of other persons: "Defendants have not cited any persuasive authorities to support their view that Washington, the successor, is tainted in equity by the *malfeasance* of Oaks, its predecessor." "The contract shall not cover any loss of production due to the neglect or *malfeasance* of the insured."

The legislative drafter of the following statutory provision was not unorthodox in using both *malfeasance* and *misfeasance*: "Respondents were classified civil service employees, entitled under Ohio Rev. Code Ann. § 124.34 (1984) to retain their positions "during good behaviour and efficient service," who could not be dismissed 'except for *misfeasance, malfeasance* or *nonfeasance* in office.'

Malefaction = crime, offense. It is Formal Word that has become an Archaic.

Q. Explain the word malice.

A. malice is often an ambiguous term, because it has been diluted in legal writing. Early in the twentieth century, the dilution was noted and objected to: "When all that is meant by *malice* is an intention to commit an unlawful act without reference to spite or ill-feeling, it is better to drop the word *malice* and so, avoid all misunderstanding." *South Wales Miners Federation v. Glamorgan Coal Co.*, [1905] A.C. 239, 255. Even in the nineteenth century, however, the attenuated legal meaning had taken hold: "*Malice*, in the definitions of murder, has not the same meaning as in common speech ["strong ill will"] and ..... has been thought to mean criminal intention." Holmes. *The Common Law* 53 (1881: repr. 1946).

The legal and nonlegal sense can be pointedly in contrast: "Although when used in its nonlegal sense, the word clearly denotes an evil or wicked state of mind; at law, it does not necessarily have such a connotation; at law, it simply means that the actor intentionally did something unlawful. Thus, the legal meaning of *malice* is confusing to a non-lawyer because an individual may act with good reason or from humanitarian motives but, as a matter of legal terminology, he has acted with *malice* if his act is against the law." Purer, *The Language of Murder*, 14 U.C.L.A.

L. Rev. 1306, 1306 (1967). As a non-criminal example, the *malice* requirement in proving libel of a public figure does not involve spite or ill-will, only knowing falsity or a reckless diregard for the truth.

Q. What is malice aforethought in legal vocabulary?

A. malice aforethought does not "mean a state of the defendant's mind, as is often thought, except in the sense that he knew circumstances, which did, in fact, make his conduct dangerous. It is, in truth, an allegation like that of negligence, which asserts that the party did not come up to the legal standard of action under the circumstances in which, he found himself and also, that there was no exceptional fact or excuse present, which took the case out of the general rule." Holmes, *The Common Law* 62-63 (1881; repr. 1946). A more modern writer has explained, "At the present time, *malice aforethought* is used to express the idea that the accused killed his victim intentionally; no ill-will is required. The phrase is also employed to indicate simply that the killing was under such circumstances that the accused will be punished as severely as if the killing were intentional." Purver, *The Language of Murder,* 14 U.C.L.A. L. Rev. 1306, 1308 (1967).

Q. Define malignancy.

A. malignancy; malignity. *Malignancy* should be confined to denoting any cancerous disease. *Malignity* = wicked or deep-rooted ill will or hatred, malignant feelings or actions.

Q. What is a malpractice.

A. malpractice is confined in AmE to negligence or incompetence on the part of professionals (e.g., lawyers and doctors); in BrE, however, it has this meaning as well as a sense similar to *misfeasance:* "The mortgagees are not parties to the *malpractices* of the Waites and the tenants who were the victims of those *malpractices.*" (Eng.) The *OED* records two senses that are not current in the U.S.: (1) "illegal action by which a person seeks to benefit himself at the cost of others, while in a position of trust"; and (2) "a criminal or overtly mischievous action; wrongoing; misconduct." Cf. **malfeasance.**

Q. Define malum in se.

A. malum in se; malum prohibitum. These Latinisms are frequently used by common law writers. The distinction between the terms is helpful in understanding the relationship of morality with the law. *Malum in se* = evil in itself, something inherently and universally considered to be evil. *Malum prohibitum* = wrong merely because it is prescribed, made unlawful by statute.

Thus murder is the usual example of a crime *malum in se* but running traffic lights is said to be *malum prohibitum,* e.g., "The rule is that where a condition precedent is impossible or is illegal as involving *malum prohibition,* the bequest is absolute, just as if the condition had been subsequent. When, however, the illegality of the condition does not concern anything *malum in se* but is merely against a rule or the policy of law, the condition only is void." "A *malum prohibitum* is just as much a crime as a *malum in se.*" Holmes. *The Common Law* 46 (1881; repr. 1946). "In other words, I propose it shall not longer be *malum in se* for a citizen to pummel, cow-hide, kick, gouge, cut, wound, bruise, maim, burn, club, bastinado, flay or even lynch a job holder and that it shall be *malum prohibitum* only to the extent that the punishment exceeds the job-holder's deserts." (Mencken)

The plurals are *mala in se* and *mala prohibita.*

Q. What is mandamus?

A. mandamus = A writ issued by the supreme court or the high court and directed a governmental, or semi governmental, a judicial or quasi judicial and private bodies performing public function to perform their duties.

Q. Explain mandatory.

A. mandatary, n., (= one to whom a mandate is entrusted) should be distinguished both from *mandatory,* adj. and from *mandator,* n. (= one who gives a mandate).

Q. When do we mandate?

A. mandate, v.t., for *prescribe* is merely verbal sloppiness. "The Federal Rules of Appellate Procedure *mandate* [read *prescribe*] the time for filing a notice of appeal."

Q. What is mandatory?

A. mandatory. Horwill wrote in the 1930s that *mandatory* was sparingly used in England and that *obligatory* and *compulsory* were more common. The latter two terms may still be predominant but *mandatory injunction* is now a common phrase in English law reports.

Q. What is mandatory injunction?

A. mandatory injunction; prohibitory injunction. The former court order requires a positive action; the latter requires restraint from action.

Q. What is man-killing?

A. man-killing is still occasionally used in law to refer but the action of one man against another, but rarely in nonlegal writing. "Homicidal mania is the morbid and uncontrollable appetite for *man-killing*."

Q. Who is a man of law?

A. man-of-law = a man skilled in law, a lawyer. This word, which has decidedly positive connotations, is little used today, because of the hegemony of pejorative terms.

Q. What is manslaughter?

A. It is a crime of unlawful killing but not amounting to murder under english law.

Q. Define mantle.

A. mantle, mantel. *Mantle* means, among other things, "a loose robe" and is frequently used by legal writers in a figurative sense, e.g., "The *mantle* of immunity should be withdrawn." "The court has not felt constrained by stare decisis in its expansion of the protective *mantle* of sovereign immunity."

Mantel is a different and more common word, meaning "a structure of wood or marble above or around a fireplace, a shelf."

Q. Distinguish between many and much legally speaking.

A. many, much. *Many* is used with Count Nouns (*i.e.*, those that comprise a number of discrete or separable entities). *Much* is used with mass nouns (*i.e.*, those that refer to amounts as distinguished from numbers). Hence, *many persons* but *much salt* can be cited as two examples. Here *much* is used incorrectly: "We do not have *much* [read *many*] facts here." (Cf. *less* for *fewer*, noting that *less* is the correlative of *much* whereas *fewer* is the correlative of *many*.)

Q. What is mare clausum?

A. mare clausum = a sea under one country's jurisdiction, a closed sea. *Mare liberum* = a sea open to all. If usefulness may be judged in large measure by frequency of usage, these terms are not very useful.

Q. What is a margin?

A. margin (= footnotes) occurs today primarily in legal writing, though scholars in all disciplines commonly used it in the past, e.g., "The order and decree dismissing the bill is set out in the *margin*." This usage harks back to a bygone era when notes were set out in the right and left margins rather than at the foot of the page.

Q. What is Mc Naghten Rule?
A. A rule which determine whether a person is legally insane or not under English law.

Q. What is meant by mens rea?
A. mens rea = A guilty mind.

Q. What is mercy killing?
A. mercy killing = A painless killing of a person who is convicted for death penalty by the court of law.

Q. What is meant by mesne profits?
A. mesne profits = Damages payable by tresspasers who have stayed in possession after their right to occupy land has ended.

Q. Define metes and bounds.
A. metes and bounds, lines and corners. Both terms are used in deeds and surveys to describe the territorial limits of property; the method of measurement is by distances and angles from designated landmarks and in relation to adjoining properties. The more familiar phrase is *metes and bounds*.

Q. What is a methodology in legal terms?
A. methodology is frequently misused for *method*. Correctly used, *methodology* means "the science or study of method." Here are some examples of the misuse: "Because this case involves the role of depreciation rates and *methodologies* [read *methods*] in determining the revenue requirements of a regulated utility, we begin by briefly reviewing certain basic principles of regulatory ratemaking." "The recent decision in *Chevron* elaborates on these principles and sets out the appropriate *methodology* [read *method*] for asceretaining whether to afford deference to an agency's construction of its governing statute. "The passage enumerating the factors was meant to be an expression of the *methodology* [read *method*] to be used in deciding whether an activity should be held to be within the reach of that statute's imposition of liability."

Methodlogy is correctly used in the following example; the sentence was hard to come by: "Writing in a time in which *methodology in the social sciences* [i.e., the study of method in the social sciences] has become the prevailing approach, Professor von Mehren speaks of comparative study of law rather than of comparative law." (R. Pound).

Dictionary of Legal Terms 121

Q. Who is a midwife?

A. midwife, v.t.; **midwive.** The first one is the preferred form, e.g., "This may happen when a writting judge believes with heart and soul that his position is right but he knows that his majority is shaky; here persuasiveness must *midwive* [read *midwife*] the opinion if it is to come into existence at all."

Q. Explain mien.

A. mien (= demeanor, appearance, bearing) usually carries connotations of formidableness (his forbidding mien). The word is pronounced ***meen.***

Q. What is a Millennium?

A. millenium, -ia, -iums. The preferred plural is *-ia* in the AmE, and *-iums* in BrE; but either is acceptable on both sides of the Atlantic.

Q. Define mind and memory.

A. mind and memory is a common Doublet of sound mind and memory) in the context of judging testamentary capacity. Mellinkoff calls it "a snatch of confusing nonsense ..... As in England, American lawyers have long recognised that they were using *memory* here in a special way, in the sense of understanding or more, and that *mind and memory* did no more for testamentary capacity than *mind* alone." D. Mellinkoff. *The Language of the Law* 333, 335 (1963).

The share lies in failing to recognise the phrase as an archaic doublet and in misunderstanding it as setting forth independent criteria for judging testamentary capacity, because historically, *mind = memory*. Especially, in writing to be read by laymen (as in jury instructions), the second half of this doublet should be avoided. As the law is currently understood, one may be very forgetful and still be "of sound mind and memory." *Sound mind* is quite sufficient and far less confusing.

Q. What is meant by minor?

A. minor = A person below 18 years, but where guardian oppointed for a minor than such person remains minor upto age 21 years.

Q. What is mingle mangle?

A. mingle-mangle, known in erudite circles as *macaronism, soraismus* or *cacozelia,* was a common vice of language in early English opinions. It consists in English larded with Latin or French, as in the following example from

Weaver v. Ward, decided by the King's Bench in 1616 (Hobart 134): "The defendant pleaded ..... that he was ..... a trained soldier in London, of the band of one Andrews, (captain), and so was plaintiff: and that they were skirmishing with their muskets charged with powder for their exercise in *re militari* against another captain and his band; and as they were so skirmishing, the defendant, *casualiter et per infortunium et contra voluntatem suam,* in discharging his piece, did hurt and wound the plaintiff; which is the same, etc., *absque hoc,* that he was guilty *aliter sive alio modo.*"

For modern legal readers, mingle-mangle makes for fascinating, if not entirely comprehensible, reading. The following is another Latin-English example and this is also from a well-known torts case: "Trespass *quare vi & armis clausum fregit, & herbam suam pedibus conculcando consumpsit in six acres. The defendant pleads,* that he hath an acre lying next the said six acres and upon it, a hedge of thorns and he cut the thorns and they *ipso invito fell* upon the plaintiff's land." *The Case of the Thorns,* Y.B. 6 Ed. 4, 7a., p. 18 (1466) (summarised thus in *Bessey v. Olliot & Lambert,* T. Raym. 467 (1681).

Q. What is minim?

A. minim (= something minute) is sometimes used in the context of the maxim *de minimis non curat lex,* e.g., "The *minim* of the injury here obscures and tempts neglect of the importance of the issue."

Q. What is minimal?

A. minimal, minimum, adj. Both words are used adjectivally, *minimum* as an attributive adjective in phrases such as *minimum wage.* If there is a valid nuance distinguishing these two adjectival forms, it is that *minimal* = few, little, smallest (with minimal disturbance) (minimal support) (minimal objections), whereas *minimum,* adj., = consisting in the fewest necessary things or the least acceptable or lawful amount (minimum contact as a basis for jurisdiction) (minimum wage), e.g., "Most statutes set up *minimum* requirements with respect to the corporate name." "Congress accommodated state fears by allowing the states to retain *minimal* residency requirements."

Q. What do we mean by minimise?

A. minimise; minify. These words have distinct meanings and the latter is too much neglected. Property, *minimize* = to keep to a minimum and *minify* = to belittle, degrade, to represent something as smaller than it really is. *Minimalise* is not a word.

Q. What is minimum?

A. minimum, n. Pl. *minima,* e.g., "The deprivation of his protected property interest was accomplished without adherence to due process *minimums* [read *minima*]." "The courts must recognise broad administrative discretion whether to implement procedures above the *minima* required by Congress."

Q. Who are minions of the law?

A. minions of the law is a Cliche referring to policemen or other law enforcement officers.

Q. What is a miniscule?

A. miniscule is one of the commonest wrong spellings in legal texts. The correct spelling is *minuscule,* e.g., "The selling shares owned a *miniscule* [read *minuscule*] proportion of the outstanding shares." The word has been derived from the word *minus* and has nothing to do with the prefix *mini-*.

Q. What is minutia?

A. minutia is the rare singular of the plural *minutiae,* which should always take a plural verb.

mirandise (= to read an arrestee his rights under *Miranda v. Arizona*) has become common as police-officer slang in the U.S.; it is, therefore being adopted by some criminal lawyers, and even judges, e.g., "First, defendant claims that the trial court erred in ruling inadmissible his exculpatory statements made to the officer after defendant was arrested and *Mirandised.*" *People v. Barrick,* 654 P.2d 1243, 1253 (Col. 1982) (in bank). Surely, though, it is a blemish in place of some acceptable periphrasis, such as *to read* (an arrestee) *his miranda rights."*

Q. What is misappropriate?

A. misappropriate, appropriate, v.t. The former means "to apply (as another's money) dishonestly to one's own use" e.g., "It was held to be gross negligence for an administratrix to permit an attorney in fact to handle an estate for nine years without an accounting and settlement, during which time, he *misappropriated* funds." "If he took little in his own name in bad faith, intending to *misappropriate* the property, he is liable for the full amount of the mortgage and interest thereon."

Appropriate has a more neutral connotation, meaning "to take from a particular person or organisation for a particular purpose," It is tinged with some of the negative connotations made explicit in *misappropriate. Appropriate* is the non-accusatory term.

Q. Who is a mischievious man?

A. mischievious is a common misspelling and mispronunciation of *mischievious.* Cf. **grievous.**

Q. What is meant be miscarriage?

A. miscarriage = Failure in the administration of Justice, Synonym for abortion.

Q. Who is a misdemeanant?

A. misdemeanant (= one who has been convicted of a misdemeanor) is the analogue of a *felon.* But unlike *felon,* it is little known outside the law, e.g., "Unlike with the *misdemeanant* only once convicted, we are not prepared to summarily conclude that the offender, who repeats such conduct after initial prosecution and conviction, does not represent a substantial danger to society." Whether *convicted misdemeanant* is a Redundancy, is a close question; surely most legal readers would not think that it is: "A prosecutor clearly has a considerable stake in discouraging convicted *misdemeanants* from appealing and thus obtaining a *trial de novo* in the Superior Court."

Nevertheless, the senses given in the *OED* and *W3* suggest that *misdemeanant* is not properly used of one suspected of or charged with a misdemeanor, as opposed to one who has been convicted: "The better rule seems to be that an officer is not justified in killing a mere *misdemeanant* [read *suspected misdemeanant*] to effectuate his arrests."

The *OED* includes also the lay sense "a person guilty of misconduct" but legal writers should avoid using this technical term in this ambiguously broad sense.

Q. Define misdemeanor.

A. misdemeano(u)r. The *-our* is the British spelling, *-or* the American. The word is archaically spelled *misdemesnors,* as follows: "These become either right or wrong, just or unjust, duties or misdemesnors, according as the municipal legislator sees proper, for promoting the welfare of the society, and more effectually carrying on the purposes of civil life" (Blackstone).

Q. What is misdoubt?

A. misdoubt, equivalent to *doubt,* is an unnecessary and confusing Archaism.

Q. What is misfeasance?

A. misfeasance = The improper doing of an act which a person might lawfully do.

Dictionary of Legal Terms

Q. Who is a misfeasor?

A. misfeasor (= one who commits a misfeasance) is the correct agent noun but it is no longer used.

Q. What is misnomer in law?

A. misnomer (= the use of a wrong name) in law may mean "a mistake in naming a person or place," whereas in nonlegal contexts it usually refers to a misdescription of a thing, e.g., "A *misnomer* of the plaintiff in the peti-*competition convenant* [or *agreement*]. It should be avoided in favour of either of these longer phrases, e.g., "It seems reasonably clear that some allocation of the price to a covenant is necessary if a purchaser wants to deduct any amount for a *no-compete covenant* [read *covenant not to compete*]."

Q. What is moratorium?

A. moratorium = A legal authorization to a debtor to postpone payment for a certain time.

Q. What is mortgage?

A. mortgage = A loan of money taken.

Q. What is meant by natural justice?

A. natural Justice = Justice which is founded in equity, honesty and good conscience.

Q. What do you understand by naturalization?

A. It is the act by which a foreigner requires the status of a natural born citizen.

Q. What is negligence?

A. negligence = A tort, actionable at the suit of a person suffering damage from the defendent's breach of duty to take care to refrain from injuring him.

Q. What is negotiable instrument?

A. A negotiable instrument means a promissory note, bills of exchange or cheque either to order or to bearer.

Q. What is meant by *next friend?*

A. next friend = A person who is admitted or appointed by a court as a special guardian to act for the benefit of a minor or insane person.

Q. What is *noisome?*

A. noisome is often misconstrued as meaning "noisy, loud, clamorous." In fact, it means "noxious, malodorous." (Cf. **fulsome.**) The word is related etymologically to *annoy*. Here is a correct usage of the same: "If the house is to be cleaned, it is for those who occupy and govern it, rather than for strangers, to do the *noisome* work." (Cardozo)

Q. Define *no later than.*

A. no later than (= on or before) conveys an important nuance in the language of contracts. It is not equivalent to *before,* which does not include the date specified.

Q. What is *nolens volens?*

A. nolens volens (= willingly or unwillingly) is not a justifiable Latinism in modern legal prose, e.g., "Correlative to all such legal, powers are the legal liabilities in other persons-this meaning that the latter are subject *nolens volens* [read *willingly or unwillingly*] to the changes of jural relations involved in the exercise of A's powers." (Hohfeld)

Q. Who is *noile prosequitur?*

A. nolle prosequi(tur), non prosequitur. A. As Noun. The phrase *nolle prosequi* denotes the legal notice of abandonment of suit. *Nolle* is frequently used as an ellipsis for *nolle prosequi,* e.g., ":We conclude that the nine-month period between the *nolle* and the defendant's rearrest is not properly chargeable as a pre-trial delay for purposes of speedy trial analysis." *State v. Gaston,* 502 A. 2d 594, 597 (Conn. 1986).

Nolle prosequitur is an error deriving from confusion with *non prosequitur,* which is the judgement rendered against a plaintiff who does not appear in court to prosecute his case. *Non pros* is the shortened nominal form, here functioning adjectivally: "[A]ppellants contest on appeal the trial court's opening of a *non pros* judgement entered in their favour." *Geyer v. Steinbroun,* 506 A.2d 901, 905 (Pa. Super. 1986).

B. As Verb, *Nolle prosequi* is only a noun in England but has two verb forms in the U.S., *nol-pros* and *nolle pros.* The term means "to abandon a suit or have it dismissed by a nolle prosequi" e.g., "That plaintiff was arrested but never tried and the charges against him were *nolle prossed*." The earliest known usage occurred in 1878.

Occasionally, the phrase *nolle prosequi* is used as a verb in the U.S., though the shorter forms *non-pros* or *nolle pros* is more usual, e.g., "Gruskin's decision to permit defendant to admit responsibility for careless driving and to *nolle prosequi* the OUIL [operating a motor vehicle under the influence of introxicating liquor] charge was an executive function." *People v. Stackpoole,* 375 N.W. 2d 419, 424 (Mich. App. 1985).

Nonpros = to enter a non prosequitur against. The past tense form is *nonprossed*. Blackstone wrote *nonpros'd*. This word dates from in about 1755.

Q. Which are nominative and objective cases in law?

A. Nominative and Objective Cases. One might think that a work of this type, catering as it does to the members of a learned profession, could pass over the differences between subjects and objects in pronouns. The two sentences that follow, however, belie that thought: the first was written by a lawyer, the second by a law professor. "We will need to confer with *whomever* works on this project and then, have *he* or *she* draft a motion for summary judgement." "Third, the fault is said to lie in part with *we* eccentric professors. " In the first example, *whoever* should be the subject of *works* and the pronouns should be *him* and *her* as objects of *have;* in the second example, *us* should be the object of the preposition *with.*

Q. Define the word non.

A. Non- (= not) is the general-purpose negative prefix that has gained a great deal of ground since the nineteenth century. *Non-* often contrasts with *in-* or *un-* in expressing a nongradable contrast, rather than the opposite end of a scale, e.g., *nonlegal* as compared to *illegal,* or *nonscientific* as compared to *unscientific* **(See Also—Nonconstitutional) (PP 121).** Ordinarily, in both AmE and BrE, the prefix is not hyphenated. A number of pitfalls lie in the way of its usage, as categorized below.

A. With Nouns. Before adding *non-* to a noun, one should determine whether the noun being negated has an antonym that would suffice. For example, if *nonpretextual* means merely 'valid' or 'legitimate', it makes little sense to write: "The company showed that the reason for discharging the employee was *nonpretextual* [read, if appropriate, *legitimate*]." This infelicity may sometimes derive from tracking too closely statutory language without searching for the most appropriate word.

Another disadvantage in the usage of *non-* is that it is beginning to displace the simplest negative *not.* For example: "The cases relied upon in the opinion are *non-§ 1983 cases* [read *not § 1983 cases*]." *Grandstaff v. City of Borger,* 779 F.2d 1129, 1133 (5th Cir. 1986) (Hill, J., dissenting). As this example suggests, the usage of this prefix to construct phrasal nouns can be especially awkward: "The critical issue before us concerns the order and allocation of proof in a *private, non-class action* [read *private suit, not a class action,*] challenging employment discrimination."

B. With Adjectives. When adding *non-* to a compound adjective, the meaning can become especially murky: "noncivil rights suit"; "*nonper stirpes* distribution." e.g., "In *non-community property states* [read *common-law states*] the most troublesome issue confronting the courts and legislatures arises out of the rapid expansion of a variety of devices for bypassing probate." *Noncriminal* can usually be rendered more straightforwardly *civil;* hence, *civil trial is preferred* rather than *noncriminal trial; private school* (in AmE) is preferred rather than *nonpublic school.*

*Non-*adjectives should be avoided wherever possible, even if the avoidance means using more words. "In *automobile cases* [read *cases not involving automobile accidents*] there may be a homeowner's policy that triggers the lawsuit and protects the parent in a direct suit or in an apportionment." "Chapman transferred *his only other non-cash asset,* [read *his only remaining asset other than cash*], a used car lot, to his two minor sons." "A Tennessee statute that allows police officers to employ deadly force to prevent fleeing feldons from escaping is unconstitutional insofar as it authorises the use of such force to stop an apparently *unarmed and non-dangerous suspect* [*unarmed* probably suffices; if not, then read *unarmed suspect who does not appear to be dangerous*]." "A *non-negligent plaintiff* [read *A plaintiff who is not contributorily negligent*] may recover her total damages regardless of allocated damages." "We must therefore, affirm the district court's declaratory judgement that the challenged provisions of the Arizona Constitution and statutes as *applied to exclude non-property owners from elections* [read *applied to exclude those who do not own property from elections*] for the approval of the issuance of general obligation bonds, violated the Equal Protection Clause of the United States Constitution."

As with phrasal nouns, use of *non-* with phrasal adjectives produces awkward results, e.g., *nonincome-producing, noninterest-bearing, nonpar-value, nontaxpaid,* e.g., "It is undisputed that soyabean production is a *non-water dependant activity* [read *is an activity not dependant on water*]." "A couple *in a non-common-law jurisdiction*], one spouse being poorer than the other, will be subject to no gift taxation in interspousal transfers of property and will thus have the same tax advantages."

C. As a Separable Prefix. *Non-* is properly an inseparable prefix only, although some writers have tried to make it separable, e.g., "The Code seems to reflect a congressional perception that the taxation of the exercise of *non qualified* [read *nonqualified,* if not *unqualified*] stock options should be tightened up." "Rather, proof must be presented that the *non parties* [read *nonparties*] actively participated with the named party in violating the decree."

Q. Define nonage.

A. nonage (= legal infancy; the condition of being under age) is rare today except in legal contexts, e.g., "The two major grounds for testamentary incapacity are *nonage* and mental disability." Cf. *minority.*

Q. What is meant by non-cognizable offence?

A. This is an offence where the police has no legal authority to arrest the accused person without a warrant from the court.

Q. What is noncompete clause?

A. noncompete clause or *agreement* is inferior to *noncompetition clause* (or *agreement*). The prefix *non-* may be joined to adjectives (as with *nonexistent, nonfatal* and *nonreponsive),* to nouns (as with *nonoccurrence, nonissue* and *nonacceptance)* or to present participles (as with *nonpaying, nonsmoking* and *nonvoting*). It is not at its best, however, when joined to a verb to make an adjective, as in *noncompete,* e.g., "The plaintiffs rely on four cases that they claim, support their position that the amounts received pursuant to the *non-compete* [read *noncompetition*] agreements are personal service income. "*Furman v. United States,* 602 F.Supp. 444, 451 (D.S.C. 1984). *Noncompete* is not in the dictionaries and we may justifiably hope that it never gains their approval. The better phrase is *agreement not to compete* or *noncompetition covenant.*

Q. Illustrate the term non-compos mentis.

A. non compos mentis, compos mentis. These Latinisms are now little used, though as long as words such as *insane* and similar words are used figuratively as terms of disparagement, these learned terms (meaning "not in one's right mind" and "in one's right mind") may be useful. The phrase *non compos mentis* once gave rise to the slang expression *non compos* that is not used now.

Q. Distinguish between nonconstitutional and unconstitutional.

A. nonconstitutional, unconstitutional. As used by American practitioners, these terms have distinct meanings. *Nonconstitutional* = of or relating to some legal basis or principle other than those of the U.S. Constitution, e.g., "*Miranda* established a *nonconstitutional* prophylactic rule, the violation of which, creates an irrebuttable presumption of coercion that is applicable in only a limited number of circumstances." "*Kent v. Dulles* did invalidate a burden on the right to travel; however, the restriction was voided on the *nonconstitutional* basis that Congress did not intend to give the Secretary of State power to create the restriction at issue."

The more familiar word, *unconstitutional* = in violation of or not in accordance with principles found in the U.S. Constitution, e.g., "The three-judge district court held that the Act and regulations in question were *unconstitutional,* both under the equal protection clause of the Fourteenth Amendment [of the U.S. Constitution] and under the Constitution of Alaska."

Q. What is meant by nominee?

A. nominee = A person who has been selected by a party as its candidate for a public office.

Q. Who is none?

A. none = (1) not one; or (2) not any. Hence, it may correctly take either a singular or a plural verb. Here is an example of the singular: "No judgement could be entered for such refunds, if found in favour of the purchasers themselves, because *none was a* party to the proceeding." *None were* would also be correct but *none was* is more emphatic.

Q. Define the term non est factum.

A. non est factum is legal Argot denoting the plea denying the execution of an instrument sued on, e.g., "The plea of *non est factum* was not available but the case fell within the statute." (Eng.) "The exception is that if the defendant thought that the document he signed belonged to an entirely different legal category from that to which, it-in fact-belonged, he can plead *non est factum* and escape liability although he did not trouble to read the document and although he misled the plaintiff into supposing that he was agreeing." (Eng.) Pl. *non est factums.*

Q. What is nonfeasance?

A. nonfeasance, nonact. The two are distinguishable. Whereas *nonact* means merely the failure to act, *nonfeasance* implies the failure to act where a duty to act existed, e.g., "There is a presumption of adequate representation, which may be overcome by the intervenor only upon a showing of adversity of interest, the representative's collusion with the opposing party, or *nonfeasance* by the representative."

Dictionary of Legal Terms 131

Q. What is nonjury trial?

A. nonjury trial is generally inferior to *bench trial* or *trial to the bench,* as the better practice is to name something for what it is rather than for what it is not, e.g., "After a *nonjury trial* [read *bench trial* or *trial to the bench*], the district court dismissed the remaining civil rights claims at the conclusion of the plaintiff's case."

Q. Who is nonlawer?

A. nonlawyer. It is a curious practice that lawyers (and others also write about law) divide the universe into *lawyers* and *nonlawyers;* but speakers of English do it of other professions and occupations as well, e.g., "The Supreme Court later expressly limited the vessel owner's duty to *nonseamen* to situations where the workers were doing 'ship's work." *Layman* is usually unambiguous, though it has the potential disadvantage of Sexism, q.v.,; *nonlawyer* is clearly better than *layperson.*

Q. What is nonliability?

A. nonliability is an unnecessary equivalent of *no liability* or *lack of liability.*

nonobjectionable is a Needless Variant of *unobjectionable,* e.g., "Their attack concentrated upon provisions that permitted modifiction of a secured claim by reducing the amount of the periodic installments due thereon, as contrasted with the *nonobjectionable* [read *unobjectionable*] curing of a default and maintaining those payments."

Q. What is non obstante veredicto?

A. non obstante veredicto (= notwithstanding the verdict) is sometimes used in the shortened form *non obstante,* e.g., "This appeal requires us to determine whether the trial judge's action in granting judgement *non obstante* for the defendant was correct."

Q. Where do we use non participating royalty?

A. nonparticipating royalty, used often in oil and gas law, is a venial Redundancy: all mineral royalties are nonparticipating.

Q. What is nonpretextual?

A. nonpretextual. "Appellant's lawful dismissal was found by the jury to be *nonpretextual.*" Actually, the jury found that the dismissal was not pretextual; thus the finding was a negative one. To say that it "found the dismissal to be nonpretextual" wrongly suggests that the jury answered a question asking whether the dismissal was *nonpretextual;* instead, the jury was asked whether the dismissal was *pretextual* and it answered 'no.'

Q. Who is nonprobate?

A. nonprobate = other than by will; of or relating to some method of disposition apart from wills, e.g., "Today, the proportion of property passing under probate is decreasing and the proportion of property passing by *nonprobate* methods is increasing."

Q. What is nonprofit?

A. nonprofit, non-for-profit. The former is more common but the latter is increasingly used in the U.S. for greater accuracy: *nonprofit corporation* misleadingly suggests that the corporation makes no profits; but such a corporation actuallly *does* earn profits and then, applies them for charitable purposes. *Not-for-profit* is thought to reveal more accurately that the purpose is not for private gain, though indeed, the organisation may earn profits, e.g., "*Not-for-profit* corporations and public interest groups petitioned for writ of mandamus to compel the Federal Communications Commission to decide certain unresolved matters pending before a state agency."

Q. The terms nonrebuttable and irrebuttable are the same. Explain.

A. nonrebuttable is a Needless Variant of *irrebuttable,* e.g., "In actual operation, therefore, the three statutes enact what, in effect, are *nonrebuttable* [read *irrebuttable*] presumptions that every applicant for assistance in his first year of residency came to the jurisdiction solely to obtain higher benefits."

Q. What is non sequitur?

A. non sequitur should be spelled as two words, not hyphenated.

Q. What is nonstatutory?

A. nonstatutory. This word can sometimes, be replaced by *judicial, administrative* or some other desprictive word, as in *judicial policy-making* rather than *nonstatutory policy-making.* If it fits, the more specific word should eliminate *nonstatutory.*

Q. Which one is a non suit?

A. nonsuit, v.t. (= to subject to a nonsuit) has been a part of lawyers' language since the sixteenth century. "Eyre, C.J., *nonsuited* the plaintiff." (Eng.) "It is submitted that the appellants should be *nonsuited* on the ground that the publication was privileged." (Eng.) "The court *nonsuited* him and rendered judgement dismissing the action."

Q. Where is nonsuitability?

A. nonsuitability. The preferred antonyms of *suitable* and *suitability* are *unsuitable* and *unsuitableness*. *Nonsuitability,* a Needless Variant of *unsuitableness,* unsuitably suggests a relationship with *nonsuit,* q.v. Yet, it is perversely used in AmE legal contexts, e.g., "The Secretary of Agriculture shall, within ten years after September 3, 1964, review, as to its suitability or *nonsuitability* [read *unsuitableness*], each area." Wilderness Act, 16 U.S.C. § 1132(b) (1982).

Q. Who is a nontaxpaid?

A. nontaxpaid is an opaque and ugly word and is to be avoided, e.g., "Defendant has had a reputation with me for over four years as being a trafficker or *nontaxpaid* distilled spirits." A less concise wording should be used, e.g., *trafficker of distilled spirits upon which, no taxes had been paid.*

Q. Who is nontriggerman?

A. nontriggerman = a murder defendant who did not actually kill the decedent but who intended to do so, e.g., "The conduct of a *nontriggerman* during the planning and aftermath of a prison break, which eventually resulted in a quadruple murder, was sufficient for the imposition of a death penalty." The word is odd-looking but perhaps, necessary; quite often, *accomplice* suffices.

Q. Is no one is a singular noun?

A. no one is a singular noun, and therefore acts as a singular **Antecedent**, e.g., "This means that *no one* should be punished for speaking unless *their* [read *his*] speech will immediately lead to a definite dangerous act."

Q. What is no question but that?

A. no question but that. The *but* in this phrase is unnecessary; the better phrase is *no question that,* e.g., "There can be *no question but that* [read *no question that*] jurisdiction to review and to affirm or set aside the Secretary's order became fully vested in the court upon the filling of the partnership's petition."

Q. What is nor?

A. nor for *or.* Where the negative of a clause has already appeared and a disjunctive conjunction is needed *or* is generally better than *nor.* The initial negative carries through to all the elements in an enumeration, e.g., "Religiosity insists that there is something called religion wholly a part from any spceific relgion, something that has no creed *nor* [read or] dogma, no theology or scriptures, something that may be felt and need not be understood." "Her symptoms were all subjective and not supported by any medical *nor* [read *or*] other corroborating evidence." "When on the witness stand on the trial of this case, however, he could not see the trial judge *nor* [read *or*] the examiner who was five feet away."

Q. Define normalcy in a legal way.

A. normalcy is inferior to *normality*, e.g., "The *normalcy* [read *normality*] of these operations changed when Press was told by his delegate that Monatana-Austria requested a stop-off in Johannesburg." Born in the mid-nineteenth century and later, used by President Harding, *normalcy* has never been accepted as standard by the best writing authorities.

nostrum (= panacea) forms the plural *nostrums,* e.g., "But advertiesement of *nostrums* for restoration of 'lost manhood' have appeared in the daily newspapers for at least fifty years."

not. A. Placement of. When used in constructions with *all* and *every,* not is usually best placed just before those words, e.g., "*Every disclosure of a trade secret does not result* [read *not every disclosure of a trade secret results*] in an abandonment of its element of secrecy." "*All writers did not accept* [read *Not all writers accepted*] Coke's dictum." (D. Mellinkoff) *"Justice Holmes reminded us that every moral question cannot* [read *Justice Holmes reminded us that not every moral question can*] be submitted to the law and that though morality might impose restraints on legal actions, there is a vast difference between the two concepts."

B. *Not only ..... but also .....* These Correlative Conjunctions must frame syntactic parts that match, e.g., "The offer *had to not only be made in good faith, but it had to also be* [read *had not only to be made in good faith but also to be*] in such a form that it could, by an acceptance of the offeree, ripen into a valid and binding contract that could be enforced by any party to it." "These disclosures *led not only to new calls for greater social responsibility of corporations but also focused on* [read *not only led to ....., but also focussed on*] the role of the board of directors and the need for better control mechanisms to ensure that corporate management conform with legal and moral principles of conduct."

Not only ..... but also and *not only ..... but ..... as well* are correct. *Not only ..... but also ..... as well* is redundant, e.g., "But we cannot quarrel with a conclusion of a school administrator that treating a particular student with such care might to be to the advantage *not only* of the pupil *but also* [read *but*] of the other students in the school *as well.*"

C. *Not ..... nor* should usually (where short clauses are involved) be *not ..... or,* e.g., "Finding the lessee culpable is *not inherently inconsistent nor contrary to* [read *not inherently inconsistent with or contrary to*] the 'instructions.' "

Q. Who is notable?

A. notable, noteworthy, noticeable. *Noticeable* = easily seen or noticed (as e.g., scars); it is generally confined to physical senses. *Notable,* having basically the same meaning, is applied to qualities as well as to material things, e.g., "The most *notable* thing about these observations is that quite obviously the word 'res,' describing a thing, has a quite different connotation from subject matter." "Some jurisdictions, *notably* New York, have attempted to solve this problem by applying more flexible and equitable standards."

Noteworthy = worthy of notice or observation; remarkable, e.g., "It is *noteworthy* that the decree and codicil attached express conditions of survivorship to the interests of Joseph and to any wife or child of Joseph but do not add any words of that character to the limitation describing Mary Silva's interest."

Q. What is notarial?

A. notarial is the adjectival form of *notary.*

Q. What is meant by notary?

A. notery = A solicitor who attests deeds or one who in the case of a dishonoured bills, notes or deeds or protests it. Notery is also known as notary public.

Q. What is a note and a draft?

A. note; draft. A *note* is a simple promise by one party to pay money to another party or to a bearer. A *draft* is an order by one person (the drawer) to pay another person (the drawee), demanding that the drawee pay money to a third person (the payee) or to bearer.

Q. What is note up?

A. note up is the approximate British equivalent of the American term *Shepardise,* q.v. The British call their citators *noter-ups* or, in some Commonwealth countries, *noter-uppers.*

Q. Explain a notice?

A. notice, v.t. (= to give legal notice to or of) is a Legalism, e.g., "Under the present practice, however, the objecting party has not duty to *notice* a hearing, the initiative being shifted to the party seeking discovery." Or, "We have not been *noticed* [i.e., received notice] to bring the records." "The magistrate heard the motions to set aside the default judgement apparently by virtue of the fact that they were *noticed* for a hearing before the magistrate rather than before the district court." "Unless you have already done so, *notice* the depositions of all expert witnesses being offered by your opponent."

Notice should be reserved for giving the legal notice; legal writers should not use the word non-legally, as here; 'TACA International Airlines, in the midst of collective bargaining negotiations, *noticed* [read *let be known*] its intent to relocate its pilot base." (To the layman this usage confusingly suggests *notice* in the sense "to observe.") "It has been *noticed* [read *noted, i.e.*, previously, in a book] that some lawyers and judges were of the opinion that ....."

Q. What is notice to quit?
A. notice to quit (BrE) = *notice to vacate* (AmE).

Q. Who is a notorious man?
A. notorious may mean either 'famous' or 'infamous', though it usually carries connotations of the latter, *i.e.*, unfavourably known. *Notoriety* is generally more neutral, though it is, sometimes, tinged with the connotations of its adjectival form.

Q. Explain the term notwithstanding.
A. notwithstanding, when introducing a clause, should be usually followed by *that,* e.g., "The law is in accord in favouring free competition since ordinarily, it is essential to the general welfare of society, *notwithstanding* [insert *that*] competition is not alruistic but is fundamentally the play of interest against interest." "The instrument is likely to be upheld *notwithstanding* [insert *that*] it includes additionally, the reservation of power to amend the trust in whole or in part."

When introducing a verbless phrase, *notwithstanding* need not be followed by *that,* e.g., "Section 1322(b)(5) was amended to provide that its provisions were unchanged, *notwithstanding* section 1322 (b)(2)."

Q. Explain the term notwithstanding anything to the contrary contained herein.
A. notwithstanding anything to the contrary contained herein, an ungainly phrase often placed in complex contracts to introduce the most important provisions, can be fairly said to mean "the true agreement is as follows." It is best used when the contract needs to spell out explicitly that a certain provision is to override another, arguably, an inconsistent provision.

———◇◇◇———

Q. What do you understand by obiter dicta?

A. obiter dicta = Remarks of a judge which are said by the way and are not directly relevant to the case at hand.

Q. What is meant by offender?

A. offender = An accused person, one who is under accusation of having committed an offence, one who is guilty of an offence.

Q. What is onus?

A. onus = A burden

Q. What is an order?

A. order = the formal expression of any decision of a civil court which is not a decree.

Q. What do you understand by original jurisdiction?

A. original jurisdiction = Jurisdiction to entertain cases is the first instance as distinguished from appellate jurisdiction.

Q. What is overall?

A. overall is a Vague Term. "Conclusory [q.v.] findings as to each of the *Zimmer* criteria are no more helpful than an *overall* conclusory finding of dilution." "The *overall* effect of the *Gibbs* decision has been to broaden pendent jurisdiction."

Q. What is overflown?

A. overflown is the correct preterit, for *overfly,* q.v., but not for *overflow* form which properly makes *overflowed.*

Q. What is overfly?

A. overfly (= to fly over in an airplane) is uncommon except in legal usage and pilots' argot. Following are examples from legal writing: "No prescriptive easement to *overfly* plaintiff's land was acquired." "During these five years, plaintiffs did not actually use the *overflown* land; thus the airplanes harmed no one."

Q. Give the meanings of overlook and oversee.

A. overlook, oversee. The first is sometimes misused for the second. To *overlook* is to neglect or disregard. To *oversee* is to supervise or superintend. *Look over it* has also been differentiated from *overlook*; it means "to examine."

Q. What is *overly?*

A. overly is old, dating from about the twelfth century but is to be avoided. *Overly* is almost always unnecessary because *over-* may be prefixed at will as follows— *overbroad, overrefined, overoptimistic, overripe.* When it is not unnecessary, it is merely ugly. Some authorities consider *overly* semiliterate, though the editors of *W9* have used it in a number of definitions. Certainly, this adverb should be avoided whenever possible, though admittedly *over-* as a prefix is sometimes ill-sounding. Yet, it usually serves well, e.g., "It assists the legislature to avoid cumbersome and *overelaborate* wording." (Eng.) When *over-* is awkward or ugly-sounding, one might have recourse to *too.*

Another possible substitute is *unduly.* "An *overly lax* [read unduly lax] standard would provide antitrust plaintiffs with a windfall and would violate the established principle that an injury without damage creates no right to compensation."

In any event, one should always be consistent within a piece of writing. In the opinion of the U.S. Supreme Court, we find, in successive paragraphs: "The Supreme Court affirmed, rejecting the contention that the statute violated the First and Fourteenth Amendments as being vague and *overbroad* ..... It was held that a person could attack a statute as being *overly broad.*" (*Overbroad* is always preferable to *overly broad*).

Other specimens follow, with suggested improvements: "The old "legal memorandum rule" is now generally regarded as an *overly technical doctrine* [read *as an overtechnical doctine* or *as too technical a doctrine*]." "The loss must be foreseeable when the contract is entered into; it cannot be *overly* [read *unduly*] speculative." "Courts have been eager to prevent direct interference without forcing one tribunal to be *overly cautious* [read *overcautious*] about the possibility that a prior suit in another forum may involve the property."

Q. Define the term *to overreach.*

A. overreach = (1) to circumvent, outwit or to get the better of something by cunning or artifice; or (2) to defeat one's object by going too far. Sense (1) often holds in legal contexts as follows: "If, from a consideration of all the facts concerning the situation of the parties at the time the contract was made, the trial court concludes that the intended wife was not *overreached,* the contract should be sustained."

Q. What is meant by *overruling?*

A. overrule, overturn, reverse, set aside, vacate. *Overrule* is usually employed in reference to procedural points throughout a trial, as in evidence

Dictionary of Legal Terms 139

("Objection!" "Overruled"). *Overrule* is also used to describe what a superior court does to a precedent that it decides, should no longer be the controlling law, whether that precedent is of a lower court or its own. Overturn and *reverse* are terms to describe an appellate court's shift to an opposite result from that by the lower court in a given case.

Set aside and *vacate* are synonymously used to denote an appellate court's wiping clean the judgement-slate. The effect is to nullify the previous decision, usually of a lower court but not necessarily to dictate a contrary result in further proceedings.

Q. Define oversight.

A. oversight = (1) an unintentional error or (2) intentional and watchful supervision.

Q. What is an overstatement?

A. overstatement. Such words as *clearly, patently, obviously* and *indisputably* are generally rightly seen as weakening rather than strengthening the statements they preface. They have been debased. Some legal scholars have noted that when a writer begins a sentence with one of these words, he is likely to be leading up to something very questionable.

Unconscious overstatement is also a problem in legal discourse. It is never good to overstate one's case, even in minor unconscious ways, for the writing will lose credibility. Good writers are very wary of injudicious exaggeration. A common pitfall is the *more ..... than all* construction: "More black students are presently enrolled at the University of Texas Law School *than have attended the school in all its history* [read *than have attended the school in previous years cumulatively* or *than have, all told, been heretofore admitted* or *in all its history up to three years ago*]. "The approach used *in the United States* [read *in the judicial system of the United States*] to achieve information input [q.v.] and accurate output is mainly adversarial in nature."

"In 1971, Congress enacted two important statutes—the Federal Election Compaign Fund Act and the Federal Election Campaign Act—both designed to reduce the corrupting influence of money on the political process." No doubt, the writer intended to say that 1971 saw the enactment of two major statutes designed to reduce financial corruption in campaigns; what he has said, however, is that 1971 saw the enactment of two major statutes, which, incidentally, had to do with reducing ..... The problem is most easily indentifiable if one reads the sentence without the names of the statutes set off by long dashes. The root of the problem is *both,* which makes the clause it introduces non-restrictive rather than restrictive. The unconscious mis-statement is eliminated when we omit *both.*

Shoddy overstatements occur frequently in popular journalism: "Perhaps Senator Kennedy is at his best with those who count most in the world — his family." Though one might get the impression from various tabloids that the Kennedy family *does* comprise with "those who count most in the world," this is not what the writer intended to convey. [Read *who, for him, count most in the world* or *who count most in the world to him.*]

Q. Distinguish between owing and owed.

A. owing, owed. Although *owing* in the sense of *owed* is an old and established usage, the more logical course is simply to write *owed* where one means *owed*. The active participle may sometimes cause ambiguities or mislead the reader if only for a second, e.g., "In the present case, we must consider whether to recognise a new liability *owing from* [read *owed by*] parents to their children for negligent supervision." "This was a claim for the sum of £ 1108 alleged to be *owing* [read *owing*] by the defendant to the plaintiff under a contract alleged to have been made between the plaintiff and the defendant for the construction of concrete foundation work" (Aus.). "No claim was filed in the estate by the mortgagee of the real property, though a balance of approximately $5,000 was still *owing* [read *owed*]." "A promise will normally be implied from an unqualified acknowledgment that the debt is *owing* [read *owed*], or from a part payment of the debt."

Q. What is ownership?

A. ownership = An absolute right over property for something based on rightful title.

Q. What are oxymorons?

A. Oxymorons are immediate contradictions in terms, as in the word *bittersweet*. Any number of relative oxymorons exist in legal parlance, e.g., *ordered liberty, equitable servitude* (servitude in equity), *all deliberate speed* (from the U.S. desegregation cases) and *substantive due process* (substantive process?) Examples are more ostensibly contradictory, e.g., "The Government is *advancing backwards* toward the regulation of share dealing."

Q. Oyez is crying. Explain.

A. oyez, oyez, oyez is the cry heard in court to call the courtroom to order the beginning of a session. The word *oyez* was the Law French equivalent of *hear ye,* q.v., in the Middle Ages. The pronunciation was first *oh-yets,* later *oh-yes* or *oh-yez.* Hence, in Anglo-American courts the word has traditionally been pronounced "oh yes;" that is the pronunciation given in the *OED*. Sometimes, *oyez* is given the French pronunciation *oh-yay. Oyes,* a variant spelling, is not now current.

———◇◇◇———

Q. What is the meaning of the word pace?

A. pace is pronounced as *pay*-*say* = with all due respect to, with the approval of. The expression is used in expressing a contrary position.

Q. Who is a pacifist?

A. pacifist, pacificist. *Pacifist* is the established form. Etymologists formerly argued that *pacificist* is the better-formed word but it has never seemed to be so.

Q. What is paction?

A. paction = (1) the act of making a bargain or pact or (2) the pact so made. In sense (2), the word is merely a Needless Variant of *pact, agreement* or *bargain*. In sense (1), the word is useful, but rare.

Q. Explain pain of and pain on.

A. pain of, pain on. The phrase *on pain of death* was once common in law to express prohibitions the violation of which, would result in punishment by execution. The phrase has passed into lay contexts in which, it is used facetiously. But it remains as a shortened phrase *on pain of* in legal usage, e.g., "Is it reasonable to require prison employees to have foreseen, *on pain of* section 1983, damage liability, the future of prisoners' rights to the degree evolved under *Ruiz*."

Q. What is a pair?

A. pair is incorrect as a plural form as in: "He bought two pair of shoe." *Pairs* is the plural.

Q. Pale, beyond the, is used to depict jurisdiction. Comment.

A. pale, beyond the. This phrase, which has passed into lay parlance in the sense "bizarre; outside the bounds of civilised behaviour." derives from the legal sense of *pale* from English history ("a district or territory within determined bounds or subject to a particular jurisdiction"). In legal writing the phrase is best used with awareness of its derivation, as here: "The jurisdiction of the Court of Appeals below turned on its determination that an interpretation of Rule 68 to include attorneys' fees is *beyond the pale* of the judiciary's rule making authority."

Q. What is palimony?

A. palimony (= a court-ordered allowance paid by one member of a couple formerly living together out of wedlock to the other [*W9*]) is a Portmanteau Word, first recorded in 1979. It has become rather common and may justify its existence by its usefulness. It is unlikely to be anything other than a jocular word however, *Galimony,* a similar form, though more jocular, has been used for describing *palimony* between lesbians.

Q. What is palming off?

A. palming off; passing off. The two terms are perfectly synonymous ("putting into circulation or dispersing of fraudulently" [*OED*]), both being used with almost equal frequency in the AmE and BrE. *Passing off* is more peculiarly legal, e.g., "Unfair competition is almost universally regarded as a question of whether the defendant is *passing off* his goods or services as those of the plaintiff." "*Passing off* may be found only where the defendant subjectively and knowingly intended to confuse buyers." *Palming off* is used additionally in metaphorical lay senses, e.g., "Have you not tried to *palm off* yesterday's pun?"

Q. What is palpable?

A. palpable (lit., "touchable") = tangible; apparent. There is nothing wrong with using this word in figurative senses (palpable weaknesses in the argument) as it has been used since (at least) the fifteenth century.

Q. Pronounce the word pamphlet.

A. pamphlet. This word is pronounced with the *-ph-* as if it were an *-f-*. Many people incorrectly say *pam-plet.* Cf. **ophthalmotogy, amphitheater.**

Q. What is panacea?

A. panacea (= cure-all; nostrum) is sometimes confused with other words, e.g., "To allow the state to raise new matters not brought out in the original appeal or on re-hearing would *open up a panacea* [read *bring on a plethora?* or *open up a pandora's box?*] of problems by way of precedent." This is a Malapropism.

Q. What is pandemic?

A. pandemic (= [of a disease] prevalent oover the whole of a country or continent or over the whole world). The word is usually adjectival but may be used as a noun: "The strain was related to the one that was prevalent during the 1918-19 swine flu *panedmic* that was responsible for 20 million deaths worldwide, including the deaths of 5,00,000 Americans."

Dictionary of Legal Terms 143

Q. What is panel-shopping?

A. panel-shopping is analogous to *forum-shopping* in reference to panels usually consisting of three members of a court, e.g., "[The law of the case doctrine] discourages *panel shopping* at the circuit level, for in today's climate, it is most likely that a different panel will hear subsequent appeals." *Lehrman v. Gulf Oil Corp.,* 500 F.2d 659, 662 (5th Cir. 1974).

Q. Is panic a transitive verb?

A. panic, v.i., makes *panicked* and *panicking.* Usually intransitive, *panic* has appeared as a transitive verb, meaning "to affect with panic" e.g., "She did not want to *panic* the audience."

Q. What is a paper?

A. paper has a special legal sense in the phrase *commercial paper* (= negotiable documents and bills of exchange). The plural *papers* often refers to pleadings and other court documents: "We filed all the necessary papers."

Q. Who is a parajudge?

A. parajudge has been used to refer to U.S. Magistrates who have some adjudicative power but not the extent of power vested in Article III judges: "Under the 'parajudge' rationale, the Magistrates Act comports with Article III [of the U.S. Constitution] because it subjects magistrates' rulings to de novo determination by a federal district judge." *United States v. Saunders,* 641 F. 2d 654, 663 (9th Cir. 1980).

Q. What is paralegaling?

A. paralegaling is a **Colloquialism** to name what it is that a paralegal (or *legal assistant*) does. The term is similar to *bailiffing.*

Q. What is paraleipsis?

A. Paraleipsis is a rhetorical tactic in which, a speaker or writer mentions something in disclaiming any mention of it. For example, a less than scrupulous cross-examiner would engage in paraleipsis if he stated, "Mr. Smith, I won't bring up your unsavoury past as a wife-beater and pimp but I would like to ask you some questions about your prior business dealings with the plaintiff." To which, the fitting response is "Objection!," preferably after *unsavoury.*

The following is an example of judicial paraleipsis in which, the judge appears to be suggesting a tactic to one of the parties: "I purposely refrain from commenting on the posibility of any relief against Malcolm Dever's attorney,

Dalona, which may be available to the defendants or any title company that may have insured a Radner Heights fee for one of them." *Devers v. Chateau Corp.,* 792 F.2d 1278, 1299 (4th Cir. 1986) (Murnaghan, J., dissenting).

Q. Define parallelism in legal terms.

A. Parallelism refers to matching parts, *i.e.*, analogous sentence-parts that must match if the sentence has to make a logical sense. The problem of unparallel sentence-parts usually crops up in the usage of correlative conjunctions and in lists. The following are some examples, with corrections in brackets within quotations or in parentheses following the quotations: "The 1975 rule, abolishing sovereign immunity, will not take effect until 1976 and will not apply to the case at bar or [to] any pending cases." "The essential elements of recklessness are present in this case, viz., proceeding through the intersection on a green light *and* [read *that was*] plainly visible on a broad well-lighted thoroughfare." "For federal diversity purposes, a corporation is a 'citizen' *of not only* [read *not only of*] the state in which, it is incorporated, *but also of* the state where it has its principal place of business." "Marketing quotas *not only embrace* [read *embrace not only*] all that may be sold without penalty, *but also* what may be consumed on the premises" (Jackson, J.). "*Its continuance is contingent upon legally recognized rights of tenure, transfer and succession* [delete second *of* or insert *of* before *transfer*] in use and occupancy." "Defendants object to the request for production of documents on the grounds of relevancy, overbreadth, *burdensome* [read *burdensomeness*], oppression and confidentiality." (This sentence contains Illogic as well because each item in the list spells out why the defendants object to it; hence *irrelevancy* should appear where *relevancy* does.). "The trial court was correct in excluding both the testimony of V.T.W. and *in excluding* [delete *in excluding* and insert *the*] defendant's exhibits 7 and 11."

Failures of parallelism are especially common in cumulative sentences as exemplified here: "The defendants *admitted* that they published the article, *disavowed* any intention to defame and injure the plaintiff in his good name and reputation, *denied* that the article was maliciously composed, printed or published [read *and asserted*] and *that* the article appeared simply as a news item and was brought in by of its news-gatherers." "Cars may be seized if they constitute a traffic hazard, are evidences *or if they are* [read *or are*] subject to forfeiture proceedings." If the writer wished to be more emphatic, whatever the cost of repetition, he could write: "Cars may be seized if they constitute a traffic hazard, if they are evidences, or if they are subject to forfeiture proceedings."

Less troubling is a lack of parallelism where two or more sentence-parts are balanced by *and;* but even this should be avoided: "The boy's operation of the car was unlawful and *negligence* [read *negligent*] per se." "Johann was a tall, thin man, dark-haired, near-sighted, not bad-looking and a *fop* [read *foppish*]." (Here, we have a string of adjectives-all implicitly modifying *man,* the antecedent of which is *Johann;* but the writer changes the last in the string to a noun phrase.)

Q. Is paramount used for most important?
A. paramount means "most important," not merely "important."

Q. What is paramountcy?
A. paramountcy is the nominal form of *paramount,* not often seen but quite proper.

Q. How is paraphrase rendered?
A. paraphrase is occasionally misrendered as *paraphraze,* as in *Endes v. Darke,* 332 S.W. 2d 553, 556 (Tex. 1960).

Q. What is parasitic?
A. parasitic, in reference to damages, does not mean merely 'additional.' Rather, the term means, in the words of Lord Denning—M.R.—that there are some heads of damage which, if they stood alone, would not be recoverable; but, nevertheless, if they can be annexed to some other legitimate claim for damages, may yet be recoverable. They are said to be *parasitic* because, like a parasite, in biology, they cannot exist on their own but depend upon others for life or nourishment. "I do not like the very word *parasite.* A *parasite* is one who is a useless hanger-on sucking the substance of others. *Parasitic* is the adjective derived from it. It is a term of abuse. It is an opprobrious epithet. The phrase *parastic damages* conveys to my mind the idea of damages, which ought not—in justice—to be awarded but which, somehow or other have been allowed to get through by hanging on to others. If such be the concept underlying the doctrine, then the sooner it is got rid of, the better ..... I hope it will disappear from [the textbooks] after this case. *Spartan Steel & Alloys Ltd. v. Martin & Co.,*1970 A.C. 506-07.

Q. What is meant by pardon?
A. pardon = Decision of the Head of state to forgive a person who has given punishment incurred for some offence.

Q. What is parole?
A. parole = process by which a prisoner is allowed to be conditionally released during the turm of imprisonment.

Q. What is passing off?

A. passing off = A tort, where by a wrong committed by person who sells goods or carries on business etc. thereby making the buyers believe that the goods actually come from the former.

Q. What do you understand by Patent?

A. patent = Exclusively privilege granted by the authority to an inventor who invent something new.

Q. What is per incurrium ?

A. A mistaken decision by a court.

Q. What is perjury?

A. perjury = An offence of giving a false statement before the court which a person known to be false.

Q. Describe place-names as adjectives.

A. place-names as adjectives. The practice of using place-names as adjectives is to be resisted, though it is increasingly common, e.g., "A *Marion County, Indiana jury* [read *A jury in Marion County, Indiana,*] convicted petitioner of theft, a Class D felony, on November 19, 1979." "*The Gulfport, Mississppi law firm of Jones & Jones* [read *The law firm of Jones & Jones in Gulfport, Mississippi*] represented appellant's parents before this litigation began." Such constructions contribute to noun plague. lessen readability, and offend sensitive and literate readers.

Q. What is plain?

A. plain english. A. General Drafting.

B. Jury Instructions.

Q. What is a plaint?

A. plaint = the statement in writing of the cause of action in a suit.

Q. Who is a plaintiff?

A. plaintiff, complainant, demandant, objectant, exceptor. *Plaintiff* = the party who brings a suit into a court of law (*OED*). This party may have other special names, depending upon the jurisdiction and the cause of action asserted. *Complainant* is used in even more general senses of any party who brings a compalint. *Demandant* = one who makes a demand or claim; the *OED* suggests that this term may be used of a plaintiff in a civil action.

The remaining terms are quite distinct from the others. *Objectant* = one who objects. *Exceptor* = one who objects or takes exception.

Q. What do you understand by plaintiff?

A. plaintiff = A person, who brings a suit to a court of law.

Q. Who is plaintiff in error?

A. plaintiff in error, defendant in error. In some jurisdictions, the first term is an equivalent of *appellant* or *petitioner, the latter an equivalent* of *appellee* or *respondent* when the appeal is by writ of error, e.g., "The railway company and Mercer each filed an application for a writ of error and each application was granted from which, it results that in this court, each party is both *plaintiff in error* and *defendant in error."*

Q. What is a plaintive?

A. Plaintive was, for centuries, used interchangeably with *plaintiff* in legal prose. But now, the sense "being or pertaining to the plaintiff in a suit" (*OED*) is an Archaism, and is probably obsolete. The sole current meaning of *plaintive* is as an adjective- "sorrowful, mournful."

Q. What do you understand by plea bargaining ?

A. plea bargaining = where the accused instead of defending his case in proper defence simply pleaded guilty under a promise or assurance that he would be let off lightly and then in appeal or revision to enhance the sentence.

Q. Is pleading an answer in a criminal case?

A. plea, pleading, n. A *plea* is now given only in criminal cases, though at common law a defendant's answer to the plaintiff's complaint was termed as a *plea*. A *pleading* is the complaint or answer in a civil case or the criminal indictment and the answer in a criminal case.

Q. What is meant to plead in legal terms?

A. plead does not mean, as some laymen think, "to argue in court." Eric Partridge ameneded his note on *Lawyer* in *Usage and Abusage* by quoting a British man-of-law who corrected Partridge's "layman's misusages" as follows: "A barrister does not 'plead' in Court. He argues a case in Court, or- colloquially-*does* a case in Court. Pleadings are the written documents preparatory to a case-e.g., Statement of Claim, Defence in a civil action, Petition or Answer in divorce." *Usage and Abusage* 379 (1973).

Q. What is pleadable?

A. pleadable = that may be pleaded; that may be legally maintained in a court of law (*OED*), e.g., "This feature would not prevent a like construction if the language, intendment—and history thereof—convinced us it was a *pleadable* position."

Q. What is a pleading and a prayer?

A. pleading, prayer. The *pleading* is the document in which, a party in legal action sets out the cause of action of defense. A *pleading* consists of: (1) a commencement; (2) a body (or charging part); (3) a prayer or demand for judgement; (4) a signature; and, when required, (5) a verification. The *prayer,* which usually appears at the end of the pleading, is the request of relief from the court, e.g., "The court merely held that if there is a requirement that the complainant specifically plead for prejudgement interest, a *prayer* for general relief will not satisfy the requirement if the *pleadings* also contain a specific *prayer* for a different kind of interest." A typical *prayer* might read: "Wherefore, defendant prays that plaintiff take nothing in this action (etc.)."

Q. What is meant by plead innocent?

A. plead innocent. Earlier, only newspapermen used to make the mistake of writing *plead innocent* rather than *plead not guilty* but now, this phrase has made it even into judges' writings: "He refused to take urine, blood or breath sobriety tests and *pleaded innocent* [read *pleaded not guilty*] to the two charges." Lawyers should avoid the phrase. There is no such thing in criminal law as *a plea of innocent.*

Q. What is the usual form of plea in abatement?

A. plea in abatement, plea of abatement. In jurisdictions, in which, the plea is used, *plea in abatement* is the usual form.

Q. What is the latest form of please find enclosed?

A. please find enclosed is, like its inverted sibling, *enclosed please find,* q.v., an old-fashioned, stilted phrase that lawyers are fond of using in letters. A better and more modern substitute is *I am sending with this letter* or *I have enclosed.*

Q. What is a pledge?

A. It is a contract where a bailment of personal property as security for some debt or engagement.

Q. Plenary is a formal word for full. Explain.

A. plenary is a Formal Word for *full*. E.g.: "A *plenary trial* is hardly necessary to apprise the court that what it saw really happened." Here, *full trial* would be better.

Q. Differentiate between plentiful and plenteous.

A. plentiful, plenteous. No distinction in meaning being possible, writers should prefer the prevalent modern form *plentiful*. *Plenteous* is Archaic and poetic.

Q. What is plurality opinion?

A. plurality opinion = an appellate opinion without enough votes of the Judges to constitute a majority but having received the greatest number of votes of any of the opinions filed.

Q. What are plurals in legal terms?

A. Plurals. A. Borrowed Words. Words transported into the English language from other languages, especially Greek and Latin, present some of the most troublesome aspects of English plurals. At a certain point, borrowed words become thoroughly anglicised and take English plurals. But while Classical words are still new and only questionably naturalised, writers, who refer to the words as primarily foreign ones, use the plurals of the language. Then again, with certain words, the foreign plurals become so well established that anglicisation never takes place.

So many variations on this theme have occurred that it is impossible to make valid generalisations. *Minimum* makes *minima* but *premium* makes *premiums; pudendum* makes *pudena* but *memorandum* makes either *-dums* or *-da; colloquium* generally makes *-quia* in BrE, *-quiums* in AmE. The only reliable guide is a certain knowledge of specific words or habitual reference to a work of this type. In words with a choice of endings, one English and the other foreign, we should generally prefer the English plural. It is an affectation for college professors to insist on using *syllabi* rather than *-buses;* the fear of being wrong or sounding unacademic leads some of them to use forms like *auditoria* and *stadia*.

Fowler called the benighted stab at correctness "out of the frying pan into the fire" and many writers, who try to be sophisticated in their use of language, are susceptible to writing, e.g., *ignorami* and *octopi*, unware that neither is a Latin noun in *-us* that, when inflected as a plural, becomes *-i*. The proper plural of the Greek word *octopus* is *octopodes;* the proper English plural is *octopuses*. *Ignoramus* makes only *ignoramuses*, for in Latin, the word is a verb, not a noun.

French words also present problems. *Fait accompli* becomes *faits accomplis* and *force majure* becomes *forces majeures*. But then, we have the Law French words such as *feme sole*, which becomes *femes sole* and *feme covert* (or *femme couverte*), which as a plural becomes *femes covert* (or *femmes couvertes*). The best policy is to make a habit of consulting a good dictionary and to use it discriminatingly.

B. Mass (Noncount) Nouns. A recent trend in the language is to make plurals for mass nouns-general and abstract nouns that cannot be broken down into discrete units and that therefore, should not have plural forms. One example of this phenomenon is the psychologists' and sociologists' term *behaviours*, as if the ways in which, one behaves, are readily categorisable and therefore, countable. Granted, one can have good or bad behavior, but not properly *a* good behaviour or *a* bad behaviour. Following are some examples of other words infected by the contagion.

1. *Coverages*. "The policy allowed for separate *coverages* of the three cars."

2. *Discriminations*. "The statute disadvantages those who would benefit from laws barring racial, religious, or ancestral *discriminations* as against those who would bar other *discriminations* or who would otherwise regulate the real estate market in their favour."

3. *Inactions*. "The findings of the district court on the actions and *inactions* by the defendants are supported by substantial evidence and are not clearly erroneous."

4. *Languages*. Speaking of different passages in a statute or of different statutes, a writer states: "The statutory *languages* are not enough to persuade us that the Secretary's interpretation is incorrect."

5. *Litigations*. "Indeed, just as antitrust actions occupied the attentions of the litigation bar in the 1960s and class action *litigations* proliferated in the 1970s, insurance-coverage *litigations* are currently engaging the *attentions* of many of the nation's most prominent litigators." "Under the circumstances, there need not be two *litigations* when one will suffice."

6. *Managements*. "If followed, these procedures would have a beneficial effect on the *managements* of brokerage firms and those charged with supervision." (Does *managements* refer to managerial departments or to methods to management? The plural causes this ambiguity).

7. *Outputs*. "Interpersonal relationships of the justices have been shown to have measurable effects on the court's public *outputs*."

8. *Participations*. Sometimes, this phenomenon occurs through attributive usage where *participation* is substituted for *unit of participation*: "The D.C. Circuit has declared that the Glass-Steagall Act does not prohibit banks from

marking *participations* in collective investment trusts for I.R.A. assets." The same principle is at work when *proofs* is substituted for *elements of proof.*

C. -O(E)S. Fowler laid down a number of guiding principles for words ending in *-o:* firstly, monosyllables and words used as freely in the plural as in the singular usually have *-oes* (*embargoes, heroes, noes, potatoes* and *vetoes*); secondly, alien-looking words, proper names and words that are seldom used as plurals— words in which *-o-* is preceded by a vowel and shortened words (e.g., *photo*) do not take the *-e-* (*hippos, kilos, embryos, ratios*). Good dictionaries contain the preferred spellings.

D. Attributive Past-Participal Adjectives. These are usually awkward and alien-looking to a laymen, e.g., "The firm represented one of the company's *insureds* in an action that had been brought against the insured in County court."

E. Compound Nouns, Plurals of compound nouns made up of a noun and a Postpositive Adjective are formed by adding *-s* to the noun: such as *courts martial, heirs persumptive.* The British and Americans differ on the method of pluralising *attorney general,* q.v. Those words, in which, the noun is now disguised, add *-s* at the end of the word, as with all compounds ending in *ful* such as *lungfuls, and spoonfuls, handfuls.*

Q. What is poetic justice?

A. poetic justice, nowadays a Cliche, refers to the system exemplified in older fiction in which, villains always receive condign punishments and heroes their fitting rewards.

Q. What is meant by point out?

A. point out, point to, point up. *Point out* = (1) to observe; (2 to call to others' attention. *Point to* = to direct attention to (as an answer or solution). *Point up* = illustrate. *Point up* is perhaps, comparatively more frequent in legal than in non-legal writing, e.g., "We mention *Lowe* not to intimate any view on the merits of the decision here but rather, because it *points up* how the present case falls so clearly within the first amendment exception for pure commercial speech that is both misleading and tends to promote illegal conduct." "Philosophical criticism has *pointed up* a lack or precision in the language of the law as a facet of the basic deficiency of all languages."

Q. What is a pole star?

A. pole star = lodestar, q.v., e.g., "The intention of the testator as expressed in the testamentary instrument is always the *pole star* in the interpretation of a will."

Q. Differentiate between policy and polity.

A. policy, polity. *Policy,* by far the more common of these words, means "a concerted course of action followed to achieve certain ends, a plan." It is more restricted in sense than polity, which means: (1) "the principal upon which, a government is based"; or (2) "The total governmental organisation as based on its goals and policies" e.g., in the more usual sense (2): "The ancient doctrine of the common law, founded on the principles of the feudal system that a private wrong is merged in a felony, is not applicable to the civil *polity* of this country."

Q. What is meant by Polygamy?

A. polygamy = Having more than one wife or husband.

Q. What is meant by post mortem?

A. post mortem = An examination of dead body to ascertain the actual cause of death.

Q. What is power of attorney?

A. power of attorney = An authority given by one person to another to act on his behalf.

Q. What is pre-emption?

A. pre-emption = A right to purchase property before other persons.

Q. What do you understand by perscription?

A. prescription = Method of acquiring rights over another's land by long period of adverse possession.

Q. What do you understand by presumption of death?

A. presumption of death = If a person has not been heared of as alive, for seven years, there is presumption in law that he is dead.

Q. What is meant by prima facie?

A. prima facie = on the face of it, based on the first impression.

Q. What do you understand by private law?

A. private law = That part of law which deals with relations between private individuals.

Q. What is probate?

A. probate = The copy of a will ratified under the seal of a court of competant jurisdiction with a grant of administration to the estate of the testator.

Q. What is prohibition?

A. prohibition = An order of a higher court (Supreme Court, High Court) preventing on interior court from doing something.

Q. What is meant by pro-rata?

A. pro-rata = Proportionately.

Q. What is prorogation?

A. prorogation = The act of bringing a session of parliament or other legislative assembly to an end.

Q. What is menat by proviso?

A. proviso = A condition.

Q. What do you understand by public law?

A. public law = The body of laws, which deals with the relations between private individuals and the governments.

Q. What is meant by public policy?

A. public policy = A policy that is in the interest of the state and community.

Q. What is putative?

A. putative = supposed, believed, reputed, e.g., "The facts of causation were in the control of the *putative* defendant but unavailable to the plaintiff or at least very difficult to obtain." *Putative marriage,* a term originally from canon law, denotes a marriage that, though legally invalid, was contracted in good faith by at least one of the parties, e.g., "The court of civil appeals held that the *putative* wife's knowledge of pending divorce involving husband terminated the *putative* marriage." "A *putative* marriage is one into which, one or both spouses enter in good faith but which is invalid because of an existing impediment."

Q. What is qua?

A. qua = in the capacity of, as, in the role of. The word is often misused and little needed in English. "The real occasion for the use of *qua*," wrote Fowler, "occurs when a person or thing spoken of can be regarded from more than one point of view or as the holder of various coexistent functions and a statement about him (or it) is to be limited to him in one of these aspects." (*MEUI* 477). Fowler's example of a justifiable use of the term is as follows: *"Qua* lover he must be condemned for doing what *qua* citizen he would be condemned for not doing." Alas, this proper usage of the term is rarely if ever seen today.

One is hard-pressed to divine any purpose but rhetorical emphasis in the examples following: "We seek simply to keep the government, *qua* government, neutral with respect to any religious controversy." "The question of res, *qua* res, causes us no difficulty." "The only immunities in an official-capacity action are forms of sovereign immunity that the entity, *qua* entity, may possess."

Nor are the unemphatic modern uses of a nature that would justify the choice of *qua* over *as*. Indeed, these are the very types of uses that Fowler rightly objected to: "Hudspeth can challenge the FSLIC's behaviour *qua* [read *as*] receiver before the FHLBB and, if unsatisfied, can seek judicial review under the APA." "*Qua* [read *To test its claim as a*] patent, we should at least have to decide, as tabula rasa, whether the design or machine was a new and required invertion." "The right of fair comment, though shared by the public, is the right of every individual who asserts it and is, *qua* [read *as claimed by*] him, an individual right whatever name it be called by and comment by him, which is coloured by malice cannot from his standpoint be deemed fair." (Eng.)

Q. What is quaere?

A. quaere, query. *Quaere* is the Latin word meaning 'question,' sometimes appended or prefixed to doubtful statements, e.g., "Whether a plea in abatement is not the proper mode of defense when the facts relied on do not appear of record, quaere." *Engelke & Feiner Milling Co. v. Grunthal*, 46 Fla. 349, 35 So. 17, 18 (1903). The term is used occasionally in modern pedagogical writing: "One can affix one's signature to a document by writing thereon and one can affix one sheet of paper to another with a staple or sticky tape but *quaere* as to a paper clip." Leff, *The Leff Dictionary of Law,* 94 Yale L.J. 1855, 1969 (1985). The original form of *query, quaere* is now but a Needless Variant in other than this technical usage.

Dictionary of Legal Terms 155

Q. What is meant by qualifiedly?

A. qualifiedly = in a qualified fashion. Often the adjective works better than the adverb. "*Although the sheriff is not qualifiedly privileged,* [read *Although the sheriff has no qualified privilege*], the summary judgement was entered in favour of the parish and not the sheriff." Unfortunately, adverbs in *-edly* are unqualifiedly fashionable in modern legal writing.

Q. What is meant by the term qualitative?

A. qualit(at)ive. The longer form is preferred. The adjective corresponds to *quality* in the sense of character or nature, not in the sense of merit or excellence.

Q. What is a quality?

A. quality, adj., (= of high quality) is a Vogue Word and a casualism (a *quality* law firm). One is better advised to use *good* or *fine* or some other mundane adjective that is not branded as a cant term.

Q. Is quandary used for a mental state of perplexity?

A. quandary is a word naming a mental state of perplexity or confusion. It is, most emphatically, descriptive of a state of mind and should not be detached from mental processes, as here: "Conflicting state interests may make the use of either state's law inappropriate; the asbestos cases present this precise *quandary* [read *dilemma, engima* or *problem*]."

Q. What is meant by to quantify?

A. quantify, quantitate. The latter is a Needless Variant, no popular with social scientists whose choice of terms has never been a strong recommendation for the usage of those terms.

Q. What is quantitative?

A. quanti(ta)tive. The preferred form is *quantitative,* not *quantitive.* Variants such as *quantificational* should be avoided. Cf. **qualit(at)ive.**

Q. Is quantity a portion or an amount?

A. quality (usu. "portion, amount") has been used by legal theorists in a sense borrowed from logic, "the extent in which, a term in a given logical proposition is to be taken." (*W3*), e.g., "While, no doubt, in the great majority of cases, no harm results from the use of such expressions, yet these forms of statement seem to represent a blending of non-legal and legal *quantities* which, in any problem requiring careful reasoning, should preferably be kept distinct." "If, however, the problem is analysed, it will be seen that as of primary importance, the grantor has two legal *quantities:* the privilege of entering and the power, by means of such entry, to divest the estate of the grantee."

The *OED* notes that *quantity* in the sense "length or duration of time" exists now only in the legal phrase *quantity of estate* (the quantity of estate is 99 years).

Q. Define quantum.

A. quantum, a favourite word of lawyers and judges, means "amount, share, portion, the required, desired or allowed amount." The term should not be used for *degree,* as here: "The injury suffered by Lyons was several *quanta* [read *degrees*] greater than Raley's." "The scope of instrusiveness of a particular search and thus the corresponding *quantum* [read *degree*] of suspicion, is determined in the light of three factors."

The only accepted plural of this word is *quanta.* The erroneous form *quantums* is occasionally used, e.g., "Without regard to the number of rungs that appellant may climb on an appellate ladder, if minimum evidentiary *quantums* [read *quanta*] have been satisfied, the American tradition generally does not permit a reviewing court to disturb findings of facts."

Q. What is meant by quash?

A. quash = To render null or void by a superior court, to set aside or put an end to by an order of a higher court.

Q. What is meant by quasi?

A. quasi = It were analogous to, semi.

Q. What do you understand by quasi contract?

A. quasi contract = A quasi contract is an act for event from which, though not consensual contract, an obligation arises from a contract.

Q. What is quo-warranto?

A. quo warranto = A writ of quo warranto issued by the supreme court or the High court against a person who claims or who usurps any office, franchise of liberty to enquire by what authority he supports his claim.

Q. What is meant by quorum?

A. quorum = Minimum number of persons necessary for conduct of proceeding.

———✧✧✧———

Q. What is meant by Ratification?

A. ratification = Approval by word or writing or conduct.

Q. What is meant by ratio decidendi?

A. ratio decidendi = opinion given by the judge and such opinion is necessary for the decision of particular case.

Q. Is reasonable the correct usage?

A. reasonableness, reasonability. The latter is a Needless Variant of the former.

Q. Explain the term reason is because.

A. reason is because. This construction is incorrect. After a *be*-verb or other copula, there should be a noun phrase or a clause introduced by *that,* e.g., "The *reason* such matters are not material and need not be disclosed *is because* [read *is that*] public disclosure of tentative, indefinite and contingent facts would itself be misleading."

Variations on this phrase, such as *reason is due to* and *reason is based on,* are no better, e.g., "Two prosecutors stated in affidavits that the *reason* the state moved to dismiss the enhancement counts *was due to* [omit *due to*] difficulty of proof." "The *reason* for the requirement of delivery, as provided for in the statute, is *based upon* public policy." [Read *The requirement of delivery, as provided for in the statute, is based on public policy.*]

Q. Explain reason of.

A. reason of for *rationale* for is an Archaism. "Clearly, the *reason of* [read *rationale for*] section 2-202 is sensible and should be applied by analogy to article eight."

Q. What is the term reason that?

A. reason why, reason that. Both forms are correct. "The district court found that there was no *reason that* [or *why*] Hauser could not have joined in her husband's earlier action."

Q. What is rebut?

A. rebut, refute. *Rebut* means "to attempt to refute." *Refute* means "to defeat (countervailing arguments)." Thus one who *rebuts* certainly hopes to *refute*; it is immodest to assume, however, that one has *refuted* another's arguments. *Rebut* is sometimes wrongly written *rebutt*.

Q. What is redemption?

A. redemption = The paying of a loan by a mortgagor, a buying back of the legal estate after it has passed to the mortgagee.

Q. Explain the term rebuttable presumption.

A. rebuttable presumption (= a legal presumption subject to valid rebuttal) becomes illogical when turned into a adverb and a verb, e.g., "Texas courts *rebuttably presume* that such warnings will be read and heeded." This suggests that the courts *presume in a rebuttable manner,* which is not the sense; a better way of phrasing the thought is to write: "Texas courts *adopt the rebuttable presumption* that such warnings will be read and heeded."

Q. Rebuttal is an act of rebutting. Explain.

A. rebuttal, surrebuttal. *Rebuttal* = the act of rebutting. The term is used especially in legal sense and is much broader than *rebutter* q.v., which is the name of the pleading intended to rebut. *Surrebuttal* is not an answer to a rebuttal but is a variant name for the pleading called *surrebutter* q.v. and is a Needless Variant of that term.

Q. Rebutter is an answer to a plaintiff. Explain.

A. rebutter = (1) (formerly) a defendant's answer to a plaintiff's surrenjoinder; the pleading that followed the rejoinder and surrejoinder and that might, in turn be answered by the surrebutter and (2) one who rebuts. Sense (1) is the only strictly legal sense of the term.

Q. What is a receipt?

A. receipt, as a verb, began as an American word in the eighteenth century and has now spread to G.B. It is Commercialese but there is no grammatical problem in writing, "The bill must be *receipted*" or "The sale was *receipted.*" *Receipt* is ordinarily used in the Passive Voice: The preceding sentence shall not be construed Statute Drafting (A) to mean that new receipts are to be obtained every year from continuing employees who have previously been *receipted* for copies of identical provisions." Still, the Phrasal Verb *to be receipted for* is a Redundancy as well as a graceless phrase: "Each certificate issued by the corporation shall *be receipted for* by the person receiving it or by his duly authorised agent." [Read *The person, who receives a certificate issued by the organisation or his duly authorised agent, shall execute a receipt for it.*]

Dictionary of Legal Terms 159

Q. What is receipt of?

A. receipt of, be in. This insipid phrase, which usually occurs in letters, is to be avoided as Officialese or commercialese or Legalese.

Q. Who is a receiptor?

A. receiptor (= a person who receipts property attached by a sheriff, a bailee) is noted as being an American word by the *OED*. It dates from the early nineteenth century. The *-or* spelling is preferred to *-er*.

Q. What are receivables?

A. receivables (= debts owed to a business and regarded as assets) began in the mid-nineteenth century as an American but is now current in BrE as well. It is the antonym of *payables*.

Q. Who is a receiver?

A. receiver is used in both the U.S. and G.B. in the specific legal sense of "a person appointed by a court or by a corporation or other person for the protection or collection of property." Usually the *receiver* administers the property of a bankrupt, or a property that is subject to litigation, pending the outcome of a lawsuit.

Q. Explain recension.

A. recension (= the revision of a text) is not to be confused with *recession* q.v.

Q. What is receptioning?

A. receptioning (= to do the job of a receptionist) is the American law-firm word that illustrates the same tendency in modern usage as *paralegaling* and *bailiffing,* qq.v.

Q. What is recital?

A. recital, recitation. These words overlap but are distinguishable. The term from drafting is *recital,* meaning "the formal statement or setting forth of some related matter of fact in any deed or writing, as to explain the reasons for a transaction, to evidence the existence of facts or, in pleading, to introduce a positive allegation." (*W2*), e.g., "The version of the parties' proposed consent decree contains no *recital,* finding or adjudication of any illegality." "*Recitations* [read *recitals*] of consideration and use in a recorded deed are not binding upon a complainant who seeks a purchase money resulting trust." More generally, *recital* may mean "a rehearsal, account or description of something, fact or incident" e.g., "The facts are sordid but a brief *recital* of them must be made."

Recitation often connotes an oral delivery before an audience, whether in the classroom or on stage. Yet, it is often the general noun, meaning "the act of reciting." "The interrogator's *recitation* of the suspect's rights was sufficient." "The carnage caused by drunken driving is well documented and needs no detailed *recitation* here." "This court's *recitation* of the history of the case is replete with examples of the district court's having placed extreme requirements of particularised proof upon the government."

Q. Give the meaning of reckon.

A. reckon (= to count or compute) is probably an Archaism M., e.g., "The law *reckons* in days—not commonly in fractions of days—and an agreement made at six o'clock in the morning stands on the same footing with one made at eleven o'clock in the evening." The word is dialectal in the sense "to suppose, think" ("I reckon the judges will affirm").

Q. What is recognizance?

A. recognizance, reconnaissance, reconnoisance. *Recognizance* = a bond or obligation, entered into and recorded before a court or magistrate by which, a person engages himself to perform some act or observe some condition (as to appear when called on, to pay a debt or to keep the peace)." (*OED*), e.g., "The suspect was released on his own *recognizance*." *Reconnaisance* = a preliminary survey; a military or intelligence-gathering examination of a region. *Reconnoisance* is an older spelling of *reconnaissance;* it is also a Needless Variant of *recognizance* and of *recognition*. The verb corresponding to *reconnaisance* is *reconnoiter, -re*, q.v.

Q. Explain recommend against.

A. recommend against. *Recommend* is a word with positive connotations; in all the examples in the *OED*, it is construed with *to*. The antonym of *recommend* is *discommend*, which should appear in place of *reconmend against* in the following sentence: "Shortly thereafter, 45 college hours were required for applicants, even though civil-service officials *recommended against* [read *discommended*] this increase in the number of required hours."

Q. Give the meaning of recompense.

A. recompense is both a transitive verb ("to repay, compensate") and a noun ("payment in return for something"); the word is more learned than *compensate* or *compensation*. In G.B., the noun is sometimes spelled *-ce*. The nominal use is more frequent than the use as a verb: "Although foreseeability may be a proper test for determining damages for unintentional tort violations of civil rights yet it is not a proper prerequisite to obtaining *recompense* for intentional violations." "The statute does not assure the prevailing party munificient *recompense,* for it remains for the district court to determine what fee is reasonable." "Punitive damages are not only a *recompense* to the sufferer, but also a punishment to the offender and an example for the community."

Q. What is recompensive?

A. recompensive (= compensatory) is a rare term whose usage in modern prose strikes the reader as a straining for the recherche term.

Q. Give the meaning of reconnoiter.

A. reconnoiter, -re. The verb form corresponding to the noun *reconnaissance* is preferably spelled *-er* in AmE and *re* in BrE.

Q. Define the word record.

A. record frequently occurs in law in the phrases *in the record* and *of record* (attorney of record). Usually, *record* refers to the official report of the proceedings in any case coming before a court, together with the judgement given in the case, taken down by a court reporter. The *record* is read on appeal by the judges who review it for reversible errors. In administrative law, *record* refers to all considerations actually taken into account in deciding an issue.

Record has come to be used adjectivally as a shorthand for *in the record,* e.g., "We find no *record support* [*i.e.,* support in the record] for this contention." It is preferable not to collapse the prepositions into a nominal adjective in this manner. [Read *We find no support in the record for this contention*].

Q. What is recordation?

A. recordation, recordal. The latter is not a proper word, though it has erroneously appeared in such phrases as "*recordal* of a trademark with the Treasury Department." *Recordation* is the word, e.g., "The supplemental complaint requests that both the Customes Service and Art's Way remove the *recordal* [read *recordation*] of the dion registration to permit unimpeded entry of the machinery into the United States." *B. & R. Choiniere Ltd. v. Art's-Way Manufacturing Co.,* 207 U.S.P.Q. (BNA) 969, 971 (N.D.N.Y. 1979)."

Q. Define recourse.

A. recourse; resort. *Recourse* (= application) is used in the idiomatic phrases *without recourse* and *have recourse to.* To former is the peculiarly legal phrase, which, when added to the endorsement of commercial paper, protects the endorser from liability to the indorsee and later holders: "When an inter partes proceeding has been conducted the only *recourse* is an appeal from the decision of the court." *Resort* = that which one turns to for refuge or aid.

Q. To recover means to recover damages. Explain.

A. recover, in legal Argot, is an elliptical form of *recover damages,* e.g., "The United States filed suit against Central Gulf to *recover* for the missing soyabean oil."

recover (= to secure by legal process) takes *from* or *against* in modern usage. The collocation *recover of* is an Archaism for *recover from,* e.g., "It is equally well-settled that the reasonable expenses incurred by an indemnitee in defending a claim against him may be *recovered of* [read *recover from*] his indemnitor." "This is an action of tort to *recover of* [read *recover from*] the defendant damages for a malicious abuse of process." Cf. **purchase of & of** (E).

Q. What is recoverable?

A. recoverable = compensable, q.v. The term originally meant "capable of being recovered or regained" but was extended in legal usage, because of the nature of damages, to "capable of being legally obtained" e.g., "The rule is that special damages for breach of contract are not *recoverable* unless they can fairly and reasonably be considered as arising naturally from the breach." Strictly speaking, the special damages are not to be *recovered,* for they are being awarded for the first time to the complainant; but this usage is quite permissible in the legal idiom.

Q. What is meant by recover back?

A. recover back might appear to be a legal Redundancy, e.g., "Generally, a co-owner, who pays a disproportionate share of the necessary expenses of the property, may *recover back* the excess in an action for contribution, accounting or partition." But in common-law terminology, a distinction exists between *to recover* (= to obtain, as in recovering damages) and *to recover back* (= to secure the return of, as in recovering back money paid by mistake).

Q. What is meant by to recreate?

A. recreate, re-create. The former means either (of a pastime or relaxation)" to refresh or agreeably occupy" or "to amuse oneself, indulge in recreation" (*COD*); the latter means "to create anew." The hyphen makes a great difference: "The words of the witness cannot 'give' or *recreate* [read *re-create*] the 'facts,' that is, the objective situations or happenings about which, the witness is testifying." "The company's termination of the positions was a pretext for unfair labour practices, which demonstrates that these positions must now be *re-created* to provide an efficacious remedy."

Q. What is recreational?

A. recreational, recreative. The former is the preferred adjective corresponding to the noun *recreation,* e.g., "In the first few months of army training, the emphasis was on athletic activities for their *recreative* [read *recreational*] value but soon, the need for exercise as physical training became evident."

Q. Differentiate between rectal and rictal.

A. rectal, rictal. Both words are related to orifices but there are the similarities end. *Rectal* = of or relating to the rectum. *Rictal* = of or relating to the mouth or to a gaping grin.

Q. What is recurrence?

A. recurrence, recurrency, reoccurrence. *Recurrence* is the preferred form, *reocurrence* being a secondary variant meriting only careful avoidance. *Recurrency* is likewise a Needless Variant.

Q. What is recusal?

A. recusal, recusation, recusement, recusancy, recusance. The preferred nominal form of the verb *recuse* (= to remove oneself as a judge considering a case) is *recusal,* though its earliest known usage is only 1958 (*OED Supp.*). The word appeared in the *Manchester Guardian* in August, 1958 (see *OED Supp.)* and in the same year in the reported opinion from Alabama: "[T]he statute on *recusal* rests on kinship or pecuniary interest ....." *Wiggins v. State,* 104 So. 2d 560, 564 (Ala. App. 1958).

Q. Explain the term redemptive.

A. redemptive, -tory, -tional. *Redemptive* = tending to redeem, redeeming. *Redemptional* = of or pertaining to redemption. *Redemptory* is a Needless Variant of *redemptive.*

Q. Define reduce.

A. reduce should not be used as a reflexive verb, e.g., "The question *reduces itself* [read *is reducible or may be reduced*] to one of statutory interpretation." "The government's case *reduces itself* [read *is reducible*] to this:" the defendant was in a public restaurant at a time when someone said that a drug deal might be going on."

Q. What is redundancy in legal terms?

A. Redundancy. Washington Irving wrote that "redundancy of language is never found with deep reflection. Verbiage may indicate observation but not thinking. He, who thinks much, says but little in proportion to his thoughts." Lawyers should think much acout those words, and begin to write less. Following are some of the typical manifestations of redundancy in legal writing.

A. General Redundancy. This linguistic pitfall is best exemplified rather than discoursed on; comments follow the less obvious redundancies here listed, "No one need fight city hall unnecessarily." [Read *one need not fight city hall.* Or, *It is unnecessary to fight city hall.*] "This type of obligation imposes an undue restriction on alienation or an *onerous burden* in perpetuity." (*Onus = burden,* hence *onerous burden* is redundant.) "National is discharged from all its *obligations* as an *obligor*." [Read *National is discharged as obligor.* Or, *National is discharged from all its obligations.*] "By allowing representatives of the tenants, who obviously *shared a common interest* [read *shared an interest* or had an *interest in common*], to maintain a single action, the equity court eliminated the necessity of trying the common questions repetitively in separate actions." "These two paragraphs are the least legible and the most difficult to read [omit *and the most difficult to read*] in the instrument but they are most important in the evaluation of the rights of the contesting parties." " The mere fact that association acquired its knowledge *later in point of time* [omit *in point of time*] gave the appellant no superior legal position over the association." "The purpose of the statute is to ensure a high standard of education for Texas citizens *while at the same time* lessening the incentive for aliens to enter the United States illegally."

B. Awkward Repetitions. Samuel Johnson once advised his readers to "avoid ponderous ponderosity." The repetition of roots was purposeful, of course. Many legal writers, however, engage in such repetitions with no sense of irony, as in the phrases *build a building, refer to a reference, point out points* and *an individualistic individual.* As great a writer as he was, Chief Justice Marshall seems not to have had a stylistic design in the repetition here: "The question is, *in truth, a question of supremacy* [read *is, in truth, one of supremacy*]." *McCulloch v. Maryland,* 4 U.S. (4 Wheat.) 316, 433 (1819). Then again, Justice Marshall may have been striving for a rhetorical effect; in the sentences that follow, however, the repetitions are mere thoughtless errors: "Said *use of the trademark* [read *trademark*] has been *used* in foreign commerce and interstate commerce in the United States continuously since 1926." The *use* has not been used but rather the *trademark.* This sentence exemplifies one strain of **Illogic.** "The plaintiffs' number was number 37." [Read *The plaintiffs' number was 37.*] "*This judicially required warrant requirement* [read *This judicial requirement*

Dictionary of Legal Terms 165

warrant requirement or, This judicial requirement of a warrant] has been described as a narrow one. "Notice was mailed by registered mail." [Read *Notice was sent by registered mail.*] "*But the basis of his liability here was based* [read *His liability was based*] on a legal relationship only, not on his primary negligence." "The subdivided lots were sold as individual lots *with deed restrictions restricting development to single-family homes* [read *with deeds restricting development to signle-family homes*]." "The resolution of the board of directors accepting property for shares must *specify the specific* [omit *spceific*] property involved." "By cheating, he avoids pursuing *knowledge* that he, according to his transcript, should *know* [read *have*]." (One does not know knowledge; one has it.)

C. Common Redundancies. Many of these have been treated in separate entries. It is useful to be aware that phrases such as the following are redundant: *named nominee, adult parent* (but may be this is no longer redundant), *to plead a plea, cost-expensive, active agent, end result, integral part, past history* (arguably established), *connect up or together, future forecast, merge together, mingle together* and *join together* (arguably acceptable), *mix together.*

Q. Give the meaning of reek.

A. reek, wreak. These homophones are occasionally confused. *Reed* = to give off an odour or vapour. As a noun, *reek* = an odorous vapour. *Wreak* = to inflict (to wreak havoc).

Q. What is re-examination?

A. re-examination, primarily a BrE term, is equivalent to the AmE term *redirect examination.* The following are examples of the corresponding verb: "Witnesses examined in opencourt must be first examined in chief, then cross-examined and then, *re-examined.*" (Eng.) "After the cross-examination is concluded, the party, who called the witness, has a right to *re-examine* him." (Eng.)

Q. Where do we use refer back?

A. refer back is a common Redundancy, *refer* alone almost always being sufficient, e.g., "As to the use of memoranda, *refer back to* [read *refer to*] *Ward v. Morr Transfer & Storage Co.,* at page 446 *supra.*" "Section 72411.5 simply *refers us back to* [read *refers us to*] the contract." Cf. **relate back.** *Refer back* may be justified in those rare instances in which, it means "to send back to one who or that which has previously been involved," as here: "The case is simply *referred back* to the arbitrator for a re-wording of his opinion."

Q. Give the meaning of reference as a verb.

A. reference, as a verb meaning "to provide with references," is defensible, e.g., "The cross-*referenced* statute contains two subsections." It should not, however, be used for *refer,* as here: "He stated that, without *referencing* [read *referring*] to that file, he could not answer the question."

referendary, -al. The latter is a Needless Variant for the term meaning "of or relating to a referendum."

Q. Which is referrable?

A. refer(r)able, -ible. The preferred form is *referable,* which is accented on the first syllable; otherwise, the final -*r*- would be doubled. The sense is "capable of being referred to" e.g., "The maxim of clean hands will not be invoked unless the inequitable conduct sought to be attributed to plaintiff is *referable* to the very transaction that is the source of the instant controversy."

Referrable often mistakenly appears; the form is old but has long been held inferior to *referable,* e.g., "The only other causes of action pleaded by plaintiff *referrable* [read *referable*] to reimbursement are those of constructive fraud arising out of Tony's alleged operation of the corporation as his alter ego."/ "After review of the procedure followed, the board decided that the dispute was not *referrable* [read *referable*] to a public law board for reconsideration on merits."

Q. What is a referral?

A. referral, reference. Both mean "the act of referring." *Referrence* is the broader and general term. *Referral,* which began as an American word in the early twentieth century but now used commonly in BrE as well, means specifically "The referring to a third party of personal information concerning another" or "The referring of a person to an expoert or specialist for advice."

Q. Which is the correct term, reflection or reflexion?

A. reflection, reflexion. The former spelling is preferred in both AmE and BrE. *Reflexion* was formerly common in British writing. Fowler recommended -*ction* in all senses.

Q. What is a refractory?

A. refractory, -tive. These terms have undergone Differentiation. *Refractory* = stubborn, unmanageable, rebellious, e.g., "Under such circumstances, the disappointed legatee may, in a court of equity, compel the sequestration of the legacy of the *refractory* legatee for the purpose of diminishing the amount of his disappointment." *Refractive* = that refracts light.

Dictionary of Legal Terms 167

Q. When do we refrain?

A. refrain, restrain. Both mean generally "to put restraints upon" but *refrain* is used of oneself in the sense "to abstain" (he refrained from exchanging scurrilities with his accuser), whereas *restrain* is used of another (the police illegally restrained the complainant from going into the stadium).

Q. Who is a refusenik?

A. refus(e)nik = a Jew in the Soviet Union, who has been refused permission to emigrate. The spelling *refusenik* is coming to be the standard spelling for this decade-old word.

Q. What is refutation?

A. refutation; refutal. The latter is an unnecessary and ill-formed variant of *refutation*.

refute is not synonymous with *rebut*. It does not mean merely "to counter an argument" but "to disprove beyond doubt, to prove a statement false." Yet, the word is commonly misused for *rebut,* as here: "The findings of the Commissioner carry a presumption of correctness and the taxpayer has the burden of *refuting* [read *rebutting*] them." "Appellant was allowed to put on witnesses to *refute* [read *rebut*] the sexual harassment charges and he or his lawyer or both were present to cross-examine all the university's witnesses."

Q. What is meant by regard?

A. regard. This word is correctly used in the phrases *with regard to* and *in regard to*. The forms *with regards to* and *in regards to* are, to put it charitably, poor usages. The acceptable forms are best used as introductory phrases. Usually, however, they may advantageously be replaced by some simpler phrase such as *concerning, regarding, considering* or even the simple prepositions *in, about* or *for*.

The plural form, *regards,* is acceptable only in the phrase *as regardsa* as follows: "*With regards to* [read *With regard to*] the 1962 adoption of the at large election scheme, plaintiffs argue with some merit that more should have been said about this event."

Q. What is regardless?

A. regardless (= without regard to) should not be used for *despite* (= in spite of), e.g., "The appellants voted to reject the plan, reiterating the grounds for their suit against Martin; *regardless of* [read *despite*] the appellants' vote, the plan was approved with two-thirds of the creditors voting for the plan."

Q. What is *regardless whether?*

A. regardless whether is incorrect for *regardless of whether,* e.g., "*Regardless whether* [read *Regardless of whether*] COGSA or Texas state law controls, appellee is not liable for any damages caused by the delay that was not its fault."

Q. What is *registerable?*

A. regist(e)rable. The preferred from is *registrable* (a registrable trademark).

Q. Who is *registrant?*

A. registrant is pronounced as ***rej**-i-strant* does not rhyme, in the final syllable, with *restaurant.*

Q. What is *regretful?*

A. regretful; regrettable. Errors made are *re-grettable;* the persons who have committed them, assuming a normal level of contrition, are *regretful.* Here, the wrong word appears: "Many of the grievances appear justified; yet, *regretfully* [read *regrettably*], as the Supreme Court stated in *Radovich,* we are not here writing on a clean slate."

Q. Which is *regulable?*

A. regulable = able to be regulated; susceptible to regulation. *Regulatable* is incorrect.

Q. What is *regulatory?*

A. regulatory, -tive. The two forms of the adjective are used about equally often. *Regulatory* is accented in AmE on the first syllable, in BrE often on the third.

Q. What is meant by *reify?*

A. reify (= to make material, or convert mentally into a thing) is transitive only. Here, it is misused as an intransitive verb: "As soon as Schultz's objective *reifies* [read *materialises*], critics will have a more solid basis on which, to evaluate his policies."

Q. Give the meaning of *reinforce.*

A. reinforce (= to strengthen) is the universal form, though the noun is *enforce,* not *inforce.* (Likewise with *reinstate.*) Rather than hyphenate or use a diaeresis and retain the *-e-* in such words (e.g., re-enforce, re-enstate), the *-e-* in each word is changed to *-i-* when the prefix is added. *Re-enforce* (= to enforce again) is sometimes seen in AmE.

Q. What is rein in?

A. rein in, not *reign in,* is the correct form of the phrase meaning "to check, restrain." The metaphorical image is of the rider pulling on the reins of his horse to slow down (i.e., "hold his horses"), e.g., "Even when we make law judicially, we can tighten up the product dramatically if we *reign in* [read *rein in*] the staff attorneys and law clerks." Moreover, we can tighten up the product if we use idioms correctly.

Q. Define the term reintegration.

A. reintegration, redintegration. *Reintegration* is the usual form of the word in the sense "the act of restoring to a state of wholeness, renewal, reconstruction." *Redintegration* was formerly more common in this sense; it is still used in scientific and other technical contexts.

Q. Give the meaning of reiterate.

A. reiterate, iterate. It is perhaps not too literalistic to use *literate* in the sense "to repeat" and *reiterate* in the sense "to repeat a second time [*i.e.,* to state a third time]." The distinction is observed only by the most punctilious writers, *reiterate* being the usual term in either sense.

Q. What is a rejoinder in legal parlance?

A. rejoinder, surrejoinder. A *rejoinder,* in British practice, is the pleading served by a defendant in an answer to the plaintiff's reply (the pleading in an answer to the defence). In older practice, a *surrejoinder* is a plaintiff's pleading in reply to a defendant's rejoinder. The *CDL* notes that these pleadings are very rare in modern practice and can be served only with permission of the court.

Q. What is meant by relate back?

A. related back is not a Redundancy in law. It is the verbal invocation of the doctrine of *relation back,* q.v.: "whenever the claim or defense asserted in the amended pleading arose out of the conduct, transaction or occurrence set forth or attempted to be set forth in the original pleading, the amendment *relates back* to the date of the original pleading." Fed.R.Civ.P. 15(c). "Because the 1982 mortgages are between different parties from the 1977 mortgages, their priority does not *related back*."

Q. What is relatedly?

A. relatedly is an adverb inferior even to *reportedly,* q.v., e.g., "*Relatedly,* Idaho also adheres to the tenets of concurrent causation." Some better connective such as *moreover* or furthermore should be used.

Q. Give the meaning of *relate to.*

A. relate to (the jury can relate to that experience), when used as in the example just given, is a an expression that is characteristic of popular American cant during the 1970s and 1980s. It is unlikely to lose that stigma.

Q. What is a *relator?*

A. relatter, -or. The former is the preferred spelling in the sense "narrator, one who relates." *Relator* is the legal term meaning "a private person, at whose relation or in whose behalf, an application for a *quo warranto* or *mandamus* is filed" e.g., "Members of the charitable organisation can bring suit as *relators* in the name of the attorney general but this is not always a practical remedy; not only do the *relators* bear the cost of the suit, but also the conduct of the litigation is controlled by the attorney general."

relation. A. And *relative.* These terms are interchangeable in the sense "a kinsman," though currently, *relative* is slightly more usual.

B. And *relationship. Relation* is the broader term in this pair, inasmuch as *relationship* refers either to kinship or to the fact of being related by some bond. The phrase *in relationship with* is almost always incorrect for *in relation to.* To be correct, the phrase would almost have to be *in his* (or *its*) *relationship with,* etc.

C. Legal Sense. Some legal scholars, most notably Professor Leon Green, have used *relation* as "the best term available to express the value of one human being to another ..... Relations may be classified as family relations, trade relations, professional and political relations, labor relations and general social relations." L. Green, *Cases on Injuries to Relations* I (1940).

Q. Give the meaning of *relation back?*

A. relation back, in legal Argot, refers to the doctrine that an act done at a later time is considered in the eyes of the law to have occurred at a prior time, e.g., "To the extent that a power of appointment has been thought of as a mere authority to act for the donor in the completion of a disposition initiated by the donor, the agency factor has dominated and the doctrine of *relation back* has been applied." "How a magistrate who has acted within his jurisdiction up to the point at which the missing evidence should have been, but was not, given, can thereafter be said, by a kind of *relation back,* to have had no jurisdiction over the charge at all, it is hard to see." (Eng.)

Q. What is *relational?*

A. relational = of or relating to relations between persons, e.g., "Out of the mass of decisions and scholarly writings it is now possible to chart a course of study for the lawyer whose professional activities will more and more be concerned with the protection of the *relational* interests of his clients" (i.e., interests in other human beings). The term is thus distinct from the adjective *relative*.

Q. What is the meaning of the term relatively?

A. relative(ly) to. *Relative to* is a variant of *inrelation to* or *in comparison with;* usually one of these longer phrases adds clarity. Partridge called *relative to* Gobbledygook. In no event is *relatively* to proper: *"Relatively to* [read *In relation to*] her, his act was not negligent."

The phrase is also an awkward substitute for *concerning* or *regarding:* "The latter part of the paragraph contains language similar to that of paragraph (a) *relative to* [read *concerning*] the discharge of the corporation's liability if an agreement is signed by the parties."

Q. To relegate is to consign to an inferior position. Explain.

A. relegate, delegate. To *relegate* is to consign to an inferior position or to transfer for decision or execution, e.g., "The administratrix of the prisoner's estate was not *relegated* exclusively to an FTCA remedy." To *delegate* is to commit (as powers) to an agent or representative or to depute (someone).

Q. What is relevancy?

A. relevance, -cy. The former is preferred in both AmE and BrE. *Relevancy* was the predominant form in American and British writings on evidence of the nineteenth century but now, *relevance* is more common except in Scotland.

Q. What is relevant?

A. relevant is often misused for *applicable* or *appropriate,* e.g., "The board of directors might then allocate such amounts among the several outstanding series of stock on the basis of any criteria it deems *relevant* [read *applicable* or *appropriate*]."

Q. Give the meaning of relitigate.

A. relitigate (= to litigate again) is not recorded in the dictionaries but is an implied form that is unquestionably useful, e.g., "The mere fact that the *en banc* court affirmed the district court's vacation of the consent decree and has remanded for further proceedings fails to establish any reason to *relitigate* the grant of limited intervenor status."

Q. What is a remainder?

A. remainder, reversion. These terms are to be distinguished. "A *remainder* is defined as 'what is left' of an entire grant of lands or tenements after a preceding part of the same grant or estate has been disposed of in possession whose regular expiration the remainder must await ..... A *reversion* is the remnant of an estate continuing in the grantor, undisposed of, after the grant of a part of his interest. It differs from a *remainder* in that it arises by act of law whereas a *remainder* is by act of the parties. A *reversion,* moreover, is the remnant left in the grantor, whilst a *remainder* is the remnant of the whole estate disposed of, after a proceding part of the same has been given away." I J.B. Minor, *Law of Real Property* 916, 1005 (2d ed. 1910).

Q. Who is a remainderman?

A. remainderman (= the person to whom, a remainder is devised) was formerly two words but is now regularly spelled as a single word, e.g., "A court may find for example—that the donees take the property as joint tenants, as tenants in common or that one donee takes as life tenant and the others as *remaindermen.*"

Q. What is meant by remand?

A. remand, v.t. **A.** Objects. People as well as causes may be *remanded* (or "sent back"), e.g., "Fagan, who pleaded not guilty to the charge, was *remanded* to Brixton Prison for psychiatric and medical reports." (Eng.)

B. *Remand back* is a Redundancy. "*Maine v. Thornton* has been *remanded back* [omit *back*] to the Maine Supreme Judicial Court for action not inconsistent with the Supreme Court's decision." "The court *remanded* the case *back* [omit *back*] to the circuit court for a new hearing."

C. Pronunciation. *Remand* is pronounced /ri-**mand**/ both as a noun and as a verb.

Q. What is remediable?

A. remediable, remedial. *Remedial* (= providing a remedy; corrective; curative) is frequently pejorative in lay language (remedial learning). In law, however, it usually acts as the adjective for *legal remedy:* "The constructive trust is a *remedial* device imposed to prevent a person from retaining title to property if the retention would unjustly enrich him at the expense of another."

Remediable = capable of being remedied, e.g., "A refusal to enforce that stems from a conflict of interest, that is the result of a bribe, vindictiveness or retaliation or that traces to personal or other corrupt motives ought to be judicially *remediable.*"

Q. What is remediless?

A. remediless, remedyless. The former form is correct (by analogy with *merciless* or *penniless*). The term is equivalent to *irremediable*.

Q. Give the meaning of remise.

A. remise = to give up, surrender, make over to another, release (any right, property etc.) (*OED*). The term is fast becoming a legal Archaism, for a number of words are more specific and more widely understood.

Q. What is a remission?

A. remission. As a noun meaning "the act of remanding," *remission* is a Needless Variant of *remand,* n., q.v. Here is an example suggesting the writer's indulgence in Inelegant Variation: "[A]n appellate court 'may *remand* the cause .....' The procedure for *remission* [read *remand*] of the cause to the lower court ..... is further regulated and controlled generally by the rules of the appellate courts." 14A S. Flanagan, *Cyclopedia of Federal Procedure* § 69.01 at 65 (1984).

Q. Give the meaning of remit.

A. remit = (1) to pardon; (2) to abate, slacken, mitigate; (3) to refer (a matter for decision) to some authority, send back (a case) to a lower court; (4) to send or put back; or (5) to transmit (as money). Senses (1) and (2) are uncommon today. Sense (4) is frequent in legal writing: "[T]he breach by the landlord of his covenant does not justify the refusal of the tenant to perform his covenant to pay rent ..... The tenant is *remitted* to the right to recoup himself in the damages resulting from the landlord's breach of his covenant to repair." *Mitchell v. Weiss,* 26 S. W. 2d 699, 700-01 (Tex. Civ. App.-El Paso 1930). "In *remitting* the members of this class to a solution at the ballot box, rather than dangling the carrot of reform by judicial injunction before them, the district court followed the course of wisdom and practicality."

Sense (3) was formerly common in legal prose. *Remit* is used here synonymously with *remand:* "The order should be reversed, with costs to the appellant payable out of the estate and the proceedings *remitted* to the surrogate for entry of a decree in accordance with this opinion." "Nolan, Presiding Justice, dissents and votes to reverse and to *remit* the proceeding to surrogate's Court for the entry of a decree as prayed for in the objections interposed by appellants." "The case is *remitted* to the Superior Court for the entry of a judgement on the verdict as directed." Sense (5) is also quite common: "upon receiving the demand letter, she promptly remitted the amount due."

Q. What is a remittance?

A. remittance, remittal, remission, remitment. *Remission* is the noun corresponding to senses (1) through (4) of *remit*, q.v.; it means either forgiveness or "diminution of force, effect, degree or violence." *Remittal* is a Needless Variant. *Remittance* corresponds to sense (5) of *remit* and means "money sent to a person" e.g., "On the other hand, is the innocent shipper who paid the full amount of the charges to such defaulting party for *remittance* to the agent." *Remitment* is a Needless Variant.

Q. Who is a remitter?

A. remitter, -or, remittitur. A *remitter* is one who sends a remittance. (See the previous entry.) The *-or* spelling is inferior. Formerly, it was used as a technical term for the relation back of a later defective title to an earlier valid title to an estate. A *remittitur* is the process by which, the court reduces the damages awarded in a jury verdict.

Remittitur of record is entirely distinct; it refers to the return of the trial record by a court of appeal to the trial court.

Q. Give the meaning of remonstrate.

A. remonstrate. The second syllable is accented *ri-**mon**-strayt* in AmE, the first syllable ***rem**-on-strayt* in BrE.

Q. What is meant by remote?

A. remote has a special legal meaning in contexts involving the rule against perpetuities: "beyond the 21 years after some life in being by which, a devise must vest" e.g., "In *Leake v. Robinson,* there actually were afterborn children with respect to whom the remainder might have vested *remotely*."

Q. What is a removal?

A. remove, -al. These terms have procedural senses in law that are generally unknown to laymen. *Removal* = the transfer of an action from a court on one jurisdictional level to a court on another level. Therefore, in the U.S., some state-court actions may be *removed* to federal court if the proper statutory basis exists. (The correlative term for transferring the action back to state court is *remand*, q.v.) in G.B., *removal* is the transfer of a High Court action from a district registry to London (or vice versa) or of a County court action to the High court (or vice versa) (CDL).

Q. What is remuneration?

A. remuneration. So spelled, *renumeration* is an all-too-common misspelling and mispronunciation.

semble (= it seems) is used in law reports as a technical expression of uncertainty, usually, in introducing an obiter dictum. In the first two examples, the brackets are those of the original authors of the sentences: "This judgement is not conclusive in an action by the owner of ship A, for the damage done to ship B. [*Semple,* it is deemed to be irrelevant.]" (Eng.) "It is the duty of all judges to take judicial notice of the accession and [*semble*] the sign manual of her Majesty and her successors." "A bequest to X and/or Y, where both survived, was held to create a joint tenancy; *semble,* if either predeceased, the survivor would take the whole."

Q. What is meant by repeal?

A. repeal = To rescind, to revoke.

Q. What is repudiate?

A. repudiate = The renunciation of a right, contract or obligation.

Q. What is meant by repugnant?

A. rupugnant = A cause or suit already decided.

Q. What is meant by retrospective legislation?

A. retrospective legislation = An act that applies to a period before the act was passed.

Q. What do you understand by the right of re-entry?

A. right of Re-entry = Right of land lord to take possession if tenant breaks the terms of tenancy.

Q. What is robbery?

A. robbery = crime of using force or causing fear of force in order to steal.

Q. What do you understand by sale?
A. sale = Transfer of ownership in exchange of price paid.

Q. What is meant by sedition?
A. sedition = The inducing of a girl or women to part with her virtue.

Q. What is meant by send back?
A. send back is occasionally used in place of *remand*, q.v., the more formal legal term, e.g., "This was clearly error and of such vital importance that the case must be reversed and *sent back* for a new trial." Cf. **return back.**

Q. How do we sensitise?
A. sensitise; sensitivise. Although Fowler championed the latter, the former is now usual in AmE and BrE.

Q. What is sensory?
A. sensory, sensatory, sensorial. *Sensory* = of sensation or the senses. *Sensatory* is a Needless Variant. *Sensorial* = primarily responsive to sensations. This word may also be a Needless Variant of *sensory*, however.

Q. Sensuous is an appeal to the senses. Explain.
A. sensuous, sensual. These words derive from the same root, meaning "appeal to the senses" but the precise meanings have undergone Differentiation. *Sensuous* = of or relating to the five senses, arousing any of the five senses. The word properly has no risqué connotations, though it is gravely distorted by hack novelists. *Sensual* = sexual, salacious, voluptuous (sensual desires). *This* is the word intended by the hack novelists who erroneously believe that *sensuous* carries sexy overtones.

Q. Sentences are imposed by judges and not by jury. Explain.
A. sentence. In most jurisdictions, criminal *sentences* are imposed by judges and not by juries, e.g., "The Supreme Court of Alabama agrees that the jury is not the sentencing authority in Alabama and has described the sentencing judge not as a reviewer of the jury's sentence but as *the* sentencer." *Baldwin v. Alabama*, 472 U.S. 372, 384 (1985).

Q. What are the sentence adverbs, give in detail?

A. sentence adverbs are adverbs conveying the speaker's comment on the statement being made rather than qualifying a single word in the sentence. A sentence adverb does not resolve itself into the form *in a-manner,* as most adverbs do. Therefore, in *Happily, the bill did not go beyond the committee,* the introductory adverb *happily* conveys the writer's opinion on the message he imparts. Similar adverbs are *fortunately, sadly, ironically, curiously, regrettably, strangely, oddly, interstingly, importantly, accordingly, consequently, admittedly* and *concededly.*

These and a few other words are the conventional sentence adverbs in *-ly.* Improvising sentence adverbs from traditional adverbs like *hopefully* (= in a hopeful manner) and *thankfully* (= in a thankful manner), qq.v., is objectionable to many stylists but this improvising trend seems to be on the rise, e.g., "Explanatorily [read *By way of explanation*], these consolidated causes were positioned as the ordinary and uncomplicated condemnation case." *O' Neil Corp. v. Perry Gas Transmission, Inc.,* 648 S.W. 2d 335, 341 (Tex. App.— Amarillo 1983). Newfangled sentence adverbs of this type are to be discouraged. In formal prose, even those like *hopefully* and *thankfully*, with a short, beleaguered history but increasingly common, should be eschewed.

Because sentence adverbs contain the writer's own thoughts and reveal his biases, lawyers often overuse them in argumentation; the danger here, lurks in words like *clearly, undoubtedly* and *indisputably.*

Q. Separate means to segregate. Explain.

A. separate means "to segregate" and in the legal phrase, *to separate the jury.* The word *OED* suggests that this usage of the word is "chiefly in Biblical language" and does not mention the legal usage.

Q. What is a sepulcher?

A. sepulcher, -re, sepulture. The preferred spelling of the first term is *sepulcher* in AmE and *-re* in BrE. The word means "burial place, tomb" and is pronounced ***sep***-el-ker. *Sepulture,* sometimes a Needless Variant of *sepulcher,* justifies its separate form in the sense burial. These words are very formal, even literary. They should be used cautiously.

Q. What is the meaning of sequential?

A. sequential, sequacious. *Sequential* means "forming a sequence or consequence." *Sequacious* means "intellectually servile."

Q. What is sequential order?

A. sequential order is a Redundancy, e.g., "The computer placed the checks *in sequential order* [read *in order* or *in sequence*] by account number."

Q. Who is meant by the word sequester?

A. sequester, sequestrate. *Sequestrate* means nothing that *sequester,* the more common term, does not also mean. Both terms are old: *sequester* dates from the fourteenth century, *sequestrate* from the early sixteenth century. In law, *sequester* = to remove (as property) from the possession of the owner temporarily, to seize and hold the effects of a debtor until the claims of creditors are satisfied (*OED*). The lay meaning of the term, of course, is "to set aside, separate," *as to sequester* (or *separate*) the jury.

Sequestrate is given two slightly different senses by the *OED,* in addition to the overlaping senses: (1) "to divert the income of an estate or benefice, temporarily or permanently, from its owner into other hands"; and (2) (in Scots law) "to place (lands belonging to a bankrupt or of disputed ownership) in the hands of a judicial factor or trustee for the prevention of waste." However, these two senses are rare and the advice here is to avoid *sequestrate* as a Needless Variant unless a nuance conveyed by one of these specialized senses is intended. The sole weakness of this advice is illustrated in the next entry—namely that the agent noun is *sequestrator* and not, ordinarily, *sequesterer.*

In the following examples, no such nuance was intended and *sequester* would have been the better word: "It is difficult to see why a plaintiff in any action for a personal judgement in tort or contract may not also apply to the chancellor for a so-called injunction *sequestrating* [read *sequestering*] his opponent's assets pending recovery and satisfaction of a judgement in such a law action." "The practice of *sequestrating* [read *sequestering*] the property of the defendant to coerce his obedience to the decree was soon developed."

Q. Who is a sequestor?

A. sequestrator = one who sequesters property, e.g., "The court appointed *sequestrators* to take possession of defendant's chattels."

Q. What is the meaning of the term sergenty?

A. sergeanty (or *serjeanty*) is the term for a form of feudal tenure under which, a specified personal service was rendered to the king. The spelling *sergeantry* is incorrect.

Dictionary of Legal Terms 179

Q. What is seriatim?

A. seriatim = in turn, serially, one after another, in sequence; successively. Though not uncommon, the word is a Latinism to be eschewed in favour of its anglicised siblings *serially* and *in series,* e.g., "After presenting the factual and procedural setting, we dispose of the issues *seriatim* [read *serially*]." "One court refused to sever the civil-right claims or to dismiss the state law ones, electing to submit all claims *serially* to the same jury."

Q. Explain series.

A. series is ordinarily used as a singular, though it serves as a plural where more than one series in intended. Here, the verb is incorrectly plural: "There *have* [read *has*] been a *series* of efforts made by the central P.L.O. but also splinter groups to move through Jordan into the West Bank."

Boswell quoted Samuel Johnson as using the now-obsolete plural *serieses* in a legal context: "Entails are good, because it is good to preserve in a country, *serieses* of men, to whom, people are accustomed to look up as leaders."

Q. What is meant by the term serve?

A. serve (= to make legal delivery of process or a writ) as a legal term dated back to the fifteenth century. In the legal idiom, one who serves process may either *serve* a writ *on* or *upon* another or *serve* another *with* a writ.

Q. Define the meaning of the word service.

A. service was once only a noun but since the late nineteenth century, it has been used as a transitive verb as well. It may mean "to provide service for" *(the mechanic serviced the copying machine),* "to pay interest on" (to service a debt), or generally "to perform services for." Ordinarily, the verb *to serve* ought to be used in broad senses; *service,* v.t., should be used only where the writer believes that *serve* would not be suitable in idiom or sense.

Q. What is servitude in law?

A. servitude. A. And *easement. Servitude* is primarily a civil-law term, deriving from L. *servitus* (= easement) and equivalent to the term *easement* in common law. But even in the common law, *servitude* has a restricted currency in referring to a servient tenement (i.e., land subject to an easement). Hence, the Differentiation usually observed in commonlaw countries is that *easement* refers to the personal enjoyment of the burdened property and *servitude* to the burdened property itself.

An extension of *servitude* in this sense is its acceptance in international law: "an international agreement impressing on a territory a permanent status, such as one demilitarising or neutralising a State or creating rights over water." (adapted fr. *OCL*).

B. And *slavery*. "[The] word *servitude* is of larger meaning than *slavery* as the latter is popularly understood in this country and the obvious purpose [of the thirteenth amendment] was to forbid all shades and conditions of African slavery." *Slaughter-house Cases,* 83 U.S. (16 Wall.) 36, 69 (1873). Both terms, in addition to denoting "the condition of being a slave or serf or of being the property of another person," carry the notion of subjection to excessive labour.

Q. What is meant by setting aside?

A. setting aside = cancelling, making valid.

Q. Give the meaning of set-off.

A. set-off, n., is older than *offset* and is considered to be more correct by purists, e.g., "That payment had been made only in respect of the plaintiff's claim and not in respect of the claim less the equitable *set-off*." (Aus.) The *OCL* includes *set-off*, which is usual in BrE but not offset.

Q. What are set of facts?

A. set of facts is more elegant, dignified and descriptive than either *factual situation* or *fact situation.*, q.v.

Q. What is meant by set over?

A. set over = to alienate, convey, e.g., "Vendor does—by these presents—grant, bargain, sell, assign, convey, transfer, *set over* and deliver to the purchaser, the following described property."

Q. What are set phrases?

A. Set phrases. Fossilised language should not be consciously de-fossilised— that is to say that one should not try to vary what has been set in stone. Thus *set in stone* should never become *set in shale* or whatever variation one might lamely invent. One should not change *madding crowd* to *maddening crowd,* for instance. Cf. Intelligent Variation. Set phrases are sometimes, changed out of a sense of cleverness and sometimes, out of ignorance. A maladroit example appears in the following sentence: "Time is the essence of this subcontract." [Read *Time is of the essence in this subcontract.*] Indeed, so well entrenched in the language are many expressions that the slightest change will make them non-English, e.g., we have the phrase *out from under,* ruined by a metamorphosis in this sentence: "Plaintiff was injured when the back of the teller stool on which, she was sitting, fell off and the chair rolled *out from underneath her* [read *out from under her*]."

Follett called set phrases 'inviolable' (if not quite inviolate): "the attempt to liven up old cliches by inserting modifiers into the set phrase is a mistake: the distended phrase is neither original, nor unobtrusive, nor bried and sometimes, it has ceased to be immediately clear, as in *They have been reticent to a tactical fault.*" *Modern American Usage* 303 (1966). In addition to the fault of inserting modifiers into set phrases, three other faults commonly occur. Firstly, it is wrong to wrench a set phrase into ungrammatical contexts, as here: "This was reported to *we the people.*" The phrase *we the people,* of course, derives from the U.S. Constitution but the sentence calls for the objective *us.* Secondly, it is a bad style to substitute an alien word for the familiar one in a well-known phrase, e.g., changing in *large part or in large measure* to *in large degree* does not work: "The prejudice to appellant is attributable *in large degree* [read *in large part*] to appellant's own conduct." Thirdly, it is poor to aim at novelty by reversing the usual order of a phrase: "Many persons must rely upon Medicaid for their well-being and health." (The standard phrase is *health and well-being.*)

Q. Is settler the creator of a trust?

A. settler, -or. The two forms usually convey different senses. *Settler* = (1) one who settles; or (2) a homesteader. *Settlor* = the creator of a trust, a party to an instrument. *Settlor* has also been used, however as the one who settles a case: "The *settlors* [read *settlers*] have agreed between themselves that the worker shall retain the face value of the settlement and that the third party shall be responsible for satisfaction of the compensation lien."

Q. What is meant by settlor?

A. settlor, trustor, donor, creator. These four terms are used to name the person who establishes a trust. The first is the commonest. It should be spelled with the -or suffix to differentiate it from the quite different word *settler.*

Q. What is meant by several in legal terms?

A. several for *separate* is an Archaism of Shakespearean vintage that has survived only in the legal language. The usage survives primarily in the phrase *joint and several liability* but thrives in other contexts as well: "It was early established that the inheriting daughters did not hold as joint tenants; they were not subject to procedural rules, which governed joint tenancy and each had a *several* interest." "The share of each tenant in common is, unlike that of joint tenant, *several* and distinct from the shares of his contenants." "The constitutional rule requiring bills to be read on three *several* days in each house is hereby suspended." "The dispute does not cease to be a priori because it is a matter of the cumulative effect of *severally* inconclusive premises." (Eng.)

Q. What is the meaning of the legal phrase severalty?

A. severalty = the condition of being separate or distinct. The legal phrase *in severalty* is used in law in reference to land and means "held in a person's own right without being joined in interest with another" (*OED*), e.g., "The whole transaction required the cooperation of all for its success; the division of the shares among them was as much a part of it as any other; they selected each other as owners in severalty; and they should be held liable for any defaults of those whom they chose, though their liability is secondary."

Q. What is sexual?

A. sex, adj., **sexual.** Both *sex discrimination* and *sexual discrimination* appear in law reports. The former is perhaps better, inasmuch as *sexual* has come to refer more to sexual intercourse and things pertaining to it than to gender.

Q. What is meant by sine-die?

A. sine-die = Indefinitely.

Q. What is slander?

A. slander = Defamatory words spoken of another.

Q. What is sovereignty?

A. sovereignty = Apex authority or higher authority, Indian possess the sovereignty.

Q. What is speaking order?

A. speaking order = An order which contains matters which is explanatory or illustrative of the direction which is given by it.

Q. What do you understand by specific performance?

A. specific performance = The performance of a contract exactly or substantially according to its terms.

Q. What is stare decisis?

A. stare decisis = The principal that decisions of courts in previous cases must be followed in subsequent cases of similar nature.

Q. What is status quo?
A. status quo = The existing state of things.

Q. What is meant by statute?
A. statute = An act of parliament.

Q. What is subpoena?
A. sub poena = An order of a court to a person to appear and give evidence before it.

Q. What do you understand by substantive law?
A. substantive law = That part of a law which creates and defines right.

Q. What is a suit?
A. A process instituted in a court of justice for recovery of protection of a right.

Q. What do you understand by summary proceedings?
A. summary proceeding = A proceeding without following the strict rules of procedure for trials.

Q. What do you understand by summons?
A. summon = An order by which a person is called to appear before a court, judicial officer etc.

Q. What is surety?
A. surety = the person who gives the guarantee?

Q. What is meant by surrogate mother?
A. surrogate mother = A women who carries a child pursuance of an arrangement made before she began to carry the child and with a view to any child carried is pursuance of it being handed over to and the parental rights being exercised by another person to person.

Q. Differentiate between systemic and systematic.
A. systemic, systematic. *Systemic* should be *systematic* unless the reference is systems of the body, as in *systemic* disorders, e.g., "The plaintiffs alleged *systemic* [read *systematic*] disparate treatment of minority groups." "The complaint alleged across—the board *systemic* [read *systematic*] discrimination against black employees."

———❖❖❖———

Q. What is a taboo?

A. taboo, tabu. The former spelling is standard. For the verb *to taboo* (= to exclude or prohibit by authority or social influence [*COD*]), the preterite and past participle is *tabooed* rather than *taboo'd*, e.g., "A copyrighted work is not *tabooed* to subsequent workers in the same field."

Q. What is the meaning of tactile?

A. tactile, tactual. The latter has become merely a Needless Variant. *Tactile* is the usual word, meaning either "of or relating to touch" or "touchable; tangible."

Q. What is a tail?

A. tail, in the legal sense denoting a type of limited freehold estate, is a Law French term, deriving ultimately from the Old French verb *taillier* "to cut, shape, hence to fix the precise form of, to limit." Formerly, it was spelled *taille*. It commonly appears in the phrase *in tail*, e.g., "It has been repeatedly determined that if there be tenant for life, remainder to his first son *in tail*, remainder over and he is brought before the court before he has issue, the contingent remaindermen are barred." Sometimes, the word is used without *in*, as in the phrases *fee tail*, q.v. and *estate-tail*, as here: "Under the first rule, if A devises his lands to B and B's children or issue and B has not any issue at the time of the devise, the same is an *estate-tail*."

Tail may be a noun taking Positive Adjectives (*tail female, tail special*) or may itself be a postpositive adjective (*fee tail*).

Q. Give the meaning of take.

A. take (= to receive by inheritance) is peculiar to the legal idiom, e.g., "The will itself indicates the proportions according to which, the beneficiaries shall *take*."

Q. What is meant by taking exception?

A. take exception. This phrase means "to object" in general lay contexts but is used in legal writing in the sense "to posit an error on appeal," e.g., "The defendants *took* five *exceptions;* the questions raised by *exceptions* as we have shown are four."

Q. What is taken?

A. taken. Appeals to higher courts are said, in the legal idiom, to be *taken*, e.g., "We do not discuss various objections to the plan of merger filed after this *appeal* was *taken.*"

Q. Explain taken back. What is take nothing judgement?

A. take-nothing judgement (= a judgement for the defendant providing that the plaintiff recover nothing) should be hyphenated thus.

Q. Who is a taker?

A. taker = one who receives property by inheritance, e.g., "With respect to real estate, such a gift over, in the event of the indefinite failure of the issue of the *first taker*, was construed to cut down and limit the interest of the *first taker* to an estate tail." "The fact that the trust agreement reserved a power of appointment is an evidence that the settlor believed she had created an interest in the property on the part of others and reserved the power in order to defeat that interest or to postpone until a later date, the naming of specific *takers.*"

Q. Who is a talesman?

A. talesman, tales-juror. The usual form has been *talesman, tales-juror* being a variant. Both terms are coming to be Archaisms, as methods of selecting veniremen become more sophisticated, e.g., "While it is still proper in some places to select additional jurors from bystanders, the modern practice to supply a deficiency in the jury panel is a drawing from the jury wheel or box and the issuance of a special venire, the object of which, is to get a body of men less liable to causes of challenge than would be *tales-jurors* picked up in the courtroom."

Q. What is a talisman?

A. talisman (= a charm, amulet or other thing supposed to be capable of working wonders), a favorite word of judges, is not to be confused with *talesman*, q.v., e.g., "The law has outgrown its primitive stage of formation when the precise word was the sovereign *talisman*, and every slip was fatal." (Cardozo) "Freedom of choice is not a sacred talisman; it is only a means to a constitutionally required end—the abolition of the system of segregation and its effects." The plural form is *talismans*, not *talismen*.

The adjective is *talismanic*, e.g., "Ritual and *talismanic* recitations of boilerplate affidavits are a thing of the past." "Libel law can claim no *talismanic* immunity from constitutional limitations and must be measured by standards that satisfy the First Amendment."

Q. What is talk to and talk with?

A. talk to, talk with. The former suggests a conversation in which, the remarks strongly preponderate from one side, as between a superior and an inferior. The latter suggests a conversation between equals with equal participation.

Q. Give the meaning of Tantalize.

A. tantalise (= to torment or test [a person] by sight or promise of a desired thing withheld or kept just out of reach [*COD*]) is not infrequently confused with *titillate* (= to excite plesantly or tickel)

The verb *tantalise* has been derived from the Greek myth about Tantalus, the king of Sipylos, born out of the union of Zeus and the nymph Pluto. Tantalus offended the gods by stealing some of their food and giving it to mortals. Because the father of Tantalus was divine, Tantalus was himself immortal (though not a god) and thus could not be executed for his crime. Instead, as an eternal punishment, he was placed in a pool of fresh water up to his chin while overhead boughs of edible fruit hung temptingly near. Whenever he dipped to drink, the water receded; whenever he stretched to eat, a wind blew the laden boughs out of reach.

Q. What is the meaning of tantamount?

A. tantamount used as a verb is incorrect; it is an adjective only, meaning "equivalent." This lapse is probably rare: "The legal effect of the judgement in the class action *tantamounts* [read *is tantamount*], we think, to removing Humphery from the representative class."

Q. Give the meaning of tautologous?

A. tautologous, tautological. The latter, though older, has become a Needless Variant of the former, e.g., "It is not enough to say that the legislature sought to prefer one class of litigants over another and succeeded in doing so, for that is a mere *tautological* [read *tautologous*] recognition of the fact that the legislature did what it intended to do."

Q. What is tautology?

A. tautology. "What's the first excellence in a lawyer? Tautology. What is the second? Tautology. What is the third? Tautology." R. Steele, *The Funeral I* (1701). It is wroth pointing out, lest the irony escape those who have used this book at all and still are fond of Legalese that the words quoted are derisive not serious. Yet tautologies continue to proliferate; "Wide public participation in rulemakng *obviates* the problem of *singling out a single defendant* among a group of competitors for intial imposition of a new and inevitably costly legal obligation."

Dictionary of Legal Terms 187

Q. What is taxable?

A. taxable = (1) subject to taxation (taxable income); or (2) (of legal costs or (fees) assessable (taxable expenses). Sense (2) has been illustrated in this sentence: "Expert-witness fees are not *taxable* as costs of court."

Q. What is a tear gas?

A. tear gas, n.;, **teargas,** v.t. This term is spelled as two words for the noun and as one for the verb.

Q. What is technical?

A. technical, technological. The distinction is sometimes a fine one. *Technical* = of or in a particular science, art or handicraft; of or in vocational training. *Technological* = pertaining to the science of practical or industrial sciences. *Technological* connotes recent experimental methods and development whereas *technical* has no such connotation.

Q. What is meant by telephonic?

A. telephonic is a highfalutin adjectival form of *telephone,* which ordinarily serves as its own adjective. "*Ross* makes no reference to *telephonic warrants* nor have any cases been found following *Ross* that involve *telephinic* warrants [read, in both instances, *warrants issued over the telephone*]." "On request, the clerk will notify counsel who desire immediate collect *telephinic* notification when the decision is rendered." [Read *The clerk will call counsel collect, if they so desire, when the decision is rendered.*]

Q. Give the meaning of tell.

A. tell for *say. Tell* is a transitive verb that demands an indirect as well as a direct object, e.g., "One of the industry's major producers *told* [read *said*] recently that a large studio receives 20,000 stories or ideas per year of which, but twenty are made into motion pictures."

Q. What is temperature?

A. temperature is pronounced ***tem**-pe-ra-chur,* not |***tem**-pe-ra-tyur*|, which is precious or ***tem**-pa-chur,* which is slovenly. A combination of the precious and the slovenly, ***tem**-pa-tyur* is humorously affected.

Q. What is temporal?

A. temporal = (1) of relating to time, (2) worldly, (3) nonecclesiastical, (4) transitory, (5) pertaining to the temple (part of one's head), or (6) pertaining to bones in the vertebrae. In other words, this is a classic Chameleon-hued Word. Usually, *temporal* refers to time (sense 1) in legal writing, e.g.: "Although not *temporally* clear from the record, it appears that while the attorneys and the trial judge were in chambers, the court coordinator and the bailiff conducted a shuffle of the panel."

Temporal was a favorite word of Justice Holmes who used it in the special legal sense, a variation on sense (3) given above, "civil or common as opposed to criminal or ecclesiastical" e.g., "In numberless instances, the law warrants the intentional infliction of *temporal* damage because it regards it as justified." (Holmes, J.) "Actions of tort are brought for *temporal* damage; the law recognises *temporal* damage as an evil, which its object is to prevent or to address." (Holmes, J.) "The *temporal* rights of the complainant were prejudiced."

Sense (2) is also common: 'The reason behind the exception is a simple one of human relationship, implicit in the principle that human laws and other *temporal* things, are for the living."

Q. What is a temporal limit?

A. temporal limit is unidiomatic and stuffy in place of *time limit*, which is well-established, e.g., "The Supreme Court has yet to decide how long an auto search may be delayed before a warrant must be obtained or indeed whether there is a *temporal limit* [read *time limit*]."

Q. Give the meaning of temporise.

A. temporise has three important senses: (1) "to act so as to gain time" (defendant temporized by filling dilatory pleas); (2) "to comply with the requirements of the occasion" (Politicians are adept at temporising); and (3) to negotiate or discuss terms of a compromise" (defendant attempted to temporize with plaintiff rather than go for a top trial).

Q. What is tenancy? Explain its various forms in detail.

A. tenancy, tenantship, tenantry. The first one is, of course, the usual term, meaning: (1) "a holding or possession of lands or tenements, by any title of ownership"; (2) "occupancy of lands or tenements under a lease"; or (3) "that which is held by a tenant." *Tenantship* is a Needless Variant. To the extent that *tenantry* overlaps with any of the senses outlined above, it too is a Needless Variant; yet *tenantry* may stand on its own in the senses: (1) "property leased to tenants" (*i.e.*, from the point of view of the lessor) (his tenantry, an apartment complex, proved to be a sound investment); and (2) "the body of tenants" (the tenantry is dissatisfied with the proposed improvement).

tenancy by the entireties, -ty. The plural is slightly more common in both the U.S. and G.B., though *Black's* (4th ed.) contains its definiton under *tenancy by the entirety*, which is also widespread, e.g., "But a conveyance by one *tenant by the entirety* does not defeat the survivorship rights of the other."

tenancy per la verge, tenancy by the verge, tenancy by the rod. These equivalent phrases denote "a copyhold." The first is Law French, the second seomwhat anglicised Law French, and the third an anglicised Loan Translation of the first phrase. The terms are little used but in historical contexts (the rod having been delivered for purposes of conveying seisin). Any of the phrases would require explanation by the user.

tenant at sufferance; tenant by sufferance. The former is the traditional idiomatic phrase.

Q. What is meant by tenant?

A. tenant = One who hold lands by any kind of title, whether for years, for life.

Q. Explain the meaning of tendentious.

A. tendentious means 'biased (usually in favour of something), prejudiced." Its meaning is often misapprehended, as in this specimen, in which, the writer apparently thought the world means 'frivolous:' "Even though Texas did not move to dismiss the appeal as frivolous, the fact is that it patently has not merit. The removal petition does not even colorably fall within the strict tests set out in *Johnson.* We believe the appellant had ample reason to know that his appeal lacked merit and that it was *merely tendentious.*" The phrase *merely tendentious* gives away the writer's ignorance of the meaning of the word *tendentious.* *Tendencious* is a variant spelling to be eschewed.

Q. What is tendinitis?

A. tendinitis, tendonitis. *Tendinitis* = inflamation of a tendon. *Tendonitis* is incorreclty arrived at by association with the spelling of the noun *tendon.*

Q. What is a tenement?

A. tenement (= [in law] an estate in land) usually denotes in lay contexts "a building or house."

Q. Explain the term tenurial.

A. tenurial is the adjective corresponding to *tenure;* it is almost exclusively a legal term, e.g., "The importance of a lease to such a tenant today is not to create a *tenurial* relationship but to arrange for a habitable dwelling."

Q. What is meant by the word term?

A. term, n. (= a limit in space or duration), has the special legal senses "an estate or interest in hand for a certain period" (terms of years) and as a plural (*terms*), "conditions or stipulations limiting what is proposed to be granted or done" (*OED*).

Q. What is terminus?

A. terminus, terminal, n. *Terminus* = the city at the end of a railroad or a bus line. Pl. *termini. Terminal* = the station of a transportation line.

Q. What is terminus a quo?

A. terminus a quo, terminus ad quem. The former means "departure point"; the latter, "destination." Figuratively, the words are used at the beginning and ending points of an argument. Both figuratively and literally, the phrases are pomposities.

Q. What is meant by term of years?

A. term of years, term for years. The *CDL* contains its entry under *term of years* (BrE), whereas *W2* and *Black's* list *term for years* (AmE).

Q. What is termor?

A. termor = one who holds lands or tenements for a term of years or for life (*OED*). Generally, however, the word is not used of those with life estates, e.g., "But when today, we speak of someone taking on "a new lease on life," we do not think of him as a *termor*."

Q. Explain terms.

A. terms has increasingly been used as an elliptical form of *terms of the contract* or *terms of payment*.

Q. Who is a terre-tenant?

A. terre-tenant, tertenant. The latter, a Middle English anglicised version of the former, a Law French term, has never displaced the older term. In the *OED*'s only listed sense, "one who has the actual possession of land; the occupant of land," the word hardly seems justified. But *W3* adds the following definition, probably purely AmE: "one other than a judgement debtor owning an interest in the debtor's land after the lien of the judgement creditor attached thereto," a sense that *Black's* (4th ed.) limits to Pennsylvania. *Terre-tenant* should not be used unless the writer understands and makes clear the precise sense in which, he uses it and has a reason for doing so.

Q. What is a territory?

A. territory, dependency, commonwealth. The distinctions in AmE usage are as follows. A *territory* = a part of the U.S. not included within any state but organised with a separate legislature (*W9*). Guam and the U.S. Virgin Islands are *territories* of the United States; Alaska and Hawaii were formerly *territories*. *Dependency* = a land or territory geographically distinct from the country governing it but belonging to it and governed by its laws. The Phillippines was once a *dependency* of the U.S. *Commonwealth* = a political unit having local autonomy but voluntarily united with the U.S. Puerto Rico and the Northern Mariana Islands are *commonwealth*. Puerto Rico is sometimes referred to as a *dependency* but its proper designation is *commonwealth*.

Q. What is tertius gaudens?

A. tertius gaudens = a third party, who profits when two others have a dispute. Literally, the term means "a rejoicing third." It is good to have a word for this concept, which is not uncommon in law, but it is unfortunate that the word is so abstruse.

testacy, intestacy. *Testacy* = the condition of leaving a valid will at death. *Intestacy* is its antonym.

Q. What is meant by testae?

A. testae = Dying after having made a will.

Q. What is testament?

A. testament is not, as is sometimes supposed, obsolete outside the phrase *last will and testament,* q.v. In legal prose, it is still sometimes contrasted with *devise,* for in the legal idiom *testament* has come generally to signify a will disposing of personal property, whereas *devise* is traditionally, the word for a will disposing of land, e.g., "The Wills Acts of 1837 eliminated subtantive distinctions between devises and *testaments.*"

Usually, however, the word is used not for reasons of fastidiousness but for less good reasons. Here, it is an archaic pomposity to which, *will* is preferred: "A valid *testament* [read *will*] includes two essential elements: there must be a sufficient designation of the beneficiary and of the property given to him." "In *In re Bluestein's Will,* both the language of the *testament* [read *will*] and the attendant circumstances were said to support the conclusion that, in context, the testator's 'request' bespoke a direction, imposing an obligation upon the legatee."

Q. What is testamentary?

A. testamentary. A. And *testorial*. The latter, a Needless Variant without foundation, does not appear in the *OED, W3* or *Black's*. But it has occurred in American legal writing: "[I]t is enough if the circumstances, taken together, leave no doubt as to the *testorial* [read *testamentary*] intention and in some cases, it is said that the implication may be drawn from a slight circumstance appearing in the will." 57 Am. Jur. *Wills* § 1192 (1948).

Testamentary (= of or relating to a will) is not ordinarily confined to contexts involving testaments of personal property (as opposed to devises of real property), e.g., "It is everywhere recognised that the purpose of the law of will to give effect to the last valid *testamentary* act of the testator." "This court points out that man's last will may consist of several *testamentary* papers of different dates and that it is not indispensable that they should be probated at the same time." *Testamental*, a variant of *testamentary*, is not used in legal contexts.

B. For *testimonial*. Surprisingly, this error has appeared in reported opinions: "Appellee filed a motion to remand the contractual indemnity claim to allow procurement of documentary and *testamentary* [read *testimonial*] evidences." Here the distinction has been made clear: "Lay witnesses, before they express a *testimonial* opinion as to *testamentary* capacity must first testify to facts inconsistent with sanity." *In re Powers's Estate*, 134 N.W.2d 148 161 (Mich. 1965).

Q. What is a testate person?

A. testate (= a testate person), though corresponding in form to *intestate*, n., is generally, a Needless Variant of *testator*. *Testatus* is the civil-law term.

Q. What is a testation?

A. testation = the disposal of property by will (power of testation), e.g., "The loss of chartible trusts such as Baconsfied is part of the price we pay for permitting deceased persons to exercise a continuing control over assets owned by them at death; this aspect of freedom of *testation*, like most things, has its advantages and disadvantages."

Q. Who is testator?

A. testator, devisor. He who makes will. Because *testament* historically came to be more or less confined to dispositions of personal property and *devise* to those of real property, it has been thought the *testator* was at one time confined to a person who left personal, as opposed to real, property. See, e.g., M.S. Freeman, *A Treasury for Word Lovers* 173 (1983). "No such crabbed meaning ever attached to the word, however," Blackstone wrote, in 1766, "that all devises of lands and tenements shall not only be in writing, but signed by the *testator*." (quoted in *OED*).

Q. Teste is the date of insuance. Explain.

A. teste is the name in Drafting of the clause that states the name of a witness and evidences the act of witnessing, e.g., "Judgements did not bind chattels but at early common law, a writ of *fieri facias* bound chattels from the date of the *teste*, i.e., the date of the issuance, thereby invalidating all subsequent alienations." In older instruments, *teste* was used in much the same way as some legal writers use *witnesseth*, q.v., today. Cf. **testimonium.**

Q. What is testimony?

A. testimony = statement made by witness under oath.

Q. What is tort?

A. tort = A civil wrong which is not exclusively the breach of contract or the breach of trust.

Q. What is meant by tort feasor?

A. tort feasor = one who commits or is guilty of a tort.

Q. What is meant by trade mark?

A. tort = A mark used by a manufactures or traders to distinguish his goods from the goods for other.

Q. What is trespass?

A. trespass = To pass beyond.

Q. What is meant by trial?

A. trial = It means any hearing before the court at which evidence is taken.

Q. What is uberrimae fides?

A. uberrimae fides = Abundant faith, mutual good faith between persons in a particular relationship, for ex. physician and patient, guardian and ward, attorney and client.

Q. What is ultima ratio?

A. ultima ratio = the final argument, a last resort (often a force).

Q. What is the ultimate destination?

A. ultimate destination is not necessarily a Redundancy, as is often assumed. Where a shipment has a series of stops or transfers—*i.e.*, a series of "immediate destinations,"—it may be appropriate to use the phrase *final* or *ultimate destination*. One may be on one's way to Bangkok, with a stopover in Tokyo. If, on that flight to Tokyo someone asks about one's destination, it would not be inappropriate to characterise Tokyo as the *immediate destination* (i.e., the destination of that particular flight) and Bangkok as the *ultimate destination* (the destination of the entire trip).

Yet the phrase *final destination* or *ultimate destination* should not be used (as it commonly is) in contexts in which, such specificity is not called for. Cf. **final wrap-up.**

Q. What is ultimately?

A. ultimately = (1) in the end (she ultimately reached her destination) or (2) at the beginning (the two doctrines are ultimately related).

Q. What is meant by ultra?

A ultra (= [1] beyond due limit; extreme or [2] extremist; fanatical), when used for *beyond*, is erroneous, e.g., "Exemplary damages are therefore damages *ultra* [read *beyond*] compensation."

Q. What is ultra vires?

A. ultra vires = unauthorised, beyond one's power. The word is classically used as an adverb, as here: "Petitioner maintains that the commission acted *ultra vires* when it applied its new interpretation of its suspension powers to him."

Q. What is meant by unavailing?

A. unavailing = of no avail, e.g., "If Johnson lacks sufficient assets, reversing the district court of this issue as a part of this judgement would be *unavailing*."

Q. Explain the term *unbeknown*.

A. unbeknown(st). Krapp suggested that both forms are humorous, colloquial and dialectal. G.P. Krapp, *A Comprehensive Guide to Good English* 602 (1927). The *COD* likewise suggests that both are colloquial. Eric Partridge and John Simon have written—in conformity with the *OED*—that *unbeknown* is the preferred form in the phrase *unbeknown to* and that *unbeknownst* is dialectal.

These inconsistent pronouncements serve as confusing guides. We can perhaps accept (as British orthodoxy) the pronouncement of the *COD* that in BrE, the forms are colloquial (for *unknown*). In AmE, neither can really be called dialectal or colloquial, for the word is essentially literary. In current AmE usage, *unbeknownst* far outranges *unbeknown* in frequency of usage, and it must therefore, be considered at least acceptable. We have always preferred *unbeknown*, however, for the *-st* forms (e.g. *whilst, amidst*) uniformly come less naturally to AmE. The following are some examples of typical usage: "*Unbeknown* to appellant, appellee. Horn sent a plane ticket to her son." "The court upheld the admissibility of a statement given by a defendant in the absence of counsel after his lawyer, *unbeknownst* [read *unbeknown*] to the defendant, had called the police station." "The fact that, *unbeknownst* [read *unbeknown*] to Towers and Parks, undercover government involvement made any actual export impossible does not alter the jury's finding." *Unknown*, q.v., would be equally good, if not better, in the sentences quoted.

Q. Who is *unconscionable?*

A. unconscionable = (1) (of persons) having no conscience or (2) (of actions) showing no regard for conscience, not in accordance with what is right or reasonable. Lawyers use the word a great deal, often without fastidiously observing its meaning.

Q. What is *uncovered?*

A. uncovered is inherently ambiguous; it may mean (1) "not covered," or (2) "having had the cover removed."

Q. What is *unctious?*

A. unctious is not an uncommon misspelling of *unctuous*.

Q. What is *underhand?*

A. underhand(ed). The shorter form is much older, e.g., "And what shall we say to the *underhand* manner in which the incompetence of the worker and hence, his lack of right to a share of the world's goods, are suggested in these verses." "Pettifogger" was also shortened as the sixteenth-century 'fogger,' applied mostly to lawyers but also to others given to *underhand* practice for gain." *Underhanded* is also perfectly acceptable, however.

Q. Explain the term, under my signature.
A. under my signature. This expression should not be taken too literally. It means "under my authorisation" and has nothing to do with the physical placement of one's signature.

Q. Who is called undersigned?
A. undersigned is little used outside of legal contexts. Usually, it is an attributive noun (the undersigned agrees to forbear from execution).

Q. What are understood words?
A. understood words are common in English and usually are not very troublesome if we are able to mentally supply them. Often, they occur at the outset of sentences. *More important* is short for *What is more important; as pointed out earlier* is an ellipsis of *as was pointed out earlier.* Objects, too, are often elided with the understanding that the reader will know and will mentally supply the missing term, e.g., "Not mentioned was the fact that the standard auto liability also obligates the insurer to *defend.*" (After *defend,* the object *suit* is understood.) On verbs supposedly 'understood' whose absence detracts from clarity.

Q. What is under submission in the court of law?
A. under submission = being considered by the court, under advisement, e.g., "*Norton v. National Bank of Commerce* remained *under submission* for nine months."

Q. What is meant by under law?
A. under law, in law, at law, by law. These idioms have long been common in Anglo-American legal writing.

Certain verbose phrases recur in statutes, e.g.:

Verbose Expression	Kernel Expression
at the time of his death	when he dies
have need of	need
have knowledge of	know
give consideration to	consider
give recognition to	recognise
make an application	apply
make payment	pay
make provision for	provide for

Judicial writing is also a sanctuary for verbosity. The following are some typical specimens, with recommended ways of Cutting Out The Chaff: "He contends that while assisting in hooking cables to the cover of said barge, while assisting in the offloading of it, he was injured when the cover of said barge was moved, causing him to sustain a downward fall." [This sentence appears to have been dictated and unedited. Read *While offloading the barge and, in particuler, assisting in hooking cables to its cover, he fell when the cover was moved.*] "Upon *the filing of the petition* [read *Upon filing the petition*], appellant was appointed special guardian and attorney for all persons known or unknown who had any interest in the income of the common trust fund." "The court should not attempt to enforce any variation of the relations between insured and insurer while the insurance contract is *in process of performance* [read *being performed, in effect,* or *under way*]." "With the benefit of *hindsight and its unerring superb visual acquity,* one might suggest that the trial strategy chosen by Austin's appointed counsel left much to be desired." (Omit that desultory amplification of hindsight, the qualities of which, people know well enough.) "The testator devised "all my real estate now had by me wheresoever the same may be located" to his four sons." [Read *The testator devised all his real estate to his four sons.*] "A *venture,* to constitute a joint *adventure,* must be for *profit in a financial or commercial sense* [read *financial profit*]." "The existing partners and incoming partners desire by this amendatory agreement to admit the incoming partners as partners in the partnership." (This bit of verbosity needs no comment.)

Q. What is unicameral legislat?
A. unicameral legislat = A legislature consisting only one house. For ex. state like Bihar, U.P., Maharashtra, J & K, Karnataka has bi-cameral legislative and other remaining state consists of uni-cameral legislative.

Q. What is Unilateral?
A. unilateral = one sided.

Q. What is unilateral contract?
A. unilateral contract = When the party to whom an angagement is made, makes no express agreement on his part, the contract is called unilateral contract, binding only one party.

Q. What is meant by Uterine blood?
A. uterine blood. To persons are said to be uterine blood when they are descended from a common ancestral but by diffirent husband.

———◇◇◇———

Q. What is meant by vacantia bona?

A. vacantia bona = Goods unclaimed or without an owner.

Q. What is meant by verbiage?

A. verbiage was formerly unerringly pejorative. It referred to prolific language and redundancies. More recently, it has come to signify, esp. to American lawyers, "wording, diction," in a neutral sense. Perhaps, it is neutral because lawyers have become inured to their prolixities and inelegancies: "Mr. Smithson was preparing the *verbiage* for the agreement." Strictly, the word should maintain the negative connotations it has always had; *verbiage* describes a vice of lnguage. Note that in the sentence just quoted, the writer might have Cut Out The Chaff by writing: "Mr. Smithson was preparing the agreement." A somewhat different error has been illustrated in this specimen: "It is well settled that the exact *verbiage* [read *wording*] of the statute need not be alleged in an indictment when there is no material difference between the language of the *statute* and the allegations employed."

Verbage, for *verbiage,* is a common error.

Q. What is verbosity?

A. verbosity. Samuel Johnson once said, "It is unjust, sir, to censure lawyers for multiplying words when they argue; it is often necessary for them to multiply words." (quoted in *Boswell's Life of Johnson* (1781)). Perhaps it is so. But lawyers must at least attempt to distinguish between those occasions when it is necessary and those when it is not.

For example, verbosity is virtually never appropriate (much less necessary) in statutes. Yet, it is especially common in Statute Drafting. The following statute says nothing more than that the industrial commission is to lay down rules to ensure safety in the handling of liquefied petroleum gases:

"The industrial commission shall ascertain, fix, and order such reasonable standards, rules or regulitons for the design, construction, location, installation, operation, repair and maintenance of equipment for storage, handling, use and transportation by tank, truck or tank-trailer, of liquefied petroleum gases for fuel purposes and for the odorisation of the said gases used therewith, as shall render such equipment safe."

Q. What are verb phrases?

A. verb phrases, incomplete or the Problem of Non-transferable Auxiliaries. This problem plagues a great deal of legal writing, primarily because lwyers frequently attempt to express themselves alternatively, or with elaboration, e.g., "They were not liable at law for the continued suffering of the man who fell among thieves, *which they night, and morally ought to have, prevented* [read *which they might have, and morally ought to have, prevented*]."/ "But many of these holdings *have or will be overruled* [read *have been, or will be, overruled*]."/ "Plaintiff claims that he *has and will continue to receive* [read *has received and will continue to receive*] fewer benefits from the trust than he should."

Q. What is a legal verdict?

A. verdict. A. Juries, not judges, hand down verdicts (both civil and criminal). Strictly, verdicts are *returned* by juries, though we have the lay colloquialisms *to pass a verdict on* and *to give a vedict on.* Cf. **sentence.**

B. *Verdict* for *vote*. The jury collectively renders a *verdict;* individual jurors tender *votes,* not *verdicts,* e.g., "A prejudice against the defense of insanity will not qualify one from sitting as juror where the nature of the prejudice is such that the court is satisfied that it will not influence the juror's *verdict* [read *vote*]."

Voir dire, q.v., is etymologically equivalent to *verdict,* having passed into English through French. *Verdict* came through Anglo-Norman (*verdict*) but was refashioned after the medieval Latin *verdictum,* itself based on the Anglo-Norman *verdit.*

Q. What is meant by versus?

A. versus = Against a prefix symbol of opposite part written as (vs) or (v) e.g. Golaknath vs. Union of India or Golaknath V. Union of India.

Q. What are the various uses of the word very?

A. very. A. As a **Weasel Word**. Often, this intensive actually has the effect of weakening a statement rather than strengthening it, e.g., "We are *very* reluctant to substitute our views on damages for those of the jury." Here, the word *very* weakens the adjective that follows. Indeed, *very* has been used irresponsibly for so long that its actual effect is often just the opposite of its intended effect. A simple statement is usually more forceful.

B. *Very disappointed,* etc. *Very* modifies adjectives (*sorry, sick,* etc.) and not properly past participle (*disappointed, uninterested,* etc.). Follett wrote that "finer ears are offended by past participles modified by *very* without the intervention of the quantitative *much,* which respects the verbal sense of an action undergone. Such writers require *very much disappointed, very much pleased, very much engrossed very well satisfied* etc. Only a few adjectives from verbs—*tired, drunk* and possibly *depressed*—have shed enough of their verbal quality to stand an immediately proceding *very."* W. Follett, *Modern American Usage* 343 (1966). *Very interested* is another acceptable idiom, though *very much interested* seems preferable in formal contexts. When a past participle has become thoroughly established as an adjective (e.g., *drunk*). it takes *very* rather than *very much.*

Q. The term vest is used in a number of legal and lay idioms. Explain.

A. vest, v.t. & v.i., is used in a number of legal and lay idioms, particulrly *to vest in* and *to vest with,* e.g., "The parties' clear and unambiguous expressions of consent were required to *vest* a United States Magistrate *with* plenary civil jurisdiction." At common law, in the ceremony known as investiture, the lord handed over to his vassal some object representing the land: "The vassal was thus *vested with* the fief and the fief was *vested in* him: from these terms developed the modern meanings of *to vest,* as first, to place or secure something in the possession of a person; secondly, to place or establish a person in possession or occupation of something; and, thirdly, to pass into possession—the senses, in other words, which are represented in the current idioms *vest in* or *be vested in* and *vest with* or *be vested with."* Simon, *English Idioms from the Law,* 78 Law Q. Rev. 245, 249 (1962).

Q. What is veto?

A. This power has given to the permanent member of security council who have power of any permanant member of the security of the United Nations to refuse to agree to a proposed course of action; power to prohibit or refuse; refusal to assent to a parliamentary bill.

Q. What is vicarious liability?

A. vicarious liability = Liability incurred upon a person for acts of another. For ex. principle's liability for acts of his agent.

Q. Comment on the usage of the word via in legal matters?

A. via = (1) by way of (a place), passing through (they flew to Amarillo via Dallaa); (2) by means of, through the agency of (we booked our flight via Qantas). Sense (2) is considered to be "certainly acceptable in informal use."

Q. What is meant by vis-major?

A. vis-major = Act of God, irresistable force.

Q. What is meant by void?

A. void = Not valid, of no effect.

Q. What is meant by voidable?

A. voidable = Capable of being set aside as void at the opinion of a party.

Q. What are vowel clusters?

A. vowel clusters are not indigenous to the English language, though one finds them in our imported vocabulary, in words such as *onomatopoeia* (= the use of imitative or echoic words, such as *fizz* and *buzz*), *maicutic* (= Socratic) and *giaour* (= one outside the Muslim faith). In forming **Neologisms**, especially by agglutination, one should be wary of clumping vowels together in a way that would strike readers as non-English. Even three consecutive vowels may have this effect, as in *antiaircraft,* which appears far more natural as *anti-aircraft.*

Q. What is meant by wager?

A. wager = A bet or something laid down and hazarded on the issue of an uncertain event.

Q. What is meant by waifs and (e)strays?

A. waifs and (e)strays. This legal phrase has passed into common parlance in the sense "abandoned or neglected children," which is an extension of the original sense "unclimed property, wandering animals." In lay usage, the second element is usually *strays*. Technically, in law, *waifs* came to mean, at common law, things stolen and thrown away by the thief in flight but not things left behind or hidden; they belonged to the Crown by prerogative right if they had been seized on its behalf (*OCL*). *Estrays,* q.v., = valuable tame animals, found wandering and ownerless; at common law, they belonged to the Crown or, by virtue of grant or prescriptive right, to the lord of the manor (*id.*).

Q. What is waiver?

A. waiver = The intentional or voluntary relinquishment of a known right.

Q. Define wake.

A. wake, awake, awaken, wake up, woke, waked, waked up, woke up, awakened, awaked, awoke. The preterit and participial forms of *wake* and its various siblings are perhaps, the most vexing in the language. The following are the preferred declensions:

        wake > woke > waked (or woken)
        awake > awoke > awaked (or awoken)
        awaken > awakened > awakened
        wake up > woke up > waked up

Q. What is wakf?

A. wakf = Permanant dedication of property for religious or charitable purpose under muslim law.

Q. Define wane and wax.

A. wane, wax. *Wane* = to decrease in strength or importance, e.g., "The aspect of *Lochner* that curtailed economic regultion has clearly *waned* since the 1930s." "The imperative of a pre-deprivation hearing *wanes* when impractical, as in a negligent tort situation." *Wax* (= [1] to increase in strength or importance or [2] to become is used primarily (in sense (2)) in Cliches such as *to wax poetic, eloquent* etc. or (in sense (1)) as a correlative of *wane* (the doctrine waxed and waned).

Q. Give meaning of the word want.

A. want, n., (= lack) is an especially Formal Word, sometimes used in literary contexts but frequently in legal writing (want of prosecution), e.g., "The district court dismissed the action for *want* of jurisdiction, and this court reversed." "*Want* of probable cause and malice are seldom established by direct evidence of an ulterior motive." The participial *wanting* (= lacking) also appears often in legal prose: "We first consider the appellee's contention that federal jurisdiction is *wanting*." "Authority on these points is *wanting*." (Eng.)

Q. What are wards?

A. -ward(s). In AmE, the preferred practice is to use the *-ward* form of Directional Words, as in *toward, forward, backward* and *westward*. Words in *-ward* may be either adjectives or adverbs whereas words in *-wards*, common in BrE, may be adverbs only.

Dictionary of Legal Terms 203

Q. What is warning of caveat?

A. warning of caveat (= a notice given to a person who has entered a caveat [q.v.] warning him to appear and state what his interested is) is a curious but established Redundancy.

Q. What is a warrant?

A. warrant, v.t. In the modern idiom, it sounds natural that objects or actions are warranted but not that people are warranted. Therefore, "Such a conclusion warrants federal judges in substituting their views for those of state legislators," reads more naturally as follow—*Such a conclusion warrants federal judges' substituting their views for those of state legislators.* To illustrate this point, we might say that acts or beliefs are *warranted* or *unwarranted* but not that actors or believers are *warranted* or *unwarranted.*

Nevertheless, the *OED* contains examples of *warrant* used with personal objects from the seventeenth century and the usage remains common in law, if not elsewhere, e.g., "The facts and circumstances must have been sufficient in themselves to *warrant* a man of reasonable caution in the belief that an offence has been or is being committed."

Q. What is warrantable?

A. warrantable (= that may be authorised or permitted; justifiable) should not be used in the sense "capable of or justifying having a judicial warrant issue."

Q. What is meant by warranted?

A. warranted (= authorised by a search warrant) is common in American legal writing. *Warranted* has had the sense "furnished with a legal or official warrant" (*OED*) since the mid-eighteenth century, e.g., "The United States appeals the suppression of evidence obtained during a *warranted* search." The antonym of *warranted,* in this sense, is *warrantless,* q.v., not *unwarranted* (= unjustified).

Q. Who is warrantee or warranty?

A. warrantee is incorrect for *warranty.* **warranty** = A promise by the seller to repair goods during the specified period. However the purchaser here does not have a right to ask for replacement of goods.

Q. What is warrantless?

A. warrantless = (1) without a warrant (a *warrantless* entry of police upon defendant's premises) or (2) unjustified (completely warrantless accusation).

Q. What is wastage?

A. wastage, as Gowers has noted, "is properly used of loss caused by wastefulness, decay, leakage etc. or, in a staff, by death or resignation. It would be well if it were confined to this meaning instead of being used, as it habitually is, as long variant of *waste*." (*MEU2* 688).

Q. Give the meaning of waste.

A. waste, as a legal Term of Art, carries the sense "spoil, destruction or injury done to an estate by a tenant (for life or for years) to the prejudice of the heir or of the reversioner or remainderman." The following is a typical specimen: "Such injunctions include those against *waste* where a person, having only a limited interest in an estate in his occupation, threatens to wastefully cut down timber, or otherwise injure the freehold." (quoted in *OED*). The usual legal phrase is *to commit waste*.

Q. Comment on way which.

A. way which is used erroneous for *way in which,* e.g., "One of the *ways which* [read *ways in which*] the consignor may protect his interests is by filing under Article 9 pursuant to section 2-326 (3) (c)."

Q. Explain the phrase we are persuaded that.

A. we are persuaded that is often just so much verbal baggage in judicial opinions, e.g., "*We are persuaded that* the principles announced in *Tabacalera* and *Maltina* are dispositive here" becomes much more forceful thus: "The principles announced in *Tabacalera* and *Maltina* are dispositive here."

Q. What are weasel words?

A. weasel words. Theodore Roosevelt said, in a speech in St. Louis, May 31, 1916, "One of our defects as a nation is a tendency to use what have been called weasel words. When a weasel sucks eggs, it sucks the meat out of the egg and leaves the shell. If you use a weasel word after another, there is nothing left of the other." Some writers have incorrectly suggested that the metaphor suggested itself because of the wriggling and evasive character of the weasel. In any event, sensitive writers are aware of how supposed intensives (e.g., *very,* q.v.) actually have the effect of weakening a statement. Many other words merely have the effect of rendering uncertain or toothless the statements in which, they appear. Among these are *significantly, sustantially, reasonable, meaningful, compelling, undue, clear, obviously, manifestly, if practicable, with all deliberate speed* (orig. a weasel phrase, now with a history), *all reasonable means, or as soon thereafter as may be, rather, somewhat* and *quite.*

Dictionary of Legal Terms

Q. Give the meaning of the word wed.

A. wed is often used metaphorically in American legal prose for *adopt* or *endorse*, e.g., "But, though our Supreme Court has not yet *wedded* this new doctrine, it has certainly at least paid ardent courtship."

Q. What is wedded?

A. wedded is the past participal form but in the negative, the proper form is *unwed*. *Wed* is a variant past participle to be avoided.

Q. Define well.

A. well, when forming an adjective with a past participle verb, is hyphenated.

Q. Define the word widow.

A. widow, n. Mellinkoff has rightly pointed out the Redundancy in the Supreme Court's phrase *surviving widows who administer estates.* See *Reed v. Reed,* 404 U.S. 71, 75 (1971) (paraphrased). Mellinkoff, *The Myth of Precision and the Law Dictionary,* 31 U.C.L.A. L. Rev. 423, 440 (1983).

widow, v.t., may apply to a spouse of either sex. Thus *widowed man* is unobjectionable, though to many it may seem at first unnatural.

Q. Who is widower?

A. widow(er). Is one still a widow(er) when he remarries? No.

Q. Give the meaning of the word wield.

A. wield, weald. The former is the verb meaning "to control, handle, hold and use" (he wields his power with good judgement). The latter is the noun meaning "a forest" or "an uncultivated upland region."

Q. What is a will?

A. will, testament. Will = A person's declaration in writing of his intention as to disposal of his property after his death. A common belief among lawyers is that, in the Middle Ages, a *will* disposed of real personal property. This belief is, strictly speaking, erroneous, though from the eighteenth century, such a distinction is usage (unfounded in the substantive law) began to emerge. The distinction is now obsolete, however, so that in mdoern legal usage the words are interchangeable, though *will* remains the usual term.

The archaic distinction between the words is said to have grown out of the historical development of property dispositions. Ecclesiastical courts had jurisdiction of cases involving the distribution and usage of personal property; appeals from these courts were to Rome, under the Catholic hierarchy, until 1533. The common-law courts of England, in the meanwhile, decided cases involving the usage and disposition of real property. The two court systems developed distinct terms for decedents' estates, e.g., "The common-law courts took the position that a *will* was ambulatory in its revocatory effect; the ecclesiastical courts held that a *testament* was revoked at the time the revoking instrument was executed." As a result of the bifurcated judicial system, the myth goes, the terminology for real property dispositions was Anglo-Saxon (*will*) and that for personal property dispositions Latinate (*testament*), the latter terms having derived from Roman law.

History, especially linguistic history, never comes so neatly packaged, however. It is not surprising, then, to discover that medieval writers are recorded as having used *will* in reference to personal property and *testament* in reference to land. Even so, the myth concerning these terms may be valid insofar is it explains the tendencies in usage that would later give rise to an idiomatic Differentiation. It is at least possible that the Doublet *last will and testament,* q.v., had, in its origins, a purpose for the inclusion of both real and personal property. In any event, *will* now denotes the entire testamentary instrument, a place formerly said to be occupied by *devise,* q.v.,

Q. Define will.

A. will, as a verb meaning to dispose of by will, is always transitive, e.g., "In Louisiana, a testator can *will* no more than one-tenth of his estate to a woman with whom, he has lived in open concubinage."/ "Aliens could, at common law, *will* personalty and devise land but the state could seize the land in the hands of his devisees." "I *will* and bequeath all my effects to my brothers and sisters, to be divided equally among them."

Q. What is willable?

A. willable = transferable by will, e.g., "Land became *willable* with the Statute of Wills." The *OED* traces this sense back only to 1880.

Q. Define wilful.

A. wil(l)ful. *Wilful* is the preferred spelling in BrE, *willful* in AmE, *Willfull,* a misspelling, occasionally appears in the U.S.

Q. What is wilfulness?

a. wil(l) fulness, malice aforethought. These terms are sometimes confused in criminal contexts. *Willfulness* is the braoder term. "An act is done *willfully* if done volutnarily and intentionally and with the specific intent to do something the law forbids. I E. Devitt & C. Blackmar, *Federal Jury Practice and Instructions* 384 (1977).

Malice aforethough, q.v., is used in the context of homicide: "*Malice aforethought* means an intent, at the time of a killing, wilfully to take the life of a human being or an intent wilfully to act in callous or wanton disregard of the consequences to human life; but *malice aforethought* does not necessarily imply any ill will, spite or hatred toward the individual killed." 2E. Devitt & C. Blackmar, *Federal Jury Practice and instructions* 215 (1977).

Q. What is meant by the idiom willy-nilly?

A. willy-nilly is an English equivalent of the Latinism *nolens volens,* q.v., e.g., "If a federal courts is to do it, it must act in its traditional manner, not as a military commander ordering people to work *willy-nilly* nor as the President's Administrative Assistant." (Douglas, J.) It is sometimes, as the *OED* reamarks, erroneously used for "undecided, shilly-shally" (a willy-nilly disposition).

Q. What is meant by the phrase-wise?

A. -wise. Phrases arrived at with this combining form are generally to be discouraged, for they often displace a more direct wording and they are invariably graceless and inelegant, e.g., "[W]e must ..... respond to [the] claims ..... that even if acceptable *population wise* [read *as applied to the population as a whole*], the ..... plan was invidiously discriminatory because a "political fairness principle" was followed." *Gaffney v. Cummings,* 412 U.S. 735, 751-52 (1973). "Whether accmulation of earnings in the corporation is *cheaper tax-wise* [read *cheaper from the standpoint of taxes*] than accumulation in the partnership depends on a comparison of the corporate tax rate and the applicable rate to the individuals involved." "There are several other *advantages tax-wise* [read *tax advantages*] but these illustrate the tax inducements for making *inter vivos* transfers." "To continue this litigation, even though the parents should ultimately prevail, may well be, *at least money-wise* [read *at least financially*], like digging a hole to get the dirt to fill another hole." "A notice, signed by the commissioners, was filestamped on the day of the hearing; *contentwise* [omit *content-wise* altogether] this notice met the statutory requirements."

wise (= manner, fashion, way) is an Archaism that still appears infrequently in legal writing, e.g., "The testamentary revocation may be express, in order that the testator may do his new testamentary work without being *in any wise* [read *in any way*] fettered by the contents of his former will." "The judgement commands the defendant to refrain fropm *in any wise interfering* [read *interfering in any way*] with plaintiffs in the conduct of the business of their stable."

Q. What is meant by withholding?

A. withhold is sometimes used incorrectly for *deprive of or deny*, e.g., "Petitioner filed suit under 42 U.S.C. § 1983 seeking monetary damages and injunctive relief for being forced to work beyond his physical capabilities and for being *withheld* [read *denied* or *deprived of*] necessary medical treatment."

Q. Define within.

A. within, adj. "The legal tone is still too strong for common use in *the within letter.*" W. Follett, *Modern American Usage* 45 (1966). Indeed, it is perhaps too strong even for usage by legal writers, for *enclosed* is far more common and more natural, e.g., "The *within* property shall not be sold or encumbered without the express written consent of the *within* mortgagees." (This usage is apparently elliptical for *within-named;* the writer should have omitted the word or phrase completely, for it adds nothing.) "Opposing counsel is being furnished with a copy of the *with* in [read *enclosed*] response."

Q. Illustrate the meaning of the term without.

A. without for *outside.* Usually, *without* is contrasted to *with;* but in law, it is frequently an opposite of *within.* Though somewhat archaic, in formal legal prose this usage should be considered unexceptionable, e.g., "Grants or devises are constructed to bring them *within* or *without* the operation of the Rule in Shelly's Case." "The plaintiff put himself *without* the pale of the comprative negligence rule."

Q. What do you understand by witness?

A. witness = A person who is a reporter of a crime. He has personal knowledge of occurrence. His name is recorded in chargesheet and helps the court in trial stage.

Q. What is wraparound mortgage?

A. wraparound mortgage is current American legal Argot, meaning "a deed of trust whereby a purchaser incorporates into agreed payments to a grantor or third-party the grantor's obligation in the initial mortgage." A court recently defined it as "a junior mortgage the secures a promissory note with a face amount equal to the sum of the principal balance of an existing mortgage note plus any additional funds advanced by the second lender." *Mitchell v. Trustees,* 375 N. W. 2d 424, 428 (Mich. App. 1985) (with minor differences in wording).

Q. Writ is a legal document. Explain.

A. writ, n., = a legal document to be submitted to or issuing from court. The *OED* records the verbal sense of *writ* " to serve (a person) with a writ or summons" (he was writted) and notes that it is Anglo-Irish. *Writ* is an **Archaism** as a past participle of *write*, except in the **Cliche** *writ-large*, e.g., "If article 9 were *writ large* it would set out that a director is not to be removed against his will." (Eng.)

Q. What is writ?

A. writ = A judicial process of written command or order issued by a court directing or enjoining the person or person's to whom it is addressed to do or restrain from doing some act specified therein.

Q. Who is a writer?

A. writer is an obsolescent Scottishism in the sense "an attorney or law-agent, an ordinary legal practitioner in country towns, a law clerk" (*OED*).

Q. How do we write specially or illustrate?

A. write specially = to concur in a separate opinion, e.g., "I fully concur in the opinion written by judge Politz; however, I *write specially* to say that I believe the Secretary of Health and Human Services is right on track." "The three justices who voted for rehearing when the case was before them on appeal voted to deny the writ; these justices *specially* stated that although each of them voted for a rehearing on the question of appellate review of the proportionality of the sentence, that issue was presented to the Court in a writ application and that application was denied."

Q. What is wrongful according to law?

A. wrong, wrongful. The distinction is an important one in law. *Wrong* = (1) out of order, (2) contrary to law or morality, wicked, or (3) other than the right or suitable or the more or most desirable (*COD*). *Wrongful* = characterised by unmfairness or injustice, contrary to law, (of a person) not entitled to the position occupied (the wrongful possessor). Occasionally, the words happen to be coextensive, e.g., "It is a malicious act, which is in law and, in fact, a *wrong* act and therefore, a *wrongful* act and therefore an actionable act if injury ensues from it." (Eng.)

Q. What is wrong doer?

A. wrongdoer = one who violates the law. The term is used of tortfeasors as well as of criminals, e.g., "But the circumstance that the wife of one of the *wrongdoers* benefited by the imposition does not afford opportunity for relief of that character." "The policy of preventing the *wrongoer* from escaping the penalties for his wrong—in this case, punitive damages—is inapplicable."

Q. What is wrongful discharge?

A. wrongful discharge (AmE) = *wrongful dismissal* (BrE), e.g., "The only other damages the plaintiff could claim if he had been *wrongfully dismissed* would have been purely nominal." (Aus.) *Wrongful termination* is sometimes used in the U.S.

Q. What is wrongly in law?

A. wrong(ly). Both forms are proper adverbs; *wrongly*, which is less common, appears before the verb modified (the suspects were wrongly detained) whereas *wrong* should be used if the adverb follows the noun (he answered the question wrong).

Q. What is wrongous?

A. wrongous, in Scotish law, means "wrongful, illegal, unjust." It should be avoided by other than Scottish lawyers.

Q. What is xerox?

A. xerox, v.t., is a registered trademark that is nevertheless used as a noun (he made a xerox of the document), adjective (a xerox copy) and verb (to xerox a will). Careful speakers use *photocopy* or some other similar word. *Zerox* is a common misspelling.

Q. What is an X-ray?

A. X-ray, x-ray. Either form is correct, though the former is perhaps more common. *W9* suggests that the term is hyphenated as an adjective and verb (*X-ray*) and not hyphenated as a noun (*X ray*). The *COD* hyphenates the term in all the parts of speech.

Q. What is yellow dog contract?

A. yellow dog contract (= an employment contract in which, a worker disavows membership in and agrees not to join a labor union during the period of his employment [*W9*]) has become a part of American legal Argot. The term dates from 1920.

Q. What is your petitioner in law?

A. your petitioner and like phrases are quaint Archaisms to be avoided, e.g., "*Your petitioner* [read *The petitioner*] has reliable information and believes that the defendant intends to leave the jurisdiction before April 19, 1985." "*Your relator* [read *The relator*], George W. Strake, Jr., Chairman of the State Republican.

Q. What is zetetic?

A. zetetic(k). The adjective, meaning "proceeding by inquiry or investigation," is preferably spelled *zetetic* (*OEd* & *W3*), though *Black's* spells it *zetetick*.

Q. What is zeugma?

A. zeugma = a figure of speech by which, a single word is made to refer to two or more words in the sentence, especially when properly applying in sense to only one of them or applying to them in different senses, e.g., "If one party represents that he *has* (or *will*) *put* an oral agreement in writing and the other party relies on this to his substantial detriment, the first party may be estopped to set up the Statute of Frauds as a defense." (*Put* is made to be both preterit and present.) Fowler gives this example: "Sir Charles Wilson, the newly elected member for Central Leeds, *tools* the *oath* and his *seat*." (*Take* has been given two different senses here.)

Q. What is meant by the term zonate?

A. zonate(d). The term meaning "arranged in zones" is best made *zonate* rather than *zonated*.

LEGAL MAXIM

ab abusu ad usum non valet consequentia: Consequences of abuse do not aply to general use
ab actu ad posse valet illatio: From the past one can infer the future
ab aeterno: From the beginning of time
abeunt studia in mores: Pursuits change into habits
ab extra: From the outside
abiit, excessit, evasit, erupit: He has departed, gone off, escaped, broken out
ab inconvenienti: From the inconvenience involved
ab incunabulis: From infancy (from the cradle)
ab initio: From the beginning
ab intra: From within
ab invito: Against the will; unwillingly
ab origine: From the origin; from the first
abscisio infiniti: Cutting off an infinite part
absense haeres non erit: The absent one will not be heir
absente reo: The defendant being absent
absit invidia: May ill will be absent (i.e., no offence intended)
absolvo: I absolve; I acquit
absque: Without; but for
absque hoc: But for this; apart from this
absque ulla nota: Without any marks
ab uno ad omnes: From one to all
ab uno disce omnes: From one example, learn all
abusus non tollit usum: Abuse of a right does not invalidate use
abyssus abyssum invocat: Hells calls hell
a capite ad calcem: From head to heel (totally, entirely)
accedas ad curiam: You may approach the court
accipiunt leges, populus quibus legibus ex lex: They consent to laws which place people beyond the pale of the law
accusare nemo se debit, nisi coram Deo: No one is bound to accuse herself/himself, unless before God
acerbus et ingens: Fierce and mighty
ac etiam: And also
Acheruntis pabulum: Food for Acheron (i.e., food for the gallows)
acta eruditorum: Contributions to a cause

Dictionary of Legal Terms

actio ex delicto: Cause of action (i.e., reason for lawsuit)
actio personalis moritur cum personal: Personal action dies with the person
actum agere: To do what has already been done
actum est de re publica: It is all over with the republic/commonwealth
actum ne agas: Do not redo that which has been done
actus curiae: Act of the court
actus Dei: Act of God
actus reus: The criminal act; the guilty act
ab absurdum: To the absurd
ad alium diem: At another day
ad amussim: According to a rule (i.e., accurately)
ad aperturam libri: At the opening of a book
ad arbitrium: At will (i.e., at pleasure)
ad astra: To the starts (i.e., to the top)
a dato: From the date
ad baculum: To the rod (i.e., appeal to force, not reason)
ad augusta per angusta: To honour through difficulties
ad captandum: For the sake of pleasing
ad captandum vulgus: Appealing to the emotions of the crowd
ad clerum: To the clergy
ad crumenam: To the purse (i.e., appealing to self-interest)
ad damnum: To the damages (i.e., amount demanded)
addendum: Something to be added
additur: Let it be increased
ad effectum: Until effectual
adeo in teneris consuescere multum est: [It is] imperative to form habits in the early years
adesse: To be present
ad eundem gradum: To the same degree (i.e., equal blame or praise)
ad extra: To the outside
ad extremum: To the extreme (i.e., to the end)
ad fidem: To faith (i.e., in allegiance)
ad filum aquae: To the center of the stream
ad filum viae: To the centre of the road
ad finem: To the end; at the end of the page
ad finem fidelis: Faithful to the end
ad gloriam: For the glory
ad gustum: To one's taste
ad hanc vocem: To this word
adhibenda est in iocando moderatio: One should employ restraint in his/her jests

adhibendus: To be administered
ad hoc: To this; for a specific occasion; impromptu
ad hominem: Personal attack relating to the individual
adhuc sub iudice lis est: The case is still before the court
ad hunc locum: At this place
ad idem: To the same point
a die: From that day
ad ignorantium: To ignorance [of the facts of an argument]
ad infinitum: Without an end; to infinity; without limit
ad initium: At the beginning
ad instar omnium: In the likeness of all
ad interim: In the meantime; for the time being
ad internecionem: To extermination
ad invidiam: To envy; to prejudice
ad iudicium: To judgement; to common sense
ad litem: For the specific lawsuit
ad litteram: To the letter (i.e., precisely)
ad locum: At the place, at a specific location
ad manum: At hand (i.e., ready and prepared)
ad misericordiam: To pity (i.e., appealing to mercy)
ad modum: In the manner of
ad multos annos: After many years
ad nauseam: To the point of sickness; to the point of being disgusted
ad nocendum patentes sumus: We all have power to do harm
ad partes dolentes: To the painful parts
ad patres: To the fathers (i.e., dead)
ad paucos dies: For a few days
ad perpetuam rei memoriam: For the eternal/perpetual rememberance of the thing
ad personal: To the person; relating to the individual
ad populum: To the people
ad quem: To or for whom; to or for which
ad quod: To which; for which
ad quod damnum: To what damage
ad referendum: For reference; for further consideration
ad rem: To the thing; relevant to the present matter
ad saturatum: To saturation
ad sectam: At the lawsuit of
adsum: I am present; to be present
ad summam: In short; in a word

adsummum: To the highest point
adulter: Corrupter; seducer
ad usum externum: For external use
ad utrumque paratus: Ready for anything; prepared for the worst
ad valorem: According to value
ad verbum: To the word; verbatim
ad verecundiam: Appeal to modesty in an argument
adversa: Things having been noted...
adversa virtute repello: I repel adversity by valour
adversaria: That which has been turned to; commentary
adversus: Against; contrary to
adversus bonos mores: Against good morals
adversus solem ne loquitor: Don't speak against the sun (i.e., an obvious fact)
ad vitam: For life; for the duration of a person's life
ad vitam aeternam: For eternal life; for all time
ad vitam aut culpam: For life or until a misdeed
ad vivum: To the life
advocatus diaboli: Devil's advocate
aedificatum: That which is built
aegrotat: S/he is sick; certificate denoting illness
aequabiliter et diligenter: Uniformly and diligently
aequales: Equal parts
aequam servare mentem: To preserve a calm mind; equanimity
aequanimiter: With composure; with equanimity
aequilibrium indifferentiae: State of exact balance between two actions
aequitas sequitur legem: Equity follows the law
aequo animo: With a calm mind; with equanimity
aes alienum: Money belonging to another; a debt
aes triplex: Triple brass; a strong defense
aestimatio capitis: Estimation of the head; price of a man
aetatis: At the age of
aetatis suae: In the year of one's life
aeternum vale: Farewell forever
affinitas: Relationship by marriage
a fortiori: With even stronger reason; all the more
age quod agis: Do what you are doing (i.e., pay attention to what you are doing)
a latere: From the side; with confidence
albo lapillo notare diem: To mark the day with a white stone
albus: White

albus liber: White book
alere flammam: To feed the flames
alias: Otherwise; at another time
alias dictus: An assumed name; also known as
alia tendanda via est: Another way must be tried
alibi: Elsewhere
alieni appetens: Eager for another's property
alieni appetens sui profusus: Covetous of another's possession, lavish of his own
alieni generis: Of a different class
alieni iuris (alieni juris): Subject to another law
alienum est onme quicquid optando evenit: What we obtain by asking is not really ours
alimenta: Means of support (i.e., food, clothing, shelter)
alio intuitu: From another point of view
aliquant: An uneven part of the whole
aliquid: Something; somewhat
aliquis in omnibus, nullus in singulis: A somebody in general, nobody in particular
aliquot: An even part of the whole
alis volat propriis: She flies by her own wings
alitur vitium vivitque tegendo: Vice is nourished by being concealed
aliunde: From another source; from outside
alma mater: Kind/bounteous/benign mother (i.e., protective institution, as referred to by its former students)
alter: Another person; personality of another
altercatio: Forensic argumentation; cross-examination
alter ego: One's second self; very close friend
alter ego est amicus: A friend is another self
alter idem: Another thing similar in all respects
alter ipse amicus: A friend is a second self
alteri sic tibi: [Do] to another as [you do] to yourself
alternis diebus: Every other day
alternis horis: Every other hour
alternis noctibus: Every other night
alterum alterius auxilio eget: One thing needs the help of another
alterum non laedere: Not to injure others
alterum tantum: As much again; twice as much
altiora peto: I seek higher things
amari aliquid: Something bitter; a touch of bitterness

Dictionary of Legal Terms

a maximis ad minima: From the largest to the smallest
ambigendi locus: Room for doubt
a mensa et toro: From table and bed (i.e., a legal separation)
amici probantur rebus adversis: Friends are proved by adversity
amicitiae immortales mortales inimicitias debere esse: Our friendships should be immortal, our enmities mortal
amicitia semper prodest: Friendship is always of benefit
amicitia sine fraude: Friendship without deceit
amicus certus in re incerta cernitur: A friend in need is a friend indeed
amicus curiae: Friend of the court (i.e., impartial spokesperson)
amicus est tanquam alter idem: A friend is almost a second self
amicus humani generis: A friend of the human race (i.e., philanthropist)
amicus usque ad aras: A friend to the altars (i.e., a friend until death or until relilgious convictions prevent action)
a minori ad maius: From the lesser to the greater
amissum quod nescitur non amittitur: The loss that is unknown is no loss at all
amor habendi: Love of possessing
amoto quaeramus seria ludo: Setting games aside, let's get on to serious matters
ancilla theologiae: The handmaid of theology (i.e., philosophy)
anguis in herba: A snake in the grass (i.e., a hidden danger)
angulus ridet: That corner of the earth smiles
angulus terrarum: Quiet corner of the world; place of repose
amare et sapere vix deo conceditur: Even a god finds it hard to love and be wise at the same time
amicus humani generis: A friend of the human race (philanthropist)
animis opibusque parati: Prepared in minds and resources (ready for anything)
ab uno disce omnes: From one example you may judge the rest
ab urbe condita: From the founding of the city
ad finem: To the end/towards the end
ad hoc: For this purpose
ad hominem: To the man personally
a die: From that day
ad infinitum: To infinity
ad libitum: At pleasure
ad nauseam: To the point where one becomes sick/disgusted
ad rem: To the point
ad valorem: According to the value
aetatis suae: Of his or her age
a fortiori: With stronger reason
alter ego: One's second self

anno domini: In the year of our lord
anno mundi: In the year of the world
annus mirabillis: The year of wonders
ante bellum: Before the war
ante meridiem: Before noon
aqua vitae: Water of life
ars est celare artem: True art is to conceal art
ars longa vita brevis: Art is long life is short
audi alterem partem: Hear to the other side
ab absurdo: From the absurd (proving the validity of your argument by pointing out the absurdity of your opponent's position)
abusus non tollit usum: Misuse does not nullify proper use
aegrescit medendo: The disease worsens with the treatment (the remedy is worse than the disease)
aeternum vale: Farewell forever
argumentum ad hominem: An argument against the man. Directing an argument against an opponent's character rather than the subject at hand.

Ab abusu ad usum non valet consequentia. A conclusion about the use of a thing from its abuse is invalid.

Ab assuetis non fit injuria. No injury is done by things long acquiesced in.

Absentem accipere debemus eum qui non est eo loco in quo petitur. We must consider a person absent who is not in that place in which he is sought.

Absoluta sententia expositore non indiget. A simple proposition needs no expositor.

Abundans cautela non nocet. Abundant caution does no harm.

Accessorium non ducit, sed sequitur, suum principale. An accessory does not lead, but follows, its principal.

Accessorium non trahit principale. The accessory does not carry the principal with it.

Accessorius sequitur naturam sui principalis. An accessory follows the nature of his principal.

Accipere quid ut justitiam facias non est tam accipere quam extorquere. To accept anything as a reward for doing justice is rather extorting than accepting.

Accusare nemo debet se, nisi coram Deo. No one is obliged to accuse himself, except before God.

A communi observantia non est recedendum. Common observance (or usage) is not to be departed from.

Acta exteriora indicant interiora secreta. Outward acts indicate the thoughts hidden within.

Acta in uno judicio non probant in alio nisi inter easdem personas. Things done in one action cannot be taken as evidence in another, unless it is between the same parties.

Actio non datur non damnificato. An action is not given to one who is not injured.

Actio non facit reum, nisi mens sit rea. An act does not make a person guilty unless the mind is guilty.

Actionum genera maxime sunt servanda. The kinds of actions are especially to be preserved.

Actio personalis moritur cum persona. A personal action dies with the person.

Actio quaelibet it sua via. Every action proceeds in its own course.

Actore non probante, reus absolvitur. If the plaintiff does not prove his case, the defendant is acquitted.

Actori incumbit onus probandi. The burden of proof rests on the plaintiff.

Actor qui contra regulam quid adduxit non est audiendus. A pleader ought not to be heard who advances a proposition contrary to the rule (of law).

Actor sequitur forum rei. The plaintiff follows the forum of the defendant.

Actus curiae neminem gravabit. An act of the court will prejudice no one.

Actus Dei nemini facit injuriam. An act of God does wrong to no one. • That is, no one is responsible in damages for inevitable accidents.

Actus Dei nemini nocet. An act of God does wrong to no one.

Actus legis nemini est damnosus. An act of the law prejudices no one.

Actus legis nemini facit injuriam. An act of the law does no one wrong.

Actus legitimi non recipiunt modum. Acts required by law admit of no qualification.

Actus me invito factus non est meus actus. An act done (by me) against my will is not my act.

Actus non facit reum nisi mens sit rea. An act does not make a person guilty unless the mind is guilty; an act does not make the doer criminal unless his mind is criminal.

Actus repugnans non potest in esse produci. A repugnant act cannot be brought into being (that is, cannot be made effectual).

Additio probat minoritatem. An addition proves inferiority.

Ad ea quae frequentius accidunt jura adaptantur. The laws are adapted to those cases that occur more frequently.

A digniori fieri debet denominatio et resolutio. The denomination and explanation ought to be derived from the more worthy.

Adjuvari quippe nos, non decipi, beneficio oportet. Surely we ought to be helped by a benefit, not be entrapped by it.

Ad proximum antecedens fiat relatio, nisi impediatur sententia. A relative is to be referred to the nearest antecedent, unless prevented by the sense.

Ad quaestiones legis judices, et non juratores, respondent. Judges, and not jurors, answer questions of law.

Adversus extraneos vitiosa possessio prodesse solet. Possession though faulty is usually sufficient against outsiders. • Prior possession is a good title of ownership against all who cannot show a better.

Aedificare in tuo proprio solo non licet quod alteri noceat. It is not lawful to build on one's own land what may be injurious to another.

Aedificatum solo solo cedit. What is built on the land goes with the land.

Aedificia solo cedunt. Buildings go with the land.

Aequior est dispositio legis quam hominis. The law's disposition is more impartial than man's.

Aequitas agit in personam. Equity acts on the person.

Aequitas est correctio legis generaliter latae qua parte deficit. Equity is the correction of some part of the law where by reason of its generality it is defective.

Aequitas est quasi equalitas. Equity is as it were equality.

Aequitas ignorantiae opitulatur, oscitantiae non item. Equity assists ignorance but not complacency (or carelessness).

Aequitas non facit jus, sed juri auxiliatur. Equity does not create a right, but aids the right.

Aequitas nunquam contravenit leges. Equity never contravenes the laws.

Aequitas sequitur legem. Equity follows the law. Equity

Aequitas supervacua odit. Equity abhors superfluous things.

Aequum et bonum est lex legum. What is equitable and good is the law of laws.

Aestimatio praeteriti delicti ex postremo facto nunquam crescit. The assessment of a past offence never increases from a subsequent fact.

Affectio tua nomen imponit operi tuo. Your motive gives a name to your act.

Affectus punitur licet non sequatur effectus. The intention is punished even if the object is not achieved.

Affinis mei affinis non est mihi affinis. A person connected by marriage to someone connected by marriage to me is no connection of mine.

Affirmanti, non neganti, incumbit probatio. The proof is incumbent on the one who affirms, not on the one who denies.

Affirmantis est probare. The person who affirms must prove.

Agentes et consentientes pari poena plectentur. Acting and consenting parties will be liable to the same punishment.

A jure suo cadunt. They fall from their right. • That is, they lose their right.

A justitia (quasi a quodam fonte) omnia jura emanant. From justice (as from a fountain) all rights flow.

Aliena negotia exacto officio geruntur. The business of another is conducted with scrupulous attention.

Alienatio rei praefertur juri accrescendi. Alienation of property is favoured over the right to accumulate.

A l'impossible nul n'est tenu. No one is bound to do what is impossible.

Aliud est celare, aliud tacere. To conceal is one thing, to be silent another.

Aliud est distinctio, aliud separatio. Distinction is one thing, separation another.

Aliud est possidere, aliud esse in possessione. It is one thing to possess, another to be in possession.

Aliud est vendere, aliud vendenti consentire. To sell is one thing, to give consent to the seller another.

Allegans contraria non est audiendus. A person making contradictory allegations is not to be heard.

Allegans suam turpitudinem non est audiendus. A person alleging his own wrong is not to be heard.

Allegari non debuit quod probatum non relevat. What is not relevant if proved ought not to have been alleged.

Allegatio contra factum non est admittenda. An allegation contrary to the deed (or fact) is not admissible.

Alterius circumventio alii non praebet actionem. A deception practiced on one person does not give a cause of action to another.

Alternativa petitio non est audienda. An alternative petition is not to be heard.

Ambigua responsio contra proferentem est accipienda. An ambiguous answer is to be taken against the party who offers it.

Ambiguis casibus semper praesumitur pro rege. In doubtful cases the presumption is always in favour of the king.

Ambiguitas contra stipulatorem est. A dubious expression is construed against the party using it.

Ambiguitas verborum patens nulla verificatione excluditur. A patent ambiguity is not removed by extrinsic evidence (or is never helped by averment).

Ambiguum placitum interpretari debet contra proferentem. An ambiguous plea ought to be interpreted against the party pleading it.

Ambulatoria est voluntas defuncti usque ad vitae supremum exitum. The will of a decedent is ambulatory (that is, can be altered) until the last moment of life.

Ancupia verborum sunt judice indigna. Quibbling over words is unworthy of a judge.

Angliae jura in omni casu libertati dant favorem. The laws of England are favourable in every case to liberty.

Animus ad se omne jus ducit. The mind brings every right unto itself. • Often explained: It is to the intention that all law applies.

Animus hominis est anima scripti. The intention of the person is the soul of the instrument.

Annua nec debitum judex non separat ipse. Even the judge apportions neither annuities nor debt.

Apices juris non sunt jura. Legal niceties are not law.

A piratis aut latronibus capti liberi permanent. Those captured by pirates or robbers remain free.

A piratis et latronibus capta dominium non mutant. Things captured by pirates or robbers do not change their ownership.

Applicatio est vita regulae. The application is the life of a rule.

Aqua cedit solo. The water goes with the ground. • A grant of the land includes the water on it.

Arbitramentum aequum tribuit cuique suum. A just arbitration renders to each his own.

Arbitrium est judicium. An award is a judgment.

A rescriptis valet argumentum. An argument from rescripts (i.e., original writs in the register) is valid.

Argumentum ab auctoritate est fortissimum in lege. An argument drawn from authority is the strongest in law.

Argumentum ab impossibili plurimum valet in lege. An argument deduced from an impossibility has the greatest validity in law.

Argumentum ab inconvenienti plurimum valet in lege. An argument drawn from what is unsuitable (or improper) has the greatest validity in law.

Argumentum a communiter accidentibus in jure frequens est. An argument from things commonly happening is frequent in law.

Argumentum a divisione est fortissimum in jure. An argument based on a subdivision of the subject is most powerful in law.

Argumentum a majori ad minus negative non valet; valet e converso. An argument from the greater to the lesser is of no force in the negative; conversely (in the affirmative) it is valid.

Argumentum a simili valet in lege. An argument by analogy (from a similar: case) has force in law.

Arma in armatos sumere jura sinunt. The laws permit taking up arms against the armed.

Assignatus utitur jure auctoris. An assignee is clothed with the rights of the principal.

Audi alteram partem. Hear the other side. • No one should be condemned unheard.

A verbis legis non est recedendum. From the words of the law there is to be no departure.

Bancus Communium Placitorum: Court of Common Pleas
beati possidentes: Blessed are those who possess (legal doctrine, possession is nine points of the law)
bellum domesticum: Strife/war among family members
bellum internecinum: Internecine war, a war of extermination
bellum letale: Lethal war, deadly war
bellum omnium in omnes: A war of all against all
bene decessit: S/he has left (died) well (a natural death)
bene esse: Well-being
bene est tentare: It is well to try
bene exeat: Let him or her go forth. Of good character
beneficium: Kindness of favour
beneficium accipere libertatem est vendere: To accept a favour is to sell one's freedom
bene merenti: Success to those who deserve it
bene meritus: Having well deserved
billa vera: True bill
bis: Twice (to be repeated)
bis dat qui cito dat: S/he gives twice who gives quickly
bona: Good or Property
bonae fidei emptor: Purchaser in good faith
bona fide: In good faith, genuine, legitimate
bona fide polliceor: I promise in good faith
bona fides: Good faith or Documents proving identity
bona gratia: In all kindness
bona fiscalia: Public property
bonae memoriae: Of happy memory
bona mobilia: Moveable property
bona notabilia: Noteworthy things
bona peritura: Perishable goods
bona vacantia: Unclaimed property
bonis avibus: Under favourable signs
bonum omen: A good omen
bonum per se: Good in itself
bonum publicum: The public good
Baratriam committit qui propter pecuniam justitiam baractat. A person is guilty of barratry who sells justice for money.

Bastardus nullius est filius, aut filius populi. A bastard is nobody's son, or the son of the people.

Bello pacta cedunt reipublicae. In war contracts give way to the state.

Benedicta est expositio quando res redimitur a destructione. Blessed is the exposition when a thing is saved from destruction.

Beneficium invito non datur. A privilege or benefit is not granted against a person's will.

Beneficium non datum nisi propter officium. A remuneration is not given, unless on account of a duty performed.

Beneficium non datur nisi officii causa. A benefice is not granted except on account or in consideration of duty.

Beneficium principis debet esse mansurum. The benefaction of a prince ought to be be lasting.

Benignior sententia in verbis generalibus seu dubiis est preferenda. The more favourable construction is to be preferred in general or doubtful expressions.

Benignius leges interpretandae sunt quo voluntas earum conservetur. Laws are to be more liberally interpreted so that their intent may be preserved.

Bonae fidei non congruit de apicibus juris disputare. It is incompatible with good faith to insist on the extreme subtleties of the law.

Bonae fidei possessor in id tantum quod ad se pervenerit tenetur. A possessor in good faith is liable only for that which he himself has obtained (literally, what has come to him).

Bona fide possessor facit fructus consumptos suos. A possessor in good faith is entitled to the fruits (or produce) that he consumes.

Bona fides exigit ut quod convenit fiat. Good faith demands that what is agreed on shall be done.

Bona fides non patitur ut bis idem exigatur. Good faith does not allow payment to be exacted twice for the same thing.

Boni judicis est ampliare jurisdictionem (or justitiam). It is the role of a good judge to enlarge (or use liberally) his jurisdiction (or remedial authority

Boni judicis est ampliare justitiam. It is the role of a good judge to enlarge or extend justice.

Boni judicis est causas litium dirimere. It is the role of a good judge to remove causes of litigation.

Boni judicis est judicium sine dilatione mandare executioni. It is the role of a good judge to render judgment for execution without delay.

Boni judicis est lites dirimere, ne lis ex lite oriatur. It is the role of a good judge to dispose of litigations so that one suit should not grow from another.

Bonum defendentis ex integra causa; malum ex quolibet defectu. A good outcome for the defendant comes from a sound case; a bad outcome from some defect.

Dictionary of Legal Terms

Bonum necessarium extra terminos necessitatis non est bonum. A thing good from necessity is not good beyond the limits of the necessity.
Bonus judex secundum aequum et bonum judicat, et aequitatem stricto juri praefert. A good judge decides according to fairness and the good and prefers equity to strict law.
Breve ita dicitur, quia rem de qua agitur, et intentionem petentis, paucis verbis breviter enarrat. A writ is called a "breve" because it briefly states, in few words, the matter in dispute, and the object of the party seeking relief.
Breve judiciale debet sequi suum originale, et accessorium suum principale. A judicial writ ought to follow its original, and an accessory its principal.
Breve judiciale non cadit pro defectu formae. A judicial writ does not fail for a defect of form.
Brevia, tam originalia quam judicialia, patiuntur anglica nomina. Writs, original as well as judicial, bear English names.

cacoethes: Irresistible urge
cacoethes carpendi: A compulsive habit for finding fault
cacoethes loquendi: A bad habit for compulsive talking
cacoethes scribendi: A bad habit for compulsive writing
cadit quaestio: The question falls, the issue collapses
caelum non animum mutant qui mare currunt: Those who cross the sea change only their climate, not their minds
callida iunctura: Skillful joining, careful workmanship
candor dat viribus alas: Sincerity gives wings to strength
cane peius et angue: Worse than a dog or snake
cantabit vacuus coram latrone viator: the poor wayfarer will sing in the presence of travelers
capias ad audiendum: Writ ordering appearance in court
capias ad respondendum: Writ ordering the arrest of a person
capias ad satisfaciendum: Writ ordering satisfaction of an order
capiat qui capere possit: Let him/her take it who is able
captantes capti sumus: We catchers have been caught
captatio benevolentiae: Reaching after favour
caret initio et fine: It lacks a beginning and an end
cassetur billa: Let the bill be terminated
causa: Cause, precipitating factor
causa causans: Cause that causes all things
causa causata: Cause resulting from a previous cause

causa efficiens: Efficient or effective cause
causa essendi: Cause of being
causa fiendi: Cause of becoming
causa finalis: Final cause
causa formalis: Formal cause
causa latet, vis est notissima: The cause is hidden, but its force is very well known
causa mali: Cause of evil
causa materialis: Material cause
causa mortis: Cause of death, an anticipation of death
causa movens: Reason for undertaking a particular action
causa proxima: Immediate cause
causa sina qua non: Fundamental reason, necessary condition
causa secunda: Secondary cause
causa sui: Cause of itself
causa vera: True cause
caveat: Let one beware, take caution
caveat actor: Let the doer beware
caveat emptor: Let the buyer beware
caveat venditor: Let the seller beware
caveat viator: Let the traveller beware
cavendo tutus: Safe by taking heed
cave ne cadas: Take care so that you do not fall
cave quid dicis, quando, et cui: Beware of what you say, when, and to whom
certiorari: To be informed by an appellate review court
certum est quia impossible est: It is certain because it is impossible
certum vot pete finnem: Set a definite limit to your desire
cessante causa cessat effectus: Once the cause is removed, the effect will disappear
cessio bonorum: The surrender of goods
cetera desunt: The rest are lacking (the text is incomplete)
ceteris paribus: Other things being equal (other things remaining the same)
chartae libertatum: Charters of liberties
circa (ca.): About (means uncertainty about a date)
circuitus verborum: A circuit of words (a circumlocution)
circulus in probando: A circle in proof (vicious circle in logic)
circulus in definiendo: A circle in definition (vicious circle)
circulus vitiosus: A vicious circle (a logical fallacy)
cito dispensetur: Let it be dispensed quickly
civilitas successit barbarum: Civilization succeeds barbarism

Dictionary of Legal Terms

clarior e tenebris: (I shine) out of the darkness more brightly
clarum et venerabile nomen: Illustrious and venerable name
claves curiae: Keys of the court
clavis: A key; glossary in a text
codex: A volume of manuscripts; a code of laws
Codex Justinianus: the Justinian Code
cogi qui potest nescit mori: S/he who can be forced has not learned how to die
cogitatonis poenam nemo: No one is punished for her/his thoughts
cogito, ergo sum: I think, therefore I am
cognati: Relations of the mother's side
cognovit actionem: S/he has acknowledged the action
collegium: Members of a group united by common interest
colluvies vitiorum: Vile medley of vices, pit of iniquity
comitas inter communitates: Comity (friendliness) of nations
comitas inter gentes: Comity (civility) between nations
commisce: Mix together
commune bonum: The common good
commune periculum concordiam parit: Common danger begets unity
communes loci: Commonplace ideas
communibus annis: In common years, the annual average
communi consensu: By common consent
compesce mentem: Control your temper
complexus: An embracing; aggregate of parts
componere lites: To settle disputes
compos mentis: In a sound state of mind
compos sui: Master of one's self
compos voti: Having obtained one's wishes
compositus: Compounded of...
concedo: I admit, I concede
concordia discors: Harmony in discord
conditio sine qua non: Indispensable condition
coniunctis viribus: With united powers
conscia mens recti: Conscious of being right
conscientia mille testes: Conscience is as good as a thousand witnesses
consensus: By general agreement
consensus audacium: The agreement of rash men; a conspiracy
consensus facit legem: Consent makes the law
consensus gentium: Unanimity of nations; widespread agreement
consensus omnium: Agreement of all members
consequitur quodcunque petit: S/he attains whatever s/he attempts

consilio et animis: By wisdom and courage
consilio et prudentia: By wisdom and prudence
consilio manuque: By strategem and manual labour
consilio, non impetu: By deliberation, no impulse
constantia et virtute: By firmness and courage
consuetudo est altera lex: Custom is another law
consuetudo pro lege servatur: Custom is held as the law
consuetudo quasi altera natura: Habit is second nature
contra bonos mores: Contrary to good morals
contradictio in adiecto: Contradiction in terms
contra ius commune: Against common law
contra formam statuti: Against the form of the statute
contra ius gentium: Against the law of nations
contra mores: Contrary to morals
contra mundum: Against the world (i.e., an unpopular position)
contra naturam: Against nature
contra negantem principia non est disputandum: There is no disputing against one who denies the first principles
contra pacem: Against the peace
contraria contrariis curantur: Opposites are cured by opposites
copia fandi: Abundance of talk
copia verborum: Abundance of words
coram: Before [someone]; in the presence of
coram iudice: In the presence of a judge with jurisdiction
coram nobis: Before us, in our presence
coram non iudice: Before a judge without proper jurisdiction
coram paribus: Before equals, before one's peers
coram populo: In the presence of the people
corona lucis: Crown of light; a large chandelier
corpora lente augescent cito extinguuntur: Bodies grow slowly and die quickly
cornu copiae: The horn of plenty; abundance
corpus: The body; collection of law or writings
corpus delicti: Body of the crime; objective proof of crime
corpus juris: Body of law
Corpus Juris Canonici: Body of religious law
Corpus Juris Civilis: Body of civil law
corpus sine pectore: A body without a soul
corpus vile: Worthless matter
corrigendum: Something to be corrected (pl. **corrigenda**)
corruptio optimi pessima: The corruption of the best is the worst

corruptisima re publica plurimae leges: In the most corrupt state are the most laws
cras: tomorrow
cras credemus, hodie nihil: tomorrow we believe, but not today
cras mane: Tomorrow morning
cras mane sumendus: To be taken tomorrow morning
cras mihi: My turn [is] tomorrow
cras nocte: Tomorrow night
crassa negligentia: Gross negligence, criminal negligence
cras vespere: Tomorrow evening
credendum: Things to be believed, articles of faith
crede quod habes, et habes: Believe that you have it, and you do
credite posteri: Believe it, future generations
credo quia absurdum est: I believe it because it is absurd
credo quia impossibile est: I believe it because it is impossible
credo ut intelligam: I believe so that I may understand
crescat scientia, vita excolatur: Let knowledge increase, let life be perfected
crescit amornummi quantum ipsa pecunia crescit: The love of money grows as our wealth increases
crescite et multiplicamini: Increase and multiply
crescit eundo: It grows as it goes
crescit sub pondere virtus: Virtue grows under oppression
crecitur amor nummi quantum ipsa pecunia crevit: The richer you beome the more you love money
crimen: Crime; criminal
crimen falsi: Crime of falsification; perjury
crimen innominatum: Nameless crime; crime against nature
crimem laesae maiestatis: Crime of high treason
cui bono?: Whom will it benefit? Who stands to gain?
cui fortuna ipsa cedit To whom fortune herself yields
cuilibet in arte sua perito credendum est: Every skilled man is to be trusted in his own art
cui malo?: Whom will it harm?
cui placet obliviscitur, cui dolet meminit: We forget our pleasures, we remember our sufferings
cuique suum: To each his own
cuius: Of which
cuius libet: Of any that you please
cuius vis hominis est errare: It is natural for any man to make a mistake
culpa: Fault

culpae poenae par esto: Let the punishment fit the crime
culpa lata: Gross negligence
culpa levis: Ordinary negligence
culpam poena premit comes: Punishment presses hard onto the heels of crime
cum: With
cum bona venia: With good favour
cum grano salis: With a grain of salt
cum laude: With praise; with distinction
cum multis aliis: With many others
cum notis variorum: With the notes of various critics
cum onere: With the burden [of proving a charge]
cum privilegio: With privilege; an authorized edition
cum tacent clamant: When they are silent, they cry out
cuneus cuneum trudit: A wedge drives a wedge
curae level loquuntur, ingentes stupent: Slight griefs talk, great ones are speechless
curia: A court of law
curia advisari vult: The court wishes to be advised
curia Domini: The Lord's court
curia regis: The king's court
curiosa felicitas: Painstaking spontaneity
currente calamo: With the pen running on; an afterthought
cursus curiae est lex curiae: The practice of the court is the law of the court
cursus honorum: Course of honours leading to a high position
custodia legis: In the custody of law
custos: Guardian
custos morum: Guardian of the manners
custos incorruptissiumus: An incorruptible guardian
custos rotularum: Guardian of the rolls; justice of the peace
casus belli: That which causes or justifies war (reason for war, grounds for a dispute)
ceteris paribus: Other things being equal
compos mentis: Of sound mind (sane)
corum populo: In the presence of the public
corpus delicti: The substance of the crime of offence
cui bono: To whose advantage is it - who is the gainer
Carcer ad homines custodiendos, non ad puniendos, dari debet. Imprisonment should be imposed for keeping people in confinement, not for punishing them (further).

Carcer non supplicii causa sed custodiae constitutus. A prison is established not for the sake of punishment, but for detention under guard.

Casus fortuitus non est sperandus, et nemo tenetur divinare. A chance event is not to be expected, and no one is bound to foresee it.

Casus fortuitus non est supponendus. A chance event is not to be presumed.

Casus omissus et oblivioni datus dispositioni communis juris relinquitur. A case omitted and forgotten (not provided for in statute) is left to the disposal of the common law.

Casus omissus pro omisso habendus est. A case omitted is to be held as: (intentionally) omitted.

Catalla juste possessa amitti non possunt. Chattels rightly possessed cannot be lost.

Catalla reputantur inter minima in lege. Chattels are considered in law among things of least consequence.

Causa causae est causa causati. The cause of a cause is the cause of the effect.

Causa causantis causa est causati. The cause of the thing causing is the cause of the effect.

Causae dotis, vitae, libertatis, fisci sunt inter favorabilia in lege. Causes of dower, life, liberty, revenue are among the things favoured in law.

Causa patet. The reason is obvious.

Causa proxima non remota spectatur. The immediate and not the remote cause is considered.

Causa vaga et incerta non est causa rationabilis. A vague and uncertain cause is not a reasonable cause.

Caveat emptor. Let the buyer beware.

Caveat emptor qui ignorare non debuit quod jus alienum emit. Let the buyer beware; for he ought not act in ignorance when he buys what another has right to.

Caveat venditor. Let the seller beware.

Caveat viator. Let the traveler beware.

Cavendum est a fragmentis. Beware of fragments.

Certum est quod certum reddi potest. That is certain which can be rendered certain

Cessante causa, cessat effectus. The cause ceasing, the effect ceases.

Cessante ratione legis cessat et ipsa lex. When the reason of the law ceases, the law itself also ceases.

Cessante statu primitivo, cessat derivativus. When the original estate comes to an end, the derivative estate is also at an end.

Cessa regnare, si non vis judicare. Cease to reign if you wish not to adjudicate.

C'est le crime qui fait la honte, et non pas véchafaud. It is the crime that causes the shame, and not the scaffold.

Cestuy que doit inheriter al pére doit inheriter al fils. The person who should have inherited from the father should also inherit from the son.

Chacea est ad communem legem. A chase (or hunting ground) exists by common law.

Charta de non ente non valet. A deed of a thing not in being is not valid.

Charta non est nisi vestimentum donationis. A deed is nothing else than the vestment (or clothing) of a gift.

Chirographum apud debitorem repertum praesumitur solutum. When the evidence (or voucher) is found in the debtor's possession, the debt is presumed to be paid.

Chirographum non extans praesumitur solutum. When the evidence of a debt is not in existence, it is presumed to have been discharged.

Circuitus est evitandus. Circuity (roundabout proceeding) is to be avoided.

Citatio est de juri naturali. A summons is by natural right.

Clam delinquens magis punitur quam palam. A person who does wrong secretly is punished more severely than one who acts openly.

Clausulae inconsuetae semper inducunt suspicionem. Unusual clauses always arouse suspicion.

Clausula generalis non refertur ad expressa. A general clause does not refer to things expressly mentioned.

Clausula quae abrogationem excludit ab initio non valet. A clause that precludes abrogation is invalid from the beginning.

Clerici non ponentur in officiis. The clergy should not be placed in temporal offices.

Cogitationis poenam nemo meretur. No one deserves punishment for his thoughts.

Cogitationis poenam nemo patitur. No one is punished for his thoughts.

Collegium est societas plurium corporum simul habitantium. A college is a society of several people dwelling together.

Commodum ex injuria sua non habere debet. (The wrongdoer) should not derive any benefit from his own wrong.

Communis error facit jus. A common error (one often repeated) makes law.

Communis error non facit jus. A common error does not make law. • This maxim expresses a view directly contradictory to the view of the immediately preceding maxim. Both are attested in legal literature.

Compendia sunt dispendia. Abridgments are hindrances. Shortcuts or timesaving measures are often a loss.

Compromissarii sunt judices. Arbitrators are judges.

Compromissum ad similitudinem judiciorum redigitur. A compromise is brought into affinity with judgments.

Conatus quid sit non definitur in jure. What an attempt is, is not defined in law.
Concessio versus concedentem latam interpretationem habere debet. A grant ought to have a liberal interpretation against the grantor.
Concordare leges legibus est optimus interpretandi modus. To make laws agree with laws is the best mode of interpreting them.
Concordia parvae res crescunt et opulentia lites. Small means increase by concord and litigations by opulence.
Conditio illicita habetur pro non adjecta. An unlawful condition is considered unconnected.
Conditio praecedens adimpleri debet prius quam sequatur effectus. A condition precedent ought to be fulfilled before the effect can follow.
Confessio facta in judicio omni probatione major est. A confession made in court is of greater effect than any proof.
Confirmare est id quod prius infirmum fuit simul firmare. To confirm is to make firm at once what before was not firm.
Confirmare nemo potest priusquam jus ei acciderit. No one can confirm before the right accrues to him.
Confirmatio est nulla ubi donum praecedens est invalidum. A confirmation is null where the preceding gift is invalid.
Confirmat usum qui tollit abusum. One confirms a use who removes an abuse.
Conjunctio mariti et feminae est de jure naturae. The union of husband and wife derives from the law of nature.
Consensus est voluntas plurium ad quos res pertinet, simul juncta. Consent is the conjoint will of several people to whom the thing belongs.
Consensus facit legem. Consent makes law. • A contract constitutes law between the parties agreeing to be bound by it.
Consensus, non concubitus, facit matrimonium. Consent, not coition (or sharing a bed), constitutes marriage.
Consensus tollit errorem. Consent removes an error. • A person cannot object to something he has consented to.
Consensus voluntas multorum ad quos res pertinet simul juncta. Consent is the united will of several interested in one subject matter.
Consentientes et agentes pari poena plectentur. Those consenting and those perpetrating will receive the same punishment.
Consentire matrimonio non possunt infra (ante) annos nubiles. Persons cannot consent to marriage before marriageable years.
Consequentiae non est consequentia. The consequence of a consequence does not exist.
Consilia multorum quaeruntur (requiruntur) in magnis. The advice of many is sought in great affairs.

Consortio malorum me quoque malum facit. The company of wicked men makes me also wicked.
Constructio legis non facit injuriam. The construction of the law does not work an injury.
Consuetudo debet esse certa. Custom ought to be fixed.
Consuetudo debet esse certa, nam incerta pro nulla (nullius) habetur. Custom ought to be fixed, for if variable it is held as null (or of no account).
Consuetudo est altera lex. Custom is another law.
Consuetudo est optimus interpres legum. Custom is the best expounder of the law.
Consuetudo loci observanda est. The custom of the place is to be observed.
Consuetudo manerii et loci observanda est. The custom of a manor and place is to be observed.
Consuetudo neque injuria oriri neque tolli protest. A custom can neither arise nor be abolished by a wrong.
Consuetudo non habitur (trahitur) in consequentiam. Custom is not held as (or drawn into) a precedent.
Consuetudo praescripta et legitima vincit legem. A prescriptive and lawful custom overrides the law.
Consuetudo semel reprobata non potest amplius induci. A custom once disallowed cannot again be introduced.
Consuetudo tollit communem legem. Custom takes away the common law.
Consuetudo vincit communem legem. Custom overrules common law.
Consuetudo volentes ducit, lex nolentes trahit. Custom leads the willing; law drags the unwilling.
Contemporanea expositio est optima et fortissima in lege. A contemporaneous exposition is the best and most powerful in the law. • A statute is best explained by following the construction put on it by judges who lived at the time it was made, or soon after.
Contestatio litis eget terminos contradictarios. An issue requires terms of contradiction. • (That is, there can be no issue without an affirmative on one side and a negative on the other).
Contractus est quasi actus contra actum. A contract is, as it were, act against act.
Contractus ex turpi causa vel contra bonos mores nullus est. A contract founded on a wrongful consideration or against good morals is null.
Contractus legem ex conventione accipiunt. Contracts receive legal validity from the agreement of the parties.
Contra negantem principia non est disputandum. There is no disputing against one who denies first principles.

Contra non valentem agere nulla currit praescriptio. No prescription runs against a person unable to act (or bring an action)

Contra veritatem lex nunquam aliquid permittit. The law never allows anything contrary to truth.

Contrectatio rei alienae animo furandi est furtum. Touching or taking another's property with an intention of stealing is theft.

Conventio omnis intelligitur clausula rebus sic stantibus. Every contract is to be understood as being based on the assumption of things remaining as they were (that is, at the time of its conclusion).

Conventio privatorum non potest publico juri derogare. An agreement of private persons cannot derogate from public right. • That is, it cannot prevent the application of general rules of law, or render valid any contravention of law.

Conventio vincit legem. The express agreement of the parties overrides the law.

Convicia si irascaris tua divulgas; spreta exolescunt. If you are moved to anger by insults, you spread them abroad; if despised, they die out.

Copulatio verborum indicat acceptationem in eodem sensu. Coupling words together shows that they ought to be understood in the same sense.

Corporalis injuria non recipit aestimationem de futuro. A personal injury does not receive satisfaction from proceedings yet in the future.

Corpus humanum non recipit aestimationem. The person of a human being can have no price put on it.

Crescente malitia crescere debet et poena. With increase of malice, punishment ought also to increase.

Crimen laesae majestatis omnia alia crimina excedit quoad poenam. The crime of treason exceeds all other crimes in its punishment.

Crimen omnia ex se nata vitiat. Crime taints everything that springs from it.

Crimen trahit personam. The crime brings with it the person. • That is, the commission of a crime gives the courts of the place where it is committed jurisdiction over the person of the offender.

Crimina morte extinguuntur. Crimes are extinguished by death.

Cui jus est donandi eidem et vendendi et concedendi jus est. A person who has a right to give has also a right to sell and to grant.

Cuilibet in arte sua perito est credendum. Credence should be given to a person skilled in his art (that is, when speaking of matters connected with that art).

Cuilibet licet juri pro se introducto renunciare. Anyone may waive or renounce the benefit of a principle or rule of law that exists only for his protection.

Cui licet quod majus non debet quod minus est non licere. A person who has authority to do the more important act ought not to be debarred from doing what is of less importance.

Cui pater est populus non habet ille patrem. That person to whom the people is father has not a father.

Cuique in sua arte credendum est. Everyone is to be believed in his own area of expertise.

Cujus est commodum, ejus debet esse incommodum. The person who has the advantage should also have the disadvantage.

Cujus est commodum, ejus est onus. The person who has the benefit has also the burden.

Cujus est dare, ejus est disponere. The person who has a right to give has the right of disposition. • That is, the bestower of a gift has a right to regulate its disposal.

Cujus est dominium, ejus est periculum. The risk lies on the owner.

Cujus est instituere, ejus est abrogare. Whoever can institute can also abrogate.

Cujus est solum, ejus est usque ad coelum. The person who owns the soil owns up to the sky. • One who owns the surface of the ground owns, or has an exclusive right to, everything that is on or above it to an indefinite height.

Cujus est solum, ejus est usque ad coelum et ad inferos. Whoever owns the soil owns everything up to the sky and down to the depths.

Cujus juris (i.e., jurisdictionis) est principale, ejusdem juris erit accessorium. An accessory matter is subject to the same jurisdiction as its principal.

Cujus per errorem dati repetitio est, ejus consulto dati donatio est. A thing given by mistake can be recovered; if given purposely, it is a gift.

Cujusque rei potissima pars est principium. The principal part of everything is the beginning.

Culpa caret qui scit sed prohibere non potest. A person is free of blame who knows but cannot prevent.

Culpae poena par esto. Let the punishment be equal to the crime.

Culpa est immiscere se rei ad se non pertinenti. It is a fault for anyone to meddle in a matter not pertaining to him.

Culpa lata dolo aequiparatur. Gross negligence is equivalent to fraud.

Culpa tenet (teneat) suos auctores. A fault binds (or should bind) its own authors.

Cum actio fuerit mere criminalis, institui poterit ab initio criminaliter vel civiliter. When an action is purely criminal, it can be instituted from the beginning either criminally or civilly.

Cum adsunt testimonia rerum, quid opus est verbis? When the proofs of facts are present, what need is there of words?

Cum aliquis renunciaverit societati, solvitur societas. When any partner has renounced the partnership, the partnership is dissolved.

Cum confitente sponte mitius est agendum. One making a voluntary confession is to be dealt with more leniently.

Cum de lucro duorum quaeritur melior est causa possidentis. When there is a question of gain between two people, the cause of the possessor is the better.

Dictionary of Legal Terms

***Cum duo inter se pugnantia reperiuntur in testamento, ultimum ratum*: est.** When two clauses in a will are found to be contradictory, the last in order prevails.

Cum duo jura concurrunt in una persona, aequum est ac si essent in duobus. When two rights meet in one person, it is the same as if they were in two persons.

Cum in corpore dissentitur, apparet nullam esse acceptionem. When there is a disagreement in the substance, there is clearly no acceptance.

Cum legitimae nuptiae factae sunt, patrem liberi sequuntur. Children born under a legitimate marriage follow the condition of the father.

Cum quod ago non valet ut ago, valeat quantum valere potest. When that which I do is of no effect as I do it, let it have as much effect as it can (that is, in some other way).

Curatus non habet titulum. A curate has no title (to tithes).

Curia cancellariae officina justitiae. The court of chancery is the workshop of justice.

Curia parliamenti suis propriis legibus subsistit. The court of parliament is governed by its own laws.

Curiosa et captiosa interpretatio in lege reprobatur. An overnice and captious interpretation in the law is rejected.

Currit tempus contra desides et sui juris contemptores. Time runs against the indolent and those who are not mindful of their rights.

Cursus curiae est lex curiae. The practice of the court is the law of the court.

Custome serra prise stricte. Custom shall be construed strictly.

damnant quodnon intelligunt: They condemn what they do not understand
damnosa hereditas: Inheritance of damnation, ruinous legacy
damnum absque iniuria: Loss without injury, not subject to remedy
dapes inemptae: Unbought feasts; homegrown produce
dare pondus idonea fumo: Fit only to give weight to smoke
data et accepta: Things given and received; expenses and income
data fata secutus: Following what is decreed by fate
dat, donat, dicat: S/he gives, devotes, dedicates
date et dabitur vobis: Give and it shall be given unto you
de aequitate: In equity
de ambitu: In bribery
de asini umbra disceptare: To argue about the shadow of an ass
de auditu: From hearsay

debellare superbos: To overthrow the proud
de bene esse: Subject to conditions or provisions
debitum: Debt
debitum naturae: Debt of nature (death)
de bona memoria: Of good memory (of a sound mind)
de bonis asportatis: Of the goods carried away
de bonis non administratis: Of the goods not yet administered
de bonis propriis: Out of his own goods
de bono et malo: Of good and bad; come what may
de bono gestu: For good behaviour
decanus: Dean; having supervision over ten people
deceptio visus: A deception of vision; an optical illusion
decessit sine prole (DSP): Died without children
decies repetita placebit: Though ten times repeated, it will continue to please
decipimur specie rectie: We are deceived by the semblance of what is right
decipi quam fallere est tutius: It is safer to be deceived than to deceive
decipi frons prima multos: The first appearance deceives many
de claro die: By the light of day
decori decus addit avito: He adds honour to the ancestral honour
decretum: A decree; a mandate
decubitus: Lying down
decus et tutamen: Honour and defense
de die in diem: From day to day; continuously
de duobus malis, minus est semper eligendum: Of two evils, always choose the lesser one
de facto: Existing by fact
defectus sanguinis: Failure to issue
deficit omne quod nasciture: Everything that is born passes away
de fide: Of faith
de fide et officio iudicis non recipitur quaestio: No question can be allowed concerning the faith and duty of the judge
definitum: A thing defined
de fumo in flammam: Out of the smoke into the flame
degeneres animos timor arguit: Fear betrays ignoble souls
de gratia: By favour
de gustibus non est disputandum: In matters of taste, there is no argument
de integro: From the beginning; one more time
dei penates: Guardians of the household (household gods)
delictum: Offence
delineavit: S/he drew it

delirium tremens: Alcoholic distress; delusions and trembling
delphinum natare doces: You are teaching a dolphin to swim
de lunatico inquiriendo: A writ to inquire into the insanity of a person
dementia: Insanity
dementia a potu: Insanity from drinking
dementia praecox: Insanity in adolescence
deme supercilio nubem: Remove the cloud from you brow
de minimis: Of the most insignificant things
de minimis non curat lex: The law does not concern itself with trifles
de mortuis nil nisi bonum: Of the dead [say] nothing but good
de nihilo nihil: Nothing comes from nothing
denique caelum: Heaven at last
de omnibus rebus et quibusdam aliis: Concerning all things and certain other matters (circumlocution)
de omni rescibili et quibusdam aliis: Concerning everything knowable and a few other things besides
Deo volente (D. V.): God willing
de pilo pendet: It hangs by a hair (reaching a critical stage)
de plano: With ease, without difficulty
de praesenti: For the present
deprendi miserum est: It is wretched to be detected
De Profundis: From the depths; out of despair
de proprio motu: Of one's own motion (spontaneouly)
de rubus: Of things
De Rerum Natura: On the Nature of Things
desideratum: A thing much desired or needed
designatum: That which is designated
desuetudo: disuse, no longer active
desunt cetera: The rest of things is lacking; the remainder is lacking
desunt multa: Many things are lacking
de te fabula narratur: The story is told about you
de tempore in tempus: From time to time
detur aliquando otium quesque fessis: Let ease and rest be sometimes granted to the weary
detur digniori: Let it be given to the more worthy
detur pulchriori: Let it be given to the more beautiful
de verbo in verbum: Word for word
de verborum signifacatione: On the significance of words
dextras dare: To give right hands (to shake hands)
dextro tempore: At the right time

dicitur: It is said (they say)
dictis facta suppetant: Let deeds correspond to words
dictum ac factum: [No sooner] said than done
dictum de dicto: Report upon hearsay
dictum de omni et nullo: Maxim of all and nothing
dictum sapienti sat est: A word of the wise is sufficient
diebus alternis: Every other day
diebus tertiis: Every third day
diem ex die: Day by day (continuously)
dies: Day, daily
dies a quo: Day from which
dies datus: A given day
dies faustus: A day bringing good fortune; auspicious day
dies infaustus: A day bringing bad fortune; an unlucky day
dies juridicus: A day on which the court is in session
dies non: A day on which no business can be transacted
dies non juridicus: A day on which the court is not in session
difficiles nugae: Labourious trifles
difficilia quae pulchra: Things that are excellent are difficult
digito monstrari: To be pointed out with fingers
dignus vindice nodus: A knot worthy of such a liberator
di (also **dii**)**:** gods (singular: deus)
di maiores: The greater gods; men of eminence
di meliora: Heaven send us better times
dimidius: One-half
di minores: The lesser gods; men of lesser merit
dirigo: I direct
disce pati: Learn to endure
discere et docere: To learn and to teach
discere docendo: To learn through teaching
disiecta membra: Scattered limbs; fragments of a work
dispendia morae: Loss of time
dives agris, dives positis in faenore nummis: Rich in lands, rich in money lent out at interest
divide in partes aequales: Divide into equal parts
divide et impera: Divide and rule *or*: Divide and conquer *or* Divide in order to conquer
divide et regna: Divide and rule
divinae particula aurae: Particle of divine spirit
divitiae virum faciunt: Riches make the man

Dictionary of Legal Terms

dixi: I have spoken (I will say no more)
docendo discitur: One learns by teaching docendo
discimus: We learn by teaching
doce ut discas: Teach in order to learn
doctor utriusque legis: Doctor of both laws (canon and civil)
doctus cum libro: Learned with a book (having book learning)
doctus cum multis libris: Learned with many books (a polymath)
dolium volvitur: An empty cask is easily rolled
dolus: Deceit; fraud
dolus bonus: Permissable deceit
dolus malus: Unlawful deceit
duces tecum: You shall bring it with you (subpoena)
ducit amor patriae: The love of country leads [me]
ductus: Style; manner
ductus figuratus: Figurative or indirect style
ductus simplex: Straightforward or simple style
ductus subtilis: Subtle or deceiving style
dulce bellum inexpertis: War is sweet to those who have never fought
dulce et decorum est pro patria mori: It is sweet and proper to die for one's country
dum: While; on condition that...
dum docent, discunt: While they teach, they learn
dum fortuna fuit: While fortune lasted
dum loquimor fugerit invida aetas: Even as we speak, time speeds swiftly away
dum loquor, hora fugit: Time is flying while I speak
dum solus: While single
dum spiro, spero: While I breathe, I hope
dum tacent clamant: Though they are silent, they cry aloud
dum vita est spes est: While there's life, there's hope
dum vivimus, vivamus: While we live, let us live
duplici spe uti: To have a double hope
dura lex sed lex: The law is hard, but it is the law: **durante:** During
durante absentia: During [someone's] absense
durante bene placito: During good pleasure; as long as one wishes
durante dolore: While pain lasts
durante minore aetate: During minority; at an early age; while one is young
durante vita: During one's life
durum hoc est sed ita lex scripta est: This is harsh but the law is written
dux gregis: Leader of the flock

de duobus malis, minus est semper eligendum: Of two evils, the lesser is always to be chosen (choose the lesser of two evils)

dura lex sed lex: The law is hard, but it is the law

diligentia maximum etiam mediocris ingeni subsidium: Diligence is a very great help even to a mediocre intelligence.

difficile est tenere quae acceperis nisi exerceas: It is difficult to retain what you may have learned unless you should practise it.

de gustibus non disputandum: One ought not argue about tastes/there is no arguing about tastes

de facto: From the fact actual or actually

de jure: In law/by right

de mortuis nil nisi bonum: Speak nothing but good of the dead

de novo: Anew

Damnum sentit dominus. The damage falls on the owner.

Damnum sine injuria esse potest. There can be damage without any act of injustice.

Dans et retinens nihil dat. One who gives and yet retains (possession) does not give effectually (literally, gives nothing).

Da tua dum tua sunt, post mortem tunc tua non sunt. Give the things which are yours while they are yours; after death they are not yours.

Datur digniori. It is given to the more worthy.

Debet esse finis litium. There ought to be a limit to litigation.

Debet quis juri subjacere ubi delinquit. Any offender should be subject to the law of the place where he offends.

Debet sua cuique domus esse perfugium tutissimum. Every person's house should be his safest refuge.

Debile fundamentum fallit opus. A weak foundation frustrates the work (built on it).

Debita sequuntur personam debitoris. Debts follow the person of the debtor. • That is, debts belong to no locality and may be collected wherever the debtor can be found.

Debitor non praesumitur donare. A debtor is not presumed to make a gift.

Debitorum pactionibus creditorum petitio nec tolli nec minui potest. The creditors' suit can be neither quashed nor diminished by the contracts of their debtors.

Debitum et contractus sunt nullius loci. Debt and contract belong to no particular place.

Deceptis, non decipientibus, jura subveniunt. The laws help persons who have been deceived, not those deceiving.

Decimae de decimatis solvi non debent. Tithes ought not to be paid from that which is given for tithes.

Decipi quam fallere est tutius. It is safer to be deceived than to deceive.
De facto jus oritur. From fact springs law; law arises from fact.
Deficiente uno sanguine, non potest esse haeres. For lack of one blood, he cannot be heir.
De fide et officio judicis non recipitur quaestio, sed de scientia sive sit error juris sive facti. The good faith and honesty of purpose of a judge cannot be questioned, but his knowledge may be impugned if there is an error either of law or of fact.
De jure judices, de facto juratores, respondent. The judges answer regarding the law, the jury on the facts.
Delegata potestas non potest delegari. A delegated authority cannot be delegated; a delegated power cannot itself be delegated.
Delegatus non potest delegare. A delegate (or deputy) cannot appoint another; a delegate cannot himself delegate.
Deliberandum est diu quod statuendum est semel. What is to be resolved once and for all should be long deliberated on.
Delicatus debitor est odiosus in lege. A luxurious debtor is hateful in the law.
Delinquens per iram provocatus puniri debet mitius. A wrongdoer provoked by anger ought to be punished less severely.
De majori et minori non variant jura. Concerning greater and lesser, rights do not vary (or justice does vary).
De minimis non curat lex. The law does not notice or concern itself with trifling matters.
De molendino de novo erecto non jacet prohibitio. A prohibition does not lie against a newly erected mill.
De morte hominis nulla est cunctatio longa. When the death of a human being is concerned, no delay is long.
Denominatio fieri debet a dignioribus. Denomination should be made from the more worthy.
De non apparentibus et non existentibus eadem est ratio. The rule is the same respecting things that do not appear and things that do not exist.
Derivativa potestas non potest esse major primitiva. Power that is derived cannot be greater than that from which it is derived.
Derogatur legi cum pars detrahitur; abrogatur legi, cum prorsus tollitur. There is derogation from a law when part of it is taken away; there is abrogation of a law when it is abolished entirely.
Designatio justiciariorum est a rege; jurisdictio vero ordinaria a lege. The appointment of justices is by the king, but their ordinary jurisdiction is by the law.

Designatio unius est exclusio alterius, et expressum facit cessare tacitum. The designation of one is the exclusion of the other; and what is expressed prevails over what is implied.

De similibus ad similia eadem ratione procedendum est. From like things to like things we are to proceed by the same rule. • That is, we are allowed to argue from the analogy of cases.

De similibus idem est judicium. Concerning like things the judgment is the same.

Deus solus haeredem facere potest, non homo. God alone, and not man, can make an heir.

Dies dominicus non est juridicus. Sunday is not a judicial day

Dies inceptus pro completo habetur. A day begun is held as complete.

Dies incertus pro conditione habetur. An uncertain day is considered as a condition.

Dilationes in lege sunt odiosae. Delays in law are odious.

Discretio est discernere per legem quid sit justum. Discretion is to discern through law what is just.

Discretio est scire per legem quid sit justum. Discretion consists in knowing what is just in law.

Disparata non debent jungi. Dissimilar things ought not to be joined.

Dispensatio est vulnus, quod vulnerat jus commune. A dispensation is a wound, because it wounds a common right.

Dissimilium dissimilis est ratio. Of dissimilars the rule is dissimilar.

Dissimulatione tollitur injuria. Injury is wiped out by reconciliation.

Divinatio, non interpretatio, est quae omnino recedit a litera. It is a guess, not interpretation, that altogether departs from the letter.

Divortium dicitur a divertendo, quia vir divertitur ab uxore. Divorce is so called from divertendo, because a man is diverted from his wife.

Dolo facit qui petit quod redditurus est. A person acts with deceit who seeks what he will have to return.

Dolo malo pactum se non servabit. A pact made with evil intent will not be upheld.

Dolosus versatur in generalibus. A deceiver deals in generalities.

Dolum ex indiciis perspicuis probari convenit. Fraud should be proved by clear proofs.

Dolus auctoris non nocet successori. The fraud of a predecessor does not prejudice the successor.

Dolus circuitu non purgatur. Fraud is not purged by circuity.

Dolus est machinatio, cum aliud dissimulat aliud agit. Deceit is an artifice, since it pretends one thing and does another.

Dolus et fraus nemini patrocinentur (patrocinari debent). Deceit and fraud should excuse or benefit no one (they themselves require some excuse).
Dolus et fraus una in parte sanari debent. Deceit and fraud should always be remedied.
Dolus latet in generalibus. Fraud lurks in generalities.
Dominium non potest esse in pendenti. The right of property cannot be in abeyance.
Domus sua cuique est tutissimum refugium. Everyone's house is his safest refuge.
Domus tutissimum cuique refugium atque receptaculum sit. Everyone's house should be his safest refuge and shelter.
Dona clandestina sunt semper suspiciosa. Clandestine gifts are always suspicious.
Donari videtur quod nullo jure cogente conceditur. That is considered to be given which is granted when no law compels.
Donatio non praesumitur. A gift is not presumed.
Donatio perficitur possessione accipientis. A gift is rendered complete by the possession of the receiver.
Donator nunquam desinit possidere antequam donatarius incipiat possidere. A donor never ceases to have possession until the donee obtains possession.
Dormiunt aliquando leges, nunquam moriuntur. Laws sometimes sleep but never die.
Dos de dote peti non debet. Dower ought not to be sought from dower.
Doti lex favet; praemium pudoris est, ideo parcatur. The law favours dower; it is the reward of chastity; therefore let it be preserved.
Do ut des. I give that you may give.
Do ut facias. I give that you may do.
Droit ne done pluis que soit demaunde. The law gives no more than is demanded.
Droit ne poet pas morier. Right cannot die.
Duas uxores eodem tempore habere non licet. It is not lawful to have two wives at one time.
Duo non possunt in solido unam rem possidere. Two cannot possess one thing each in entirety.
Duorum in solidum dominium vel possessio esse non potest. Ownership or possession in entirety cannot belong to two persons.
Duplicationem possibilitatis lex non patitur. The law does not allow a duplication of possibility.

ecce: behold
ecce signum: behold the sign; here is the proof

e contra: on the other hand
e contrario: on the contrary
editio cum privilegio: a licensed and authorized edition of a book
editio princeps: first printed edition of a text
editio vulgata: the common edition for the majority
effectus sequitur causam: the effect follows the cause
effugere non potes necessitates, potes vincere: you cannot escape necessities, but you can overcome them
e flamma petere cibum ego et rex meus: to snatch food out of the flame
egomet mihi ignosco: I myself pardon myself
ego spem pretio non emo: I do not purchase hope for a price
ei incumbit probatio qui dicit non qui negat: the proof lies upon the one who affirms, not the one who denies
ejectamenta: ejected matter, worthless items
ejusdem farinae: of the same flour; persons of the same nature
ejusdem generis: of the same kind; of the same class
elapso tempore: the time having elapsed
elephantem ex musca facis: you are making an elephant out of a fly
elixir vitae: elixir of life
emeritus: one having served his time
empta dolore experientia docet: experience teaches when bought with pain
emptor: buyer, purchaser
emulsio: an emulsion
e necessitate: from necessity; having no alternative
ens a se: a being in itself
Ens Entium: the Supreme Being
ense et aratro: with sword and plow
ense petit placidam sub libertate quietem: by the sword she seeks peaceful repose under liberty
ens legis: a creature of the law
ens rationis: rational being
ens realissimum: the most real being
entia non sunt multiplicanda praeter necessitatem: things are not to be multiplied unless necessary
eo animo: with that intention
eo instante: at that moment
eo ipso: by that itself; by that fact
eo loco: at that very place
eo nomine: under the name
e pluribus unum: one out of many

epulis accumbere divis: to recline at the feasts of the gods
e re nata: under the present circumstance
ergo: therefore
errare est humanum: to err is human
erratum: an error in printing or writing (pi. errata)
erubuit, salva res est: he blushed, the affair is safe
eruditio et religio: learning and religion
esse: to be; being; existence
esse est percipi: to be is to be perceived
esse quam videri: to be rather than to seem
esse quam videri bonus malebat: he preferred to be good rather than to merely seem good
esse quid: to be; being thus so
est ars etiam male dicendi: there is an art even to malediction
est autem vis legem simulans: violence may also simulate the law
est brevitate opus, ut currat sententia: terseness is needed so that the thought may run free
est deus in nobis: there is a god within us
est et fideli tuta silentio merces: loyalty has its reward secure
est modus in rebus: there is a proper measure in things
esto perpetuum: let it be everlasting
esto quod esse videris: be what you seem to be
est quaedam flere voluptas: there is a certain pleasure in crying
est unusquisque faber ipsae suae fortunae: every one is the creator of his own fortune
et alia; et alii (et al.): and other things; and other people
et alibi: and elsewhere
et cetera (etc.): and the rest; and so forth
et cum spiritu tuo: and with your spirit
et decus et pretium recti: both the ornament and reward of virtue
et discere et rerum exquire re causas: both to learn and to investigate the causes of things
et hoc genus omne: and everything of the kind
etiam atque etiam: again and again
etiam peribant ruinae: even the ruins have perished
etiam sapientibus cupido gloriae novissima exuitur: the desire for glory is the last infirmity to be cast off even by the wise
et id genus omne: and everything of the kind
et mihi res, non me rebus subjungere conor: I suit life to myself, not myself to life

et nos quoque tela sparsimus: we too have hurled weapons
et nunc et semper: now and always
et passim: and everywhere; scattered thought
et sceleratis sol oritur: the sun shines even on the wicked
et sequens (et seq.): and the following
et sic de ceteris: and so the rest
et sic de similibus: and so of similar things (or people)
et sic fecit: and he or she did so
et tollens vacuum plus nimio Gloria verticem: Vain glory, who lifts her proud head too high
et uxor (et ux.): and wife
eventus stultorum magister: the result is the instructor of fools
ex abrupto: without preparation
ex abundante cautela: from excessive caution
ex abundantia: out of the abundance
ex abusu non arguitur in usum: from the abuse of a thing there is no arguing against its use
ex acervo: out of a heap
ex adverso: from the opposite side
ex aequo et bono: according to justice and right
ex animo: from the heart; sincerely
ex auctoritate commissa: by virtue of my authority
ex bona fide: out of one's honour; from good faith
ex capite: out of the head; from memory
ex cathedra: from the seat; a position of authority
excelsior: ever higher
exceptio probat regulam de rebus non exceptis: the exception proves the rule as to things not excepted
exceptis exicipiendibus: things excluded which should be excluded
excerpta: selections or excerpts
excitari, non hebescere: to be excited, not dull
ex commodo: from convenience
ex concesso: from what has been conceded
ex contractu: matter arising out of a contract
excudit: he or she cast it
ex curia: from the court
ex delicto: matter arising out of the crime
ex dono: by gift of; donated by
exeat: he or she may go out; allowing student to be absent
exempla sunt odiosa: examples are odious

exempli gratia (e. g.): odious for the sake of example
exemplum exequatur: sample; copy; model it may be executed
exercitatio optimus es magister: practice is the best teacher
ex facie: from the face of
ex facto: from the fact or act
ex facto jus oritur: the law arises out of the fact
ex fide fortis: strength through faith
ex granis fit acervus: many grains make a heap
ex gratia: as an act of grace; out of one's favour
exhibeatur: let it be given
exitus acta probat: the end justifies the means
ex lege: arising from the law
ex libris: from the library of (used on bookplates)
exlonginquo: from a distance
ex malis moribus bonae leges natae sunt: from bad usages, good laws have been born
ex mera gratia: through mere favour
ex mero motu: our of simple impulse; spontaneously
ex modo praescripto: as directed
ex more: according to custom
ex natura rei: from the nature of things
ex necessitate rei: from the necessity of the case
ex nihilo: from nothing
ex nihilo nihil fit: from nothing, nothing can be made
ex officio: by virtue of one's office
Ex ore infantium: Out of the mouth of babies
ex ore parvulorum veritas: out of the mouth of little children (comes) truth
exorire alquis nortis ex ossibus ultor: rise up from my dead bones, avenger
ex parte: from one side only; partisan
ex pede Herculem: to measure Hercules from his foot; from the sample we are able to estimate the whole
experientia docet: experience teaches
experientia docet stultos: experience teaches fools
experimentum crucis: a crucial experiment
experto credito: trust in one who has experience
expertus metuit: having had experience, he is afraid
explicit: it ends here
explorant adversa viros: misfortune tries men
ex post facto: after the fact; in retrospect

expressio unius est exclusio alterius: the expression of one thing excludes others
expressis verbis: in express terms
ex professo: in an open manner
ex proposito: of a set purpose; by design
ex propriis: from one's own resources
ex proprio motu: of one's own accord; voluntarily
ex quocunque capite: for whatever reason
ex relatione: reason upon relation or report
ex tacito: in a tacit manner
ex tempore: spontaneously, without preparation
ex silentio: in consequence of no contrary evidence
exinctus amabitur idem: the same one will be loved after he's dead
extortor bonorum legumque contortor: one who extorts good citizens and twists the laws
extra modum: beyond measure
extra muros: beyond the walls
extra pecuniam non est vita: without money there is no life
ex turpi causa non oritur actio: no immoral matter can lead to a legal action
ex ungue leonem: from the claw (we may judge) a lion; from a sample we may judge the whole
ex uno disce omnes: from one, learn of all; deductive reasoning
eiurare patriam: to renounce one's country
ex usu: of use; advantageous
ex vi termini: from the force of the term
ex voluntate: as a volunteer, without obligation
ex voto: out of a vow; in pursuance of a vow
exitus acta probat: The result validates the deeds.
ejustden generis: Of the same kind
e pluribus unum: One out of many
ex curia: Out of court
exempli gratia: By way of example
Eadem causa diversis rationibus coram judicibus ecclesiasticis et secularibus ventilatur. The same cause is argued on different principles before ecclesiastical and secular judges.
Eadem est ratio, eadem est lex. (If) the reason is the same, the law is the same.
Effectus sequitur causam. The effect follows the cause.
Ei incumbit probatio qui dicit, non qui negat. The burden of the proof rests on the person who affirms, not the one who denies
Ei nihil turpe, cui nihil satis. Nothing is immoral to the person to whom nothing is enough.

Ejus est interpretari cujus est condere. It is that person's to interpret whose it is to enact.
Ejus est nolle, qui potest velle. A person who can will (exercise volition) has a right to refuse to will (withhold consent).
Ejus est non nolle qui potest velle. A person may consent tacitly who can consent expressly.
Ejus est periculum cujus est dominium aut commodum. He who has the dominion or advantage has the risk.
Ejus nulla culpa est cui parere necesse sit. No guilt attaches to a person who is compelled to obey.
Electa una via, non datur recursus ad alteram. When one way has been chosen, no recourse is given to another.
Electiones fiant rite et libere sine interruptione aliqua. Let choices be made in due form and freely, without any interruption.
Electio semel facta, et placitum testatum, non patitur regressum. A choice once made, and a plea witnessed (or intent shown), allows no going back.
Electio semel facta non patitur regressum. An election once made cannot be recalled.
En eschange il covient que les estates soient egales. In an exchange it is desirable that the estates be equal.
Enitia pars semper praeferenda est propter privilegium aetatis. The part of the elder sister is always to be preferred on account of the privilege of age.
Enumeratio infirmat regulam in casibus non enumeratis. Enumeration disaffirms the rule in cases not enumerated.
Enumeratio unius est exclusio alterius. Specification of one thing is an exclusion of the other.
Eodem ligamine quo ligatum est dissolvitur. An obligation is dissolved by the same bond by which it is contracted.
Eodem modo quo oritur, eodem modo dissolvitur. It is discharged in the same way as it is created.
Eodem modo quo quid constituitur, dissolvitur. In the same way as anything is constituted, it is dissolved (or destroyed).
Eodem modo quo quid constituitur, eodem modo destruitur. In the same way in which something is constituted, it may be destroyed.
Equitas sequitur legem. Equity follows the law.
Errores ad sua principia referre est refellere. To refer errors to their origin is to refute them.
Errores scribentis nocere non debent. The mistakes of the scribe (or copyist) ought to do no harm.
Error juris nocet. An error of law injures.

Error nominis nunquam nocet, si de identitate rei constat. Mistake in the name never injures if the identity of the thing is certain.

Error qui non resistitur approbatur. An error that is not resisted is approved.

Error scribentis nocere non debet. The error of a scribe (or copyist) ought not to injure.

Erubescit lex filios castigare parentes. The law blushes when children correct their parents.

Est autem vis legem simulans. Violence may also put on the mask of law.

Est boni judicis ampliare jurisdictionem. It is the role of a good judge to extend the jurisdiction.

Est ipsorum legislatorum tanquam viva vox. The voice of the legislators themselves is like a living voice. • That is, the provisions of a statute are to be understood and interpreted as practical rules for real circumstances.

Est quiddam perfectius in rebus licitis. There is something more perfect in things that are permitted.

Eventus varios res nova semper habet. A novel matter always produces various results.

Ex antecedentibus et consequentibus fit optima interpretatio. The best interpretation is made from what precedes and what follows.

Exceptio ejus rei cujus petitur dissolutio nulla est. There is no exception based on the very matter for which a solution is being sought.

Exceptio falsi est omnium ultima. The exception for falsehood is last of all.

Exceptio firmat regulam in casibus non exceptis. An exception affirms the rule in cases not excepted.

Exceptio firmat regulam in contrarium. An exception affirms a rule to the contrary.

Exceptio nulla est versus actionem quae exceptionem perimit. There is no exception against an action that extinguishes the exception.

Exceptio probat regulam de rebus non exceptis. An exception proves a rule concerning things not excepted.

Exceptio quae firmat legem exponit legem. An exception that confirms the law expounds the law.

Exceptio quoque regulam declarat. The exception also declares the rule.

Exceptio semper ultima ponenda est. An exception is always to be put last.

Excessus in jure reprobatur. Excess in law is condemned.

Excessus in re qualibet jure reprobatur communi. Excess in anything at all is condemned by common law.

Excusat aut extenuat delictum in capitalibus, quod non operatur idem in civilibus. That excuses or extenuates a wrong in capital causes which does not have the same effect in civil suits.

Ex diuturnitate temporis omnia praesumuntur solenniter esse acta. From length of time, all things are presumed to have been done in due form.
Ex dolo malo non oritur actio. An action does not arise from a fraud.
Executio est executio juris secundum judicium. Execution is the execution of the law according to the judgment.
Executio est finis et fructus legis. Execution of the law is its end and fruition.
Executio legis non habet injuriam. Execution of the law cannot work an injury.
Exempla illustrant, non restringunt, legem. Examples make the law clearer, and do not restrict it.
Ex facto jus oritur. The law arises out of the fact.
Ex frequenti delicto augetur poena. Punishment increases with repeated offence.
Ex maleficio non oritur contractus. A contract does not arise out of an illegal act.
Ex malis moribus bonae leges natae sunt. Good laws are born from evil morals.
Ex multitudine signorum colligitur identitas vera. From a great number of signs true identity is ascertained.
Ex nihilo nihil fit. From nothing nothing comes.
Ex non scripto jus venit quod usus comprobavit. Unwritten law is that which custom has sanctioned.
Ex nudo pacto non oritur actio. No action arises on a contract without a consideration.
Ex pacto illicito non oritur actio. From an illicit contract no action arises.
Expedit rei publicae ne sua re quis male utatur. It is to the advantage of the state that a person should not make bad use of his own property.
Expedit rei publicae ut sit finis litium. It is to the advantage of the state that there should be a limit to litigation.
Experientia per varios actus legem facit. Experience through various acts makes law.
Ex praecedentibus et consequentibus est optima interpretatio. The best interpretation takes account of what precedes and follows.
Expressa nocent, non expressa non nocent. Things expressed do harm; things not expressed do not.
Expressa non prosunt quae non expressa proderunt. There is no benefit in expressing what will benefit when unexpressed.
Expressio eorum quae tacite insunt nihil operatur. The expression of those things that are tacitly implied is of no consequence.
Expressio unius est exclusio alterius. The expression of one thing is the exclusion of another.
Extincto subjecto, tollitur adjunctum. When the substance is gone, the adjunct disappears.

Ex tota materia emergat resolutio. The construction or explanation should arise out of the whole subject matter.
Extra legem positus est civiliter mortuus. An outlaw is dead as a citizen.
Extra territorium jus dicenti impune non paretur. One who gives a judgment outside his jurisdiction is disobeyed with impunity.
Extra territorium jus dicenti non paretur impune. One who gives a judgment outside his jurisdiction is not obeyed with impunity.
Extremis probatis praesumuntur media. Extremes having been proved, intermediate things are presumed.
Ex turpi causa non oritur actio. No action arises out of a wrongful consideration.

facere sacramentum: to take an oath
facere totum: to do everything
facies non omnibus una nec diversa tamen: the features are not the same in all respects, nor are they different
facile est inventis addere: it is easy to add to things already invented
facile largire de alieno: it is easy to be generous with things of another person
facile omnes quom valemus recta consilia aegrotis damus: when we are healthy, we all have advice for those who are sick
facile princeps: easily first; number one in the field
facilis descensus Averno: the descent to hell is easy
facilius est multa facere quam diu: it is easier to do many things than to do one thing for a long time
facinus quos inquinant aequat: guilt equates all who share in guilt
facit indignatio versum: indignation produces verse
facta armorum: facts of arms
fact non verba: deeds not words; action not speeches
facta sunt potentiora verbis: facts are more powerful than words
factotum: one who does everything; handyman
factum est: it is done, it is complete
factum infectum fieri nequit: a thing done cannot be undone
factum probandum: the fact of a case to be proved
factum probans: facts tending to prove other facts
fac ut sciam: make me know; make me aware
faex populi: the dregs of the people; the rabble
fallacia consequentis: fallacy of the consequence
falsa demonstratio: false designation; erroneous description
falsa lectio: false reading; erroneous interpretation

falsi crimem: the crime of falsification
falsus in uno, falsus in omnibus: false in one thing, false in everything
fama clamosa: noisy rumor; public scandal
fama mala quo non aliud velocius ullum: there is nothing swifter than an evil rumor
famam extendere factis: to make known his fame by deeds
fama volat: rumor flies (i.e., travels fast)
fames optimum condimentum: hunger is the best seasoning
famosus libellus: a slanderous or libelous letter
farrago libelli: miscellaneous contents of a book
fari quae sentiat: to say what one feels
fas est et ab hoste doceri: it is right to learn even from an enemy
fasti: calendar of events
fatua mulier: a foolish woman; a prostitute
favete linguis: favour with your tongue; say nothing bad lest you displease the gods
fax mentis incendium gloriae: the passion for glory is fire for the mind
fecit: he or she made it
felicitas habet multos amicos: prosperity has many friends
feliciter: happily; fortunately
felix culpa: fortunate fault
felix qui nihil debet: happy is he who owes nothing
felix qui potuit rerum cognoscere causas: fortunate is he who understands the causes of things
felo de se: one who kills himself doing an illegal act
ferae naturae: wild beasts; undomesticated animals
fere libenter homines id quod volunt credunt: men readily believe what they want to believe
ferrea non venerem sed praedam saecula laudant: the iron age celebrates not love but the acquisition of material possessions
fiat experimentum in corpore: let one experiment on a body
fiat haustus: let a draught be made let
fiat justitia: let justice be done
fiat justitia, ruat caelum: let justice be done, even though the heavens fall
fiat lux: let there be light
fiat mixtura: let a mixture be made
fiat potio: let a portion be made
fiat voluntas tua: Thy will be done
ficta voluptatis causa sint proxima veris: fictions should approximate the truth in order to please

fictio cedit veritati: fiction yields to the truth
fide et amore: by faith and love
fide et fortitudine: by fidelity and fortitude
fideli certa merces: to the faithful, reward is certain
fidelis ad urnam: faithful to the urn; faithful until death
fideliter: faithfully
fide, non armis: by faith, not by arms
fides ante intellectum: faith before understanding
fides, sed cui vide: trust, but watch out to whom
fides et justitia: faith and justice
fides et veritas: faith and truth
fides facit fidem: faith creates faith
fides non timet: faith does not fear
fides probata coronat: approved faith confers a crown
fides Punica: Punic faith; treacherous
fides servanda est: faith must be kept
fidus Achates: faithful companion
fidus et audax: faithful and courageous
fieri facias: writ authorizing execution of a judgment
figura causae: stylistic pattern of a speech
filius: a son
filius est pars patris: a son is part of the father
filius nullius: son of nobody; bastard
filius populi: son of the people
filius terrae: son of the earth; a serf
finem respice: look to the end; consider the end
flamma fumo est proxima: fire is very close to smoke
fortes fortuna iuvat: Fortune favours the brave
fortiter in re, suaviter in modo: Resolute/unhesitant in action, gentle in manner.
fallaces sunt rerum species: The appearances of things are deceptive.
favete linguis: Favour me with your tongues (be silent)
flat justitia ruat coelum: Let justice be done through the heavens fall
flat lux: Let there be light
fidei defensor: Defender of the faith
flagrante delicto: The very act
floreat: Let it flourish
fons et origo: The source and origin
fortasse: May be
Facinus quos inquinat aequat. Guilt makes equal those whom it stains.

Facta tenent multa quae fieri prohibentur. Deeds contain many things that are prohibited to be done.

Factum a judice quod ad ejus officium non spectat, non ratum est. A judge's act that does not pertain to his office is of no force.

Factum cuique suum, non adversario, nocere debet. Anyone's act should injure himself, not his adversary.

Factum infectum fieri nequit. What is done cannot be undone.

Factum negantis nulla probatio. No proof is incumbent on a person who denies a fact.

Factum non dicitur quod non perseverat. That is not said to be done which does not last.

Factum unius alteri nocere non debet. The deed of one should not hurt the other.

Facultas probationum non est angustanda. The capability of offering proofs is not to be narrowed.

Falsa causa non nocet. A false motive does no injury. • Generally, an erroneous motive does not invalidate.

Falsa demonstratione legatum non perimi. A legacy is not destroyed by an incorrect description.

Falsa demonstratio non nocet, cum de corpore (persona) constat. False description does not injure or vitiate, provided the thing or person intended has once been sufficiently described. • Mere false description does not make an instrument inoperative.

Falsa grammatica non vitiat chartam. False grammar does not vitiate a charter.

Falsa orthographia sive falsa grammatica non vitiat concessionem. Error in spelling or grammar does not vitiate a grant.

Falsus in uno, falsus in omnibus. False in one thing, false in everything

Fama, fides, et oculus non patiuntur ludum. Reputation, plighted faith, and eyesight do not endure deceit.

Fatetur facinus qui judicium fugit. A person who flees judgment confesses guilt.

Fatuus praesumitur qui in proprio nomine errat. A person is presumed to be incompetent who makes a mistake in his own name (that is, does not know his own name).

Favorabilia in lege sunt fiscus, dos, vita, libertas. The treasury, dower, life, and liberty are things favoured in law.

Favorabiliores rei potius quam actores habentur. Defendants are rather to be favoured than plaintiffs.

Favorabiliores sunt executiones aliis processibus quibuscunque. Executions are preferred to all other processes whatever.

Favores ampliandi sunt; odia restringenda. Favourable inclinations are to be enlarged; animosities restrained.

Felix qui potuit rerum cognoscere causas. Happy is he who could apprehend the causes of things.

Felonia implicatur in quolibet proditione. Felony is implied in every treason.

Fere secundum promissorem interpretamur. We generally interpret in favour of the promisor.

Festinatio justitiae est noverca infortunii. The hurrying of justice is the stepmother of misfortune.

Fiat prout fieri consuevit, nil temere novandum. Let it be done as it is accustomed to be done; let no innovation be made rashly.

Fictio est contra veritatem, sed pro veritate habetur. Fiction is contrary to the truth, but it is regarded as truth.

Fictio juris non est ubi veritas. Where truth is, fiction of law does not exist.

Fictio legis inique operatur alicui damnum vel injuriam. Fiction of law works unjustly if it works loss or injury to anyone.

Fictio legis neminem laedit. A fiction of law injures no one.

Fides est obligatio conscientiae alicujus ad intentionem alterius. Faith is an obligation of conscience of one to the will of another.

Fides servanda est. Faith must be observed. • An agent must not violate the confidence reposed in him or her.

Fides servanda est; simplicitas juris gentium praevaleat. Faith is to be preserved; the simplicity of the law of nations should prevail.

Fieri non debet, sed factum valet. It ought not to be done, but if done it is valid.

Filiatio non potest probari. Filiation cannot be proved. • That is, the husband is presumed to be the father of a child born during coverture.

Filius est nomen naturae, sed haeres nomen juris. "Son" is a name of nature, but "heir" a name of law.

Filius in utero matris est pars viscerum matris. A child in the mother's womb is part of the mother's vitals.

Finis finem litibus imponit. A fine puts an end to litigation.

Finis rei attendendus est. The end of a thing is to be attended to.

Finis unius diei est principium alterius. The end of one day is the beginning of another.

Firmior et potentior est operatio legis quam dispositio hominis. The operation of law is firmer and more powerful than the will of man.

Forma legalis forma essentialis. Legal form is essential form.

Forma non observata, infertur adnullatio actus. When form is not observed, a nullity of the act is inferred.

Fortior est custodia legis quam hominis. The custody of the law is stronger than that of man.

Fortior et potentior est dispositio legis quam hominis. The disposition of the law is stronger and more powerful than that of man.
Fractionem diei non recipit lex. The law does not regard a fraction of a day.
Frater fratri uterino non succedit in haereditate paterna. A brother shall not succeed a uterine brother in the paternal inheritance.
Fraus est celare fraudem. It is a fraud to conceal a fraud.
Fraus est odiosa et non praesumenda. Fraud is odious and not to be presumed.
Fraus et dolus nemini patrocinari debent. Fraud and deceit should excuse no one.
Fraus et jus nunquam cohabitant. Fraud and justice never dwell together.
Fraus latet in generalibus. Fraud lies hidden in general expressions.
Fraus meretur fraudem. Fraud deserves fraud.
Frequentia actus multum operatur. The frequency of an act has much effect.
Fructus augent haereditatem. Fruits enhance an inheritance.
Fructus pendentes pars fundi videntur. Hanging fruits are considered part and parcel of land.
Fructus perceptos villae non esse constat. It is agreed that gathered fruits are not a part of the farm.
Frumenta quae sata sunt solo cedere intelliguntur. Grain that has been sown is understood to belong to the soil.
Frustra agit qui judicium prosequi nequit cum effectu. A person sues in vain who cannot prosecute his judgment with effect.
Frustra est potentia quae nunquam venit in actum. Power that never comes to be exercised is useless.
Frustra expectatur eventus cujus effectus nullus sequitur. An event is vainly awaited from which no effect follows.
Frustra feruntur leges nisi subditis et obedientibus. Laws are made to no purpose except for those who are subject and obedient.
Frustra fit per plura quod fieri potest per pauciora. That is done vainly through many measures if it can be accomplished through fewer.
Frustra legis auxilium quaerit qui in legem committit. Vainly does a person who offends against the law seek the help of the law.
Frustra petis quod mox es restiturus. Vainly you seek what you are soon to restore.
Frustra petis quod statim alteri reddere cogeris. Vainly you seek what you will immediately be compelled to give back to another.
Frustra probatur quod probatum non relevat. It is useless to prove what if proved would not aid the matter in question.
Furiosi nulla voluntas est. An insane person has no will.
Furiosus absentis loco est. An insane person is considered as absent.

Furiosus solo furore punitur. An insane person is punished by insanity alone.

Furor contrahi matrimonium non sinit, quia consensu opus est. Insanity prevents marriage from being contracted, because consent is needed.

Furtum non est ubi initium habet detentionis per dominium rei. There is no theft where the holder has a beginning of detention (began holding the object) through ownership of the thing.

Generale dictum generaliter est interpretandum. A general expression is to be construed generally.

Generale nihil certi implicat. A general expression implies nothing certain.

Generalia praecedunt, specialia sequuntur. Things general precede; things special follow.

Generalia specialibus non derogant. Things general do not restrict (or detract from) things special.

Generalia sunt praeponenda singularibus. General things are to be put before particular things.

Generalia verba sunt generaliter intelligenda. General words are to be understood in a general sense.

Generalibus specialia derogant. Things special restrict things general.

Generalis clausula non porrigitur ad ea quae antea specialiter sunt comprehensa. A general clause does not extend to those things that have been previously provided for specifically.

Generalis regula generaliter est intelligenda. A general rule is to be understood generally.

Glossa viperina est quae corrodit viscera textus. It is a poisonous gloss that gnaws away the vitals of the text.

Grammatica falsa non vitiat chartam. False grammar does not vitiate a deed.

Gravius est divinam quam temporalem laedere majestatem. It is more serious to hurt divine than temporal majesty.

Haereditas est successio in universum jus quod defunctus habuerat. Inheritance is the succession to every right possessed by the late possessor.

Haereditas nunquam ascendit. An inheritance never ascends.

Haeredum appellatione veniunt haeredes haeredum in infinitum. By the title of heirs, come the heirs of heirs to infinity.

Haeres est alter ipse, et filius est pars patris. An heir is another self, and a son is a part of the father.
Haeres est aut jure proprietatis aut jure representationis. A person is an heir by either right of property or right of representation.
Haeres est eadem persona cum antecessore. The heir is the same person as the ancestor.
Haeres est nomen collectivum. "Heir" is a collective noun.
Haeres est nomen juris, filius est nomen naturae. "Heir" is a term of law; "son" is one of nature.
Haeres est pars antecessoris. An heir is a part of the ancestor.
Haeres haeredis mei est meus haeres. The heir of my heir is my heir.
Haeres legitimus est quem nuptiae demonstrant. The lawful heir is the one whom the marriage indicates (i.e., who is born in wedlock).
Haeres minor uno et viginti annis non respondebit, nisi in casu dotis. An heir under 21 years of age is not answerable, except in the matter of the dower.
Hoc servabitur quod initio convenit. That shall be preserved which is useful in the beginning.
Hominum causa jus constitutum est. Law was established for the benefit of humankind.
Homo et capax et incapax esse potest in diversis temporibus. A person may be capable and incapable at different times.
Homo vocabulum est naturae; persona juris civilis. "Man" (*homo*) is a term of nature; "person" (*persona*), a term of civil law.
hic et ubique: Here and everywhere
hic jacet: Here lies
hinc illae lacrimae: Hence come those tears
hoc genus omne: And all that sort of people
honoris causa: For the sake of honour

ignis internum: The fire within
ipsa scientia potestas est: Knowledge itself is power.
in pace, ut sapiens, aptarit idonea bello: In peace, like a wise man, he appropriately prepares for war.
idem: The same
id est: That is
in camera: In secret in a judges private room
index expurgatorius: A list of forbidden books
in excelsis: In the highest

in extenso: At full length
in extremis: At the point of death
infra dignitatem: Below ones dignity
in medias res: In the midst of things
in memoriam: In memory to the memory of
in re: In the matter of
in situ: In its original position
in statu pupillari: In the state of being a ward
integer vitae: Blameless of life
inter allia: Among other things
in toto: Entirely
ipse dixit: He himself said it
ipsissima verba: The very words
ipso facto: In the fact itself
Id certum est quod certum reddi potest. That is certain which can be made certain.
Idem agens et patiens esse non potest. The same person cannot be both agent and patient (i.e., the doer and person to whom the thing is done).
Idem est facere et nolle prohibere cum possis. It is the same thing to commit an act and to refuse to prohibit it when you can.
Idem est nihil dicere et insufficienter dicere. It is the same thing to say nothing and not to say enough. • To say a thing in an insufficient manner is the same as not to say it at all.
Idem est non esse et non apparere. It is the same thing not to be as not to appear. • What does not appear on the record is considered non-existent.
Idem est non probari et non esse; non deficit jus sed probatio. It is the same thing not to be proved and not to exist; the law is not deficient but the proof.
Idem est scire aut scire debere aut potuisse. To be bound to know or to have been able to know is the same as to know.
Idem non esse et non apparere. It is the same thing not to exist and not to appear.
Idem semper antecedenti proximo refertur. Idem (the same) always refers to the nearest antecedent.
Identitas vera colligitur ex multitudine signorum. True identity is collected from a great number of signs.
Id perfectum est quod ex omnibus suis partibus constat. That is perfect which is complete in all its parts.
Id possumus quod de jure possumus. We are able to do that which we can do lawfully.
Id quod nostrum est sine facto nostro ad alium transferri non potest. What belongs to us cannot be transferred to another without our act (or deed).

Id solum nostrum quod debitis deductis nostrum est. That alone is ours which is ours after debts have been deducted.

Id tantum possumus quod de jure possumus. We can do only what we can lawfully do.

Ignorantia eorum quae quis scire tenetur non excusat. Ignorance of those things that anyone is bound to know does not excuse.

Ignorantia excusatur non juris sed facti. Ignorance of fact is excused but not ignorance of law.

Ignorantia facti excusat, ignorantia juris non excusat. Ignorance of fact excuses; ignorance of law does not excuse. • Every person must be considered cognizant of the law; otherwise, there is no limit to the excuse of ignorance.

Ignorantia judicis est calamitas innocentis. The ignorance of the judge is the misfortune of the innocent.

Ignorantia juris non excusat. Ignorance of the law does not excuse.

Ignorantia juris quod quisque scire tenetur neminem excusat. Ignorance of the law, which everyone is bound to know, excuses no one.

Ignorantia juris sui non praejudicat juri. Ignorance of one's right does not prejudice the right.

Ignorantia legis neminem excusat. Ignorance of law excuses no one.

Ignorantia praesumitur ubi scientia non probatur. Ignorance is presumed where knowledge is not proved.

Ignorare legis est lata culpa. To be ignorant of the law is gross neglect of it.

Ignoratis terminis artis, ignoratur et ars. Where the terms of an art are unknown, the art is also unknown.

Ignoscitur ei qui sanguinem suum qualiter redemptum voluit. A person is forgiven who chose to purchase his own blood (or life) on any terms whatsoever. • Whatever a person may do under the fear of losing life or limb will not be held binding on him in law.

Illud quod alteri unitur extinguitur, neque amplius per se vacare licet. That which is united to another is extinguished, nor can it again be detached.

Immobilia situm sequuntur. Immovables follow (the law of) their locality.

Imperii majestas est tutelae salus. The majesty of the empire is the safety of its protection.

Imperitia culpae annumeratur. Unskillfulness is reckoned as a fault (as blameworthy conduct or neglect). • Also termed *Imperitia enumeratur culpae.*

Imperitia est maxima mechanicorum poena. Unskillfulness is the greatest punishment of mechanics (i.e., from its effect in making them liable to those by whom they are employed).

Impersonalitas non concludit nec ligat. Impersonality neither concludes nor binds.

Impius et crudelis judicandus est qui libertati non favet. A person is to be judged impious and cruel who does not favour liberty.
Impossibilium nulla obligatio est. There is no obligation to perform impossible things.
Impotentia excusat legem. Powerlessness excuses (or dispenses with) law. • The impossibility of doing what is required by the law excuses non-performance or non-enforcement.
Improbi rumores dissipati sunt rebellionis prodromi. Wicked rumors spread abroad are the forerunners of rebellion.
Impunitas continuum affectum tribuit delinquendi. Impunity provides a constant inclination to wrongdoing.
Impunitas semper ad deteriora invitat. Impunity invites (an offender) to ever worse offences.
In aequali jure melior est conditio possidentis. When the parties have equal rights, the condition of the possessor is the better.
In alta proditione nullus potest esse accessorius sed principalis solummodo. In high treason no one can be an accessory but only a principal.
In alternativis electio est debitoris. The debtor has the choice among alternatives.
In ambiguis casibus sempter praesumitur pro rege. In doubtful cases the presumption is always in favour of the king.
In atrocioribus delictis punitur affectus licet non sequatur effectus. In the more atrocious crimes, the intent (or attempt) is punished even if the effect does not follow.
In casu extremae necessitatis omnia sunt communia. In a case of extreme necessity, everything is in common.
Incaute factum pro non facto habetur. An alteration done carelessly (inadvertently) will be taken as not done.
Incendium aere alieno non exuit debitorem. A fire does not release a debtor from his debt.
Incerta pro nullis habentur. Things uncertain are considered as nothing.
Incerta quantitas vitiat actum. An uncertain quantity vitiates the act.
Incivile est, nisi tota sententia inspecta, de aliqua parte judicare. It is improper to give an opinion on any part of a passage without examining the whole.
In civilibus ministerium excusat, in criminalibus non item. In civil matters, agency (or service) excuses, but not so in criminal matters.
In claris non est locus conjecturis. In obvious instances there is no room for conjectures.
Incommodum non solvit argumentum. An inconvenience does not solve (or demolish) an argument.
In conjunctivis oportet utramque partem esse veram. In conjunctive constructions, each part must be true.

In consimili casu consimile debet esse remedium. In a similar case, the remedy should be similar.

In contractibus, rei veritas potius quam scriptura perspici debet. In contracts, the truth of the matter ought to be regarded rather than the writing.

In contractibus tacite insunt quae sunt moris et consuetudinis. In contracts, matters of custom and usage are tacitly implied. • A contract is understood to contain the customary clauses, although they are not expressed.

In contrahenda venditione, ambiguum pactum contra venditorem interpretandum est. In the contract of sale, an ambiguous agreement is to be interpreted against the seller.

In conventionibus, contrahentium voluntas potius quam verba spectari placuit. In agreements, the intention of the contracting parties should be regarded more than their words.

Incorporalia bello non adquiruntur. Incorporeal things are not acquired by war.

In criminalibus probationes debent esse luce clariores. In criminal cases, the proofs ought to be clearer than light.

In criminalibus sufficit generalis malitia intentionis cum facto paris gradus. In criminal cases, a general wickedness of intention is sufficient if combined with an act of equal or corresponding degree.

In criminalibus voluntas reputabitur pro facto. In criminal matters, the intent will be reckoned as the deed. • In criminal attempts or conspiracy, the intention is considered in place of the act.

Inde datae leges ne fortior omnia posset. Laws were made lest the stronger should have unlimited power.

Indefinitum aequipollet universali. The undefined is equivalent to the whole.

Indefinitum supplet locum universalis. The undefined supplies the place of the whole.

Index animi sermo. Speech is the index of the mind.

In disjunctivis sufficit alteram partem esse veram. In disjunctive constructions, it is sufficient if either part is true.

In dubiis benigniora praeferenda sunt. In doubtful cases, the more liberal constructions are to be preferred.

In dubiis magis dignum est accipiendum. In doubtful cases, the more worthy is to be accepted.

In dubiis non praesumitur pro testamento. In doubtful cases, there is not presumption in favour of the will.

In dubio, haec legis constructio quam verba ostendunt. In a doubtful case, the construction of the law is what the words indicate.

In dubio, pars mitior est sequenda. In a doubtful case, the gentler course is to be followed.

In dubio, pro lege fori. In a doubtful case, the law of the forum (is to be favoured).

In dubio, sequendum quod tutius est. In a doubtful case, the safer course is to be followed.

In eo quod plus sit semper inest et minus. The lesser is always included in the greater.

In favorabilibus magis attenditur quod prodest quam quod nocet. In things favoured, what does good is more regarded than what does harm.

In favorem vitae, libertatis, et innocentiae omnia praesumuntur. All presumptions are in favour of life, liberty, and innocence.

In fictione juris semper aequitas existit. In a fiction of law there is always equity. • A legal fiction is always consistent with equity.

In fictione juris semper subsistit aequitas. In a legal fiction equity always abides (or prevails).

Infinitum in jure reprobatur. That which is endless is condemned in law.

In generalibus latet error. Error lurks in general expressions.

In genere quicunque aliquid dicit, sive actor sive reus, necesse est ut probat. In general, whoever alleges anything, whether plaintiff or defendant, must prove it.

Iniquissima pax est anteponenda justissimo bello. The most unjust peace is to be preferred to the justest war.

Iniquum est alios permittere, alios inhibere mercaturam. It is inequitable to permit some to trade and to prohibit others to do so.

Iniquum est aliquem rei sui esse judicem. It is unjust for anyone to be judge in his own cause.

In judiciis minori aetati succurritur. In judicial proceedings, allowance is made for a minor (in age).

In judicio non creditur nisi juratis. In court no one is trusted except those sworn.

In jure non remota causa, sed proxima, spectatur. In law, the proximate, and not the remote, cause is regarded.

In jure omnis definitio periculosa est. In law every definition is dangerous.

Injuria fit ei cui convicium dictum est, vel de eo factum carmen famosum. An injury is done to the person of whom an insult was said, or concerning whom an infamous song was made.

Injuria non excusat injuriam. A wrong does not excuse a wrong.

Injuria non praesumitur. A wrong is not presumed.

Injuria propria non cadet beneficium facientis. No benefit shall accrue to a person from his own wrongdoing.

Injuria servi dominum pertingit. The servant's wrongdoing reaches the master.
• The master is liable for injury done by his servant.

In majore summa continetur minor. In the greater sum is contained the less.
In maleficiis voluntas spectatur, non exitus. In criminal offences, the intention is regarded, not the event.
In maleficio ratihabitio mandato comparatur. In delict (or tort), ratification is equivalent to authorization.
In maxima potentia minima licentia. In the greatest power there is the least license.
In mercibus illicitis non sit commercium. Let there be no commerce in illicit goods.
In novo casu novum remedium apponendum est. In a novel case a new legal remedy must be applied.
In obscuris quod minimum est sequimur. In obscure cases, we follow what is least so.
In odium spoliatoris omnia praesumuntur. Everything is presumed to the prejudice of the despoiler.
In omnibus (fere) poenalibus judiciis, et aetati et imprudentiae succurritur. In almost all penal judgments, allowance is made for age (or youth) and lack of discretion.
In omnibus quidem, maxime tamen in jure, aequitas spectanda sit. In all affairs indeed, but especially in those that concern the administration of justice, equity should be regarded.
In omni re nascitur res quae ipsam rem exterminat. In everything, the thing is born that ends the thing itself.
In pari causa possessor potior haberi debet. When two parties have equal claims, the possessor should be considered the stronger.
In pari causa potior est conditio possidentis. When two parties have equal claims, the position of the possessor is the stronger.
In pari delicto melior est conditio possidentis. When both parties are equally at fault, the position of the possessor is the better.
In pari delicto potior est conditio defendentis. Where both parties are equally in the wrong, the position of the defendant is the stronger.
In poenalibus causis benignius interpretandum est. In penal cases, the more liberal interpretation is to be made.
In praeparatoriis ad judicium favetur actori. In things preparatory to trial, the plaintiff is favoured.
In praesentia majoris cessat potentia minoris. In the presence of the superior, the power of the inferior ceases.
In propria causa nemo judex. No one can be judge in his own cause.
In quo quis delinquit, in eo de jure est puniendus. In whatever matter one offends, in that the person is rightfully to be punished.

In re dubia magis infitiatio quam affirmatio intelligenda. In a doubtful matter, the negation is to be understood rather than the affirmation.

In re lupanari testes lupanares admittentur. In a matter concerning a brothel, prostitutes will be admitted as witnesses.

In re pari potiorem causam esse prohibentis constat. Where the parties have equal rights (in common property), it is an established principle that the one prohibiting has the stronger cause.

In re propria iniquum admodum est alicui licentiam tribuere sententiae. It is extremely unjust to assign anyone the privilege of judgment in his own cause.

In republica maxime conservanda sunt jura belli. The laws of war must be especially preserved in the state.

In restitutionem, non in poenam, haeres succedit. The heir succeeds to the restitution, not the penalty.

In restitutionibus benignissima interpretatio facienda est. The most favourable construction is to be made in restitutions.

Insanus est qui, abjecta ratione, omnia cum impetu et furore facit. The person is insane who, having cast aside reason, does everything with violence and rage.

In satisfactionibus non permittitur amplius fieri quam semel factum est. In payments, it is not permitted that more be received than has been received once for all (i.e., after payment in full).

Instans est finis unius temporis et principium alterius. An instant is the end of one time and the beginning of another.

In suo quisque negotio hebetior est quam in alieno. Everyone is less perceptive (of flaws) in his own business than in that of another.

Intentio caeca mala. A concealed intention is an evil one.

Intentio inservire debet legibus, non leges intentioni. The intention ought to be subject to the laws, not the laws to the intention.

Intentio mea imponit nomen operi meo. My intent gives a name to my act.

Inter arma silent leges. Amid the arms of war the laws are silent.

Interest reipublicae ne maleficia remaneant impunita. It is in the interest of the state that crimes not remain unpunished.

Interest reipublicae ne sua quis male utatur. It is in the interest of the state that no one misuse his own property.

Interest reipublicae quod homines conserventur. It is in the interest of the state that people should be protected.

Interest reipublicae res judicatas non rescindi. It is in the interest of the state that judgments already given not be rescinded.

Interest reipublicae suprema hominum testamenta rata haberi. It is in the interest of the state that a person's last will should be held valid.

Interest reipublicae ut carceres sint in tuto. It is in the interest of the state that prisons should be secure.

Interest reipublicae ut quilibet re sua bene utatur. It is in the interest of the state that each person make good use of his own property.

Interest reipublicae ut sit finis litium. It is in the interest of the state that there be a limit to litigation.

Interpretare et concordare leges legibus est optimus interpretandi modus. To interpret and reconcile laws so they harmonize is the best mode of construction.

Interpretatio fienda est ut res magis valeat quam pereat. Such a construction should be made that the measure may take effect rather than fail.

Interruptio multiplex non tollit praescriptionem semel obtentam. Repeated interruptions do not remove a prescription (or acquisition by long use) once it has been obtained.

In testamentis plenius testatoris intentionem scrutamur. In wills we diligently examine the testator's intention.

In testamentis plenius voluntates testantium interpretantur. In wills the intentions of the testators are more fully (or liberally) construed.

In toto et pars continetur. In the whole the part also is included.

Inutilis labor et sine fructu non est effectus legis. Useless and fruitless labour is not the effect of law.

Inveniens libellum famosum et non corrumpens punitur. A person who discovers a libel and does not destroy it is punished.

In verbis non verba sed res et ratio quaerenda est. In wording, it is not the words but the substance and the meaning that is to be sought.

Invito beneficium non datur. No benefit is given to one unwilling. • No one is obliged to accept a benefit against his consent.

In vocibus videndum non a quo sed ad quid sumatur. In discourse it is not the point from which but the end to which it is drawn that should be regarded.

Ipsae leges cupiunt ut jure regantur. The laws themselves desire that they should be governed by right.

Ira furor brevis est. Anger is a short insanity.

Ita lex scripta est. So the law is written.

Ita semper fiat relatio ut valeat dispositio. Let the relation be so made that the disposition may stand.

Judex aequitatem semper spectare debet. A judge ought always to regard equity.

Judex ante oculos aequitatem semper habere debet. A judge ought always to have equity before his eyes.

Judex damnatur cum nocens absolvitur. The judge is condemned when the guilty party is acquitted.

Judex debet judicare secundum allegata et probata. The judge ought to give judgment according to the allegations and the proofs.

Judex est lex loquens. The judge is the speaking law.

Judex non potest esse testis in propria causa. A judge cannot be a witness in his own cause.

Judex non potest injuriam sibi datum punire. A judge cannot punish a wrong done to himself.

Judex non reddit plus quam quod petens ipse requirit. The judge does not give more than the plaintiff himself demands.

Judicandum est legibus non exemplis. Judgment must be given by the laws, not by examples.

Judices non tenentur exprimere causam sententiae suae. Judges are not bound to explain the reason of their judgments.

Judicia posteriora sunt in lege fortiora. The later decisions are stronger in law.

Judicia sunt tanquam juris dicta, et pro veritate accipiuntur. Judgments are, as it were, the dicta (or sayings) of the law, and are received as truth.

Judiciis posterioribus fides est adhibenda. Trust should be put in the later decisions.

Judici officium suum excedenti non paretur. A judge who exceeds his office (or jurisdiction) is not obeyed.

Judici satis poena est quod Deum habet ultorem. It is punishment enough for a judge that he has God to take vengeance on him.

Judicis est in pronuntiando sequi regulam, exceptione non probata. It is the proper role of a judge in rendering his decision to follow the rule, when the exception has not been proved.

Judicis est judicare secundum allegata et probata. It is the proper role of a judge to decide according to the allegations and proofs.

Judicis est jus dicere, non dare. It is the proper role of a judge to state the right, not to endow it. • Generally interpreted, it is the duty of the judge to administer justice and not to make law.

Judicis officium est opus diei in die suo perficere. It is the duty of a judge to finish the work of each day within that day.

Judicium a non suo judice datum nullius est momenti. A judgment given by a person who is not its proper judge (not in the proper jurisdiction) is of no consequence.

Judicium est quasi juris dictum. Judgment is, as it were, a pronouncement of the right (or a saying of the law).

Judicium non debet esse illusorium, suum effectum habere debet. A judgment ought not to be illusory (or deceptive); it ought to have its proper effect.

Judicium redditur in invitum, in praesumptione legis. In presumption of law, a judgment is given against one's will.

Judicium semper pro veritate accipitur. A judgment is always taken for truth.

Juncta juvant. Things joined together are helpful.

Jura ecclesiastica limitata sunt infra limites separatos. Ecclesiastical laws are limited within separate bounds.

Jura eodem modo destituuntur quo constituuntur. Laws are abrogated or repealed by the same means by which they are made.

Jura naturae sunt immutabilia. The laws of nature are unchangeable.

Jura publica anteferenda privatis. Public rights are to be preferred to private.

Jura publica ex privato promiscue decidi non debent. Public rights ought not to be determined in confusion, from private considerations.

Jurare est Deum in testem vocare, et est actus divini cultus. To swear is to call God to witness, and is an act of religion.

Jura regis specialia non conceduntur per generalia verba. The special rights of the king are not granted by general words.

Jura sanguinis nullo jure civili dirimi possunt. The rights of blood (or kinship) cannot be destroyed by any civil law.

Jurato creditur in judicio. In judgment credit is given to the swearer.

Juratores debent esse vicini, sufficientes et minus suspecti. Jurors ought to be neighbors, of sufficient means and free from suspicion (literally, less suspected).

Juratores sunt judices facti. The jurors are the judges of fact.

Juratus creditur in judicio. In judgment a person who has sworn an oath is believed.

Juris effectus in executione consistit. The effect of law (or of a right) consists in the execution.

Juris ignorantia est cum jus nostrum ignoramus. It is ignorance of law when we do not know our own right.

Jus accrescendi praefertur oneribus. The right of survivorship is preferred to incumbrances.

Jus accrescendi praefertur ultimae voluntati. The right of survivorship is preferred to a last will.

Jus civile est quod sibi populus constituit. The civil law is what a people has established for itself.

Jus descendit, et non terra. A right descends, and not the land.

Jus dicere (et) non jus dare. To state the right (and) not to endow it. • Generally interpreted, to declare the law (and) not to make it.

Jus est ars boni et aequi. Law is the science of what is good and just.

Jus est norma recti; et quicquid est contra normam recti est injuria. The law is the rule of right; and whatever is contrary to the rule of right is an injury.
Jus et fraus nunquam cohabitant. Right and fraud never abide together.
Jus ex injuria non oritur. A right does not arise from a wrong.
Jus in re inhaerit ossibus usufructuarii. A right in the thing cleaves to the person (literally, the bones) of the usufructuary.
Jusjurandum inter alios factum nec nocere nec prodesse debet. An oath made between third parties ought neither to hurt nor to profit.
Jus naturale est quod apud homines eandem habet potentiam. Natural right is that which has the same force among (all) mankind.
Jus non habenti tute non paretur. It is safe not to obey a person who has no right.
Jus publicum privatorum pactis mutari non potest. A public right cannot be changed by agreements of private parties.
Jus quo universitates utuntur est idem quod habent privati. The right that corporations exercise is the same as the right that individuals possess.
Jus respicit aequitatem. Law regards equity.
Jus superveniens auctori accrescit successori. An additional or enhanced right for the possessor accrues to the successor.
Justitia est virtus excellens et Altissimo complacens. Justice is an excellent virtue and pleasing to the Most High.
Justitia firmatur solium. By justice the throne is strengthened.
Justitia nemini neganda est. Justice is to be denied to no one.
Justitia non est neganda, non differenda. Justice is not to be denied or delayed.
Jus vendit quod usus approbavit. The law dispenses what use has approved.

lex non distinguitur nos non distinguere debemus: The law does not distinguish and so we ought not distinguish.
legum servi sumus ut liberi esse possimus: We are slaves of the law in order that we may be able to be free.
lapsus linguae: A slip of the tongue
lex talionis: The law of retaliation
locum tenens: A deputy
La conscience est la plus changeante des régles. Conscience is the most changing of rules.
La ley favour la vie d'un home. The law favours a man's life.
La ley favour l'inheritance d'un home. The law favours a man's inheritance.

La ley voit plus tost suffer un mischiefe que un inconvenience. The law will sooner suffer a mischief than an inconvenience.

Lata culpa dolo aequiparatur. Gross negligence is equivalent to fraud.

Le contrat fait la loi. The contract makes the law.

Legatos violare contra jus gentium est. It is contrary to the law of nations to do violence to ambassadors.

Legem enim contractus dat. The contract gives the law.

Leges figendi et refigendi consuetudo est periculosissima. The practice of adding and annulling laws is a most dangerous one.

Leges fixit pretio atque refixit. He shaped and reshaped laws for a price; he promulgated and annulled laws at a price. • The reference is to a judge who took bribes.

Leges humanae nascuntur, vivunt, et moriuntur. Laws that humans have made are born, live, and die.

Leges non verbis sed rebus sunt impositae. Laws are imposed on affairs, not words.

Leges posteriores priores contrarias abrogant. Subsequent laws repeal prior conflicting ones.

Leges suum ligent latorem. Laws should bind their own author.

Leges vigilantibus, non dormientibus subveniunt. The laws aid those who keep watch, not those who sleep (that is, the vigilant, not the negligent).

Legibus sumptis desinentibus, lege naturae utendum est. Where man-made laws fail, the law of nature must be used.

Legis constructio non facit injuriam. The construction of law does not do wrong.

Legis interpretatio legis vim obtinet. The interpretation of law obtains the force of law

Legislatorum est viva vox, rebus et non verbis legem imponere. The voice of legislators is a living voice, to impose laws on (actual) affairs and not on (mere) words.

Legitime imperanti parere necesse est. One who commands lawfully must be obeyed.

Legitimus haeres et filius est quem nuptiae demonstrant. A lawful son and heir is he whom the marriage declares to be lawful.

Le salut du peuple est la suprême loi. The safety of the people is the highest law.

Les fictions naissent de la loi, et non la loi des fictions. Fictions arise from the law, and not law from fictions.

Les lois ne se chargent de punir que les actions exterieures. Laws undertake to punish only outward actions.

Lex aequitate gaudet. Law delights in equity.

Lex aequitate gaudet; appetit perfectum; est norma recti. The law delights in equity it covets perfection; it is a rule of right.
Lex aliquando sequitur aequitatem. The law sometimes follows equity.
Lex beneficialis rei consimili remedium praestat. A beneficial law affords a remedy in a similar case.
Lex citius tolerare vult privatum damnum quam publicum malum. The law would sooner endure a private loss than a public evil.
Lex contra id quod praesumit probationem non recipit. The law accepts no proof against that which it presumes.
Lex deficere non potest in justitia exhibenda. The law cannot fail in dispensing justice.
Lex de futuro, judex de praeterito. The law (provides) for the future, the judge for the past.
Lex dilationes semper exhorret. The law always abhors delays.
Lex est ab aeterno. The law is from eternity.
Lex est dictamen rationis. Law is the dictate of reason.
Lex est exercitus judicum tutissimus ductor. The law is the safest leader of the army of judges.
Lex est norma recti. Law is a rule of right.
Lex est sanctio sancta, jubens honesta et prohibens contraria. Law is a sacred sanction, commanding what is right and prohibiting the contrary.
Lex est summa ratio. Law is the highest reason.
Lex est tutissima cassis; sub clypeo legis nemo decipitur. Law is the safest helmet; under the shield of the law no one is deceived.
Lex favet doti. The law favours dower.
Lex fingit ubi subsistit aequitas. Law creates a fiction where equity abides.
Lex intendit vicinum vicini facta scire. The law presumes that one neighbor knows the actions of another.
Lex judicat de rebus necessario faciendis quasi re ipsa factis. The law judges of things that must necessarily be done as if actually done.
Lex necessitatis est lex temporis, i.e., instantis. The law of necessity is the law of time, i.e., time present.
Lex neminem cogit ad vana seu inutilia peragenda. The law forces no one to do vain or useless things.
Lex neminem cogit ostendere quod nescire praesumitur. The law forces no one to make known what he is presumed not to know.
Lex nemini facit injuriam. The law does wrong to no one
Lex nemini operatur iniquum, nemini facit injuriam. The law works an injustice to no one and does wrong to no one

Lex nil facit frustra, nil jubet frustra. The law does nothing in vain and commands nothing in vain.
Lex non a rege est violanda. The law is not to be violated by the king.
Lex non cogit ad impossibilia. The law does not compel to impossible ends.
Lex non curat de minimis. The law is not concerned with matters of least consequence.
Lex non debet deficere conquerentibus in justitia exhibenda. The law ought not to fail in dispensing justice to those with a grievance.
Lex non deficit in justitia exhibenda. The law does not fail in showing justice.
Lex non exacte definit, sed arbitrio boni viri permittit. The law does not define exactly, but trusts in the judgment of a good man.
Lex non favet votis delicatorum. The law does not favour the wishes of the fastidious.
Lex non intendit aliquid impossibile. The law does not intend anything impossible.
Lex non novit patrem, nec matrem; solam veritatem. The law knows neither father nor mother; only the truth.
Lex non oritur ex injuria. The law does not arise from an unlawful act.
Lex non patitur fractiones et divisiones statuum. The law does not tolerate fractions and divisions of estates.
Lex non praecipit inutilia, quia inutilis labor stultus. The law does not command useless things, because useless labour is foolish.
Lex non requirit verificari quod apparet curiae. The law does not require that to be proved which is apparent to the court.
Lex plus laudatur quando ratione probatur. The law is more praised when it is consonant with reason.
Lex posterior derogat priori. A later statute repeals an earlier one.
Lex prospicit, non respicit. The law looks forward, not backward.
Lex punit mendaciam. The law punishes falsehood.
Lex rejicit superflua, pugnantia, incongrua. The law rejects superfluous, contradictory, and incongruous things.
Lex reprobat moram. The law disapproves of delay.
Lex respicit aequitatem. Law regards equity.
Lex semper dabit remedium. The law will always give a remedy.
Lex semper intendit quod convenit rationi. The law always intends what is agreeable to reason.
Lex spectat naturae ordinem. The law regards the order of nature.
Lex succurrit ignoranti. The law assists the ignorant.
Lex succurrit minoribus. The law assists minors.
Lex uno ore omnes alloquitur. The law speaks to all with one mouth.

Lex vigilantibus, non dormientibus, subvenit. Law aids the watchful, not the sleeping.

Liberata pecunia non liberat offerentem. The return of money does not free the party presenting it (from liability).

Libertas est naturalis facultas ejus quod cuique facere libet, nisi quod de jure aut vi prohibetur. Liberty is the natural power of doing whatever one pleases, except what is prevented by law or force.

Libertas est res inestimabilis. Liberty is an inestimable thing.

Libertas inaestimabilis res est. Liberty is a priceless good.

Libertas non recipit aestimationem. Freedom does not admit of valuation.

Libertas omnibus rebus favorabilior est. Liberty is more favoured than all things.

Liberum corpus nullam recipit aestimationem. The body of a free person allows no price to be set on it.

Liberum est cuique apud se explorare an expediat sibi consilium. Everyone is free to ascertain for himself whether a recommendation is advantageous to him.

Licita bene miscentur, formula nisi juris obstet. Lawful acts are well joined together, unless some form of law prevents it.

Ligeantia est quasi legis essentia; est vinculum fidei. Allegiance is, as it were, the essence of the law; it is the bond of faith.

Ligeantia est vinculum fidei; ligeantia est legis essentia. Allegiance is the bond of fealty and the essence of law.

Ligna et lapides sub armorum appellatione non continentur. Sticks and stones are not contained under the name of arms.

Linea recta est index sui et obliqui; lex est linea recta. A right line is an index of itself and of an oblique; law is a right line.

Linea recta semper praefertur transversali. The right line is always preferred to the collateral.

Literae scriptae manent. Written words last.

Litis nomen omnem actionem significat, sive in rem, sive in personam sit. The word "lis" (a lawsuit) signifies every action, whether it is in rem or in personam.

Litus est quousque maximus fluctus a mari pervenit. The shore is where the highest wave from the sea has reached.

Locus contractus regit actum. The place of the contract governs the act.

Longa patientia trahitur ad consensum. Long sufferance is construed as consent.

Longa possessio est pacis jus. Long possession is a right of peace.

Longa possessio jus parit. Long possession begets a right.

Longa possessio parit jus possidendi et tollit actionem vero domino. Long possession produces the right of possession and deprives the true owner of his action.

Loquendum ut vulgus, sentiendum ut docti. We should speak as the common people; we should think as the learned.
L'ou le ley done chose, la ceo done remedie a vener a ceo. Where the law gives a right, it gives a remedy to recover.
Lubricum linguae non facile trahendum est in poenam. A slip of the tongue ought not to be easily subject to punishment.
Lucrum facere ex pupilli tutela tutor non debet. A guardian ought not to make money out of the guardianship of his ward.
Lunaticus, qui gaudet in lucidis intervallis. A person is (still) a lunatic who enjoys lucid intervals.

mirabile dictu: Wonderful to relate
mirabile visu: Wonderful to see
mendacem memorem esse oportet: It is fitting that a liar should be a man of good memory (liars should have good memories)
minima maxima sunt: The smallest things are most important.
magnum opus: A great work
male fide: With bad faith treacherously
mea culpa: By my own fault
meo periculo: At my own risk
modus operandi: Plan of working
modus vivendi: A way of living
multum in parvo: Much in little
mutatis mutandis: With necessary changes
mutantur omnia nos et mutamur in illis: All things change, and we change with them.
Magna culpa dolus est. Great fault (or gross negligence) is equivalent to fraud.
Magna negligentia culpa est; magna culpa dolus est. Great negligence is fault; great fault is fraud.
Maihemium est homicidium inchoatum. Mayhem is incipient homicide.
Major continet in se minus. The greater includes the less.
Majore poena affectus quam legibus statuta est non est infamis. A criminal afflicted with a greater punishment than is provided by law is not infamous.
Majori summae minor inest. The lesser is included in the greater sum.
Major numerus in se continet minorem. The greater number contains in itself the less.
Majus continet minus. The greater contains the less.

Majus dignum trahit ad se minus dignum. The more worthy draws to itself the less worthy.

Majus est delictum seipsum occidere quam alium. It is a greater crime to kill one's self than another.

Maledicta expositio quae corrumpit textum. It is a cursed construction that corrupts the text.

Maleficia non debent remanere impunita, et impunitas continuum affectum tribuit delinquendi. Evil deeds ought not to remain unpunished, and impunity affords continual incitement to wrongdoing.

Maleficia propositis distinguuntur. Misdeeds are distinguished from proposals; crimes are distinguished by the intention (with which they are committed).

Malitia est acida, est mali animi affectus. Malice is sour; it is the quality of a bad mind.

Malitia supplet aetatem. Malice makes up for age.

Malitiis hominum est obviandum. The malicious designs of men must be thwarted.

Malum non habet efficientem sed deficientem causam. Evil has not an efficient but a deficient cause.

Malum non praesumitur. Evil is not presumed.

Malum quo communius eo pejus. The more common the evil, the worse.

Malus usus est abolendus. An evil custom ought to be abolished; a bad usage should be abolished.

Malus usus est abolendus, quia in consuetudinibus, non diuturnitas temporis, sed soliditas rationis est consideranda. An evil custom is to be abolished, because, in customs, not length of time, but solidity of reason, is to be considered.

Mandatarius terminos sibi positos transgredi non potest. A mandatary cannot exceed the bounds of his authority.

Mandatum nisi gratuitum nullum est. Unless a mandate is gratuitous (without payment), it is not a mandate.

Manifesta probatione non indigent. Obvious facts are not in need of proof.

Maris et faeminae conjunctio est de jure naturae. The union of male and female is founded on the law of nature.

Matrimonia debent esse libera. Marriages ought to be free.

Matrimonium subsequens tollit peccatum praecedens. A subsequent marriage removes preceding fault.

Matter en ley ne serra mise en bouche del jurors. Matter of law shall not be put into the mouths of jurors.

Maturiora sunt vota mulierum quam virorum. The wishes of women are of quicker maturity than those of men. • That is, women arrive earlier at eligibility for marriage.

Maxime paci sunt contraria vis et injuria. The greatest enemies to peace are force and wrong.
Maximus erroris populus magister. The people are the greatest master of error.
Melior est causa possidentis. The cause of the possessor is preferable.
Melior est conditio defendentis. The condition of the defendant is the better.
Melior est conditio possidentis et rei quam actoris. Better is the condition of the possessor, and that of the defendant (is better) than that of the plaintiff.
Melior est conditio possidentis, ubi neuter jus habet. Better is the condition of the possessor where neither of the two has the right.
Melior est justitia vere praeveniens quam severe puniens. Justice that truly prevents a crime is better than that which severely punishes it.
Melius est in tempore occurrere quam post causam vulneratum remedium quaerere. It is better to oppose in time than to seek a remedy after a wrong has been inflicted.
Melius est jus deficiens quam jus incertum. Law that is deficient is better than law that is uncertain.
Melius est omnia mala pati quam malo consentire. It is better to suffer every wrong than to consent to wrong.
Melius est petere fontem quam sectari rivulos. It is better to go to the fountainhead than to follow the streams.
Melius est recurrere quam male currere. It is better to run back than to run wrong (or badly). • It is better to retrace one's steps than to proceed improperly.
Mens testatoris in testamentis spectanda est. In wills, the intention of the testator is to be regarded.
Mentiri est contra mentem ire. To lie is to go against the mind.
Mercis appellatio ad res mobiles tantum pertinet. The term "merchandise" belongs to movable things only.
Mercis appellatione homines non contineri. Under the name of merchandise human beings are not included.
Merito beneficium legis amittit qui legem ipsam subvertere intendit. A person deservedly loses the protection of the law who attempts to overturn the law itself.
Merx est quidquid vendi potest. Merchandise is whatever can be sold.
Meum est promittere, non dimittere. It is mine to promise, not to discharge.
Minatur innocentibus qui parcit nocentibus. A person threatens the innocent who spares the guilty.
Minima poena corporalis est major qualibet pecuniaria. The smallest bodily punishment is greater than any pecuniary one.
Minime mutanda sunt quae certam habuerunt interpretationem. Things that have had a fixed interpretation are to be altered as little as possible.

Minimum est nihilo proximum. The least is next to nothing.

Minor jurare non potest. A minor cannot take an oath.

Minor septemdecim annis non admittitur fore executorem. A person under 17 years of age is not admitted to be an executor.

Minus solvit qui tardius solvit; nam et tempore minus solvitur. A person pays too little who pays too late; for, from the delay, the payment is less.

Misera est servitus ubi jus est vagum aut incertum. It is a miserable slavery where the law is vague or uncertain.

Mitius imperanti melius paretur. The more mildly one commands, the better is he obeyed.

Mobilia non habent situm. Movables have no fixed site or locality.

Mobilia personam sequuntur, immobilia situm. Movable things follow the person; immovable ones, their locality.

Mobilia sequuntur personam. Movables follow the person.

Modica circumstantia facti jus mutat. A small circumstance attending an act alters the right.

Modus de non decimando non valet. A prescription not to pay tithes is void.

Modus et conventio vincunt legem. Customary form and the agreement of the parties overcome the law. This is one of the first principles relative to the law of contract.

Modus legem dat donationi. Custom (or form) gives law to a gift.

Mora debitoris non debet esse creditori damnosa. Delay by a debtor ought not to be injurious to a creditor.

Mora reprobatur in lege. Delay is disapproved of in law.

Mors dicitur ultimum supplicium. Death is called the extreme penalty.

Mors omnia solvit. Death dissolves all things.

Mortis momentum est ultimum vitae momentum. The moment of death is the last moment of life.

Mortuus exitus non est exitus. A dead issue is no issue. • That is, a child born dead is no child.

Mos retinendus est fidelissimae vetustatis. A custom of the truest antiquity is to be retained.

Mulcta damnum famae non irrogat. A fine does not impose a loss of reputation.

Multa conceduntur per obliquum quae non conceduntur de directo. Many things are conceded indirectly that are not allowed directly.

Multa fidem promissa levant. Many promises lessen confidence.

Multa multo exercitatione facilius quam regulis percipies. You will perceive many things much more easily by practice than by rules.

Multa non vetat lex quae tamen tacite damnavit. The law does not forbid many things that yet it has silently condemned.

Multa transeunt cum universitate quae non per se transeunt. Many things pass with the whole that would not pass separately.
Multi multa, nemo omnia novit. Many men know many things; no one knows everything.
Multiplicata transgressione crescat poenae inflictio. The infliction of punishment should increase with the repetition of the offence.
Multitudinem decem faciunt. Ten make a multitude.
Multitudo errantium non parit errori patrocinium. The multitude of those who err does not produce indulgence for error.
Multitudo imperitorum perdit curiam. A multitude of ignorant practitioners destroys a court.

Nasciturus pro jam nato habetur quamdiu agitur de ejus commodo. One about to be born is held as already born as long as the issue is to his benefit; a child conceived is treated as born to the extent that it is to his or her benefit.
Natura appetit perfectum, ita et lex. Nature aspires to perfection, and so does the law.
Naturae vis maxima; natura bis maxima. The force of nature is greatest; (and, as some say,) nature is doubly greatest.
Naturale est quidlibet dissolvi eo modo quo ligatur. It is natural for a thing to be dissolved in the same way in which it is bound.
Natura non facit saltum, ita nec lex. Nature makes no leap, and neither does the law.
Natura non facit vacuum, nec lex supervacuum. Nature makes no vacuum, and the law nothing purposeless.
Nec curia deficeret in justitia exhibenda. Nor should the court be deficient in showing justice.
Necessarium est quod non potest aliter se habere. That is necessary which cannot be otherwise.
Necessitas est lex temporis et loci. Necessity is the law of time and place.
Necessitas facit licitum quod alias non est licitum. Necessity makes lawful what otherwise is unlawful.
Necessitas inducit privilegium quoad jura privata. Necessity creates a privilege with regard to private rights.
Necessitas non habet legem. Necessity has no law.
Necessitas publica major est quam privata. Public necessity is greater than private necessity.
Necessitas quod cogit defendit. Necessity defends what it compels.

Necessitas vincit legem. Necessity overcomes the law.
Necessitas vincit legem; legum vincula irridet. Necessity overcomes the law; it laughs at the fetters of laws.
Nec tempus nec locus occurrit regi. Neither time nor place thwarts the king.
Nec veniam effuso sanguine casus habet. Where blood has been spilled, the case is unpardonable.
Nec veniam, laeso numine, casus habet. Where the Divinity has been insulted, the case is unpardonable.
Negatio conclusionis est error in lege. The denial of a conclusion is error in law.
Negatio destruit negationem, et ambae faciunt affirmationem. A negative destroys a negative, and both make an affirmative.
Negatio duplex est affirmatio. A double negative is an affirmative.
Negligentia semper habet infortuniam comitem. Negligence always has misfortune for a companion.
Neminem laedit qui jure suo utitur. A person who exercises his own rights injures no one.
Neminem oportet esse sapientiorem legibus. No one ought to be wiser than the laws.
Nemo admittendus est inhabilitare seipsum. No one is allowed to incapacitate himself.
Nemo agit in seipsum. No one acts against himself.
Nemo alienae rei, sine satisdatione, defensor idoneus intelligitur. No one is considered a competent defender of another's property, without security.
Nemo alieno nomine lege agere potest. No one can sue at law in the name of another.
Nemo allegans suam turpitudinem audiendus est. No one testifying to his own wrong is to be heard as a witness.
Nemo auditur propriam turpitudinem allegans. No one is heard when alleging his own wickedness; no one can be heard whose claim is based on his own disgraceful behaviour.
Nemo bis punitur pro eodem delicto. No one is punished twice for the same offence.
Nemo cogitationis poenam patitur. No one suffers punishment for his thoughts.
Nemo cogitur rem suam vendere, etiam justo pretio. No one is bound to sell his property, even for a just price.
Nemo commodum capere potest de injuria sua propria. No one can derive benefit from his own wrong.
Nemo contra factum suum (proprium) venire potest. No one can contradict his own deed.

Nemo damnum facit, nisi qui id fecit quod facere jus non habet. No one does damage except the person who did what he has no right to do.
Nemo dare potest quod non habet. No one can give that which he does not have.
Nemo dat qui non habet. No one gives who does not possess.
Nemo dat quod non habet. No one gives what he does not have; no one transfers (a right) that he does not possess.
Nemo debet bis puniri pro uno delicto. No one ought to be punished twice for the same offence.
Nemo debet bis vexari pro eadem causa. No one should be twice troubled for the same cause.
Nemo debet bis vexari, si constet curiae quod sit pro una et eadem causa. No one ought to be twice troubled, if it appears to the court that it is for one and the same cause of action.
Nemo debet esse judex in propria causa. No one should be judge in his own cause.
Nemo debet immiscere se rei alienae ad se nihil pertinenti. No one should interfere in another's business that does not at all concern him.
Nemo debet in communione invitus teneri. No one should be retained in a partnership against his will.
Nemo debet locupletari aliena jactura. No one ought to be enriched at another's expense.
Nemo debet locupletari ex alterius incommodo. No one ought to be enriched out of another's disadvantage.
Nemo debet rem suam sine factu aut defectu suo amittere. No one should lose his property without his own act or negligence.
Nemo de domo sua extrahi potest. No one can be dragged (taken by force) from his own house.
Nemo duobus utatur officiis. No one should exercise two offices.
Nemo ejusdem tenementi simul potest esse haeres et dominus. No one can be both heir and owner of the same land at the same time.
Nemo est haeres viventis. No one is an heir of someone living.
Nemo est supra leges. No one is above the laws.
Nemo ex alterius facto praegravari debet. No one ought to be burdened in consequence of another's act.
Nemo ex consilio obligatur. No one is bound for the advice he gives.
Nemo ex dolo suo proprio relevetur aut auxilium capiat. Let no one be relieved or gain advantage by his own fraud.
Nemo ex proprio dolo consequitur actionem. No one acquires a right of action from his own wrong deception.

Nemo inauditus condemnari debet, si non sit contumax. No one ought to be condemned unheard, unless for contempt.

Nemo in communione potest invitus detineri. No one can be held (to act) in common against his will; no one can be forced to remain in common ownership against his will.

Nemo in propria causa testis esse debet. No one can be a witness in his own cause.

Nemo jus sibi dicere potest. No one can give judgment for himself.

Nemo militans Deo implicetur secularibus negotiis. No one warring for God should be troubled by secular business.

Nemo nascitur artifex. No one is born an expert. • Wisdom in the law is acquired only through diligent study.

Nemo plus commodi haeredi suo relinquit quam ipse habuit. No one leaves a greater asset to his heir than he had himself.

Nemo plus juris ad alienum transferre potest quam ipse haberet. No one can transfer to another a greater right than he himself might have.

Nemo potest contra recordum verificare per patriam. No one can verify by the country against a record. • Certain matters of record cannot be contested in court.

Nemo potest esse simul actor et judex. No one can be at the same time suitor and judge.

Nemo potest esse tenens et dominus. No one can be at the same time tenant and landlord (of the same tenement).

Nemo potest exuere patriam. No one can cast off his own country.

Nemo potest facere per alium quod per se non potest. No one can do through another what he cannot do by himself.

Nemo potest mutare consilium suum in alterius injuriam. No one can change his purpose to the injury of another.

Nemo potest nisi quod de jure potest. No one is able to do a thing unless he can do it lawfully.

Nemo potest plus juris ad alium transferre quam ipse habet. No one can transfer to another a greater right than he himself (actually) has.

Nemo potest sibi debere. No one can owe to himself.

Nemo praesens nisi intelligat. One is not present unless he understands.

Nemo praesumitur alienam posteritatem suae praetulisse. No one is presumed to have preferred another's posterity to his own.

Nemo praesumitur donare. No one is presumed to make a gift.

Nemo praesumitur ludere in extremis. No one is presumed to trifle at the point of death.

Nemo praesumitur malus. No one is presumed to be bad.

Nemo prohibetur plures negotiationes sive artes exercere. No one is prohibited from exercising several kinds of business or arts.

Nemo prohibetur pluribus defensionibus uti. No one is forbidden to employ several defenses.

Nemo punitur pro alieno delicto. No one is punished for the crime or wrong of another.

Nemo punitur sine injuria, facto, seu defalta. No one is punished unless for some wrong, act, or default.

Nemo qui condemnare potest absolvere non potest. No one who can condemn is unable to acquit.

Nemo sibi esse judex vel suis jus dicere debet. No one ought to be his own judge or to administer justice in cases where his relations are concerned.

Nemo tenetur ad impossibile. No one is bound to an impossibility.

Nemo tenetur armare adversarium contra se. No one is bound to arm his adversary against himself.

Nemo tenetur divinare. No one is bound to foretell the future.

Nemo tenetur edere instrumenta contra se. No one is bound to produce writings against himself.

Nemo tenetur informare qui nescit sed quisquis scire quod informat. No one who is ignorant of a thing is bound to give information of it, but everyone is bound to know what he gives information of.

Nemo tenetur jurare in suam turpitudinem. No one is bound to swear to his own criminality.

Nemo tenetur prodere seipsum. No one is bound to betray himself. • In other words, no one can be compelled to incriminate himself.

Nemo tenetur seipsum accusare. No one is bound to accuse himself. • This is a formulation of the privilege against self-incrimination.

Nemo tenetur seipsum infortuniis et periculis exponere. No one is bound to expose himself to misfortune and dangers.

Nemo tenetur seipsum prodere. No one is bound to betray himself.

Nemo unquam judicet in se. Let no one ever be a judge in his own cause.

Nemo unquam vir magnus fuit sine aliquo divino afflatu. No one was ever a great man without some divine inspiration.

Nemo videtur fraudare eos qui sciunt et consentiunt. No one is considered as deceiving those who know and consent.

Ne quid in loco publico vel itinere fiat. Let nothing be done (put or erected) in a public place or way.

Nigrum nunquam excedere debet rubrum. The black should never go beyond the red. • That is, the text of a statute should never be read in a sense more comprehensive than the rubric, or title.

Nihil aliud potest rex quam quod de jure potest. The king can do nothing but what he can do legally; the king can do nothing except by law.

Nihil consensui tam contrarium est quam vis atque metus. Nothing is so opposite to consent as force and fear.

Nihil dat qui non habet. A person gives nothing who has nothing.

Nihil dictum quod non dictum prius. Nothing is said that was not said before.

Nihil est enim liberale quod non idem justum. For there is nothing generous that is not at the same time just.

Nihil est magis rationi consentaneum quam eodem modo quodque dissolvere quo conflatum est. Nothing is more consonant to reason than that everything should be dissolved in the same way as it was made.

Nihil facit error nominis cum de corpore constat. An error in the name is nothing when there is certainty as to the person.

Nihil habet forum ex scena. The court has nothing to do with what is not before it.

Nihil iniquius quam aequitatem nimis intendere. Nothing is more unjust than to extend equity too far.

Nihil magis justum est quam quod necessarium est. Nothing is more just than what is necessary.

Nihil nequam est praesumendum. Nothing wicked is to be presumed.

Nihil perfectum est dum aliquid restat agendum. Nothing is perfect while something remains to be done.

Nihil possumus contra veritatem. We have no power against truth.

Nihil praescribitur nisi quod possidetur. There is no prescription for what is not possessed.

Nihil quod est contra rationem est licitum. Nothing that is against reason is lawful.

Nihil quod est inconveniens est licitum. Nothing that is improper is lawful.

Nihil quod est licitum est inconveniens. Nothing that is lawful is improper.

Nihil simul inventum est et perfectum. Nothing is invented and perfected at the same moment.

Nihil tam proprium imperio quam legibus vivere. Nothing is so becoming to authority as to live according to the law.

Nil agit exemplum litem quod lite resolvit. A precedent accomplishes nothing if it settles one dispute by raising another.

Nil facit error nominis cum de corpore vel persona constat. An error in the name is immaterial when the body or person is certain.

Nil sine prudenti fecit ratione vetustas. Antiquity did nothing without a good reason.

Nil temere novandum. Nothing should be rashly changed.

Nimia certitudo certitudinem ipsam destruit. Too great certainty destroys certainty itself.
Nimia subtilitas in jure reprobatur. Too much subtlety in law is condemned.
Nimium altercando veritas amittitur. By too much quarreling truth is lost.
Nobiles magis plectuntur pecunia, plebes vero in corpore. The higher classes are more punished in money, but the lower in person.
Nobilitas est duplex, superior et inferior. There are two sorts of nobility, the higher and the lower.
Nomen est quasi rei notamen. A name is, as it were, the distinctive sign (or signifier) of a thing.
Nomen non sufficit si res non sit de jure aut de facto. A name does not suffice if the thing does not exist by law or by fact.
Nomina si nescis, perit cognitio rerum. If you do not know the names of things, the knowledge of things themselves perishes.
Nomina sunt mutabilia, res autem immobiles. Names are mutable, but things immutable.
Nomina sunt notae rerum. Names are the marks of things.
Nomina sunt symbola rerum. Names are the symbols of things.
Non auditur perire volens. One who wishes to perish is not heard.
Non bis in idem (or imperative, ne bis in idem). Not twice for the same thing. • That is, a person shall not be twice tried for the same crime.
Non consentit qui errat. A person who errs does not consent.
Non dat qui non habet. A person who does not have does not give.
Non deberet alii nocere quod inter alios actum esset. A person ought not to be injured by what has taken place between other parties.
Non debet actori licere quod reo non permittitur. What is not permitted to the defendant ought not to be allowed to the plaintiff.
Non debet adduci exceptio ejus rei cujus petitur dissolutio. An exception (or plea) should not be made on the very matter of which a determination is sought (in the case at hand).
Non debet alii nocere quod inter alios actum est. A person ought not to be prejudiced by what has been done between others.
Non debet alteri per alterum iniqua conditio inferri. An unfair condition ought not to be brought on one person by the act of another.
Non debet cui plus licet quod minus est non licere. A person who is permitted to do the greater thing ought not to be forbidden to do the lesser.
Non decet homines dedere causa non cognita. It is unbecoming to surrender people when no cause has been shown.
Non decipitur qui scit se decipi. A person is not deceived who knows himself to be deceived.

Non definitur in jure quid sit conatus. What an attempt is, is not defined in law.

Non differunt quae concordant re, tametsi non in verbis iisdem. Those things that agree in substance, even if not in the same words, do not differ.

Non efficit affectus nisi sequatur effectus. The intention amounts to nothing unless some effect follows.

Non est arctius vinculum inter homines quam jusjurandum. There is no closer (or firmer) link among men than an oath.

Non est certandum de regulis juris. There is no disputing rules of law.

Non est disputandum contra principia negantem. There is no disputing against a person who denies first principles.

Non est novum ut priores leges ad posteriores trahantur. It is not an innovation to adapt earlier laws to later ones.

Non est recedendum a communi observantia. There should be no departure from a common observance.

Non est regula quin fallat. There is no rule that may not deceive (or disappoint).

Non est reus nisi mens sit rea. A person is not guilty unless his mind is guilty.

Non exemplis sed legibus judicandum est. Not by examples but by the laws must judgment be made.

Non facias malum ut inde veniat bonum. You are not to do evil that good may come of it.

Non in legendo sed in intelligendo leges consistunt. The laws consist not in reading but in understanding.

Non in tabulis est jus. It is not in books that the law is to be found.

Non jus ex regula, sed regula ex jure. The law does not arise from the rule (or maxim), but the rule from the law.

Non jus, sed seisina facit stipitem. Not right, but seisin, makes a stock (from which the inheritance must descend).

Non licet quod dispendio licet. That which is permitted only at a loss is not permitted.

Non nasci et natum mori paria sunt. Not to be born and to be born dead are equivalent.

Non obligat lex nisi promulgata. A law is not binding unless it has been promulgated.

Non observata forma, infertur adnullatio actus. When the form has not been observed, an annulment of the act is inferred.

Non officit conatus nisi sequatur effectus. An attempt does not harm unless a consequence follows.

Non omne damnum inducit injuriam. Not every loss produces an injury (i.e., gives a right to action).

Non omne quod licet honestum est. Not everything that is lawful is honourable; not everything that is allowable is morally right.

Non potest adduci exceptio ejusdem rei cujus petitur dissolutio. An exception cannot be brought on the same matter whose determination is at issue (in the action at hand).
Non potest probari quod probatum non relevat. That cannot be proved which, when proved, is irrelevant.
Non potest quis sine brevi agere. No one can sue without a writ.
Non potest videri desisse habere qui nunquam habuit. A person cannot be considered as having ceased to have a thing who never had it.
Non praestat impedimentum quod de jure non sortitur effectum. A thing that has no effect in law is not an impediment.
Non quod dictum est, sed quod factum est, inspicitur. Not what has been said but what has been done is regarded
Non refert quid ex aequipollentibus fiat. It does not matter which of two equivalents happens.
Non refert quid notum sit judici, si notum non sit in forma judicii. It matters not what is known to the judge if it is not known to him judicially.
Non refert verbis an factis fit revocatio. It does not matter whether a revocation is made by words or by acts.
Non respondebit minor, nisi in causa dotis, et hoc pro favore doti. A minor shall not answer except in a case of dower, and here in favour of dower.
Non solent quae abundant vitiare scripturas. Superfluous expressions do not usually vitiate writings.
Non sunt longa ubi nihil est quod demere possis. There is no prolixity where there is nothing that you can omit.
Non temere credere est nervus sapientae. Not to believe rashly is the sinew of wisdom.
Non valet donatio nisi subsequatur traditio. A gift is not valid unless delivery (or transference) follows.
Non valet exceptio ejusdem rei cujus petitur dissolutio. An exception based on the very matter of which the determination is sought is not valid.
Non valet impedimentum quod de jure non sortitur effectum. An impediment that does not derive its effect from the law has no force.
Non verbis sed ipsis rebus leges imponimus. Not on words, but on affairs themselves do we impose laws.
Non videntur qui errant consentire. They who err are not considered as consenting
Non videntur rem amittere quibus propria non fuit. They are not considered as losing a thing if it was not their own.
Non videtur consensum retinuisse si quis ex praescripto minantis aliquod immutavit. If a person has changed anything at the demand of a party threatening, he is not considered to have maintained his consent.

Non videtur perfecte cujusque id esse quod ex casu auferri potest. A thing is not considered completely to belong to anyone if it can be taken from him by chance (or occasion).

Non videtur quisquam id capere quod ei necesse est alii restituere. A person is not considered to acquire property in a thing that he must restore to another.

Noscitur a sociis. It is known from its associates

Noscitur ex socio qui non cognoscitur ex se. A person who is not known for himself is known from his associate

Notitia dicitur a noscendo; et notitia non debet claudicare. Notice is named from knowledge; and notice ought not to limp (that is, be imperfect).

Nova constitutio futuris formam imponere debet, non praeteritis. A new enactment ought to impose form on what is to come, not on what is past. • A new regulation should not apply retroactively but from its enactment.

Novatio non praesumitur. A novation is not presumed.

Novitas non tam utilitate prodest quam novitate perturbat. Novelty does not as much benefit by its utility as it disturbs by its novelty.

Novum judicium non dat novum jus, sed declarat antiquum. A new judgment does not make a new right, but declares the old.

Noxa caput sequitur. The liability follows the head or person. • Liability to make good an injury caused by a slave attaches to the master

Nuda ratio et nuda pactio non ligant aliquem debitorem. Bare reason and naked agreement do not bind any debtor.

Nudum pactum ex quo non oritur actio. Naked agreement (nudum pactum) is that from which no action arises.

Nulla emptio sine pretio esse potest. There can be no sale without a price.

Nulla pactione effici potest ne dolus praestetur. No agreement is sufficient to effect that there be no liability for fraud.

Nulla virtus, nulla scientia locum suum et dignitatem conservare potest sine modestia. Without moderation, no virtue, no knowledge can preserve its place and dignity.

Nulle régle sans faute. There is no rule without fault.

Nulle terre sans seigneur. There is no land without a lord.

Nulli enim res sua servit jure servitutis. No one can have a servitude over his own property.

Nullum crimen majus est inobedientia. No crime is greater than disobedience.

Nullum exemplum est idem omnibus. No example is the same for all purposes.

Nullum iniquum est praesumendum in jure. Nothing unjust is to be presumed in law.

Nullum matrimonium, ibi nulla dos. No marriage, there no dower.

Nullum simile est idem. Nothing that is like another is the same. • That is, no likeness is exactly identical.

Nullum simile est idem nisi quatuor pedibus currit. Nothing similar is identical, unless it run on all fours.

Nullum simile quatuor pedibus currit. No simile runs on four feet (on all fours). • No simile holds in every respect.

Nullus commodum capere potest de injuria sua propria. No one can gain advantage by his own wrong.

Nullus debet agere de dolo, ubi alia actio subest. Where another form of action is given, no one ought to sue in the action de dolo.

Nullus idoneus testis in re sua intelligitur. No one is understood to be a competent witness in his own cause.

Nullus jus alienum forisfacere potest. No one can forfeit another's right.

Nullus liber homo capiatur, aut imprisonetur. Let no free man be taken or imprisoned.

Nullus recedat e curia cancellaria sine remedio. Let no one depart from the court of chancery without a remedy.

Nullus videtur dolo facere qui suo jure utitur. No one is to be regarded as acting by fraud who exercises his legal right.

Nul ne doit s'enrichir aux depens des autres. No one ought to enrich himself at the expense of others.

Nul prendra advantage de son tort demesne. No one shall take advantage of his own wrong.

Nul sans damage avera error ou attaint. No one shall have error or attaint unless there has been damage.

Nunquam crescit ex post facto praeteriti delicti aestimatio. The valuation (or assessment of damage) for a past offence is never increased by what happens subsequently.

Nunquam decurritur ad extraordinarium sed ubi deficit ordinarium. One never resorts to the extraordinary but when the ordinary fails.

Nunquam fictio sine lege. There is no fiction without law.

Nunquam nimis dicitur quod nunquam satis dicitur. What is never sufficiently said is never said too much.

Nunquam praescribitur in falso. There is never prescription in case of falsehood (or forgery).

Nunquam res humanae prospere succedunt ubi negliguntur divinae. Human affairs never prosper when divine ones are neglected.

Nuptias non concubitus sed consensus facit. Not sharing a bed but consent makes the marriage.

Obedientia est legis essentia. Obedience is the essence of the law.

Obtemperandum est consuetudini rationabili tanquam legi. A reasonable custom is to be obeyed like law.

Occultatio thesauri inventi fraudulosa. The concealment of discovered treasure is fraudulent.

Occupantis fiunt derelicta. Things abandoned become the property of the (first) occupant.

Odiosa et inhonesta non sunt in lege praesumenda. Odious and dishonest acts are not to be presumed in law.

Odiosa non praesumuntur. Odious things are not presumed.

Officia judicialia non concedantur antequam vacent. Judicial offices ought not to be granted before they are vacant.

Officia magistratus non debent esse venalia. The offices of magistrates ought not to be sold.

Officit conatus si effectus sequatur. The attempt becomes of consequence if the effect follows.

Officium nemini debet esse damnosum. An office ought to be injurious to no one.

Omissio eorum quae tacite insunt nihil operatur. The omission of those things that are silently implied is of no consequence.

Omne actum ab intentione agentis est judicandum. Every act is to be judged by the intention of the doer.

Omne crimen ebrietas et incendit et detegit. Drunkenness both inflames and reveals every crime.

Omne jus aut consensus fecit, aut necessitas constituit, aut firmavit consuetudo. Every right has been derived from consent, established by necessity, or confirmed by custom.

Omne majus continet in se minus. Every greater thing contains in itself the less.

Omne majus dignum continet in se minus dignum. Every more worthy thing contains in itself the less worthy.

Omne majus minus in se complectitur. Every greater thing embraces in itself the lesser.

Omne principale trahit ad se accessorium. Every principal thing draws to itself the accessory.

Omne quod solo inaedificatur solo cedit. Everything that is built on the soil belongs to the soil.

Omne sacramentum debet esse de certa scientia. Every oath ought to be founded on certain knowledge.

Omnes actiones in mundo infra certa tempora habent limitationem. All actions in the world are limited within certain periods.

Omnes licentiam habere his quae pro se indulta sunt renunciare. All have liberty to renounce these things that have been granted in their favour.

Omnes prudentes illa admittere solent quae probantur iis qui in arte sua bene versati sunt. All prudent people are accustomed to admit those things that are approved by those who are skilled in their profession.

Omnes sorores sunt quasi unus haeres de una haereditate. All sisters are as it were one heir to one inheritance.

Omne testamentum morte consummatum est. Every will is consummated by death.

Omnia delicta in aperto leviora sunt. All crimes committed openly are considered lighter.

Omnia praesumuntur contra spoliatorem. All presumptions are against one who wrongfully dispossesses another.

Omnia praesumuntur legitime facta donec probetur in contrarium. All things are presumed to be done legitimately until the contrary is proved.

Omnia praesumuntur rite ac sollemniter esse acta. All things are presumed to be done in proper and regular form; all things are presumed to have been rightly and regularly done.

Omnia praesumuntur rite et solemniter esse acta donec probetur in contrarium. All things are presumed to have been done regularly and with due formality until the contrary is proved.

Omnia quae jure contrahuntur contrario jure pereunt. All obligations contracted under a law are destroyed by a law to the contrary.

Omnia quae sunt uxoris sunt ipsius viri. All things that are the wife's belong to her husband.

Omnia rite esse acta praesumuntur. All things are presumed to have been done in due form.

Omnis actio est loquela. Every action is a complaint.

Omnis consensus tollit errorem. Every consent removes an error.

Omnis exceptio est ipsa quoque regula. Every exception is itself also a rule.

Omnis indemnatus pro innoxio legibus habetur. Every uncondemned person is held by the law as innocent.

Omnis innovatio plus novitate perturbat quam utilitate prodest. Every innovation disturbs by its novelty more than it benefits by its usefulness.

Omnis interpretatio vel declarat, vel extendit, vel restringit. Every interpretation explains, or extends, or restricts.

Omnis nova constitutio futuris formam imponere debet, et non praeteritis. Every new enactment should regulate future, not past transactions; every new law must impose its form on future cases and not past ones.
Omnis persona est homo, sed non vicissim. Every person is a human being, but not every human being a person.
Omnis privatio praesupponit habitum. Every privation presupposes possession.
Omnis querela et omnis actio injuriarum limitata est infra certa tempora. Every plaint and every action for injuries is limited within fixed times.
Omnis ratihabitio retrotrahitur et mandato priori aequiparatur. Every subsequent ratification has a retrospective effect and is equivalent to a prior command.
Omnis regula suas patitur exceptiones. Every rule of law allows its own exceptions.
Omnium contributione sarciatur quod pro omnibus datum est. What has been given for all should be compensated by the contribution of all.
Omnium rerum quarum usus est, potest esse abusus, virtute solo excepta. Of everything of which there is a use, there can be abuse, virtue alone excepted.
Opinio quae favet testamento est tenenda. That opinion is to be followed which favours the will.
Oportet quod certa res deducatur in judicium. A thing, to be brought to judgment, must be definite.
Oportet quod certa sit res quae venditur. A thing, to be sold, must be definite.
Optima enim est legium interpres consuetudo. Custom is the best interpreter of laws.
Optima est lex quae minimum relinquit arbitrio judicis; optimus judex qui minimum sibi. It is the best law that leaves the least to the discretion of the judge; the best judge is he who leaves least to himself.
Optima legum interpres est consuetudo. Custom is the best interpreter of law.
Optimus interpres rerum usus. Usage is the best interpreter of things.
Optimus judex qui minimum sibi. He is the best judge who (leaves) the least to his own discretion.
Optimus legum interpres consuetudo. Custom is the best interpreter of laws.
Ordine placitandi servato, servatur et jus. When order of pleading has been preserved, the law is also preserved.
Origine propria neminem posse voluntate sua eximi manifestum est. It is manifest that no one by his own will can be stripped of his origin (or be banished from his place of origin).
Origo rei inspici debet. The origin of a thing ought to be regarded.
omnia mutantur nos et mutamur in illis: All things change, and we change with them
omnia causa fiunt: Everything happens for a reason.

primum non nocere: Above all do no harm/ First do not harm.
parturient montes, nascetur ridiculus mus: Mountains will be in labour, and an absurd mouse will be born (all that work and nothing to show for it).
parva leves capiunt animas: Small things occupy light minds (small things amuse small minds).
pessimum genus inimicorum laudantes: Flatterers are the worst type of enemies.
possunt quia posse videntur: They can because they seem to be able to (they can do it because they think they can do it - the power of positive thinking).
potius mori quam foedari: Rather to die than to be dishonoured (death before dishonour).
praemonitus pramunitus: Forewarned, forearmed.
proprium humani ingenii est odisse quem laeseris: It is human nature to hate a person whom you have injured.
perfer et obdura; dolor hic tibi proderit olim: Be patient and tough; some day this pain will be useful to you.
pari passu: With equal pace together
pinxit: He painted this
post hoc propter hoc: After this, therefore because of this (false reasoning)
post mortem: After death
prima facie: On the first view
primus inter pares: First among equals
proxime accessit: He came next
Pacta dant legem contractui. Agreements give law to the contract.
Pacta privata juri publico derogare non possunt. Private contracts cannot restrict (or take away from) public law.
Pacta quae turpem causam continent non sunt observanda. Contracts founded on an immoral consideration are not to be observed.
Pactis privatorum juri publico non derogatur. There is no derogation from public law by private contracts.
Pacto aliquid licitum est quod sine pacto non admittitur. By agreement (or contract) something is permitted that, without agreement, is not allowed.
Parens est nomen generale ad omne genus cognationis. "Parent" is a general name for every kind of relationship.
Parentum est liberos alere etiam nothos. It is the role of parents to support their children even when illegitimate.
Paria copulantur paribus. Similar things unite with similar.
Paribus sententiis reus absolvitur. When opinions are evenly divided, the defendant is acquitted.

Par in parem imperium non habet. An equal has no power over an equal.

Parte quacumque integrante sublata, tollitur totum. When any essential part has been removed, the whole is removed (or destroyed).

Partus sequitur ventrem. The offspring follows the condition of the mother (literally, the womb).

Parum est latam esse sententiam, nisi mandetur executioni. It is not enough that judgment has been given if it is not committed to execution.

Parum proficit scire quid fieri debet si non cognoscas quomodo sit facturum. It does little good to know what ought to happen, if you do not know how it will take effect.

Pater est quem nuptiae demonstrant. The father is the man whom the marriage indicates. • This expresses the idea that a child born to a married woman is presumed begotten by her husband.

Pater is est quem nuptiae demonstrant. The father is he whom the marriage indicates.

Patria laboribus et expensis non debet fatigari. A jury ought not to be wearied with labours and expenses.

Patria potestas in pietate debet, non in atrocitate consistere. Parental authority should consist in devotion, not dread.

Peccata contra naturam sunt gravissima. Offences against nature are the most serious.

Pendente lite nihil innovetur. During litigation, let nothing be changed.

Periculosum est res novas et inusitatas inducere. It is dangerous to introduce new and unaccustomed things.

Periculum rei venditae, nondum traditae, est emptoris. The purchaser assumes the risk for a thing sold, but not yet delivered.

Per rationes pervenitur ad legitimam rationem. By reasoning we come to legal reason.

Per rerum naturam factum negantis nulla probatio est. By the nature of things, a person who denies a fact is not bound to give proof.

Persona conjuncta aequiparatur interesse proprio. A personal connection is equivalent to one's own interest.

Persona est homo cum statu quodam consideratus. A person is a human being considered with reference to a certain status.

Personae vice fungitur municipium et decuria. Towns and boroughs act in the role of persons.

Personalia personam sequuntur. Personal things follow the person.

Perspicua vera non sunt probanda. Plain truths are not to be proved.

Per varios actus legem experientia facit. In the course of various acts, experience frames the law.

Pirata est hostis humani generis. A pirate is an enemy of the human race.
Placita negativa duo exitum non faciunt. Two negative pleas do not form an issue.
Plena et celeris justitia fiat partibus. Let the parties have full and speedy justice.
Pluralis numerus est duobus contentus. The plural number is satisfied with two.
Plus exempla quam peccata nocent. Examples hurt more than offences.
Plus peccat auctor quam actor. The instigator of a crime is a worse offender than the perpetrator.
Plus valet unus oculatus testis quam auriti decem. One eyewitness is better than ten earwitnesses.
Plus valet vulgaris consuetudo quam regalis concessio. Common custom is better than royal grant.
Plus vident oculi quam oculus. Several eyes see more than one.
Poena ad paucos, metus ad omnes perveniat. Let punishment be inflicted on a few, dread on all.
Poenae potius molliendae quam exasperandae sunt. Punishments should rather be softened than aggravated.
Poenae sunt restringendae. Punishments should be restrained.
Poena ex delicto defuncti haeres teneri non debet. The heir ought not to be penalized for the wrong (or crime) of the decedent.
Poena non potest, culpa perennis erit. Punishment cannot be, guilt will be, perpetual.
Poena suos tenere debet actores et non alios. Punishment should take hold of the guilty (who commit the wrong), and not others.
Poena tolli potest, culpa perennis erit. The punishment can be removed, but the guilt will be perpetual.
Politiae legibus, non leges politiis, adaptandae. Politics are to be adapted to the laws, not the laws to politics.
Polygamia est plurium simul virorum uxorumve connubium. Polygamy is being married to more than one husband or wife at one time.
Ponderantur testes, non numerantur. Witnesses are weighed, not counted.
Posito uno oppositorum negatur alterum. One of two opposite positions having been affirmed, the other is denied.
Possessio est quasi pedis positio. Possession is, as it were, the position of the foot.
Possessio pacifica per annos 60 facit jus. Peaceable possession for 60 years gives a right.
Posteriora derogant prioribus. Later things restrict (or detract from) earlier ones.
Posthumus pro nato habetur. A posthumous child is considered as though born (before the father's death).

Postliminium fingit eum qui captus est semper in civitate fuisse. Postliminy (restoration of rights) imagines that a person who has been captured has never left the state. • A person captured by the enemy, who later returns, is restored to all his former rights.

Potentia debet sequi justitiam, non antecedere. Power ought to follow, not to precede, justice.

Potentia inutilis frustra est. Useless power is in vain.

Potentia non est nisi ad bonum. Power is not conferred but for the (public) good.

Potestas stricte interpretatur. A power should be strictly interpreted.

Potestas suprema seipsum dissolvere potest, ligare non potest. Supreme power can dissolve (or release), but cannot bind, itself.

Potest quis renunciare, pro se et suis, jus quod pro se introductum est. A person may relinquish, for himself and his heirs, a right that was introduced for his own benefit.

Potior est conditio defendentis. Stronger is the condition of the defendant (than that of the plaintiff).

Potior est conditio possidentis. Stronger is the condition of the possessor.

Praedium servit praedio. Land is under servitude to land. • A servitude is not a personal right, but attaches to the dominant tenement.

Praepropera consilia raro sunt prospera. Hasty counsels are seldom prosperous.

Praesentare nihil aliud est quam praesto dare seu offerre. To present is nothing other than to give or offer on the spot.

Praestat cautela quam medela. Prevention is better than cure.

Praesumatur pro justitia sententiae. Let there be a presumption of sentence's justice.

Praesumitur pro legitimatione. There is a presumption in favour of legitimacy.

Praesumptio cedit veritati. A presumption yields to the truth.

Praesumptio ex eo quod plerumque fit. A presumption arises from what generally happens.

Praesumptio opponitur probationi. A presumption is distinguished from proof.

Praesumptio violenta plena probatio. Forceful presumption is full proof.

Praesumptio violenta valet in lege. Forceful presumption is effective in law.

Praetextu liciti non debet admitti illicitum. What is illegal ought not to be admitted under pretext of legality.

Praxis judicum est interpres legum. The practice of the judges is the interpreter of the laws.

Pretium succedit in locum rei. The price takes the place of the thing sold.

Prima pars aequitatis aequalitas. The first part of equity is equality.

Principalis debet semper excuti antequam perveniatur ad fideijussores. The principal should always be exhausted before resorting to the sureties.

Principia probant, non probantur. Principles prove; they are not proved.

Principiis obsta. Oppose beginnings. • Oppose a thing in its inception in order to have any success against it.

Principiorum non est ratio. There is no reasoning of principles.

Principium est potissima pars cujusque rei. The beginning is the most powerful part of each thing.

Prior tempore, potior jure. Earlier in time, stronger in right.

Privatio praesupponit habitum. Deprivation presupposes possession.

Privatis pactionibus non dubium est non laedi jus caeterorum. There is no doubt that the rights of others (not party to the agreement) cannot be prejudiced by private agreements.

Privatorum conventio juri publico non derogat. An agreement of private persons does not derogate from public law.

Privatum commodum publico cedit. Private yields to public advantage.

Privatum incommodum publico bono pensatur. Private disadvantage is made up for by public good.

Privilegium est beneficium personale et extinguitur cum persona. A privilege is a benefit belonging to a person, and it dies with the person.

Privilegium est quasi privata lex. A privilege is, as it were, a private law.

Privilegium non valet contra rempublicam. A privilege has no force against the commonwealth.

Probandi necessitas incumbit illi qui agit. The necessity of proving rests on the one who sues (or claims some right).

Probationes debent esse evidentes, (id est) perspicuae et faciles intelligi. Proofs ought to be evident, (that is) clear and easily understood.

Probatis extremis, praesumitur media. When the extremes have been proved, the intermediate proceedings are presumed.

Processus legis est gravis vexatio; executio legis coronat opus. The process of the law is heavy hardship; the execution of the law crowns (or rewards) the work.

Prohibetur ne quis faciat in suo quod nocere possit alieno. It is prohibited for anyone to do on his own property what may injure another's.

Proles sequitur sortem paternam. The offspring follows the condition of the father.

Propositio indefinita aequipollet universali. An indefinite proposition is equal to a general one.

Pro possessione praesumitur de jure. From possession arises a presumption of right.

Pro possessore habetur qui dolo injuriave desiit possidere. A person is considered a possessor who has ceased possession through fraud or injury.

Proprietas totius navis carinae causam sequitur. The property of the whole ship follows the condition of the keel.
Proprietates verborum observandae sunt. The proprieties (i.e., proper meanings) of words are to be observed.
Prosecutio legis est gravis vexatio; executio legis coronat opus. Litigation is a heavy hardship, but execution of the law crowns (or rewards) the work.
Protectio trahit subjectionem, subjectio protectionem. Protection brings submission; submission (brings) protection.
Proviso est providere praesentia et futura, non praeterita. A proviso is to provide for things present and future, not past.
Prudenter agit qui praecepto legis obtemperat. A person acts prudently who obeys the precept of law.

qui scribit bis legit: He who writes reads twice.
qui non est hodie cras minus aptus erit: He who is not prepared today will be less so tomorrow.
qui tacet consentire: Who is silent gives consent.
quis custodiet ipsos custodes?: Who will watch the watchers themselves?
quod erat demonstrandum: Which was to be proved
quod erat faciendum: Which was to be done
quot homines tot sententiac: So many men so many options
Quae ab hostibus capiuntur, statim capientium fiunt. Things taken from public enemies immediately become the property of the captors.
Quae ab initio inutilis fuit institutio, ex post facto convalescere non potest. An institution void in the beginning cannot acquire validity by a subsequent act.
Quae ab initio non valent, ex post facto convalescere non possunt. Things invalid from the beginning cannot be made valid by a subsequent act.
Quae cohaerent personae a persona separari nequeunt. Things that belong to the person cannot be separated from the person.
Quae communi legi derogant stricte interpretantur. (Statutes) that derogate from the common law should be strictly construed.
Quae incontinenti (vel certo) fiunt inesse videntur. Things that are done immediately (or with certainty) are considered part of the same transaction.
Quae in curia acta sunt rite agi praesumuntur. What is done in court is presumed to be rightly done.
Quae in partes dividi nequeunt solida a singulis praestantur. Things (such as services) that cannot be divided into parts are rendered entire by each severally.

Quae inter alios acta sunt nemini nocere debent, sed prodesse possunt. Transactions between others can benefit, but should not injure, anyone who is not party to them.

Quae legi communi derogant non sunt trahenda in exemplum. Things that derogate (or detract) from the common law are not to be drawn into precedent.

Quae legi communi derogant stricte interpretantur. Things that derogate (or detract) from the common law are construed strictly.

Quaelibet concessio fortissime contra donatorem interpretanda est. Every grant is to be construed most strongly against the grantor.

Quaelibet jurisdictio cancellos suos habet. Every jurisdiction has its boundaries.

Quae mala sunt inchoata in principio vix bono peraguntur exitu. Things bad in the commencement seldom end well.

Quae non fieri debent, facta valent. Things that ought not to be done are held valid when they have been done.

Quae non valeant singula, juncta juvant. Things that may not avail individually have effect when united.

Quae propter necessitatem recepta sunt, non debent in argumentum trahi. Things that are accepted as a matter of necessity ought not to be brought into the argument.

Quaeras de dubiis, legem bene discere si vis. Inquire into doubtful points if you wish to understand the law well.

Quaere de dubiis, quia per rationes pervenitur ad legitimam rationem. Inquire into doubtful points, because through reasoning we arrive at legal reason.

Quaerere dat sapere quae sunt legitima vere. To investigate is the way to know what things are truly lawful.

Quae rerum natura prohibentur nulla lege confirmata sunt. What is prohibited by the nature of things can be confirmed by no law.

Quae singula non prosunt, juncta juvant. Things that are of no advantage individually are helpful when taken together.

Quae sunt minoris culpae sunt majoris infamiae. Offences that are of lesser guilt are of greater infamy.

Qualitas quae inesse debet, facile praesumitur. A quality that ought to be inherent is easily presumed.

Quando aliquid conceditur, conceditur id sine quo illud fieri non possit. When anything is granted, that also is granted without which it cannot take effect.

Quando aliquid mandatur, mandatur et omne per quod pervenitur ad illud. When anything is commanded, everything by which it can be accomplished is also commanded.

Quando aliquid prohibetur ex directo, prohibetur et per obliquum. When anything is prohibited directly, it is also prohibited indirectly.

Quando aliquid prohibetur, prohibetur omne per quod devenitur ad illud. When anything is prohibited, everything by which it is arrived at is prohibited.

Quando licit id quod majus, videtur licere id quod minus. When the greater is allowed, the lesser is considered to be allowed also.

Quando plus fit quam fieri debet, videtur etiam illud fieri quod faciendum est. When more is done than ought to be done, that at least is considered as performed that should have been performed.

Quando res non valet ut ago, valeat quantum valere potest. When the thing is of no force as I do it, let it have as much as it can have.

Quando verba et mens congruunt, non est interpretationi locus. When the words and the mind agree, there is no room for interpretation.

Qui accusat integrae famae sit et non criminosus. Let the one who accuses be of honest reputation and not implicated in a crime.

Qui acquirit sibi acquirit haeredibus. A person who acquires for himself acquires for his heirs.

Qui adimit medium dirimit finem. A person who takes away the means destroys the end.

Qui alterius jure utitur, eodem jure uti debet. A person who uses the right of another ought to use the same right.

Qui bene distinguit bene docet. One who distinguishes well teaches well.

Qui bene interrogat bene docet. One who questions well teaches well.

Qui cadit a syllaba cadit a tota causa. One who fails in a syllable fails in his whole cause.

Qui confirmat nihil dat. A person who confirms gives nothing.

Qui contemnit praeceptum, contemnit praecipientem. A person who shows contempt for the precept shows contempt for the author (or advocate) of it.

Quicquid acquiritur servo, acquiritur domino. Whatever is acquired by the servant is acquired for the master.

Quicquid demonstratae rei additur satis demonstratae frustra est. Whatever is added to the description of a thing already sufficiently described is of no effect.

Quicquid est contra normam recti est injuria. Whatever is against the rule of right is a wrong.

Quicquid in excessu actum est, lege prohibetur. Whatever is done in excess is prohibited by law.

Quicquid judicis auctoritati subjicitur, novitati non subjicitur. Whatever is subject to the authority of a judge is not subject to innovation.

Quicquid plantatur solo, solo cedit. Whatever is affixed to the soil belongs to it.

Quicquid recipitur, recipitur secundum modum recipientis. Whatever is received is received according to the direction of the recipient.

Quicquid solvitur, solvitur secundum modum solventis. Whatever is paid is paid according to the direction of the payer.

Qui cum alio contrahit, vel est vel debet esse non ignarus conditionis ejus. A party who contracts with another either is or ought to be cognizant of that party's condition. • Otherwise, he is not excusable.

Qui dat finem dat media ad finem necessaria. A person who gives an end gives the necessary means to that end.

Qui destruit medium destruit finem. A person who destroys the means destroys the end.

Qui doit inheriter al pére, doit inheriter al fitz. One who ought to inherit from the father ought to inherit from the son.

Quidquid enim sive dolo et culpa venditoris accidit in eo venditor securus est. For concerning anything that occurs without deceit and guilt on the part of the vendor, the vendor is secure.

Quid sit jus, et in quo consistit injuria, legis est definire. What constitutes right, and wherein lies the injury, it is the function of the law to declare.

Quid turpi ex causa promissum est non valet. A promise arising from a wrongful cause is invalid.

Quieta non movere. Not to disturb what is settled

Qui evertit causam evertit causatum futurum. One who overthrows the cause overthrows its future effects.

Qui ex damnato coitu nascuntur, inter liberos non computentur. They who are born of an illicit union should not be counted among children.

Qui facit id quod plus est, facit id quod minus est, sed non convertitur. A person who does that which is more, does that which is less, but not vice versa.

Qui facit per alium facit per se. A person who acts through another acts himself. • The acts of an agent are considered the acts of the principal

Qui habet jurisdictionem absolvendi, habet jurisdictionem ligandi. One who has jurisdiction for dissolving (an obligation) has jurisdiction to bind.

Qui haeret in litera, haeret in cortice. One who clings to the letter clings to the shell (or surface).

Qui ignorat quantum solvere debeat, non potest improbus videri. A person who does not know what he ought to pay cannot be regarded as dishonest.

Qui in jus dominiumve alterius succedit jure ejus uti debet. One who succeeds to another's right or property ought to use that person's right. • That is, the successor has the same rights and liabilities as attached to that property or interest in the hands of the assignor.

Qui inscienter peccat, scienter emendet. One who offends unwittingly must make good knowingly.

Qui in utero est, pro jam nato habetur quoties de ejus commodo quaeritur. A child in the womb is considered as born, whenever there is a question of benefit to the child.

Qui jure suo utitur, nemini facit injuriam. A person who exercises his proper right harms no one.

Quilibet potest renunciare juri pro se inducto. Anyone may renounce a right introduced for his own benefit.

Qui male agit odit lucem. A person who does wrong hates the light (of discovery).

Qui mandat ipse fecisse videtur. A person who commands (a thing to be done) is considered to have done it himself.

Qui melius probat, melius habet. The party who gives better proof has the better (right). • Often rendered, "He who proves more recovers more."

Qui nascitur sine legitimo matrimonio, matrem sequitur. A child who is born out of lawful matrimony follows the condition of the mother.

Qui non cadunt in constantem virum, vani timores sunt aestimandi. Those fears are considered vain (or frivolous) that do not affect a man of stable character.

Qui non habet, ille non dat. Who has not, gives not.

Qui non habet in aere, luet in corpore. What a man cannot pay with his purse, he must suffer in person.

Qui non habet in aere, luet in corpore, ne quis peccetur impune. Let him who has not (the wherewithal to pay) in money, pay in his person (i.e., by corporal punishment), lest anyone be wronged with impunity.

Qui non habet potestatem alienandi habet necessitatem retinendi. A person who has not the power of alienating, is obliged to retain.

Qui non improbat approbat. A person who does not disapprove approves.

Qui non negat fatetur. A person who does not deny, admits.

Qui non obstat quod obstare potest, facere videtur. A person who does not prevent what he can prevent, is considered to act.

Qui non prohibet cum prohibere possit, jubet. A person who does not forbid when he can forbid, commands.

Qui non prohibet quod prohibere potest, assentire videtur. A person who does not forbid what he can forbid, is considered to assent.

Qui non propulsat injuriam quando potest infert. A person who does not repel an injury when he can, brings it on.

Qui obstruit aditum destruit commodum. A person who obstructs an entrance, destroys a conveniency.

Qui omne dicit nihil excludit. A person who says all excludes nothing.

Qui parcit nocentibus innocentes punit. A person who spares the guilty, punishes the innocent.

Qui peccat ebrius, luat sobrius. Let him who offends while drunk be punished when sober; one who offends when drunk must pay when sober. • The phrase is sometimes taken to mean that one who sins ignorantly must correct it knowingly.

Qui per alium facit per seipsum facere videtur. A person who does anything through another, is considered as doing it himself.

Qui per fraudem agit frustra agit. A person who acts fraudulently, acts in vain.

Qui potest et debet vetare, tacens jubet. A person who can and ought to forbid a thing (as much as) orders it, if he keeps silent.

Qui primum peccat ille facit rixam. Who first offends, causes the quarrel.

Qui prior est tempore potior est jure. The person who is prior in time is stronger in right.

Qui pro me aliquid facit, mihi fecisse videtur. A person who does something in my behalf is considered to have done it to me (for me). • "To do a service for a man is to do it to him."

Qui providet sibi, providet haeredibus. A person who provides for himself, provides for his heirs.

Qui rationem in omnibus quaerunt rationem subvertunt. They who seek a reason for everything, subvert reason.

Qui sciens solvit indebitum donandi consilio id videtur fecisse. A person who knowingly pays what is not due, is considered to have done it with the intention of making a gift.

Qui semel actionem renunciaverit, amplius repetere non potest. A litigant who has once renounced his action, cannot bring it any longer.

Qui semel malus, semper praesumitur esse malus in eodem genere. A person who is once bad, is always presumed to be bad in the same kind of affair.

Qui sentit commodum sentire debet et onus. A person who enjoys the benefit, ought also to bear the burden.

Qui sentit commodum sentire debet et onus; et e contra. A person who enjoys the benefit ought also to bear the burden; and the contrary.

Qui sentit onus, sentire debet et commodum. A person who feels the burden, ought also to feel the benefit.

Quisquis est qui velit jurisconsultus haberi, continuet studium, velit a quocunque doceri. Whoever there is who wishes to be regarded as a jurisconsult (legal expert), should prolong his study and be willing to be taught by everyone.

Qui tacet consentire videtur. A party who is silent, appears to consent.

Qui tacet consentire videtur ubi tractatur de ejus commodo. A party who is silent, is considered as assenting, when his advantage is debated

Qui tacet non utique fatetur, sed tamen verum est eum non negare. A person who is silent does not indeed confess, but yet it is true that he does not deny.

Qui tardius solvit minus solvit. A person who pays too late pays less (than he ought).

Qui vult decipi, decipiatur. Let one who wishes to be deceived, be deceived.

Quod ab initio non valet, (in) tractu temporis non convalescet. What is ill from the outset, will not be cured by passage of time.

Quod ad jus naturale attinet, omnes homines aequales sunt. All men are equal as far as natural law is concerned.

Quod aedificatur in area legata cedit legato. Whatever is built on land given by will, passes with the gift of the land.

Quod alias non fuit licitum necessitas licitum facit. Necessity makes lawful what otherwise was unlawful.

Quod approbo non reprobo. What I approve, I do not disapprove.

Quod a quoque poenae nomine exactum est id eidem restituere nemo cogitur. What has been exacted from someone as a penalty, no one is obliged to restore to him.

Quod constat clare, non debet verificari. What is clearly agreed, need not be proved.

Quod constat curiae, opere testium non indiget. What appears true to the court, needs not the help of witnesses.

Quod contra legem fit, pro infecto habetur. What is done contrary to the law, is considered as not done.

Quod contra rationem juris receptum, non est producendum ad consequentias. That which is received against the reason of the law, is not to be extended to its logical consequences.

Quodcunque aliquis ob tutelam corporis sui fecerit jure id fecisse videtur. Whatever one does in defense of his person, he is considered to have done legally.

Quod demonstrandi causa additur rei satis demonstratae, frustra fit. What is added for the sake of demonstration to a thing sufficiently demonstrated, is done to no purpose.

Quod dubitas, ne feceris. When in doubt, do not do it.

Quod enim semel aut bis existit, praetereunt legislatores. Legislators pass by that which happens but once or twice.

Quod est ex necessitate nunquam introducitur, nisi quando necessarium. What is introduced of necessity, is never introduced except when necessary.

Quod est inconveniens aut contra rationem non permissum est in lege. What is unsuitable or contrary to reason is not allowed in law.

Quod est necessarium est licitum. What is necessary, is lawful.

Quod fieri debet facile praesumitur. That which ought to be done is easily presumed.

Quod fieri non debet, factum valet. What ought not to be done, when done, is valid.

Quod inconsulto fecimus, consultius revocemus. What we have done without due consideration, we should revoke with better consideration.

Quod initio non valet, tractu temporis non valet. What is void in the beginning, does not become valid by passage of time.

Quod initio vitiosum est non potest tractu temporis convalescere. What is defective in origin, cannot be mended by passage of time.

Quod in uno similium valet, valebit in altero. What avails in one of two similar things, will avail in the other.

Quod ipsis, qui contraxerunt, obstat, et successoribus eorum obstabit. That which bars those who have contracted, will bar their successors also.

Quod jussu alterius solvitur pro eo est quasi ipsi solutum esset. That which is paid at the bidding of another, has the same effect as if it had been paid to that person himself. • The party who has a debt paid for him, is in the same position as though the money were paid to him directly.

Quod meum est sine me auferri non potest. What is mine, cannot be taken away without me (i.e., my consent).

Quod minus est in obligationem videtur deductum. That which is the lesser, is held to be imported into the contract.

Quod naturalis ratio inter omnes homines constituit, vocatur jus gentium. What natural reason has established among all men, is called the law of nations.

Quod necessarie intelligitur id non deest. What is necessarily understood, is not lacking.

Quod necessitas cogit, defendit. What necessity compels, it justifies.

Quod non apparet non est, et non apparet judicialiter ante judicium. What appears not, does not exist, and nothing appears judicially before judgment.

Quod non capit Christus, capit fiscus. What Christ (or the church) does not take, the treasury takes.

Quod non habet principium non habet finem. What has no beginning, has no end.

Quod non legitur non creditur. What is not read, is not believed.

Quod nullius esse potest, id ut alicujus fieret nulla obligatio valet efficere. What can belong to no one, no agreement (or obligation) can make property of anyone.

Quod nullius est, est domini regis. That which belongs to nobody, belongs to our lord the king.

Quod nullius est id ratione naturali occupanti conceditur. What belongs to no one, by natural reason, becomes property of the first occupant.

Quo modo quid constituitur eodem modo dissolvitur. In whatever mode a thing is constituted, in the same manner it is dissolved.

Quum de lucro duorum quaeratur, melior est conditio possidentis. When there is a question of gain (to one) of two parties, the condition of the possessor is the better.

Ratihabitio mandato aequiparatur. Ratification is equal to a command.

Ratio est formalis causa consuetudinis. Reason is the source and formal cause of custom.

Ratio est legis anima, mutata legis ratione mutatur et lex. Reason is the soul of the law; when the reason of the law has been changed, the law is also changed.

Ratio et auctoritas duo clarissima mundi lumina. Reason and authority are the two brightest lights in the world.

Ratio in jure aequitas integra. Reason in law is perfect equity.

Ratio legis est anima legis. The reason of the law is the soul of the law

Ratio non clauditur loco. Reason is not confined to any place.

Ratio potest allegari deficiente lege, sed vera et legalis et non apparens. A reason can be adduced when the law is defective, but it must be a true and legal reason, and not specious (or apparent).

Receditur a placitis juris potius quam injuriae et delicta maneant impunita. One departs from settled rules of law, rather than let crimes and wrongs remain unpunished.

Recipitur in modum recipientis. A thing is received in the way the recipient intends.

Recorda sunt vestigia vetustatis et veritatis. Records are vestiges of antiquity and truth.

Recurrendum est ad extraordinarium quando non valet ordinarium. We must have recourse to what is extraordinary when what is ordinary fails.

Reddenda singula singulis. Each must be put in each separate place. • That is, the several terms or items apply distributively, or each to its proper object.

Regula pro lege, si deficit lex. If the law is inadequate, the maxim serves in its place.

Regulariter non valet pactum de re mea non alienanda. As a rule, a contract not to alienate my property, is not binding.

Reipublicae interest voluntates defunctorum effectum sortiri. It is in the interest of the state that the wills of the dead should have their (intended) effect.

Rei turpis nullum mandatum est. There is no mandate for a thing immoral (or illegal). Hence, there is no action for failing to act on such a mandate.

Relatio est fictio juris et intenta ad unum. Relation is a fiction of law, and intended for one thing.

Relatio semper fiat ut valeat dispositio. Reference should always be made in such a manner that a disposition (in a will) may have effect.

Relativorum cognito uno, cognoscitur et alterum. Of things relating to each other, one being known, the other is also known.

Religio sequitur patrem. Religion follows the father. • The father's religion is prima facie the infant's religion.

Remissius imperanti melius paretur. A person commanding not too strictly, is better obeyed.

Remoto impedimento, emergit actio. When the impediment has been removed, the action arises.

Repellitur a sacramento infamis. An infamous person is prevented from taking an oath.

Repellitur exceptione cedendarum actionum. (The litigant) is defeated by the plea that the actions have been assigned.

Reprobata pecunia liberat solventem. Money refused releases the person paying (or offering payment).

Reputatio est vulgaris opinio ubi non est veritas. Reputation is a common opinion where there is no certain knowledge.

Rerum ordo confunditur, si unicuique jurisdictio non servetur. The order of things is confounded if the proper jurisdiction of each is not maintained.

Rerum suarum quilibet est moderator et arbiter. Every one is the manager and disposer of his own matters.

Res accendent lumina rebus. Matters will throw light on (other) matters.

Res accessoria sequitur rem principalem. An accessory follows its principal.

Rescriptum principis contra jus non valet. The prince's rescript, if contrary to law, is of no avail.

Res denominatur a principaliori parte. A thing is named from its more essential (or primary) part.

Res est misera ubi jus est vagum et incertum. It is a miserable state of things where the law is vague and uncertain.

Resignatio est juris proprii spontanea refutatio. Resignation is the spontaneous rejection of one's own right.

Res inter alios acta aliis non nocet. A thing done between two parties, does not damage other parties; a matter transacted between parties (e.g., to a contract) does not prejudice non-parties.

Res inter alios acta alteri nocere non debet. Things done between others ought not to injure an outsider (not party to them).

Res inter alios judicatae nullum aliis praejudicium faciunt. Matters adjudged in the lawsuits of others do not prejudice those who were not parties to them.

Res judicata pro veritate accipitur. A matter adjudged is taken for truth.
Res nullius naturaliter fit primi occupantis. A thing that has no owner, naturally belongs to the first taker.
Resoluto jure concedentis, resolvitur jus concessum. When the right of the grantor has been extinguished, the right granted is extinguished.
Res periit domino suo. The destruction of the thing is a loss to its owner.
Res per pecuniam aestimatur, et non pecunia per res. The value of a thing is estimated by its worth in money, and the value of money is not estimated by reference to things.
Respondeat raptor, qui ignorare non potuit quod pupillum alienum abduxit. Let the ravisher answer, for he could not be ignorant that he has taken away another's ward.
Respondeat superior. Let the principal answer
Responsio unius non omnino audiatur. The answer of one witness should not be heard at all.
Res propria est quae communis non est. A thing is private that is not common.
Res sacra non recipit aestimationem. A sacred thing does not admit of valuation.
Res sua nemini servit. No one can have a servitude over his own property.
Res transit cum suo onere. The thing passes with its burden.
Reus excipiendo fit actor. The defendant by a plea (or exception) becomes plaintiff.
Reus laesae majestatis punitur, ut pereat unus ne pereant omnes. A traitor is punished that one may die lest all perish.
Riparum usus publicus est jure gentium, sicut ipsius fluminis. The use of riverbanks is by the law of nations public, like that of the stream itself.

semper idem: Always the same
sine die: Without a day being appointed
sine qua non: Without which not an indispensable condition
status quo: The state in which things as they are now
stet: Let it stand (Do not delete)
sub judice: Under consideration
sub poena: Under penalty
sub rosa: Under the rose (privately)
sub specie: Under the appearance of
suggestio falsi: A suggestion of something false
sul generis: Of its own kind peculiar
summum bonum: The chief good

sic: Yes

Sacramentum si fatuum fuerit, licet falsum, tamen non committit perjurium. A foolish oath, though false, does not make perjury.

Sacrilegus omnium praedonum cupiditatem et scelerem superat. A sacrilegious person surpasses the greed and wickedness of all other robbers.

Saepe constitutum est res inter alios judicatas aliis non praejudicare. It has often been settled that matters adjudged between others ought not to prejudice those who were not parties.

Saepe viatorem nova, non vetus, orbita fallit. Often it is the new track, not the old one, that deceives the traveler.

Salus populi (est) suprema lex. The safety of the people is the supreme law. • The phrase is sometimes put in the imperative

Salus populi suprema lex esto. Let the safety of the people be the supreme law.

Salus reipublicae suprema lex. The safety of the state is the supreme law.

Salus ubi multi consiliarii. Where there are many counselors, there is safety.

Sanguinis conjunctio benevolentia devincit homines et caritate. A tie of blood overcomes human beings through benevolence and family affection.

Sapiens incipit a fine, et quod primum est in intentione, ultimum est in executione. A wise person begins from the end, and what is first in intention is last in execution.

Sapiens omnia agit cum consilio. A wise man does everything advisedly.

Sapientia legis nummario pretio non est aestimanda. No price in money is to be put on the wisdom of the law.

Satius est petere fontes quam sectari rivulos. It is better to seek the sources than to follow tributaries.

Scientia sciolorum est mixta ignorantia. The knowledge of smatterers is ignorance diluted.

Scientia utrimque par pares contrahentes facit. Equal knowledge on both sides makes the contracting parties equal.

Scienti et volenti non fit injuria. A wrong is not done to one who knows and assents to it.

Scire debes cum quo contrahis. You ought to know with whom you make an agreement.

Scire et scire debere aequiparantur in jure. To know a thing and to be bound to know it are regarded in law as equivalent.

Scire leges non hoc est verba earum tenere, sed vim et potestatem. To know the laws is to observe not their (mere) words, but their force and power.

Scire proprie est rem ratione et per causam cognoscere. To know properly is to know a thing in its reason and by its cause.

Scribere est agere. To write is to act.

Scripta litera manet. The written word endures.

Secta quae scripto nititur a scripto variari non debet. A suit that relies on a writing ought not to vary from the writing.

Semel civis semper civis. Once a citizen, always a citizen.

Semel malus semper praesumitur esse malus in eodem genere. Whoever is once bad is presumed to be so always in the same kind of affair.

Semper in dubiis benigniora praeferenda sunt. In dubious cases, the more favourable constructions are always to be preferred.

Semper in obscuris quod minimum est sequimur. In obscure cases we always follow what is least obscure.

Semper in stipulationibus et in caeteris contractibus id sequimur quod actum est. In stipulations and other contracts, we always follow what was done (or agreed to).

Semper ita fiat relatio ut valeat dispositio. Let the reference always be so made that the disposition may avail.

Semper necessitas probandi incumbit ei qui agit. The necessity of proving always rests on the claimant.

Semper praesumitur pro legitimatione puerorum, et filiatio non potest probari. The presumption is always in favour of legitimacy of children, and filiation cannot be proved.

Semper praesumitur pro negante. The presumption is always in favour of the one who denies.

Semper praesumitur pro sententia. The presumption is always in favour of a judgment (or sentence).

Semper pro matrimonio praesumitur. There is always a presumption in favour of marriage.

Semper qui non prohibet pro se intervenire mandare creditur. A person who does not prohibit the intervention of another in his behalf is always believed to authorize it.

Semper sexus masculinus etiam faemininum continet. The masculine gender always includes the feminine as well.

Semper specialia generalibus insunt. Special clauses are always included in general ones.

Sensus verborum est anima legis. The meaning of words is the spirit of the law.

Sententia a non judice lata nemini debet nocere. A judgment pronounced by one who is not a judge should harm no one.

Sententia contra matrimonium nunquam transit in rem judicatam. A sentence against marriage never becomes a final judgment (i.e., res judicata).

Sententia facit jus, et legis interpretatio legis vim obtinet. The judgment creates the right, and the interpretation of the law obtains the force of law.

Sententia facit jus, et res judicata pro veritate accipitur. The judgment creates the right, and what is adjudicated is taken for truth.

Sententia interlocutoria revocari potest, definitiva non potest. An interlocutory judgment may be revoked, but not a final one.

Sententia non fertur de rebus non liquidis. Judgment is not given on matters that are not clear.

Sequi debet potentia justitiam, non praecedere. Power should follow justice, not precede it.

Sermo index animi. Speech is an index of the mind.

Servanda est consuetudo loci ubi causa agitur. The custom of the place where the action is brought is to be observed.

Si aes pro auro veneat non valet. If bronze is sold for gold (the contract) is invalid.

Si a jure discedas, vagus eris et erunt omnia omnibus incerta. If you depart from the law, you will wander (without a guide), and everything will be in a state of uncertainty to everyone.

Si alicujus rei societas sit et finis negotio impositus est, finitur societas. If there is a partnership in any matter, and the business is ended, the partnership ceases.

Si aliquid ex solemnibus deficiat, cum aequitas poscit subveniendum est. If anything is lacking from formal requirements, when equity requires, it will be supplied.

Si assuetis mederi possis, nova non sunt tentanda. If you can be relieved by accustomed remedies, new ones should not be tried.

Sic interpretandum est ut verba accipiantur cum effectu. Such an interpretation is to be made that the words may be taken with effect.

Sic utere tuo ut alienum non laedas. Use your property so as not to damage another's; so use your own as not to injure another's property.

Sicut natura nil facit per saltum, ita nec lex. Just as nature does nothing with a leap, so neither does the law.

Si duo in testamento pugnantia reperientur, ultimum est ratum. If two conflicting provisions are found in a will, the latter is decisive.

Sigillum est cera impressa, quia cera sine impressione non est sigillum. A seal is a piece of wax impressed, because wax without an impression is not a seal.

Si judicas, cognosce. If you judge, understand.

Silentium in senatu est vitium. Silence in the senate is a fault.

Silent leges inter arma. Laws are silent amid arms.

Simplicitas est legibus amica, et nimia subtilitas in jure reprobatur. Simplicity is a friend to the laws, and too much subtlety in law is condemned.

Sine possessione usucapio procedere non potest. Without possession, prescription (Roman usucapio) cannot proceed.

Superflua non nocent. Superfluities do no injury.

Suppressio veri, expressio falsi. Suppression of the truth (is equivalent to) the expression of what is false.

Suppressio veri, suggestio falsi. Suppression of the truth (is equivalent to) the suggestion of what is false.

Surplusagium non nocet. Extraneous matter does no harm. • Superfluous allegations, not proper to the case, should have no effect.

Tacita quaedam habentur pro expressis. Certain things though unexpressed are considered as expressed.

Talis non est eadem, nam nullum simile est idem. "Such" is not "the same," for nothing similar is the same thing.

Tantum bona valent, quantum vendi possunt. Things are worth as much as they can be sold for.

Tantum concessum quantum scriptum. So much is granted as is written.

Tantum habent de lege, quantum habent de justitia. (Precedents) have value in the law to the extent that they represent justice.

Tantum operatur fictio in casu ficto quantum veritas in casu vero. A legal fiction operates to the same extent and effect in the supposed case as the truth does in a real case.

Tantum praescriptum quantum possessum. There is only prescription insofar as there has been possession.

Tempus ex suapte natura vim nullam effectricem habet. Time, of its own nature, has no effectual force.

Tempus mortis inspiciendum. (One must) look to the time of death.

Tenor est qui legem dat feudo. It is the tenor that gives law to the fee. • That is, the tenor of the feudal grant regulates its effect and extent.

Terminus annorum certus debet esse et determinatus. A term of years ought to be certain and definite (with a fixed end).

Terra manens vacua occupanti conceditur. Land lying unoccupied is given to the occupant.

Terra transit cum onere. Land passes with the incumbrances.

Testamenta latissimam interpretationem habere debent. Wills ought to have the broadest interpretation.

Testamentum omne morte consummatum. Every will is completed by death.

Testatoris ultima voluntas est perimplenda secundum veram intentionem suam. The last will of a testator is to be fulfilled according to his true intention.

Testibus deponentibus in pari numero, dignioribus est credendum. When the number of witnesses giving testimony is equal on both sides, the more trustworthy are to be believed.
Testibus, non testimoniis, credendum est. The witnesses must be believed, not (simply) their testimony.
Testimonia ponderanda sunt, non numeranda. Testimonies are to be weighed, not counted.
Testis de visu praeponderat aliis. An eyewitness outweighs others.
Testis lupanaris sufficit ad factum in lupanari. Someone from a brothel is a sufficient witness to a happening in a brothel.
Testis nemo in sua causa esse potest. No one can be a witness in his own cause.
Testis oculatus unus plus valet quam auriti decem. One eyewitness is worth more than ten earwitnesses.
Testmoignes ne poent testifier le negative, mes l'affirmative. Witnesses cannot testify to a negative; they must testify to an affirmative.
Timores vani sunt aestimandi qui non cadunt in constantem virum. Those fears must be considered vain (or frivolous) that do not affect a man of steady character.
Titulus est justa causa possidendi id quod nostrum est. Title is the just cause of possessing that which is ours.
Tolle voluntatem et erit omnis actus indifferens. Take away the will, and every action will be indifferent.
Totum praefertur unicuique parti. The whole is preferred to any single part.
Tout ce que la loi ne defend pas est permis. Everything that the law does not forbid is permitted.
Toute exception non surveillée tend à prendre la place du principe. Every exception not watched tends to assume the place of the principle.
Tractent fabrilia fabri. Let smiths perform the work of smiths.
Traditio loqui facit chartam. Delivery makes the deed (document) speak.
Transgressione multiplicata, crescat poenae inflictio. When transgression is repeated, let the infliction of punishment be increased.
Transit in rem judicatam. It passes into a judgment.
Transit terra cum onere. The land passes with its burdens.
Tres faciunt collegium. Three form a corporation.
Triatio ibi semper debet fieri ubi juratores meliorem possunt habere notitiam. Trial ought always to be held where the jurors can have the better information.
Triennalis pacificus possessor beneficii est inde securus. The undisturbed possessor of a benefice for three years is thereafter secure (from challenge).
Turpis est pars quae non convenit cum suo toto. The part is bad that does not accord with its whole.

Tuta est custodia quae sibimet creditur. The guardianship is secure that is entrusted to itself alone.

Tutius erratur ex parte mitiori. It is safer to err on the gentler side (or on the side of leniency).

Tutius est rei incumbere quam personae. It is safer to rely on a thing than on a person. • Real security is safer than personal security.

ubique: Everywhere

ultima thule: The utmost limit

ultra vires: Beyond ones powers

Ubi aliquid conceditur, conceditur et id sine quo res ipsa esse non potest. When anything is granted, that also is granted without which the thing itself cannot exist.

Ubi aliquid impeditur propter unum, eo remoto, tollitur impedimentum. When anything is impeded by reason of one thing, when that is removed, the impediment is removed.

Ubi cessat remedium ordinarium, ibi decurritur ad extraordinarium. When a common remedy ceases to be of service, recourse is had to an extra-ordinary one.

Ubi culpa est, ibi poena subesse debet. Where the fault is, there the punishment should be imposed.

Ubicunque est injuria, ibi damnum sequitur. Wherever there is a legal wrong, there damage follows.

Ubi damna dantur victus victori in expensis condemnari debet. Where damages are awarded, the party that did not succeed ought to be adjudged to pay expenses for the party that prevailed.

Ubi eadem ratio, ibi idem jus. Where there is the same reason, there is the same law.

Ubi eadem ratio, ibi idem jus; et de similibus idem est judicium. Where there is the same reason, there is the same law; and the same judgment should be rendered on comparable facts.

Ubi est forum, ibi ergo est jus. Where the forum (or place of jurisdiction) is, there accordingly is the law.

Ubi factum nullum, ibi fortia nulla. Where there is no fact, there are no strong points.

Ubi jus, ibi remedium. Where there is a right, there is a remedy.

Ubi jus incertum, ibi jus nullum. Where the right is uncertain, there is no right.

Ubi lex deest, praetor supplet. Where the law is deficient, the praetor supplies the deficiency.
Ubi lex est specialis et ratio ejus generalis, generaliter accipienda est. Where the law is special and the reason of it is general, it ought to be taken as general.
Ubi lex non distinguit, nec nos distinguere debemus. Where the law does not distinguish, we ought not to distinguish.
Ubi major pars est, ibi totum. Where the greater part is, there is the whole.
Ubi matrimonium, ibi dos. Where there is marriage, there is dower.
Ubi non adest norma legis, omnia quasi pro suspectis habenda sunt. Where there is no rule of law, everything must be held, as it were, suspect.
Ubi non est condendi auctoritas, ibi non est parendi necessitas. Where there is no authority to establish (a rule), there is no necessity to obey.
Ubi non est lex, ibi non est transgressio quoad mundum. Where there is not law, there is not transgression, as far as this world is concerned.
Ubi non est principalis, non potest esse accessorius. Where there is no principal, there can be no accessory.
Ubi nullum matrimonium, ibi nulla dos. Where there is no marriage, there is no dower.
Ubi onus ibi emolumentum. Where the burden is, there is the profit or advantage.
Ubi periculum, ibi et lucrum collocatur. Where the risk is, there also the profit accrues.
Ubi pugnantia inter se in testamento juberentur, neutrum ratum est. When two directions conflicting with each other were given in a will, neither is held valid.
Ubi quis delinquit ibi punietur. Where anyone commits an offence, there will he be punished.
Ubi remedium, ibi ius. Where there is a remedy, there is a right.
Ubi verba conjuncta non sunt, sufficit alterutrum esse factum. Where words are not conjoined, it is enough that one or another (of the things enumerated) has been done.
Ultima voluntas testatoris est perimplenda secundum veram intentionem suam. The last will of a testator is to be fulfilled according to his true intention.
Ultimum supplicium esse mortem solam interpretamur. We consider death alone to be the extreme punishment.
Ultra posse non potest esse et vice versa. What is beyond possibility cannot exist, and the reverse (what cannot exist is not possible).
Una persona vix potest supplere vices duarum. One person can scarcely supply the place of two.

veritas vos liberabit: The truth shall make you free
victis honor: Honour to the vanquished
vincit qui se vincit: He conquers who conquers himself.
vir sapit qui pauca loquitur: That man is wise who talks little (know when to hold your tongue).
vita non est vivere sed valere vita est: Life is more than merely staying alive.
Vocatus atque: non vocatus: Deus aderit: Invoked or not invoked, the god is present.
verbum sat sapienti: A word is enough for a wise man.
via media: A middle course
vice versa: The terms being reversed
videlicet: That is to say namely
vi et armis: By force and arms
virginibus puerisque: For girls and boys
viva voce: By the living voice (orally).
vox et praeterea nihil: A voice and nothing more
vox populi vox dei: The voice of the people is the voice of god.
Vagabundum nuncupamus eum qui nullibi domicilium contraxit habitationis. We call the person a vagabond who has acquired nowhere a domicile of residence.
Valeat quantum valere potest. Let it have effect as far as it can have effect.
Vana est illa potentia quae nunquam venit in actum. Vain is that power that never comes into action.
Vani timores sunt aestimandi, qui non cadunt in constantem virem. Those fears are to be considered groundless that do not affect a man of steady character.
Vani timoris justa excusatio non est. There is no legal excuse based on a groundless fear.
Velle non creditur qui obsequitur imperio patris vel domini. A person is not presumed to act of his own will who obeys the orders of his father or his master.
Vendens eandem rem duobus falsarius est. A vendor is fraudulent if he sells the same thing to two.
Veniae facilitas incentivum est delinquendi. Ease of winning pardon is an incentive to committing crime.
Verba accipienda sunt secundum subjectam materiam. Words are to be interpreted according to the subject matter.
Verba accipienda ut sortiantur effectum. Words are to be taken so that they may have some effect.

Verba aliquid operari debent — debent intelligi ut aliquid operentur. Words ought to have some effect—words ought to be understood so as to have some effect.
Verba aliquid operari debent; verba cum effectu sunt accipienda. Words ought to have some effect; words must be taken so as to have effect.
Verba artis ex arte. Terms of art (should be explained) from the art.
Verba chartarum fortius accipiuntur contra proferentem. The words of deeds are taken most strongly against the person offering them.
Verba cum effectu accipienda sunt. Words must be taken so as to have effect.
Verba currentis monetae tempus solutionis designant. The words "current money" refer to the time of payment.
Verba debent intelligi cum effectu. Words ought to be understood with effect.
Verba debent intelligi ut aliquid operentur. Words ought to be so understood that they may have some effect.
Verba dicta de persona intelligi debent de conditione personae. Words spoken of the person are to be understood of the condition of the person.
Verba fortius accipiuntur contra proferentem. Words are interpreted more strongly against the party who puts them forward; words are most readily accepted against the one putting them forward.
Verba generalia generaliter sunt intelligenda. General words are to be understood generally.
Verba generalia restringuntur ad habilitatem rei vel aptitudinem personae. General words are limited to the capability of the subject matter or the aptitude of the person.
Verba generalia restringuntur ad habilitatem rei vel personae. General words are limited to the capability of the subject matter or of the person.
Verba illata (relata) inesse videntur. Words referred to are considered as if incorporated.
Verba in differenti materia per prius, non per posterius, intelligenda sunt. Words referring to a different subject are to be understood by what goes before, not by what follows.
Verba intelligenda sunt in casu possibili. Words are to be understood in reference to a possible case.
Verba intentioni, et non e contra, debent inservire. Words should be subject to the intention, not the reverse.
Verba ita sunt intelligenda, ut res magis valeat quam pereat. Words are to be so understood that the matter may have effect rather than fail.
Verba nihil operari melius est quam absurde. It is better that words should have no effect than an absurd effect.
Verba pro re et subjecta materia accipi debent. Words should be taken most in favour of the thing and the subject matter.

Verba quae aliquid operari possunt non debent esse superflua. Words that can have some effect ought not to be (treated as) superfluous.

Verba relata hoc maxime operantur per referentiam ut in eis inesse videntur. Words to which reference is made have, by the reference, this particular effect, that they are considered to be incorporated in those (clauses). • Words to which reference is made in an instrument have the same effect and operation as if they were inserted in the clause referring to them.

Verba relata inesse videntur. Words to which reference is made are considered incorporated.

Verba secundum materiam subjectam intelligi nemo est qui nescit. There is no one who does not know that words should be understood according to the subject matter.

Verba semper accipienda sunt in mitiori sensu. Words are always to be taken in their milder sense.

Verba strictae significationis ad latam extendi possunt, si subsit ratio. Words of a strict signification can be given a wide signification if there is reason for it.

Verba sunt indices animi. Words are indications of the intention.

Verbis standum ubi nulla ambiguitas. One must abide by the words where there is no ambiguity.

Verborum obligatio verbis tollitur. An obligation verbally incurred is verbally extinguished.

Verbum imperfecti temporis rem adhuc imperfectam significat. The verb in the imperfect tense indicates a matter as yet incomplete.

Veredictum quasi dictum veritatis; ut judicium quasi juris dictum. A verdict is, as it were, the saying of the truth, in the same manner that a judgment is the saying of the law (or right).

Veritas, a quocunque dicitur, a Deo est. Truth, by whomsoever pronounced, is from God.

Veritas demonstrationis tollit errorem nominis. The truth of the description removes the error of the name.

Veritas est justitiae mater. Truth is the mother of justice.

Veritas habenda est in juratore; justitia et judicium in judice. Truth is the desideratum in a juror; justice and judgment in a judge.

Veritas nihil veretur nisi abscondi. Truth fears nothing but to be hidden.

Veritas nimium altercando amittitur. By too much quarreling the truth is lost.

Veritas nominis tollit errorem demonstrationis. The truth of the name takes away the error of the description.

Veritatem qui non libere pronunciat, proditor est veritatis. One who does not speak the truth freely is a traitor to the truth.

www.ingramcontent.com/pod-product-compliance
Lightning Source LLC
Chambersburg PA
CBHW071331150426
43191CB00007B/705